SHONEN JUMP GRAPHIC NOVEL

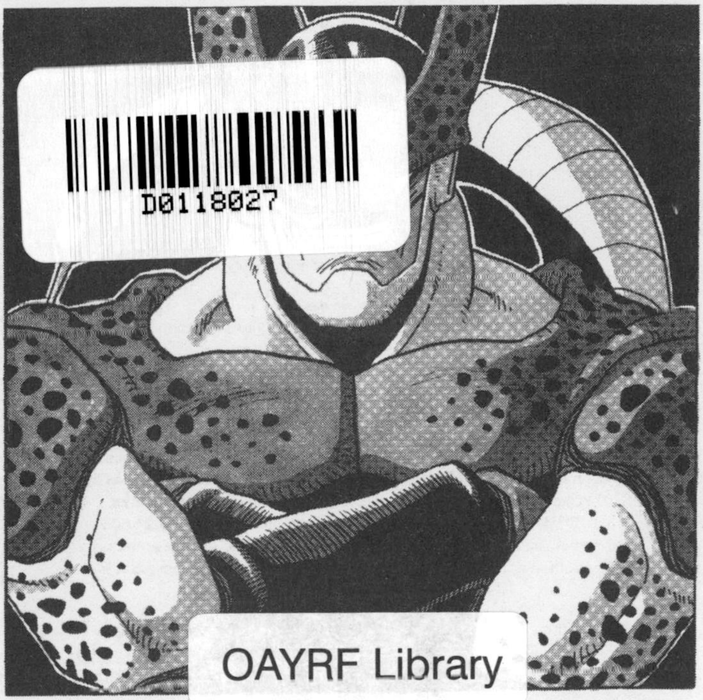

DRAGON BALL Z

Vol. 15

DB: 31 of 42

STORY AND ART BY
AKIRA TORIYAMA

THE MAIN CHARACTERS

Bulma

Goku's oldest friend, Bulma is a scientific genius. She met Goku while on a quest for the seven magical Dragon Balls which, when gathered together, can grant any wish.

Son Goku

The greatest martial artist on Earth, he is one of the last of the Saiyans, an almost extinct alien race. Like Trunks and Vegeta, he can power-up by transforming into a "Super Saiyan." Currently he's out of commission with a virus.

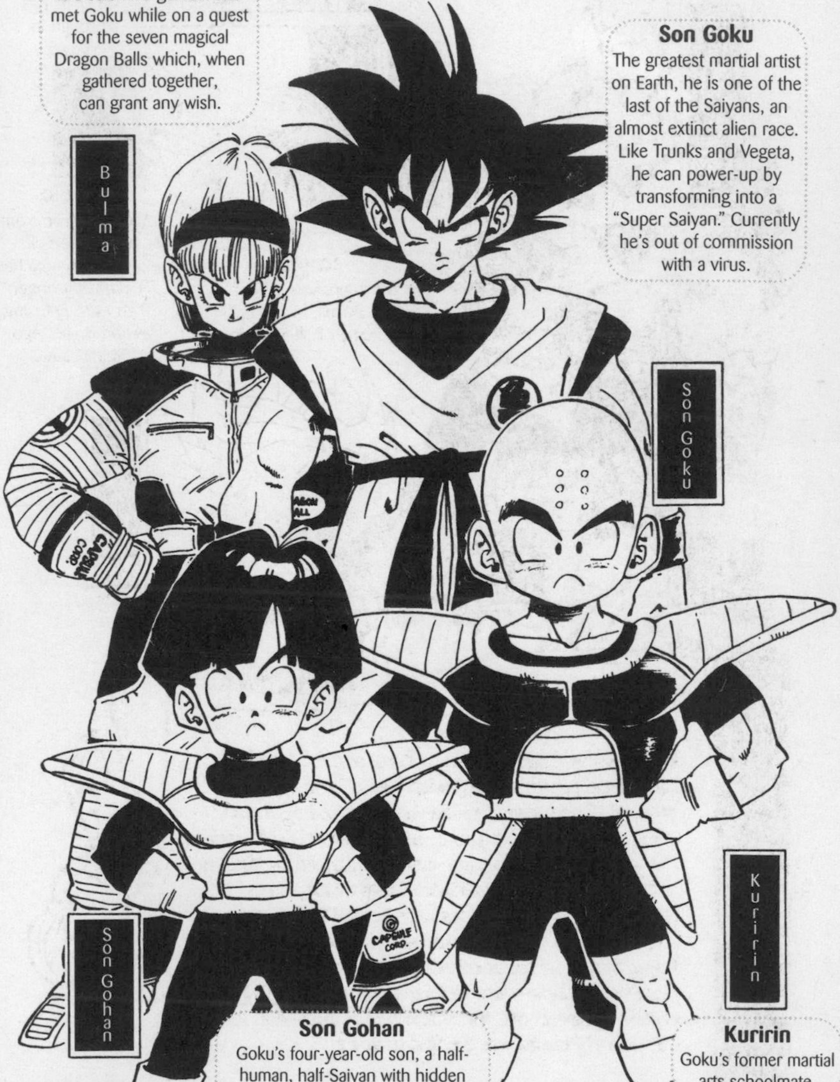
Bulma
Son Goku
Kuririn
Son Gohan
CAPSULE CORP.

Son Gohan

Goku's four-year-old son, a half-human, half-Saiyan with hidden reserves of strength. He was trained by Goku's former enemy Piccolo.

Kuririn

Goku's former martial arts schoolmate.

Androids #16, #17 and #18

Incredibly strong androids—or are they cyborgs?—created by the late Dr. Gero to destroy Son Goku.

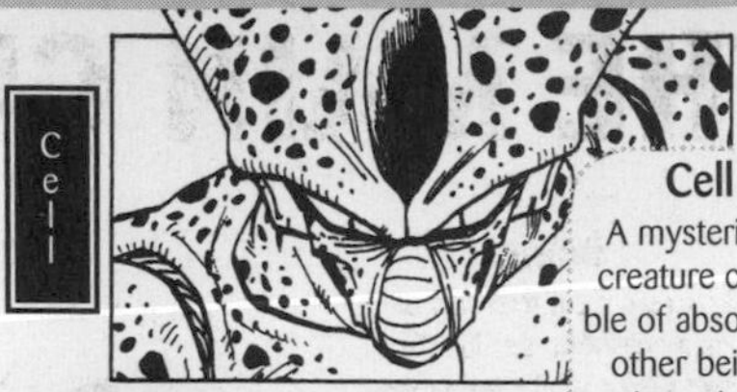
Cell

Cell

A mysterious creature capable of absorbing other beings through its stinger.

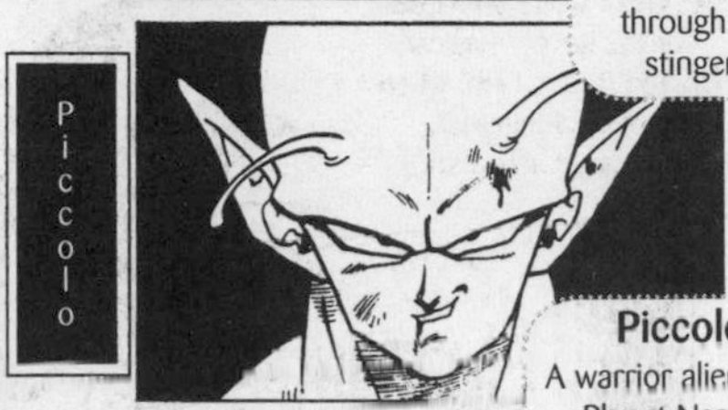
Piccolo

Piccolo

A warrior alien from Planet Namek. Recently, Piccolo has become stronger than ever by fusing with his alter ego Kami-sama.

Trunks

The future son of Vegeta and Bulma, he is a half-human, half-Saiyan.

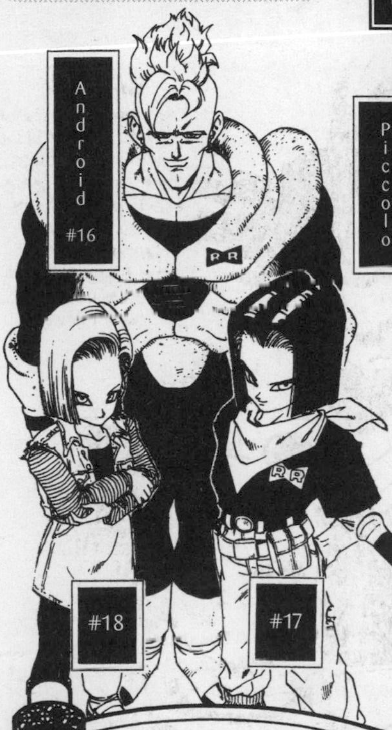
Android #16
#18
#17

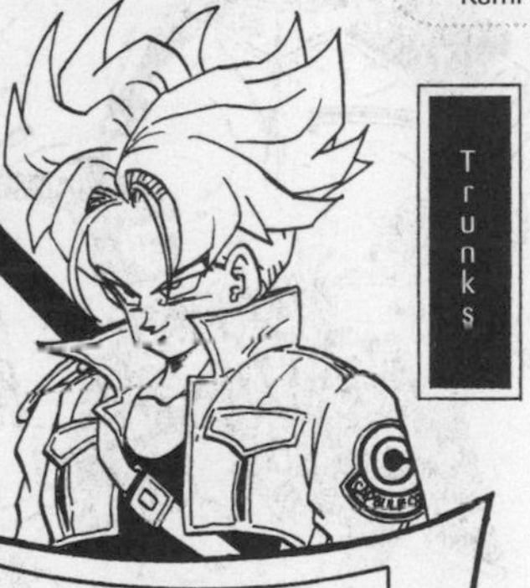
Trunks

Son Goku was Earth's greatest hero, and the Dragon Balls—which can grant any wish—were Earth's greatest treasure. Three years ago, Earth was visited by Trunks, a time traveler from the future. Trunks warned Earth's martial artists that the world would soon be attacked by terrifying androids—and Goku would develop a deadly virus! With Goku sick, the other heroes were forced to fight the androids by themselves, and lost. While our heroes were licking their wounds *another* strange enemy appeared, a monster which announced its presence by eating the entire population of a town! The heroes rushed to the scene, and Piccolo was the first to arrive…

DRAGON BALL Z 15

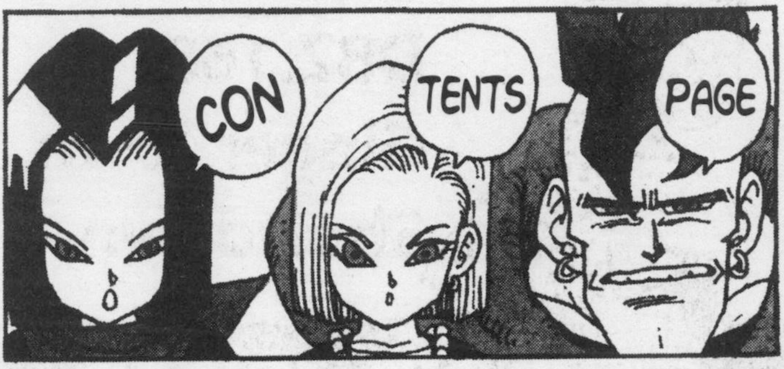
PAGE
TENTS
CON

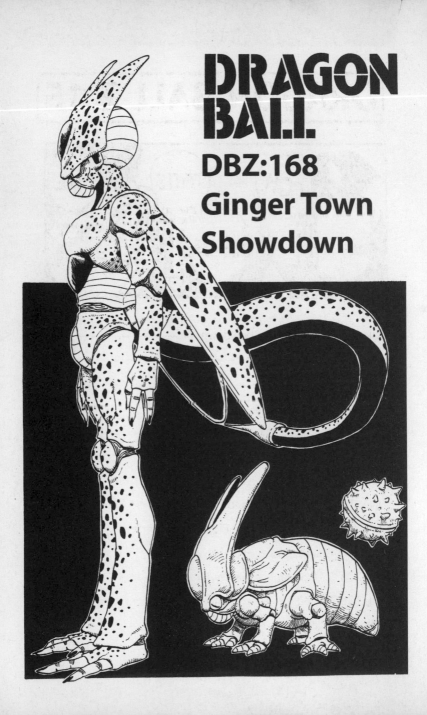

DRAGON BALL

DBZ:168
Ginger Town Showdown

READ THIS WAY

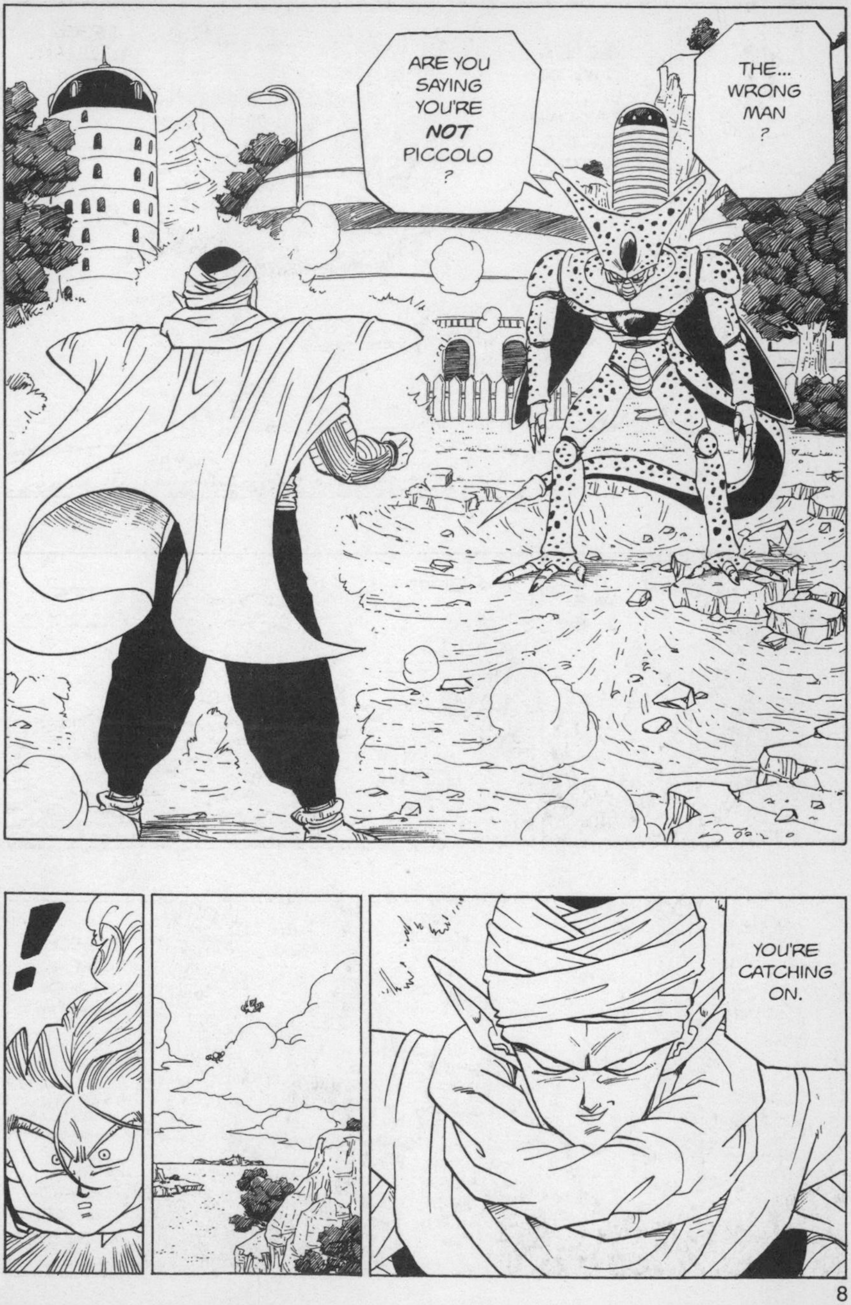
THE... WRONG MAN ?
ARE YOU SAYING YOU'RE ***NOT*** PICCOLO ?
YOU'RE CATCHING ON.
!

READ THIS WAY

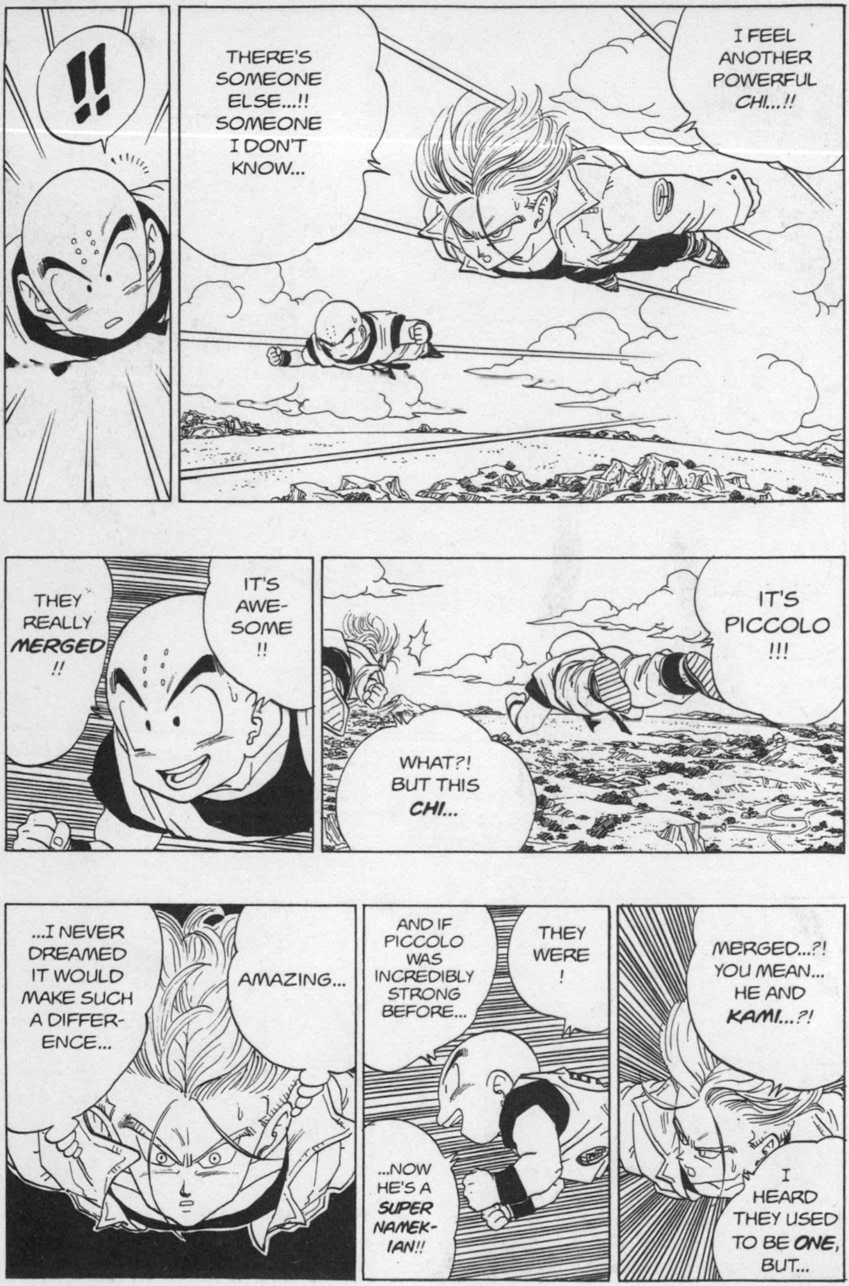
I FEEL ANOTHER POWERFUL CHI...!!
THERE'S SOMEONE ELSE...!! SOMEONE I DON'T KNOW...
!!
IT'S PICCOLO!!!
WHAT?! BUT THIS CHI...
IT'S AWESOME!!
THEY REALLY MERGED!!
MERGED...?! YOU MEAN... HE AND KAMI...?!
I HEARD THEY USED TO BE ONE, BUT...
THEY WERE!
AND IF PICCOLO WAS INCREDIBLY STRONG BEFORE...
...NOW HE'S A SUPER NAMEKIAN!!
AMAZING...
...I NEVER DREAMED IT WOULD MAKE SUCH A DIFFERENCE...

READ THIS WAY

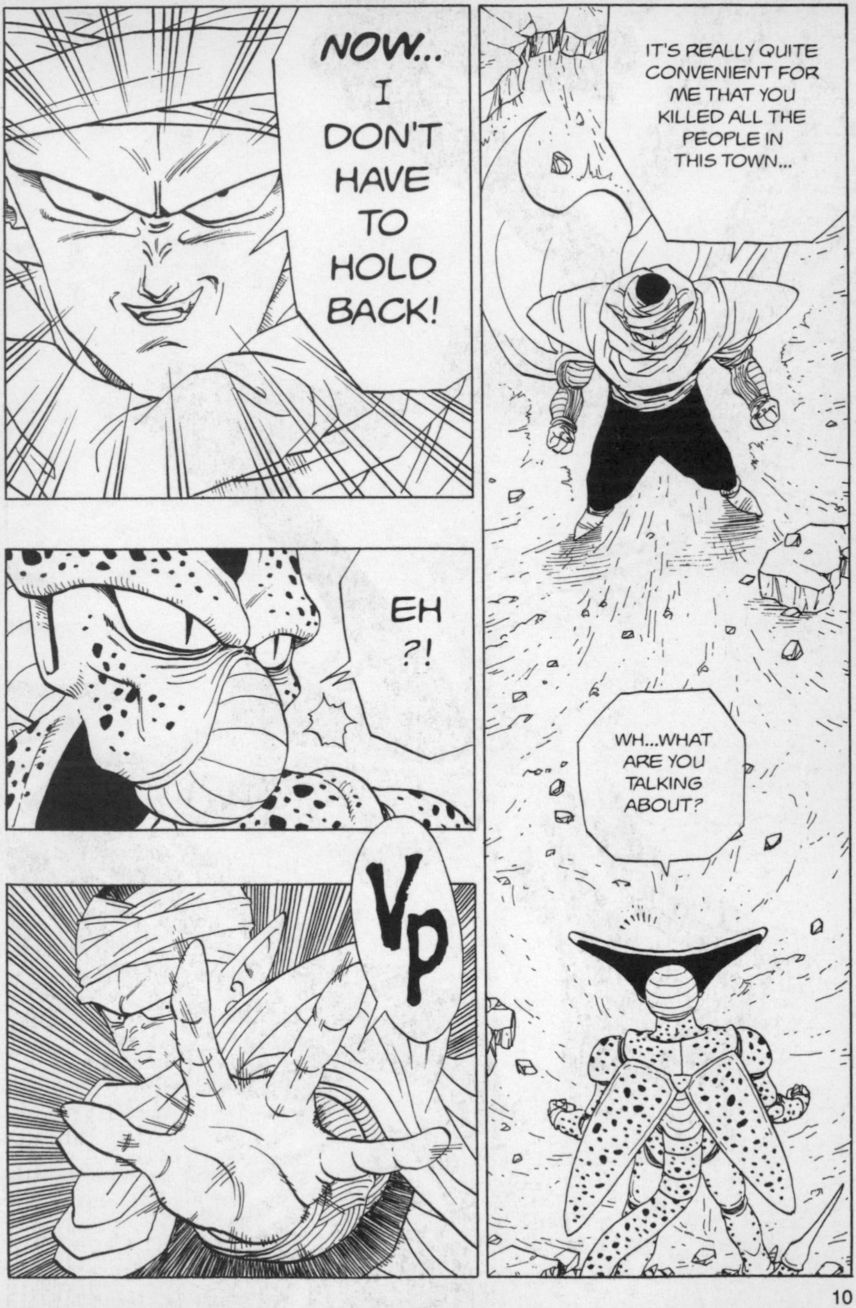
IT'S REALLY QUITE CONVENIENT FOR ME THAT YOU KILLED ALL THE PEOPLE IN THIS TOWN...
WH...WHAT ARE YOU TALKING ABOUT?
NOW... I DON'T HAVE TO HOLD BACK!
EH ?!
VP

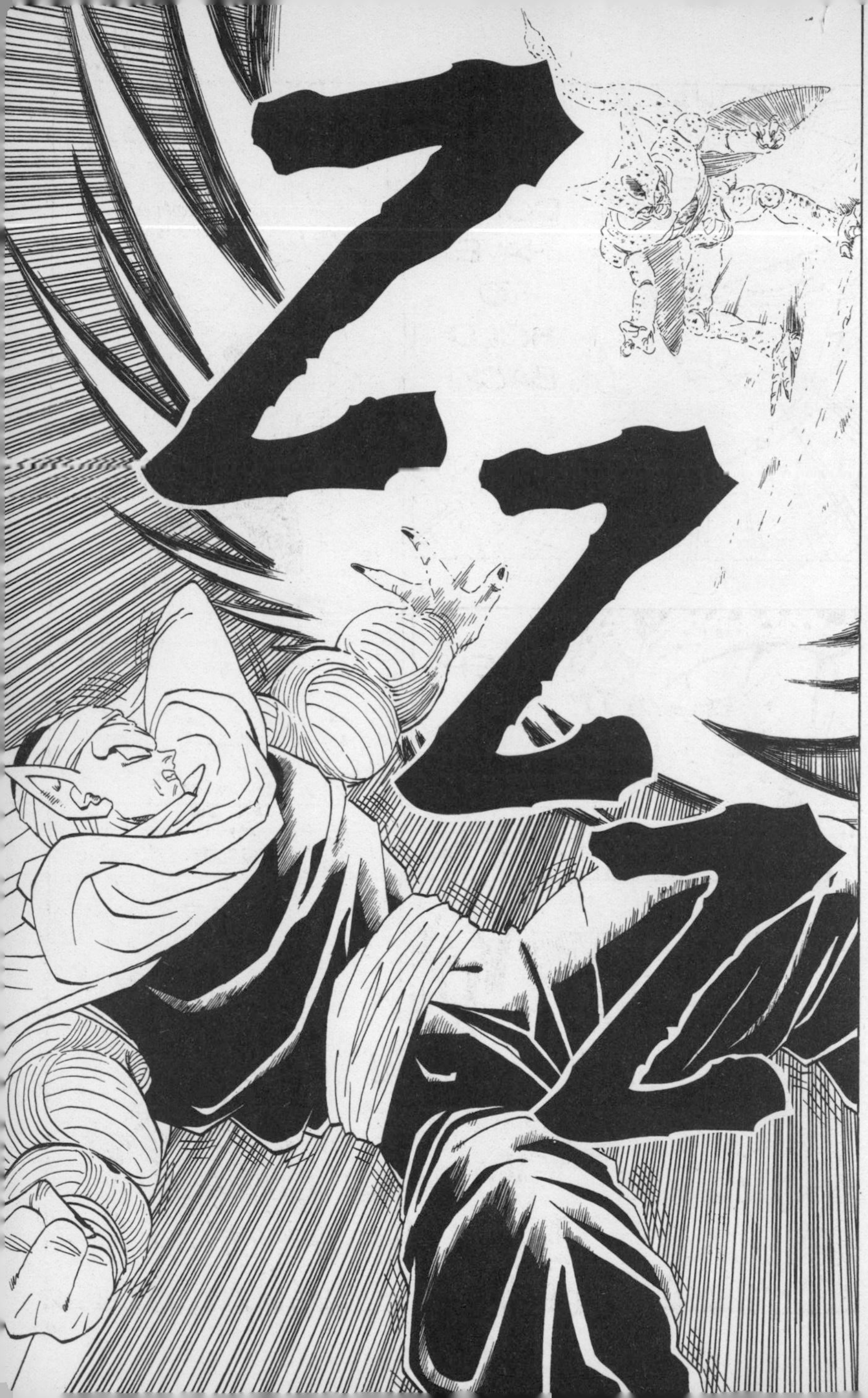

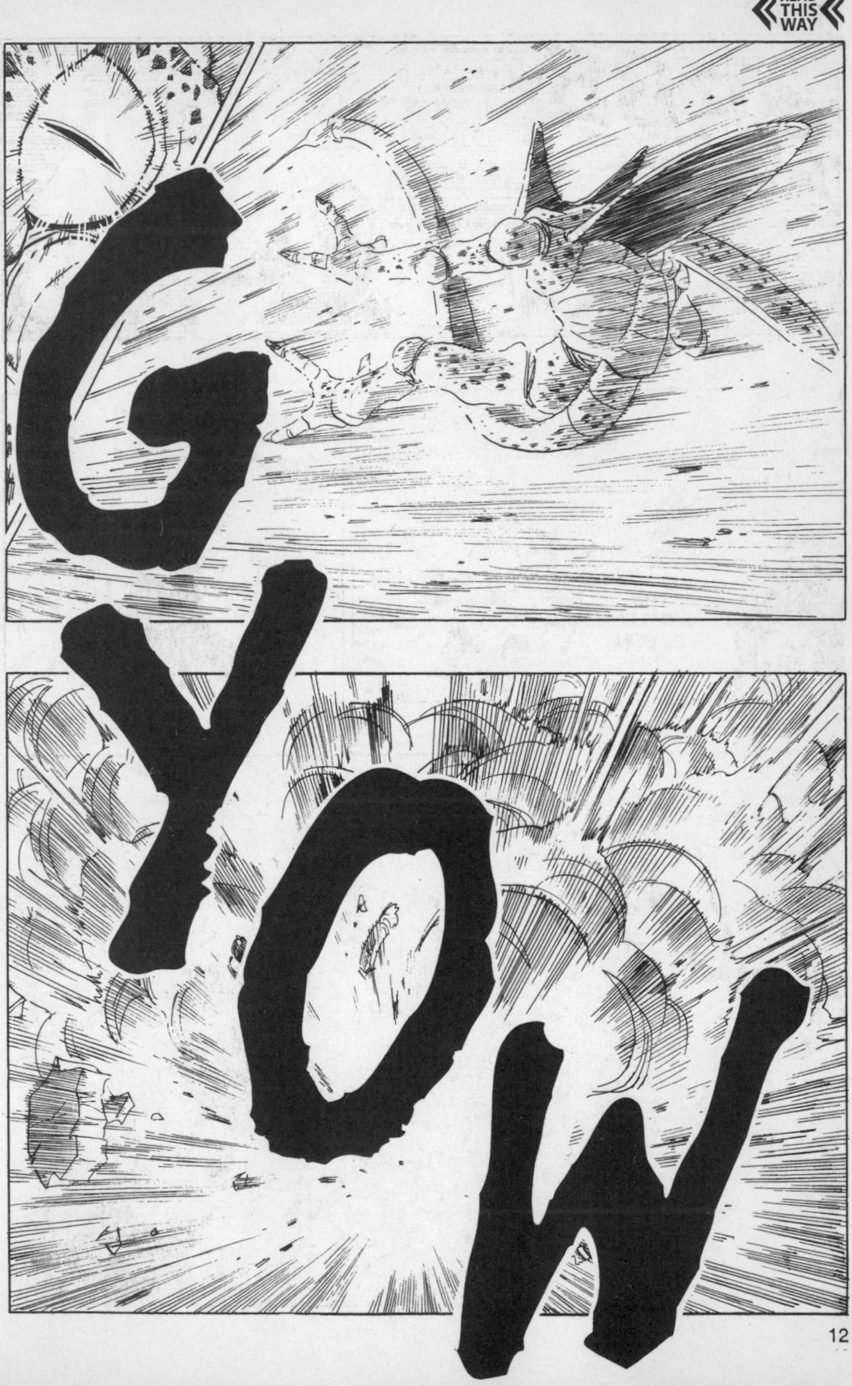
READ THIS WAY
GYOW

READ THIS WAY

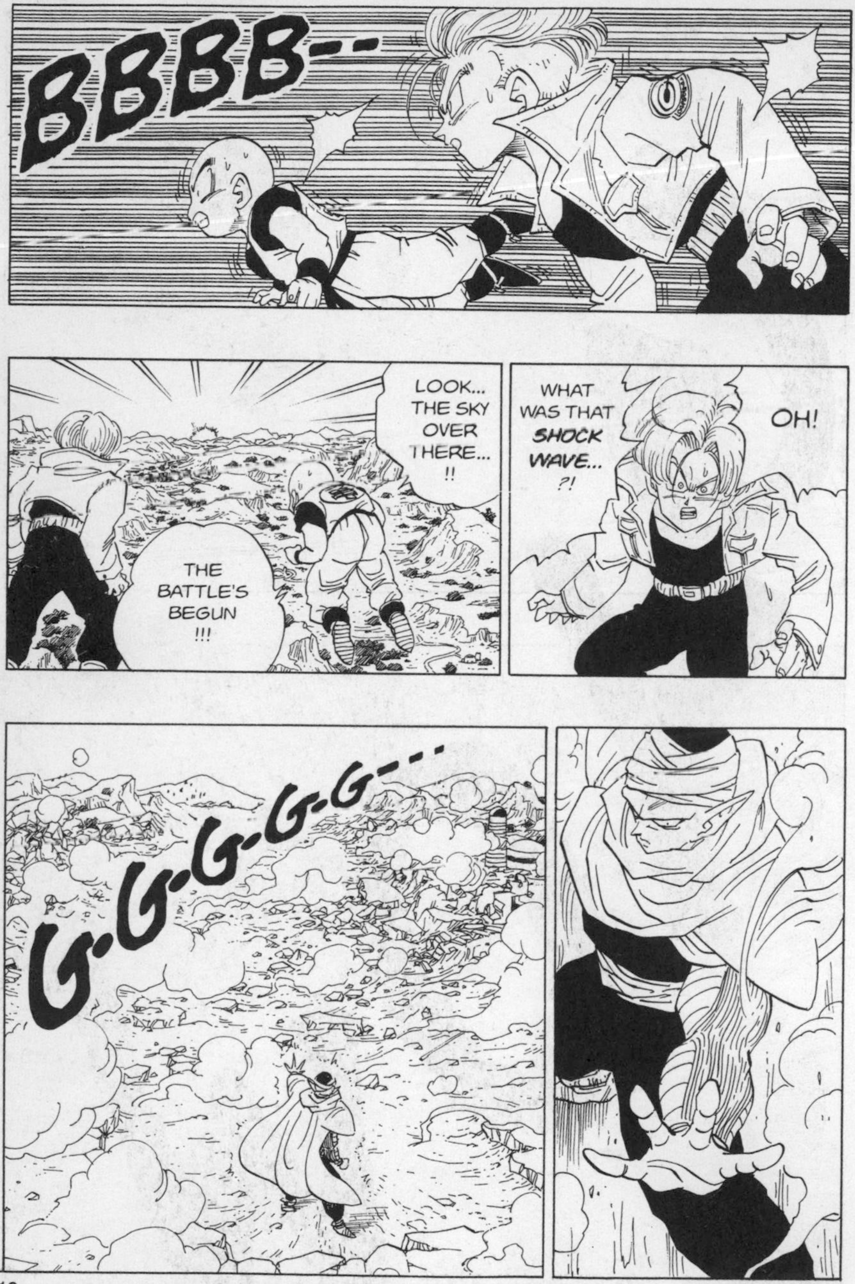
BBBB--
OH!
WHAT WAS THAT SHOCK WAVE...?!
LOOK... THE SKY OVER THERE...!!
THE BATTLE'S BEGUN!!!
G-G-G-G-G---

READ THIS WAY

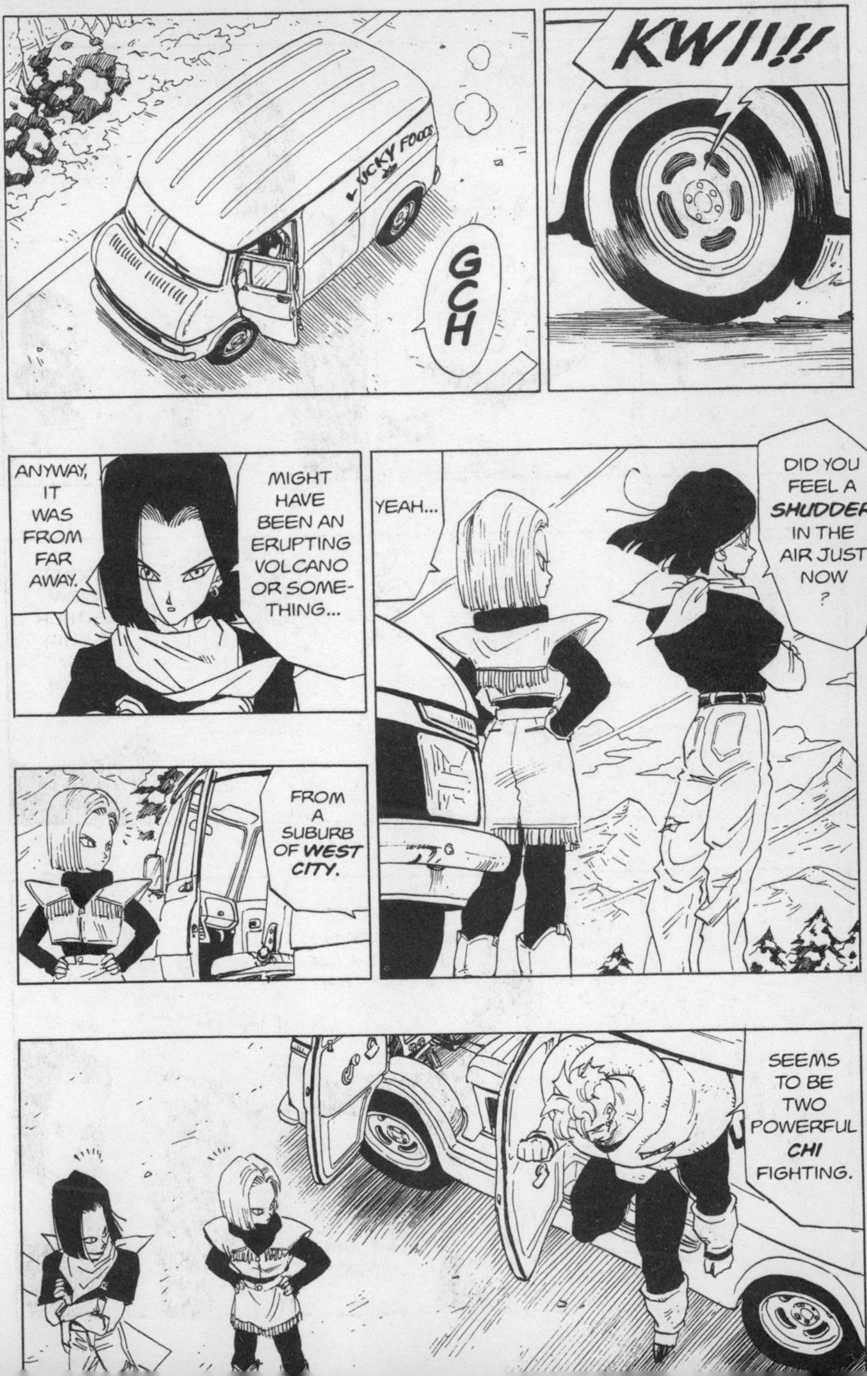
KWII!!!
GCH
DID YOU FEEL A **SHUDDER** IN THE AIR JUST NOW?
YEAH...
MIGHT HAVE BEEN AN ERUPTING VOLCANO OR SOMETHING...
ANYWAY, IT WAS FROM FAR AWAY.
FROM A SUBURB OF **WEST CITY**.
SEEMS TO BE TWO POWERFUL **CHI** FIGHTING.

READ THIS WAY

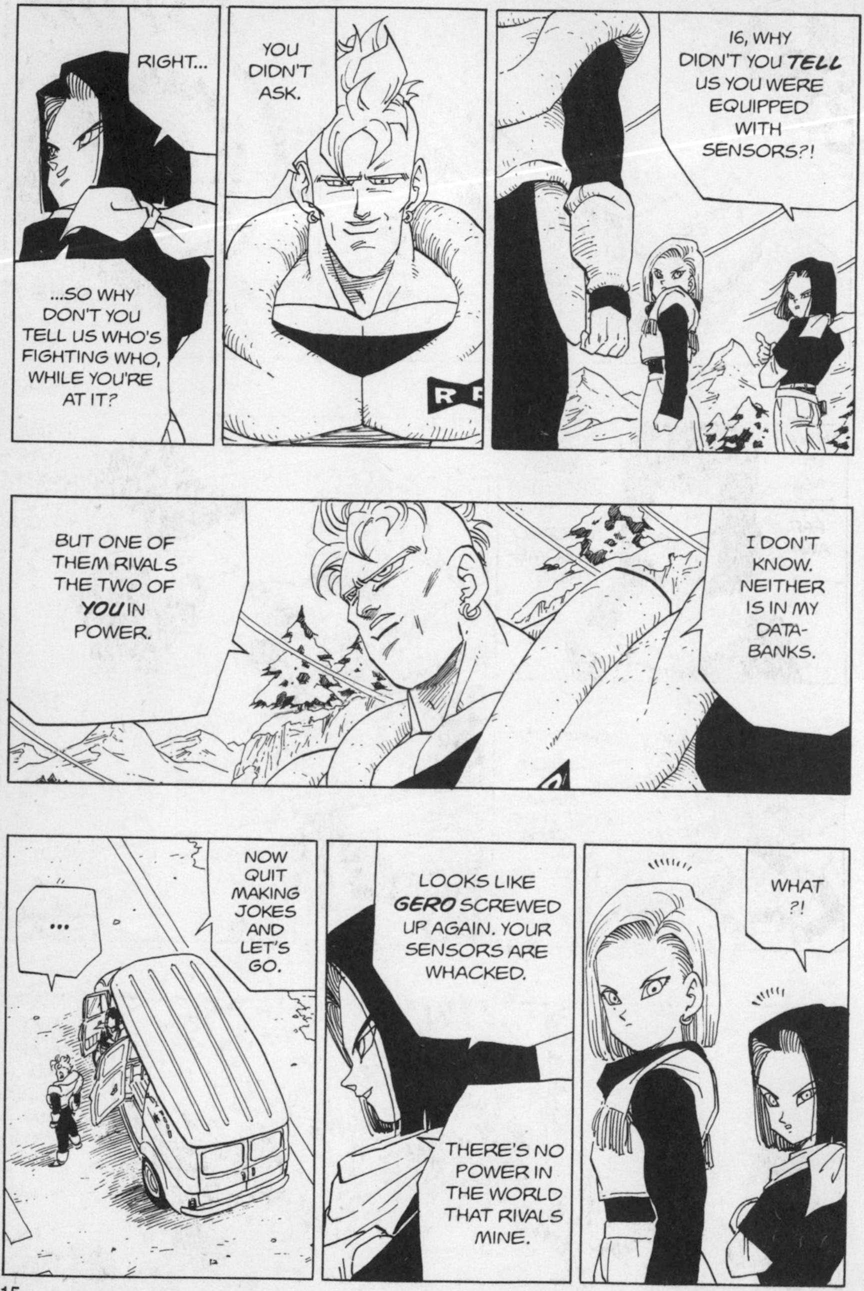
16, WHY DIDN'T YOU **TELL** US YOU WERE EQUIPPED WITH SENSORS?!
YOU DIDN'T ASK.
RIGHT...
...SO WHY DON'T YOU TELL US WHO'S FIGHTING WHO, WHILE YOU'RE AT IT?
I DON'T KNOW. NEITHER IS IN MY DATA-BANKS.
BUT ONE OF THEM RIVALS THE TWO OF **YOU** IN POWER.
WHAT?!
LOOKS LIKE **GERO** SCREWED UP AGAIN. YOUR SENSORS ARE WHACKED.
THERE'S NO POWER IN THE WORLD THAT RIVALS MINE.
NOW QUIT MAKING JOKES AND LET'S GO.
...

READ THIS WAY

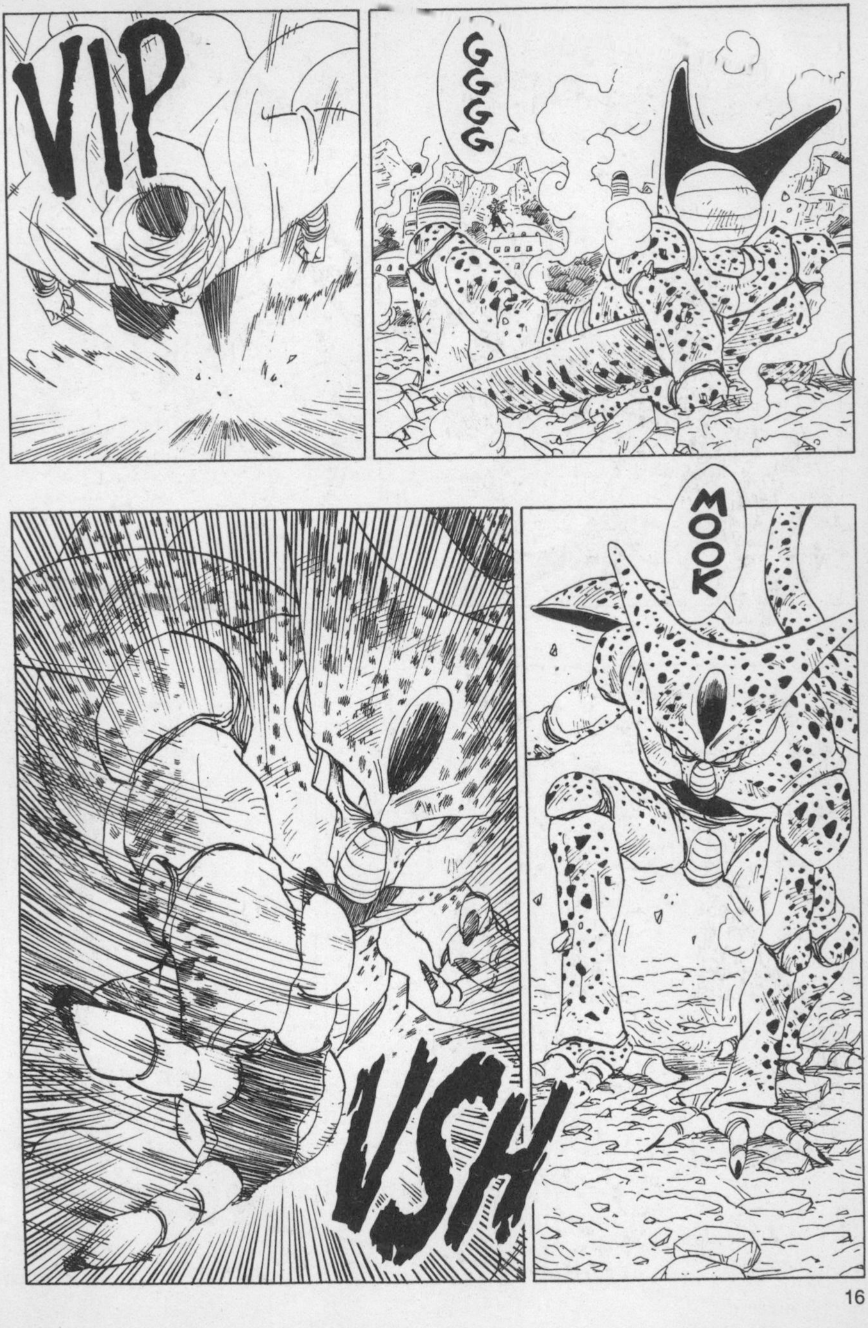
GGGG
VIP
MOOK
VSH

READ THIS WAY

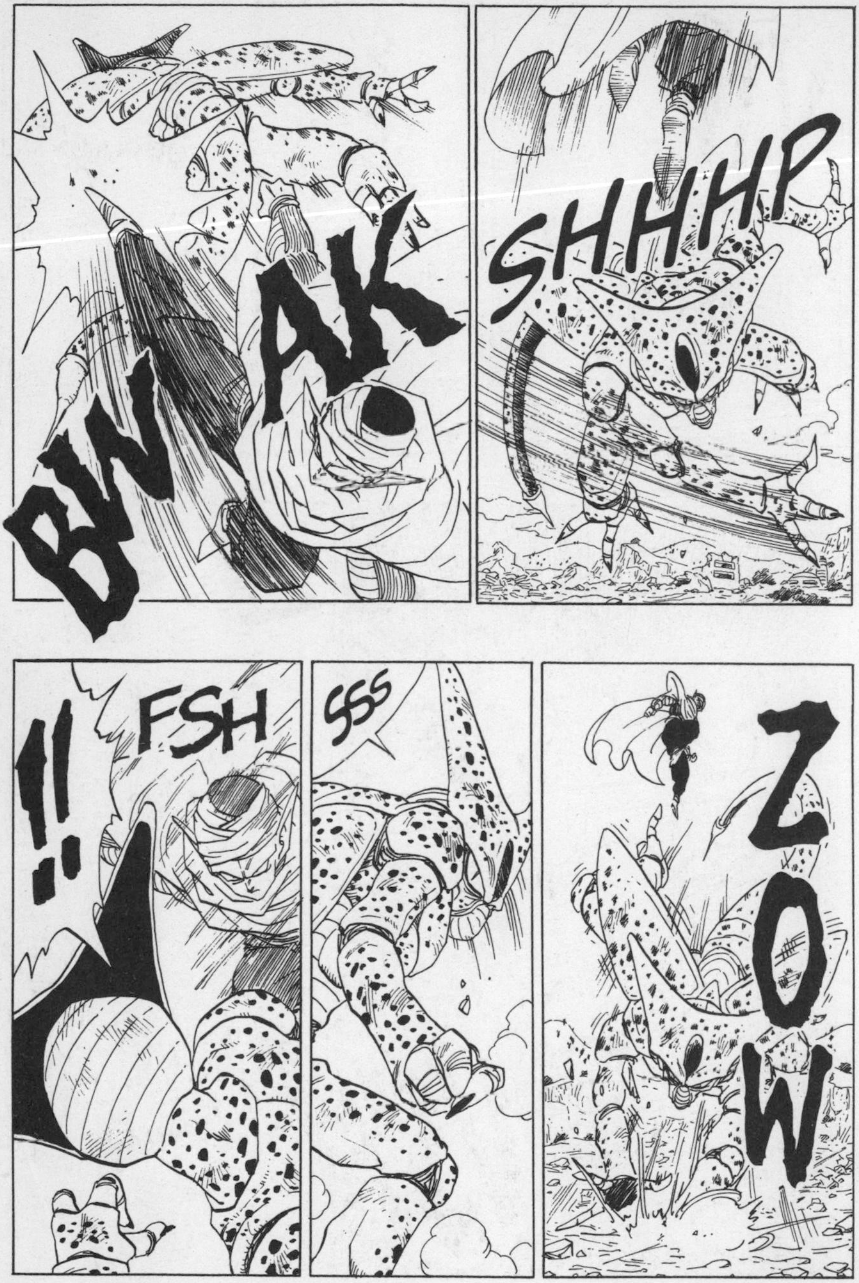
SHHHP
BWAK
ZOW
SSS
FSH
!!

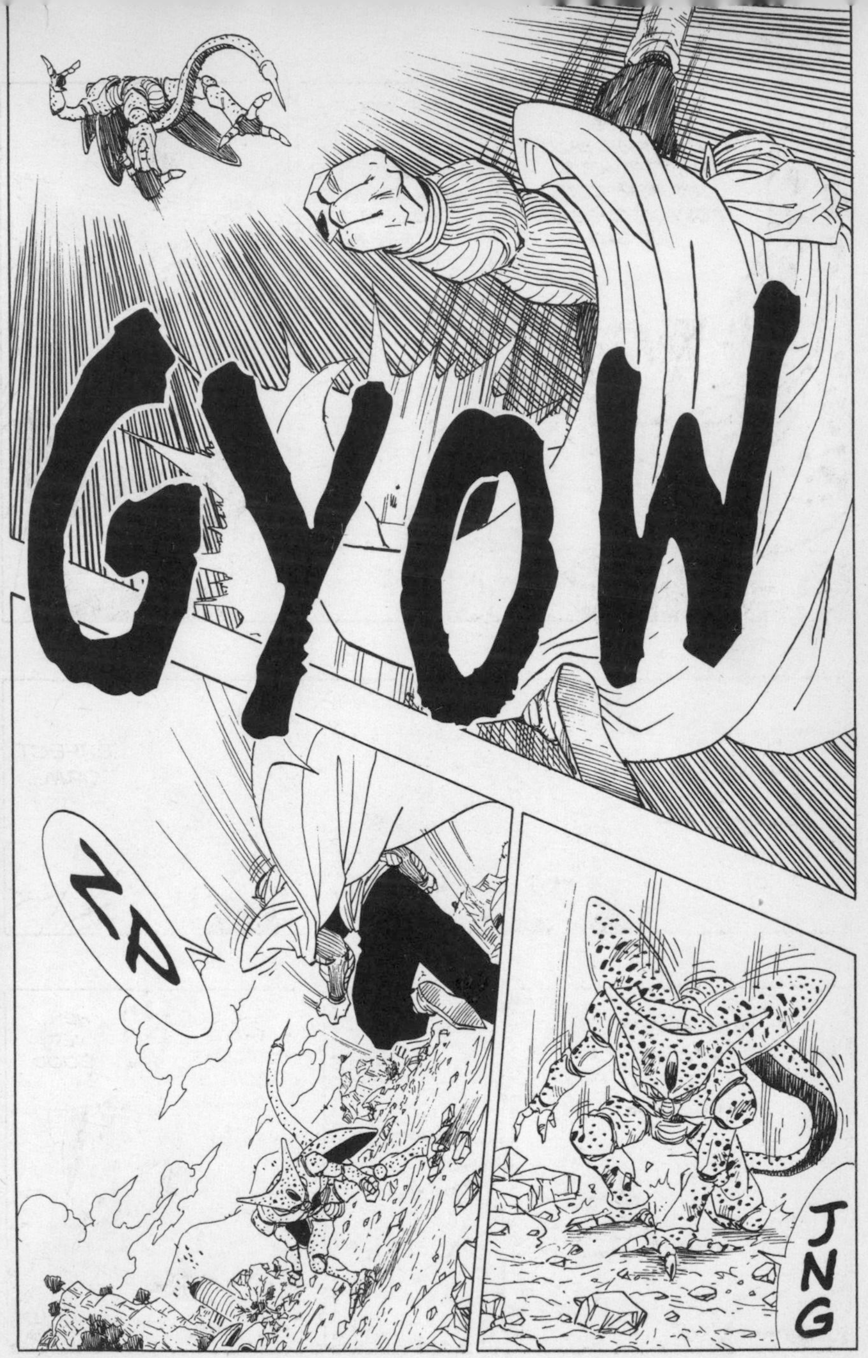
GYOW
JNG
ZIP

READ THIS WAY

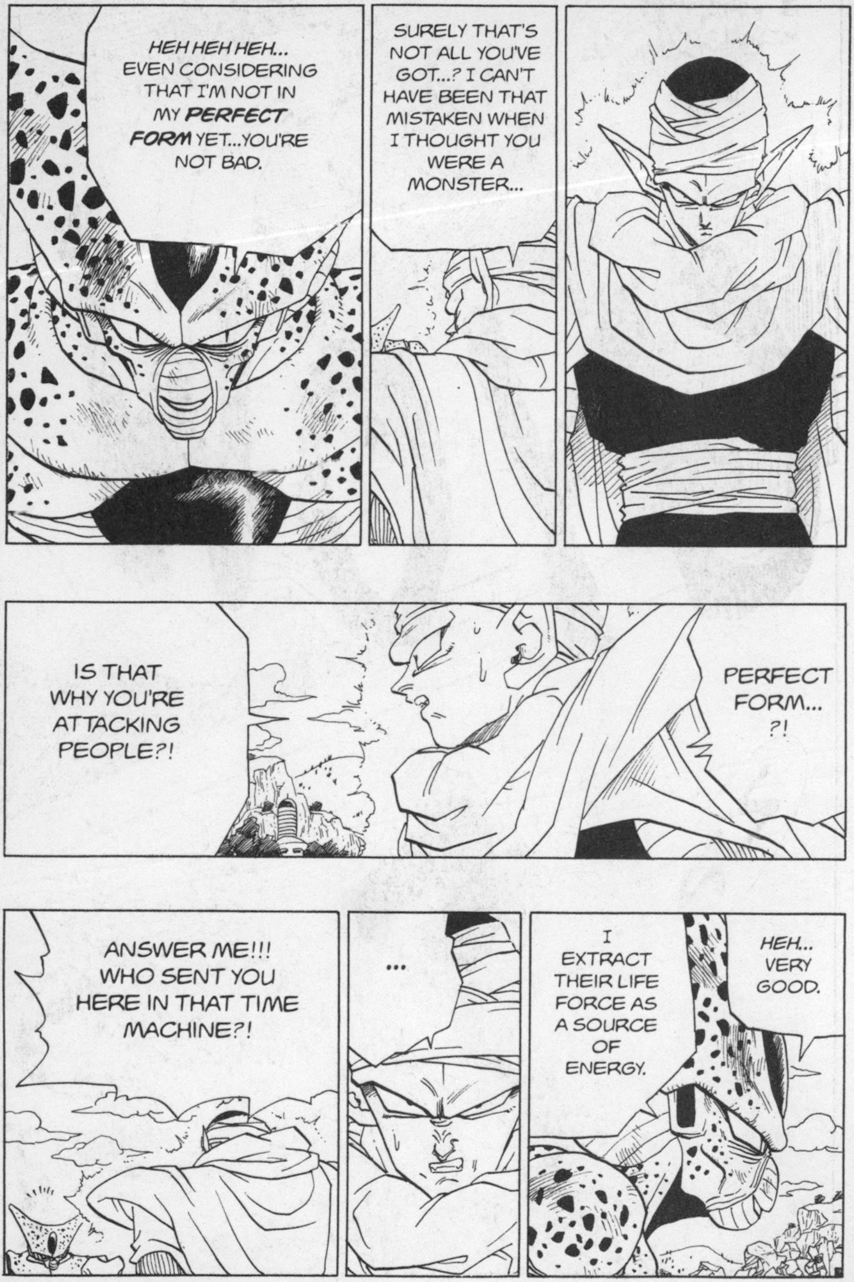

SURELY THAT'S NOT ALL YOU'VE GOT...? I CAN'T HAVE BEEN THAT MISTAKEN WHEN I THOUGHT YOU WERE A MONSTER...
HEH HEH HEH... EVEN CONSIDERING THAT I'M NOT IN MY PERFECT FORM YET...YOU'RE NOT BAD.
PERFECT FORM...?!
IS THAT WHY YOU'RE ATTACKING PEOPLE?!
HEH... VERY GOOD.
I EXTRACT THEIR LIFE FORCE AS A SOURCE OF ENERGY.
...
ANSWER ME!!! WHO SENT YOU HERE IN THAT TIME MACHINE?!

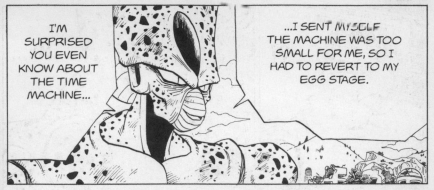

READ THIS WAY

...I SENT MYSELF THE MACHINE WAS TOO SMALL FOR ME, SO I HAD TO REVERT TO MY EGG STAGE.
I'M SURPRISED YOU EVEN KNOW ABOUT THE TIME MACHINE...
WELL...
I'LL BET YOU DON'T KNOW **THIS**...
!
SHH
KA...

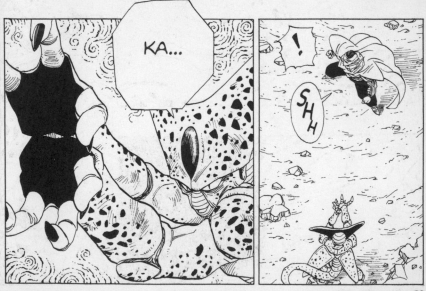

...?!

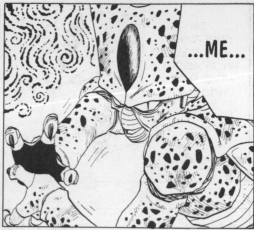

...ME...

...ME...

...HA...

TH-THAT
STANCE...!
IT CAN'T
BE...!!!

NEXT: *The Mystery Solved*

READ THIS WAY

DBZ: 169 • A Farewell to Arms

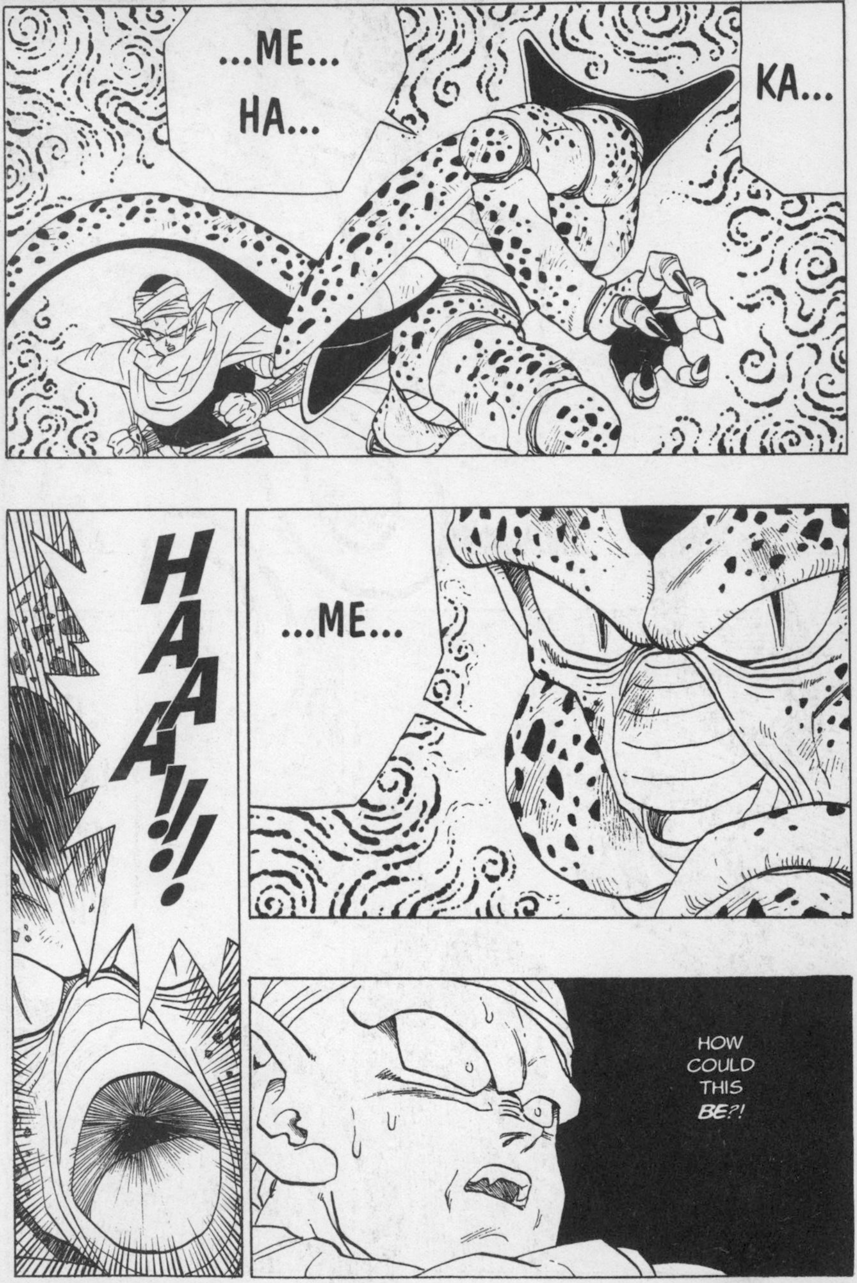
KA...
...ME...
HA...
...ME...
HOW COULD THIS *BE*?!
HAAA!!!

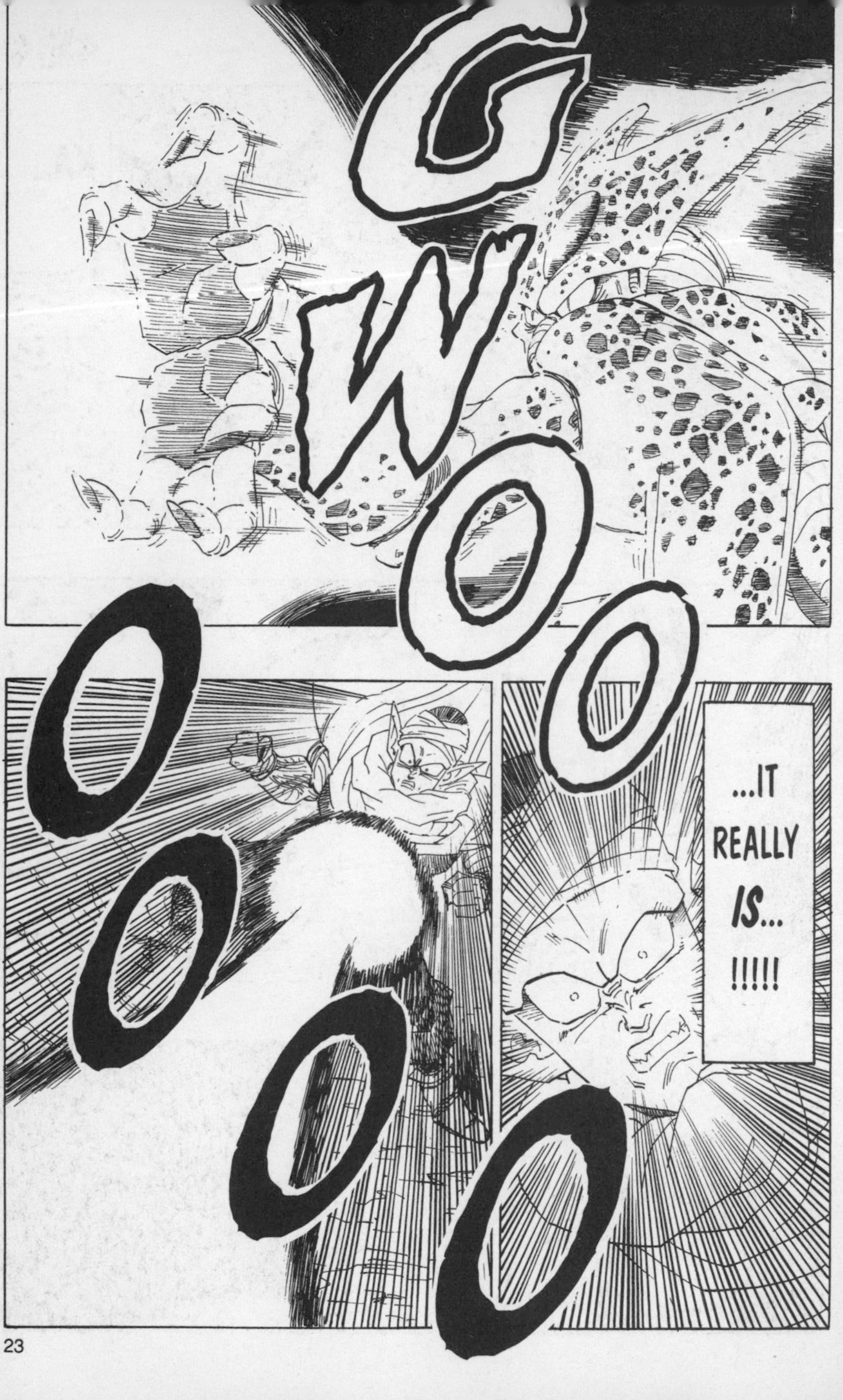
GWOOOOOO
...IT REALLY IS... !!!!!

READ THIS WAY

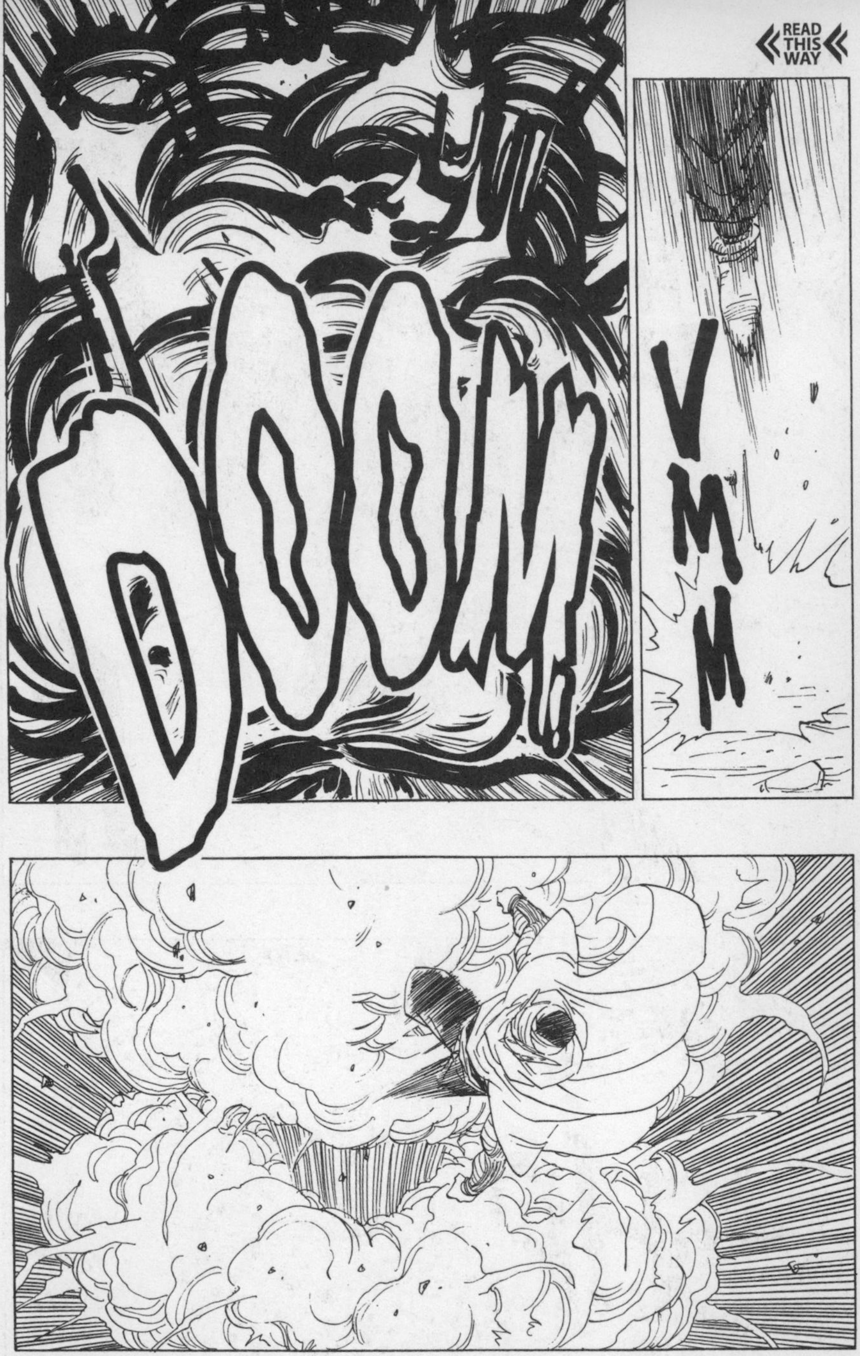
VMMM
DOOM!

READ THIS WAY

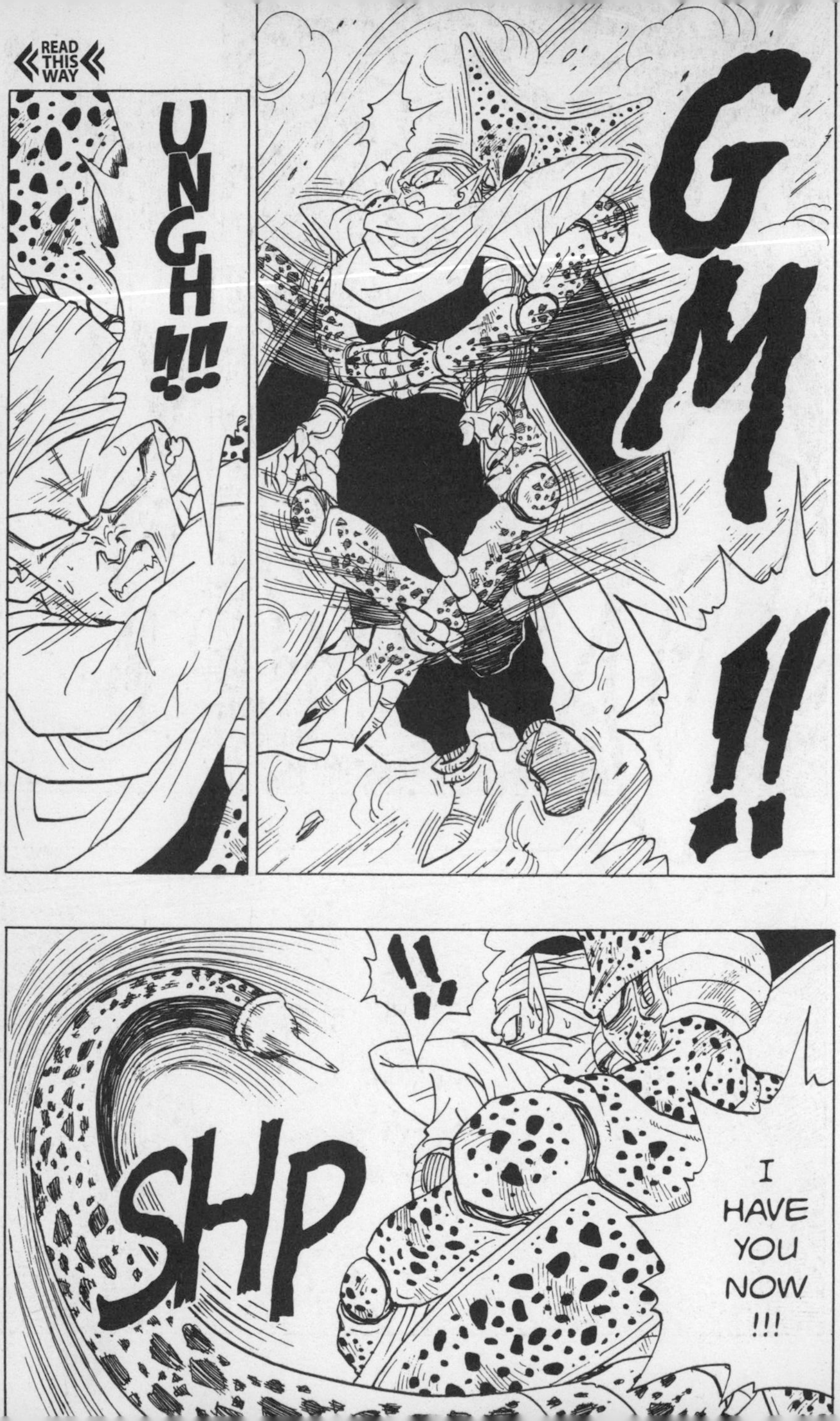
GM!!
UNGH!!
!!
I HAVE YOU NOW!!!
SHP

READ THIS WAY

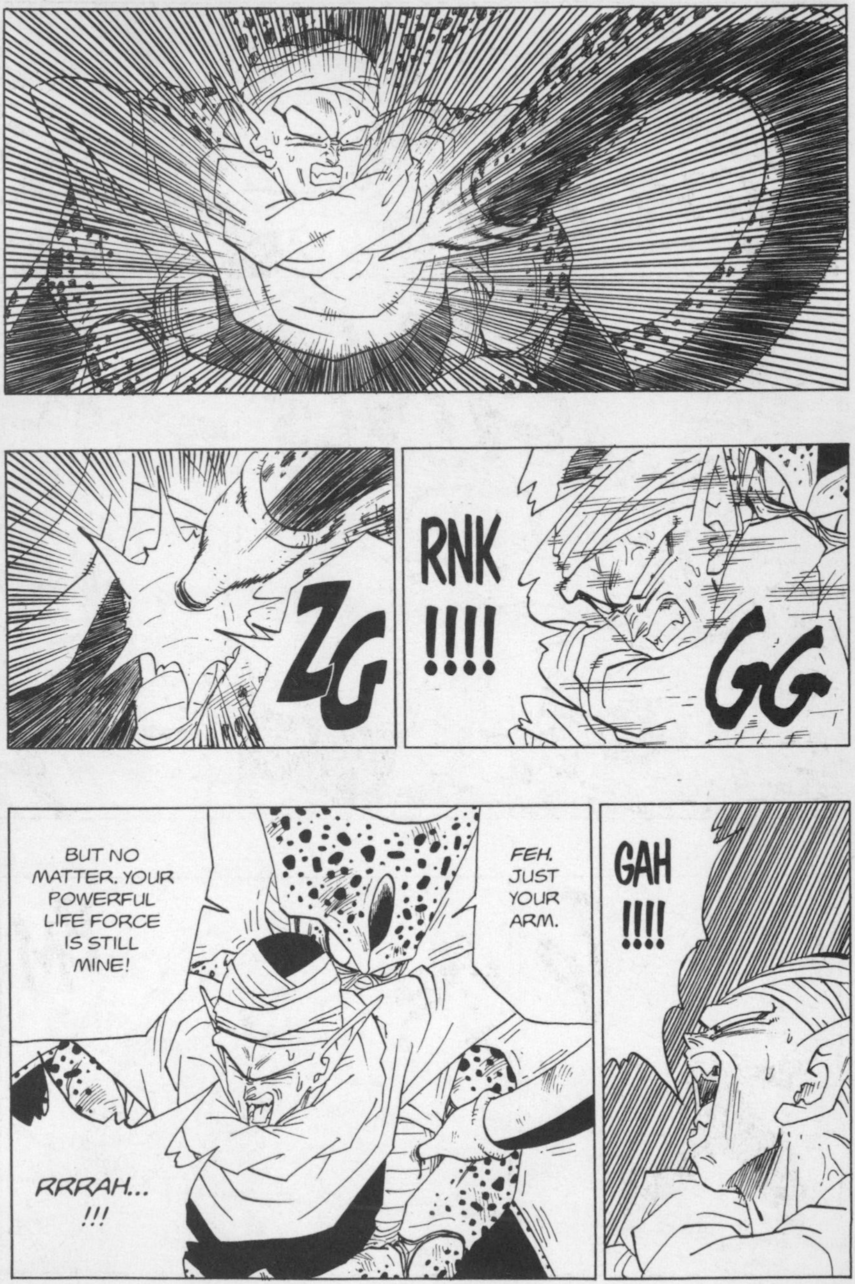
RNK !!!!
GG
ZG
GAH !!!!
FEH. JUST YOUR ARM.
BUT NO MATTER. YOUR POWERFUL LIFE FORCE IS STILL MINE!
RRRAH... !!!

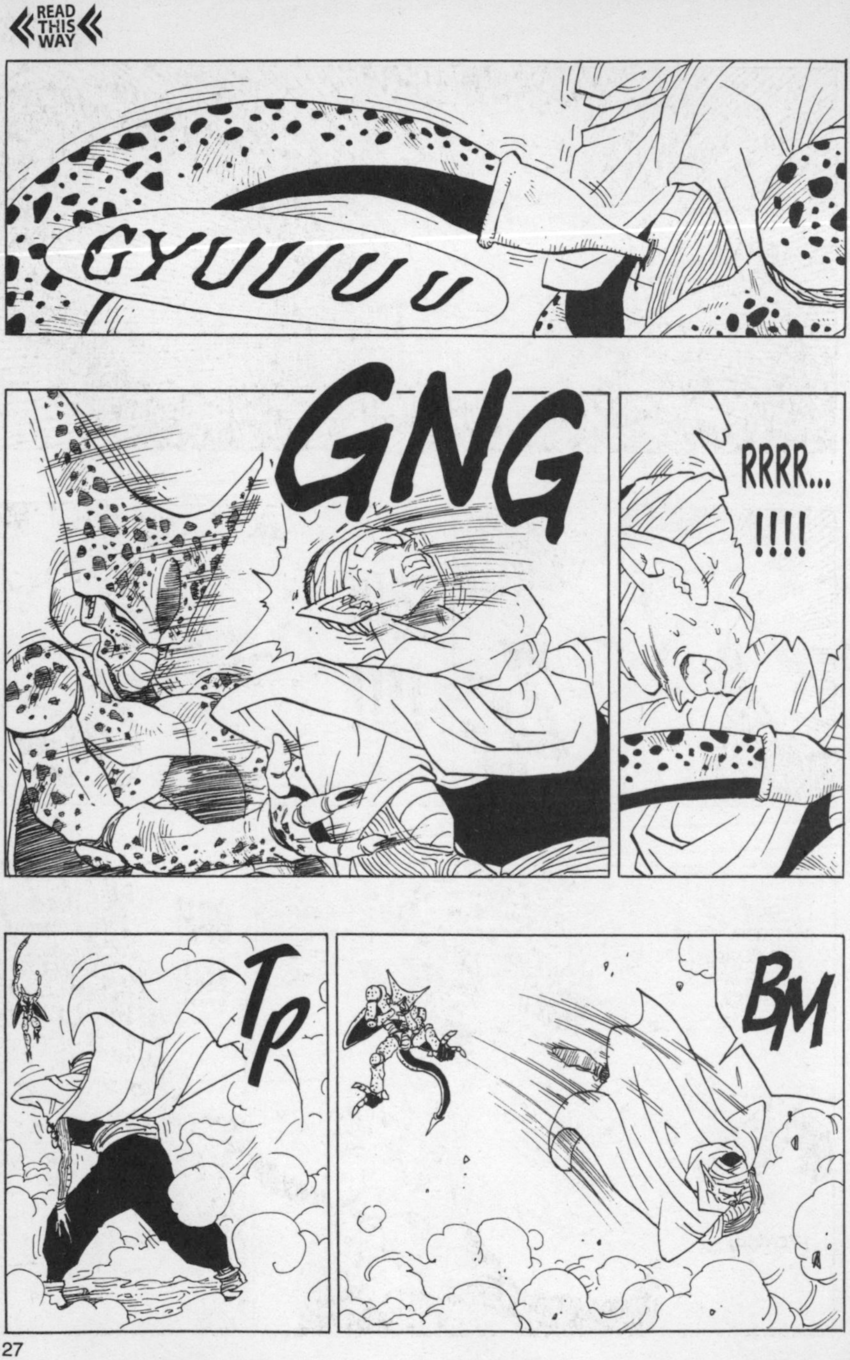
READ THIS WAY
GYUUUUU
RRRR...
!!!!
GNG
BM
TP

READ THIS WAY

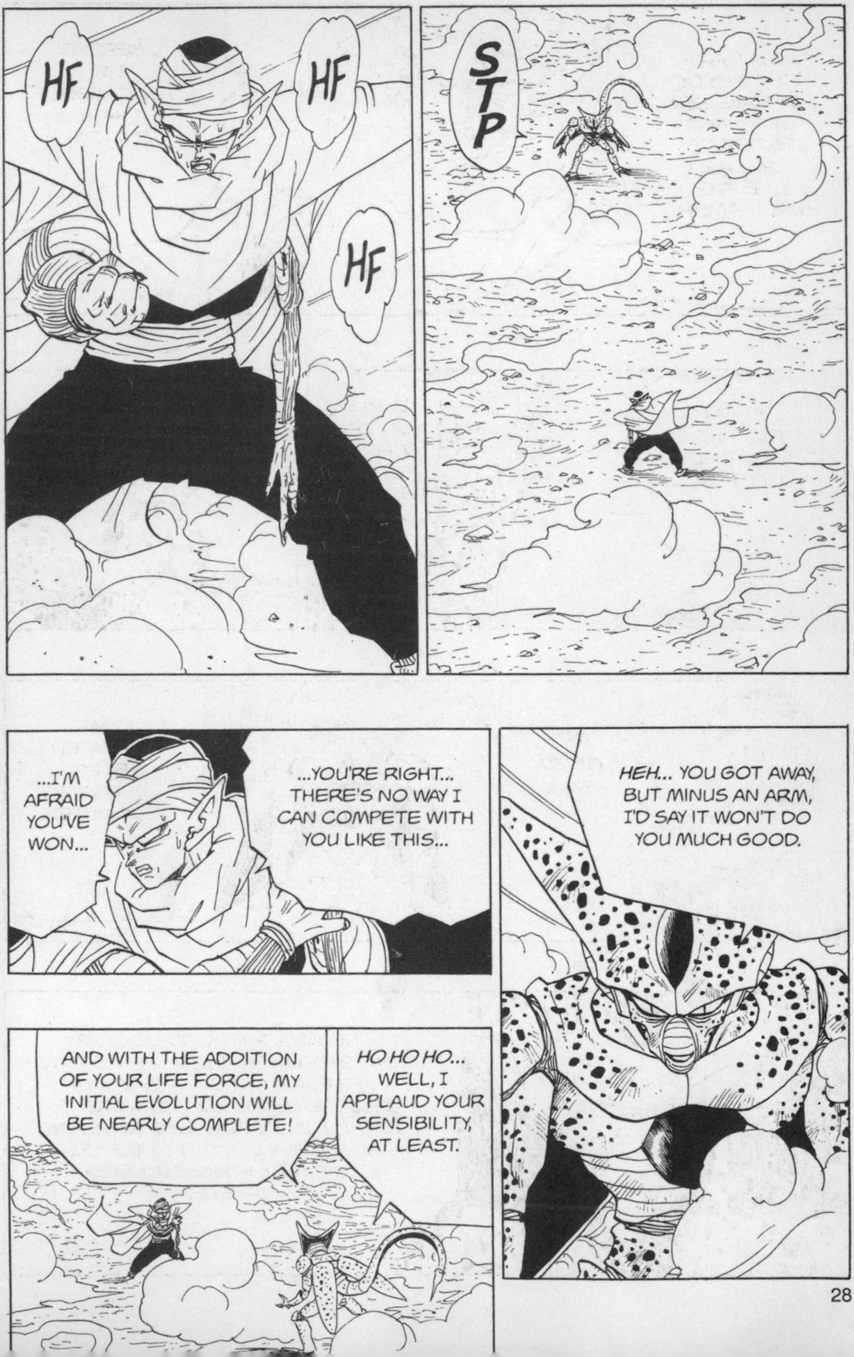

STP
HF
HF
HF
HEH... YOU GOT AWAY, BUT MINUS AN ARM, I'D SAY IT WON'T DO YOU MUCH GOOD.
...YOU'RE RIGHT... THERE'S NO WAY I CAN COMPETE WITH YOU LIKE THIS...
...I'M AFRAID YOU'VE WON...
HO HO HO... WELL, I APPLAUD YOUR SENSIBILITY, AT LEAST.
AND WITH THE ADDITION OF YOUR LIFE FORCE, MY INITIAL EVOLUTION WILL BE NEARLY COMPLETE!

READ THIS WAY

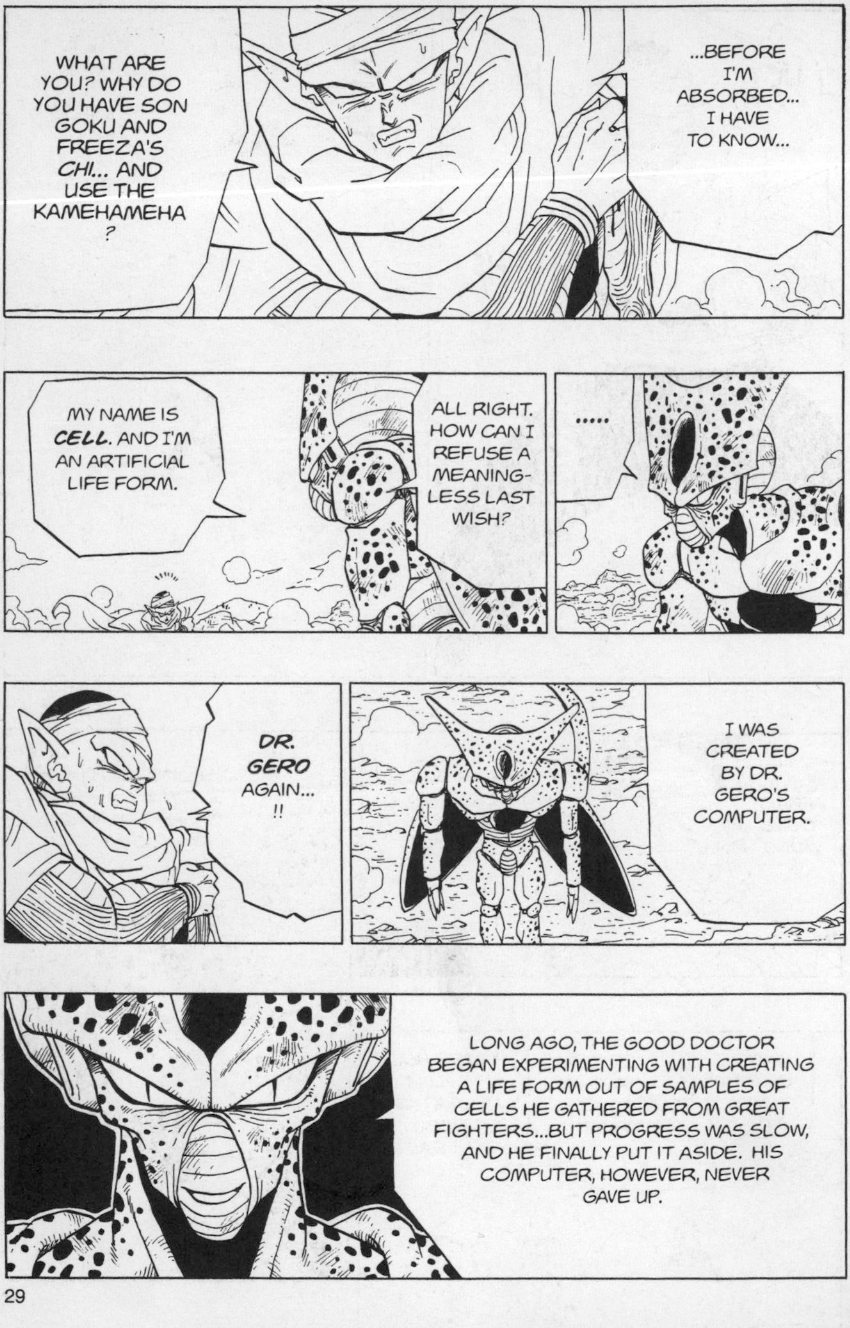
...BEFORE I'M ABSORBED... I HAVE TO KNOW...
WHAT ARE YOU? WHY DO YOU HAVE SON GOKU AND FREEZA'S *CHI*... AND USE THE KAMEHAMEHA ?
.....
ALL RIGHT. HOW CAN I REFUSE A MEANING-LESS LAST WISH?
MY NAME IS ***CELL***. AND I'M AN ARTIFICIAL LIFE FORM.
I WAS CREATED BY DR. GERO'S COMPUTER.
DR. GERO AGAIN... !!
LONG AGO, THE GOOD DOCTOR BEGAN EXPERIMENTING WITH CREATING A LIFE FORM OUT OF SAMPLES OF CELLS HE GATHERED FROM GREAT FIGHTERS...BUT PROGRESS WAS SLOW, AND HE FINALLY PUT IT ASIDE. HIS COMPUTER, HOWEVER, NEVER GAVE UP.

READ THIS WAY

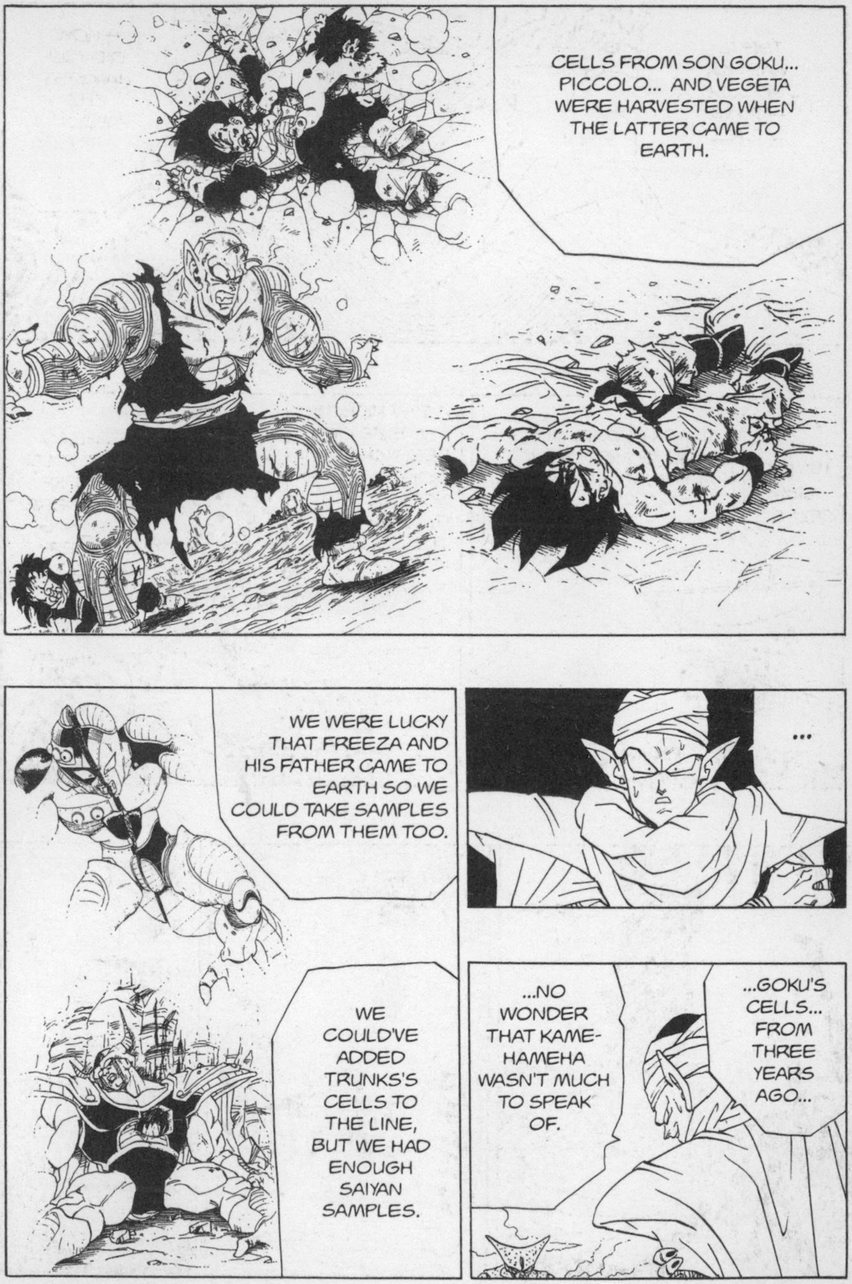

CELLS FROM SON GOKU... PICCOLO... AND VEGETA WERE HARVESTED WHEN THE LATTER CAME TO EARTH.
...
...GOKU'S CELLS... FROM THREE YEARS AGO...
...NO WONDER THAT KAME-HAMEHA WASN'T MUCH TO SPEAK OF.
WE WERE LUCKY THAT FREEZA AND HIS FATHER CAME TO EARTH SO WE COULD TAKE SAMPLES FROM THEM TOO.
WE COULD'VE ADDED TRUNKS'S CELLS TO THE LINE, BUT WE HAD ENOUGH SAIYAN SAMPLES.

READ THIS WAY

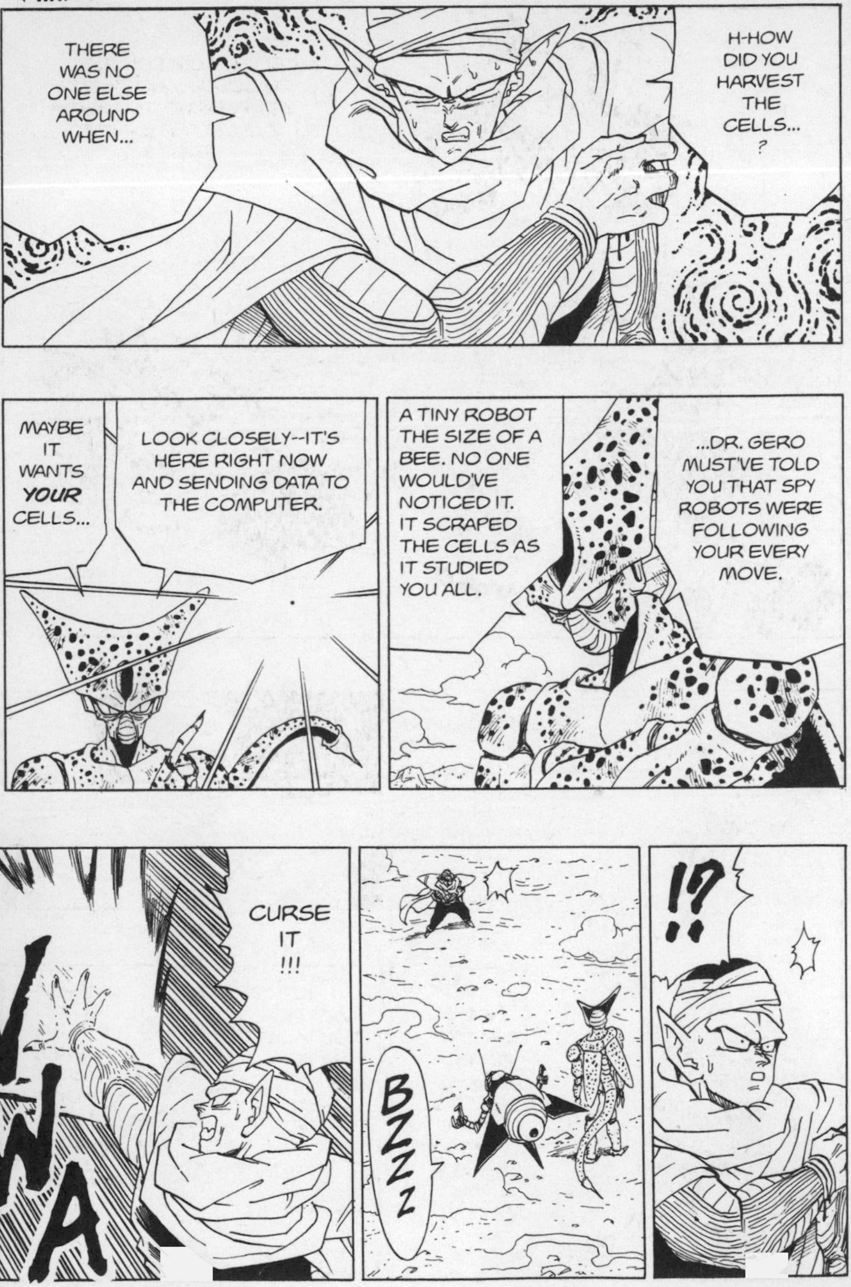

H-HOW DID YOU HARVEST THE CELLS...?
THERE WAS NO ONE ELSE AROUND WHEN...
...DR. GERO MUST'VE TOLD YOU THAT SPY ROBOTS WERE FOLLOWING YOUR EVERY MOVE.
A TINY ROBOT THE SIZE OF A BEE. NO ONE WOULD'VE NOTICED IT. IT SCRAPED THE CELLS AS IT STUDIED YOU ALL.
LOOK CLOSELY--IT'S HERE RIGHT NOW AND SENDING DATA TO THE COMPUTER.
MAYBE IT WANTS *YOUR* CELLS...
!?
BZZZ
CURSE IT!!!
VWA

READ THIS WAY

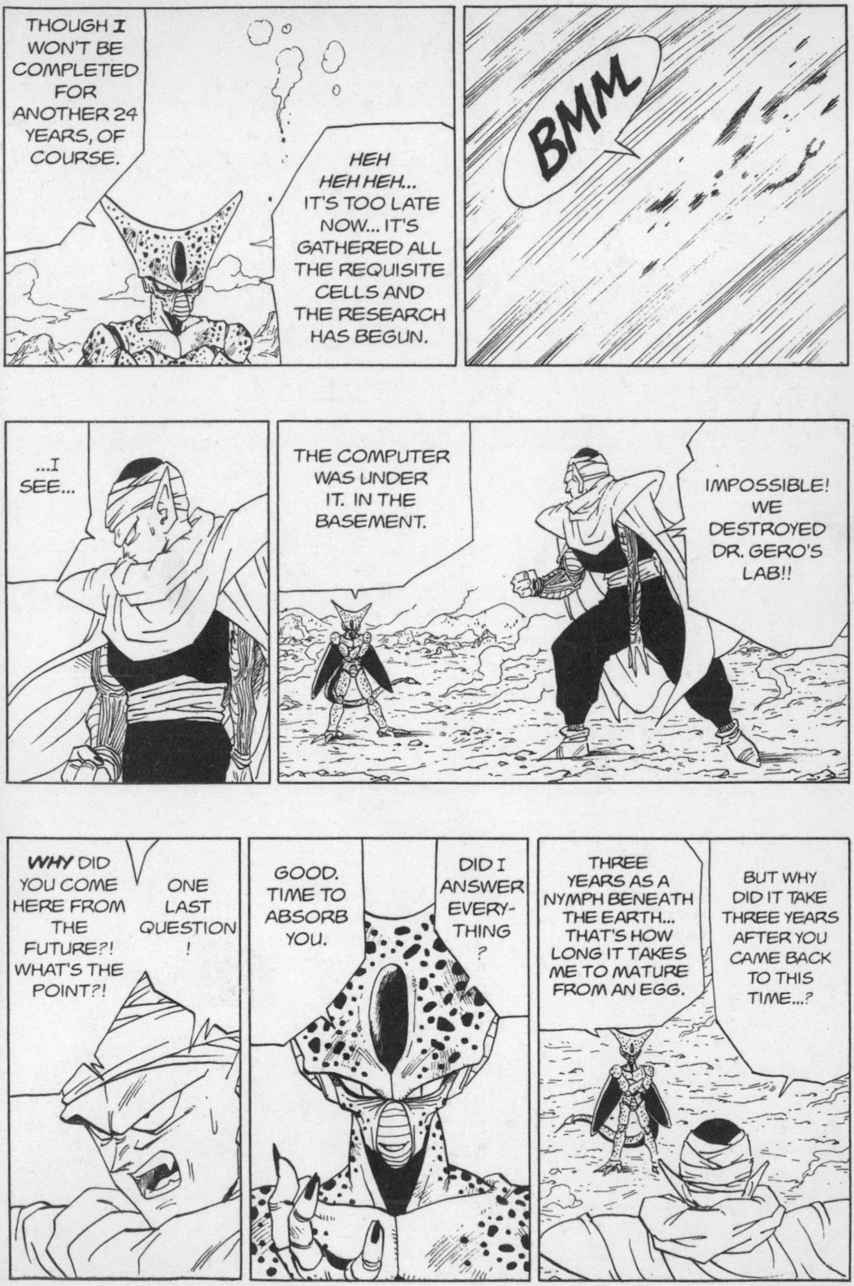

BMM
HEH HEH HEH... IT'S TOO LATE NOW... IT'S GATHERED ALL THE REQUISITE CELLS AND THE RESEARCH HAS BEGUN.
THOUGH I WON'T BE COMPLETED FOR ANOTHER 24 YEARS, OF COURSE.
IMPOSSIBLE! WE DESTROYED DR. GERO'S LAB!!
THE COMPUTER WAS UNDER IT. IN THE BASEMENT.
...I SEE...
BUT WHY DID IT TAKE THREE YEARS AFTER YOU CAME BACK TO THIS TIME...?
THREE YEARS AS A NYMPH BENEATH THE EARTH... THAT'S HOW LONG IT TAKES ME TO MATURE FROM AN EGG.
DID I ANSWER EVERY-THING?
GOOD. TIME TO ABSORB YOU.
ONE LAST QUESTION!
WHY DID YOU COME HERE FROM THE FUTURE?! WHAT'S THE POINT?!

READ THIS WAY

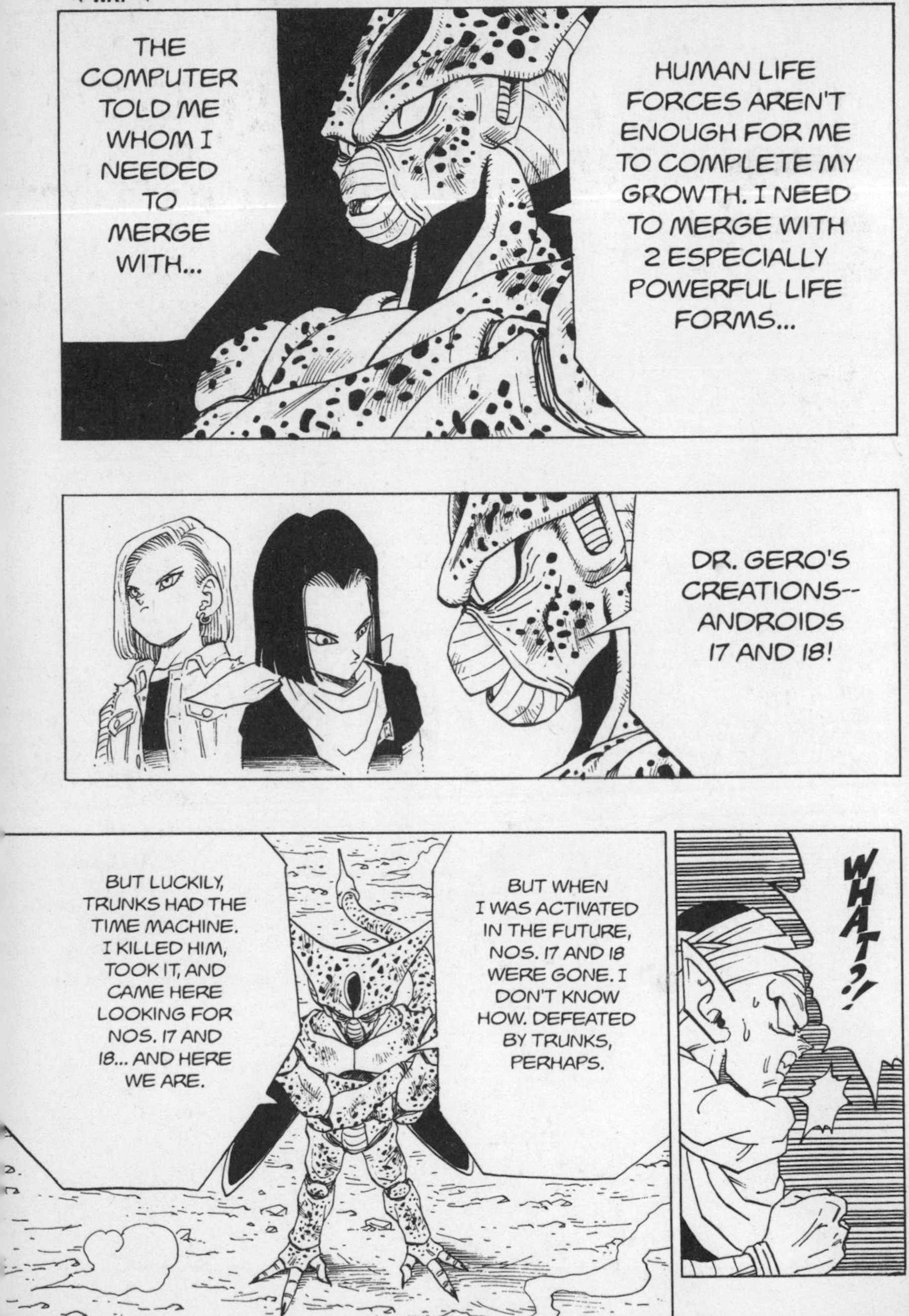

HUMAN LIFE FORCES AREN'T ENOUGH FOR ME TO COMPLETE MY GROWTH. I NEED TO MERGE WITH 2 ESPECIALLY POWERFUL LIFE FORMS...
THE COMPUTER TOLD ME WHOM I NEEDED TO MERGE WITH...
DR. GERO'S CREATIONS-- ANDROIDS 17 AND 18!
WHAT?!
BUT WHEN I WAS ACTIVATED IN THE FUTURE, NOS. 17 AND 18 WERE GONE. I DON'T KNOW HOW. DEFEATED BY TRUNKS, PERHAPS.
BUT LUCKILY, TRUNKS HAD THE TIME MACHINE. I KILLED HIM, TOOK IT, AND CAME HERE LOOKING FOR NOS. 17 AND 18... AND HERE WE ARE.

READ THIS WAY

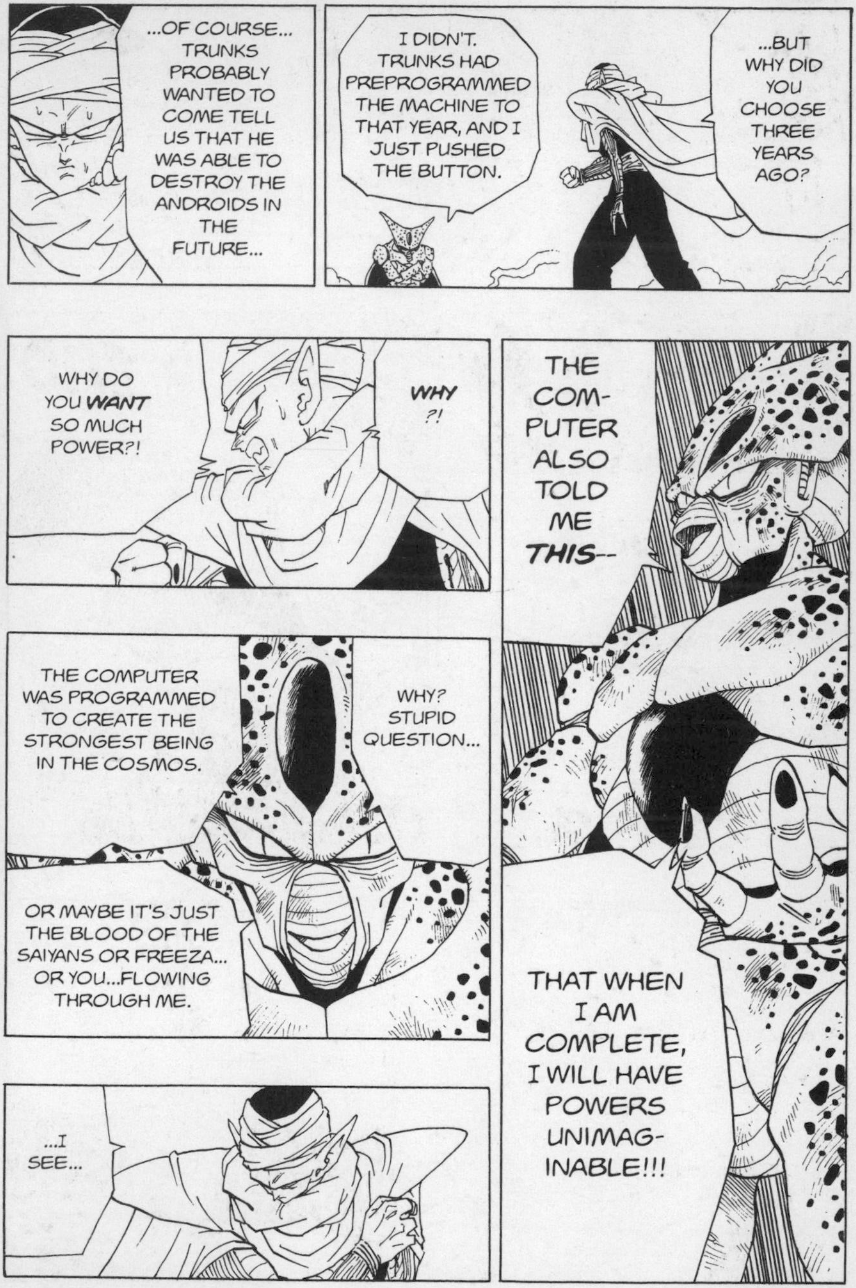
...BUT WHY DID YOU CHOOSE THREE YEARS AGO?
I DIDN'T. TRUNKS HAD PREPROGRAMMED THE MACHINE TO THAT YEAR, AND I JUST PUSHED THE BUTTON.
...OF COURSE... TRUNKS PROBABLY WANTED TO COME TELL US THAT HE WAS ABLE TO DESTROY THE ANDROIDS IN THE FUTURE...
THE COMPUTER ALSO TOLD ME *THIS*--
THAT WHEN I AM COMPLETE, I WILL HAVE POWERS UNIMAGINABLE!!!
WHY ?!
WHY DO YOU *WANT* SO MUCH POWER?!
WHY? STUPID QUESTION...
THE COMPUTER WAS PROGRAMMED TO CREATE THE STRONGEST BEING IN THE COSMOS.
OR MAYBE IT'S JUST THE BLOOD OF THE SAIYANS OR FREEZA... OR YOU...FLOWING THROUGH ME.
...I SEE...

READ THIS WAY

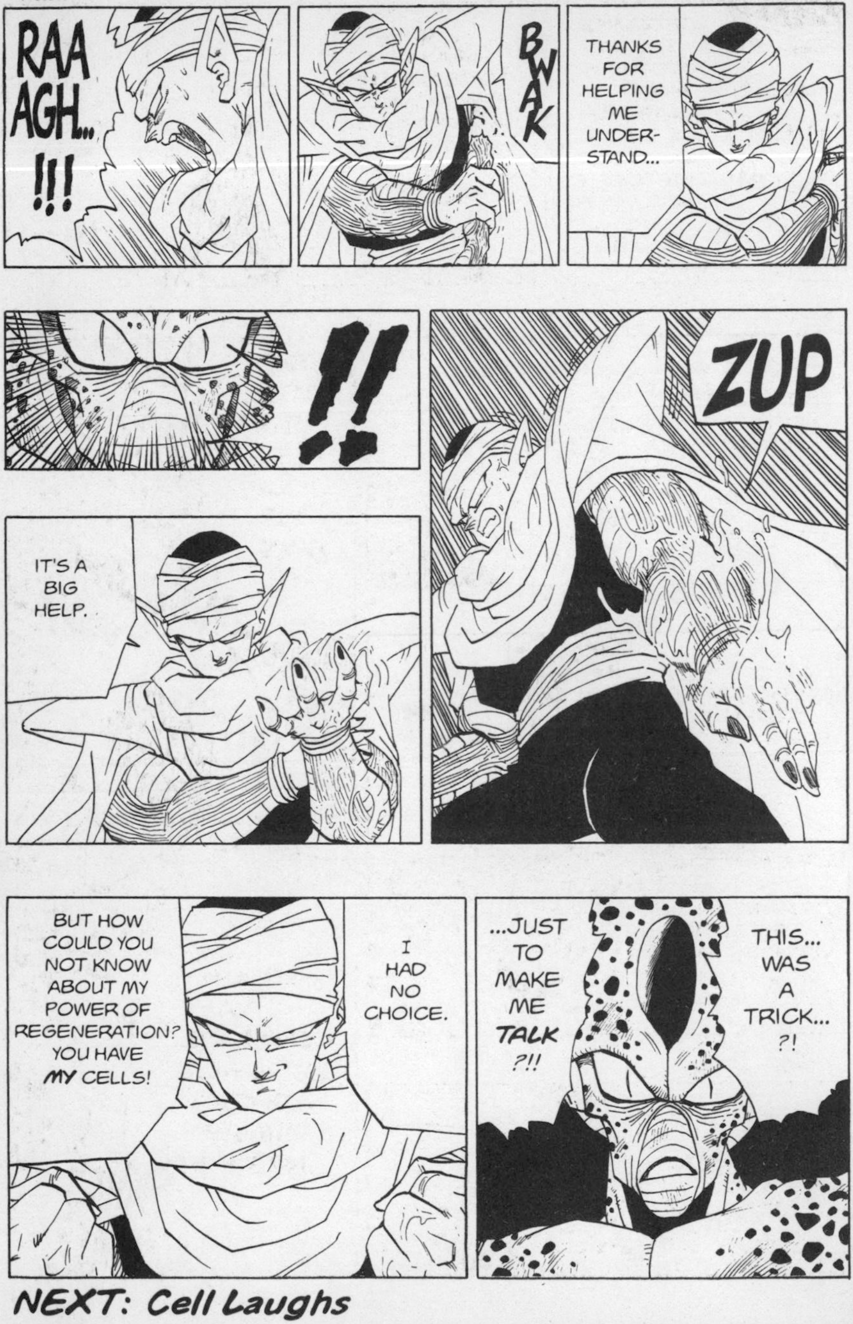
THANKS FOR HELPING ME UNDER-STAND...
BWAK
RAAAGH... !!!
ZUP
!!
IT'S A BIG HELP.
THIS... WAS A TRICK... ?!
...JUST TO MAKE ME TALK ?!!
I HAD NO CHOICE.
BUT HOW COULD YOU NOT KNOW ABOUT MY POWER OF REGENERATION? YOU HAVE MY CELLS!

NEXT: Cell Laughs

DBZ: 170 • Cell Laughs Last

READ THIS WAY

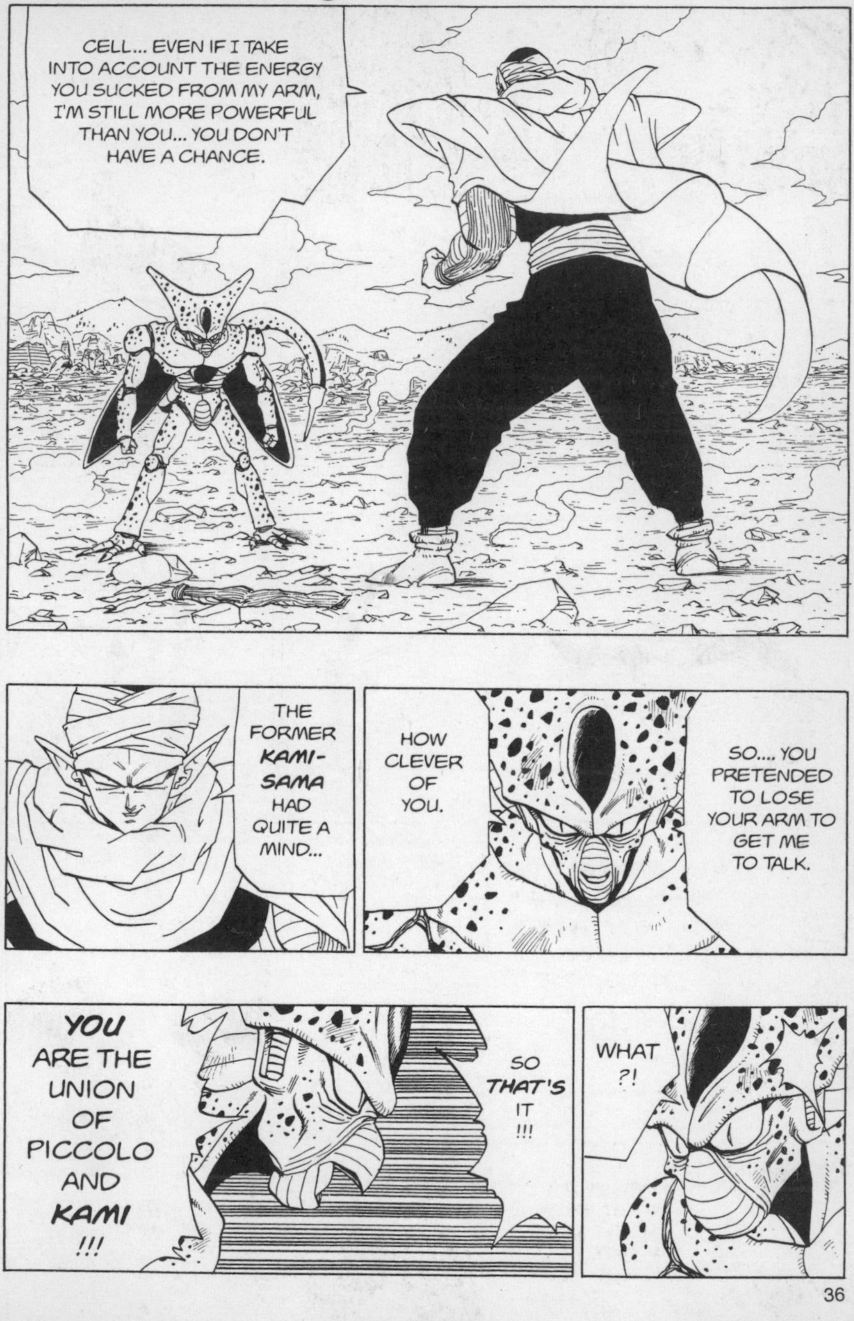

CELL... EVEN IF I TAKE INTO ACCOUNT THE ENERGY YOU SUCKED FROM MY ARM, I'M STILL MORE POWERFUL THAN YOU... YOU DON'T HAVE A CHANCE.
SO.... YOU PRETENDED TO LOSE YOUR ARM TO GET ME TO TALK.
HOW CLEVER OF YOU.
THE FORMER *KAMI-SAMA* HAD QUITE A MIND...
WHAT ?!
SO *THAT'S* IT !!!
YOU ARE THE UNION OF PICCOLO AND ***KAMI*** !!!

READ THIS WAY

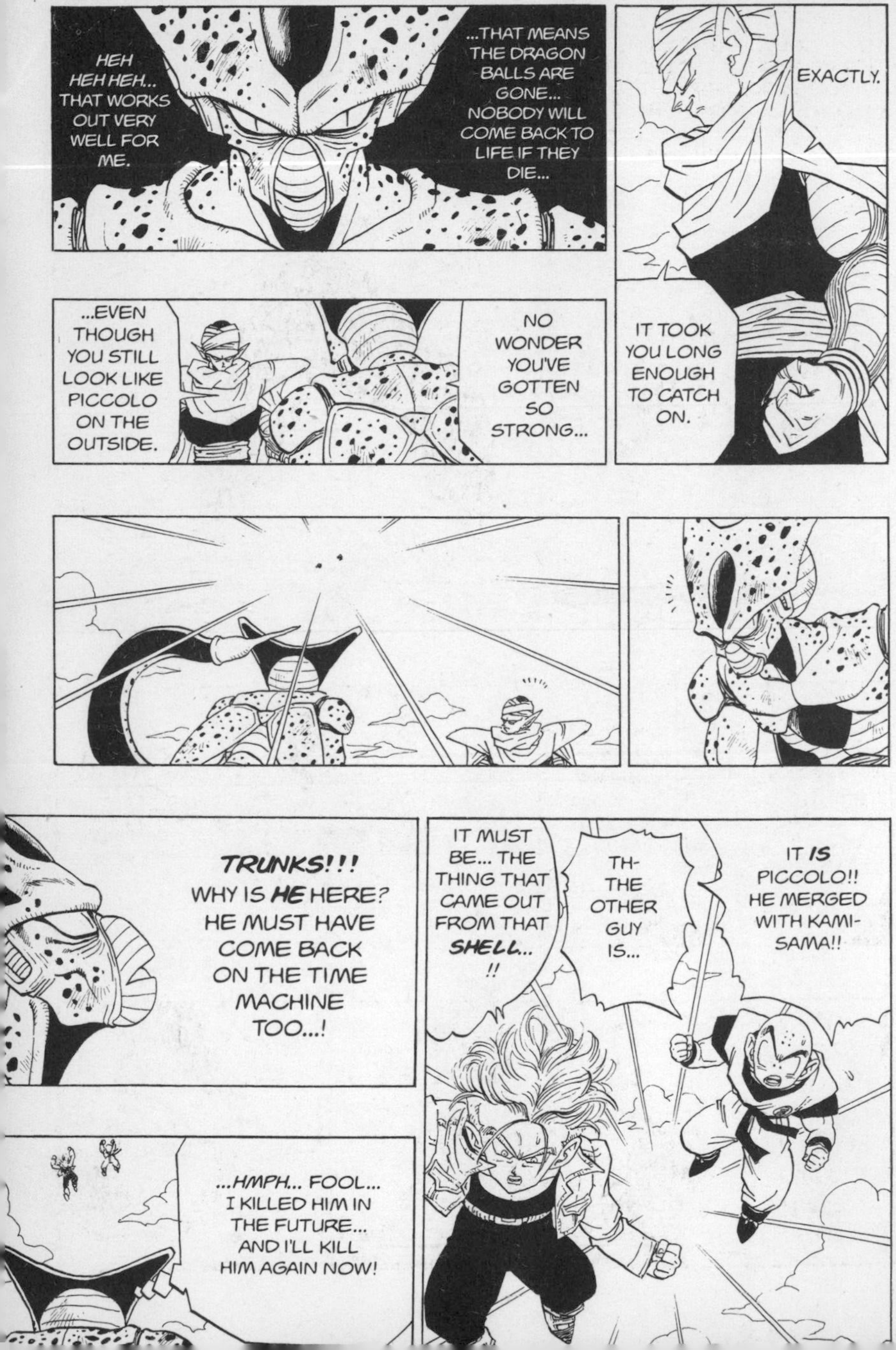
EXACTLY.
IT TOOK YOU LONG ENOUGH TO CATCH ON.
...THAT MEANS THE DRAGON BALLS ARE GONE... NOBODY WILL COME BACK TO LIFE IF THEY DIE...
HEH HEH HEH... THAT WORKS OUT VERY WELL FOR ME.
NO WONDER YOU'VE GOTTEN SO STRONG...
...EVEN THOUGH YOU STILL LOOK LIKE PICCOLO ON THE OUTSIDE.
IT *IS* PICCOLO!! HE MERGED WITH KAMI-SAMA!!
TH- THE OTHER GUY IS...
IT MUST BE... THE THING THAT CAME OUT FROM THAT *SHELL*...!!
TRUNKS!!! WHY IS *HE* HERE? HE MUST HAVE COME BACK ON THE TIME MACHINE TOO...!
...HMPH... FOOL... I KILLED HIM IN THE FUTURE... AND I'LL KILL HIM AGAIN NOW!

READ THIS WAY

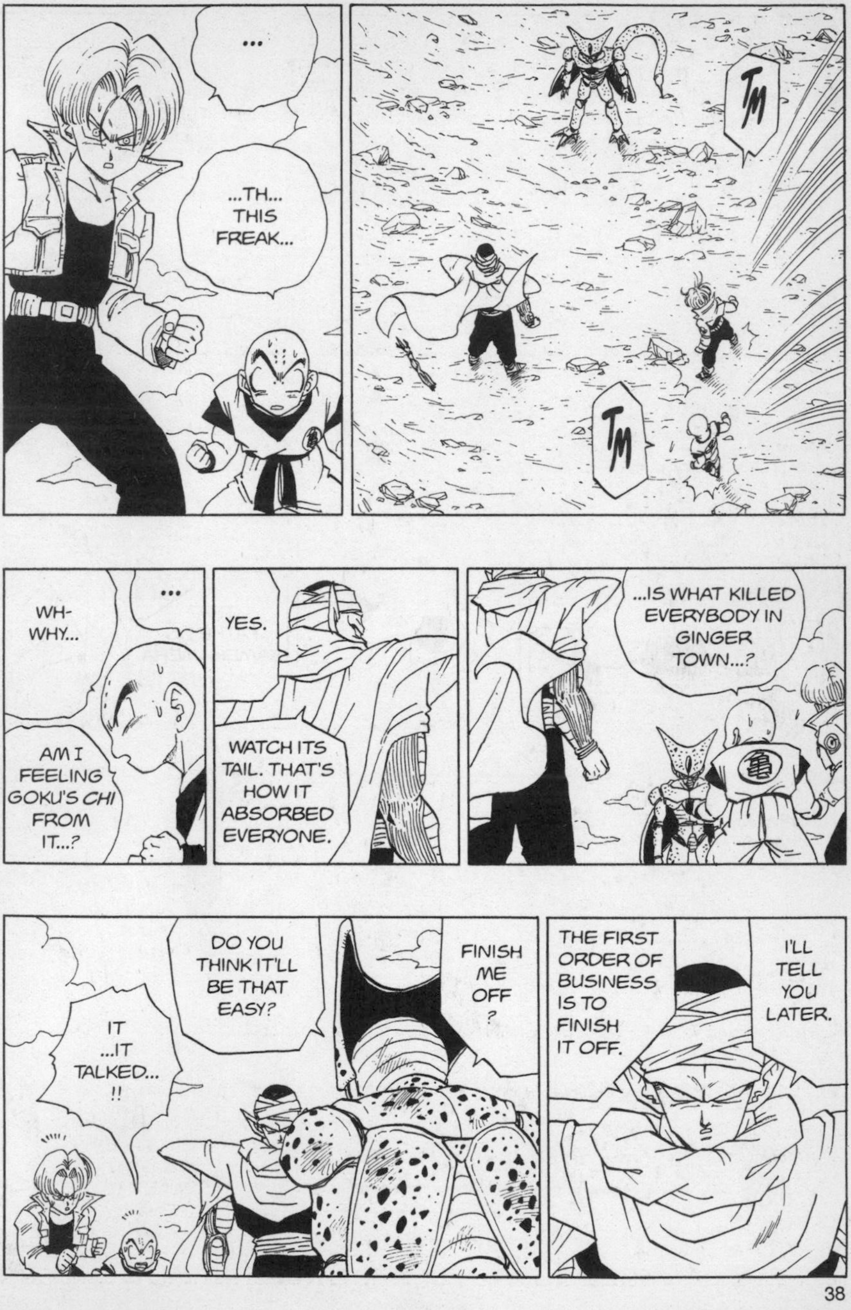
TM
TM
...
...TH... THIS FREAK...
...IS WHAT KILLED EVERYBODY IN GINGER TOWN...?
YES.
WATCH ITS TAIL. THAT'S HOW IT ABSORBED EVERYONE.
...
WH- WHY...
AM I FEELING GOKU'S *CHI* FROM IT...?
I'LL TELL YOU LATER.
THE FIRST ORDER OF BUSINESS IS TO FINISH IT OFF.
FINISH ME OFF?
DO YOU THINK IT'LL BE THAT EASY?
IT ...IT TALKED... !!

READ THIS WAY

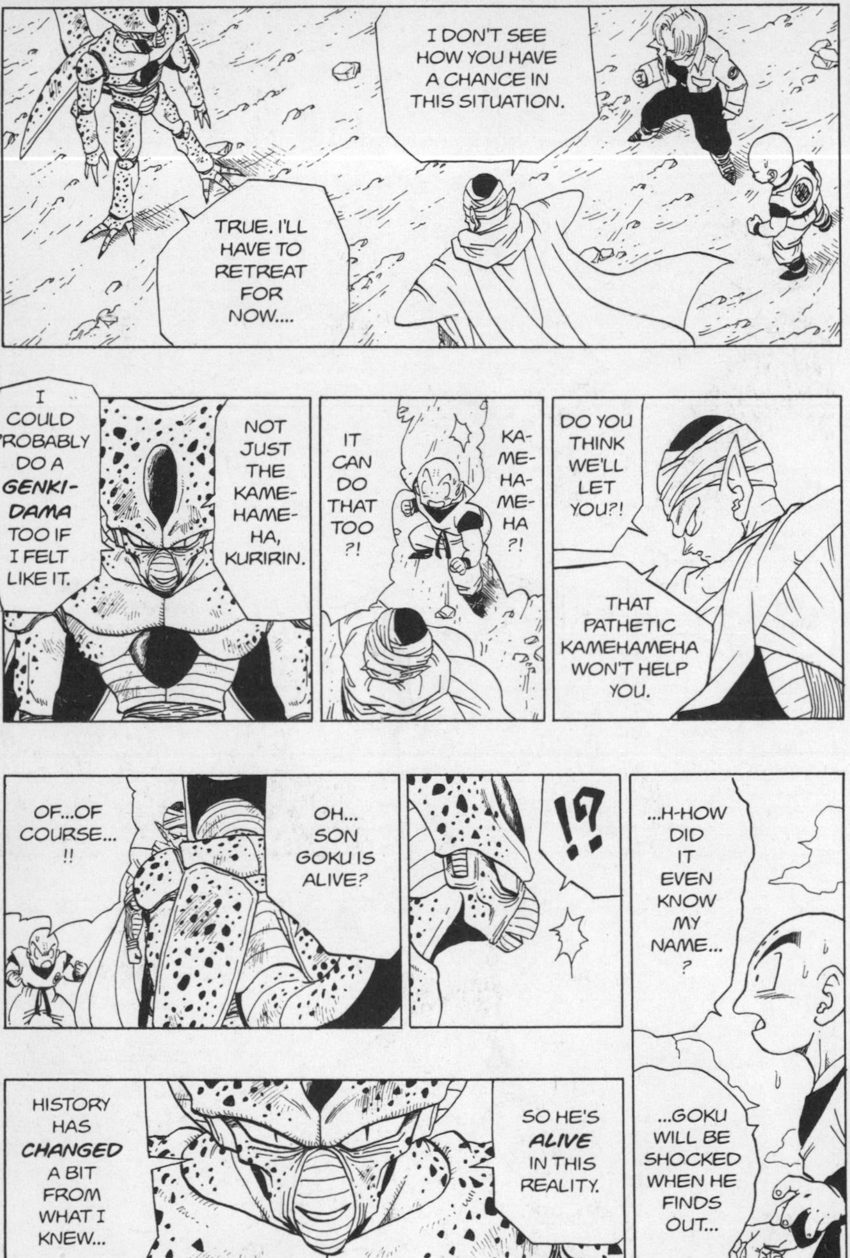

I DON'T SEE HOW YOU HAVE A CHANCE IN THIS SITUATION.
TRUE. I'LL HAVE TO RETREAT FOR NOW....
DO YOU THINK WE'LL LET YOU?!
THAT PATHETIC KAMEHAMEHA WON'T HELP YOU.
KA-ME-HA-ME-HA?!
IT CAN DO THAT TOO?!
NOT JUST THE KAME-HAME-HA, KURIRIN.
I COULD PROBABLY DO A GENKI-DAMA TOO IF I FELT LIKE IT.
...H-HOW DID IT EVEN KNOW MY NAME...?
...GOKU WILL BE SHOCKED WHEN HE FINDS OUT...
!?
OH... SON GOKU IS ALIVE?
OF...OF COURSE...!!
SO HE'S ALIVE IN THIS REALITY.
HISTORY HAS CHANGED A BIT FROM WHAT I KNEW...

READ THIS WAY

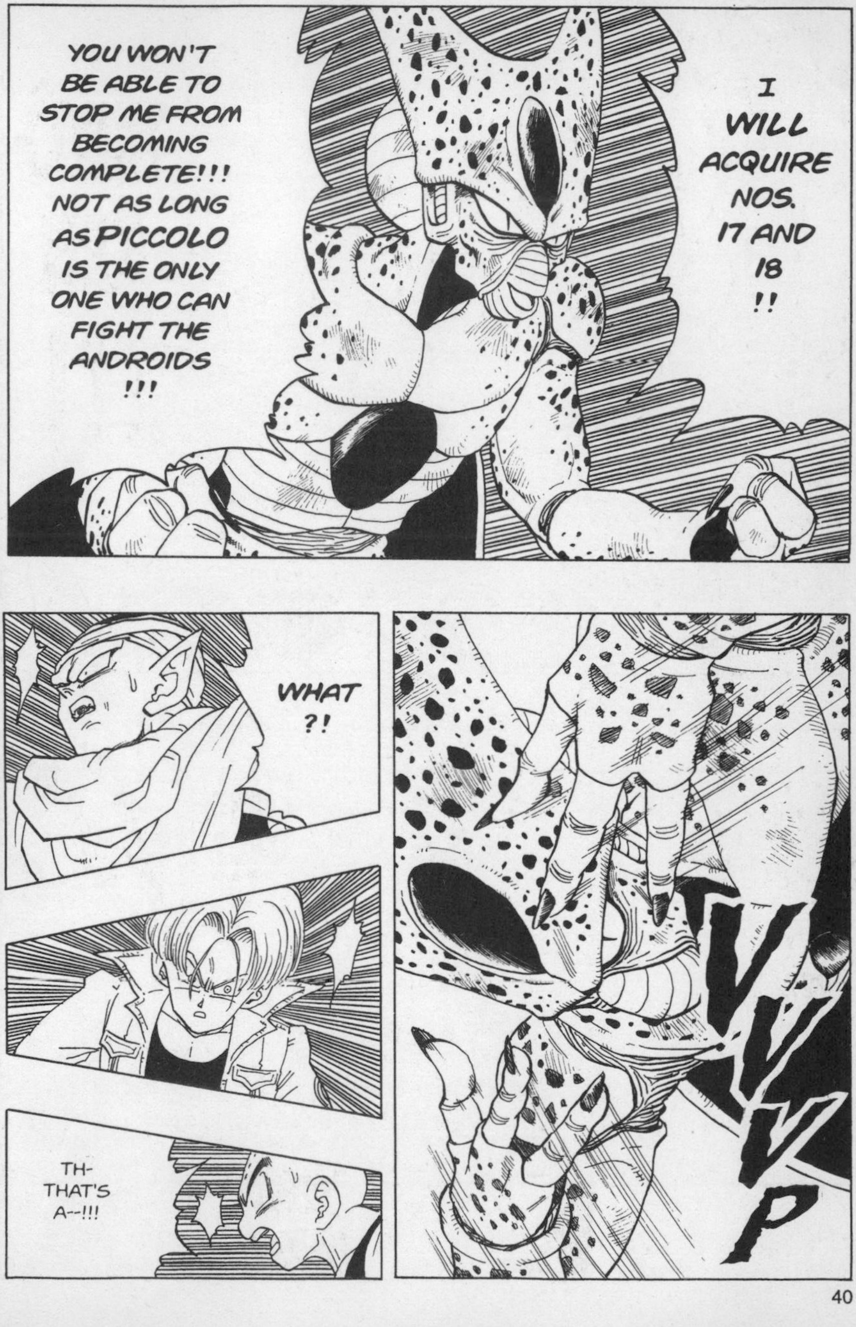
I WILL ACQUIRE NOS. 17 AND 18!!
YOU WON'T BE ABLE TO STOP ME FROM BECOMING COMPLETE!!! NOT AS LONG AS PICCOLO IS THE ONLY ONE WHO CAN FIGHT THE ANDROIDS!!!
VVVP
WHAT?!
TH-THAT'S A--!!!

READ THIS WAY

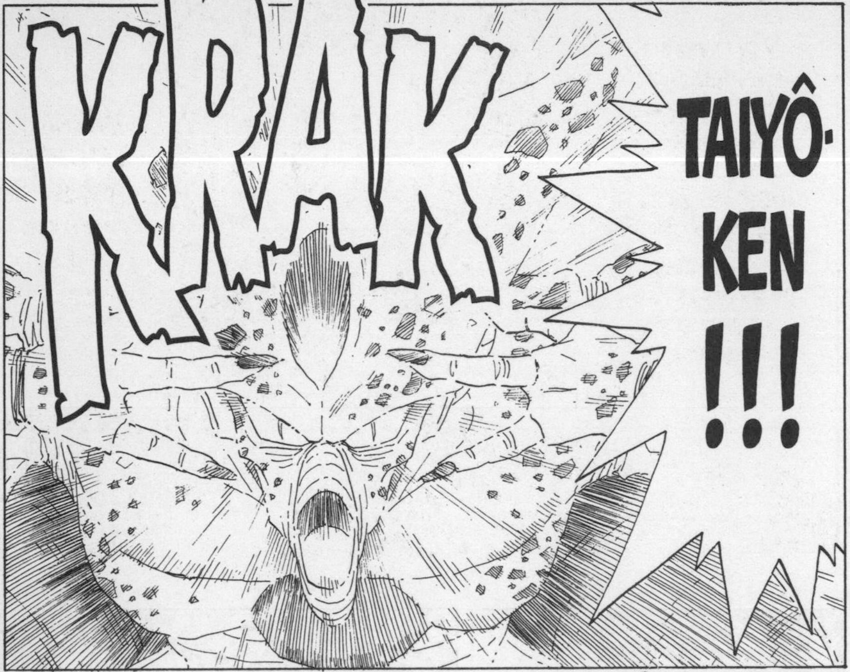
KRAK
TAIYÔ-KEN!!!

*A.K.A. "FIST OF THE SUN!"

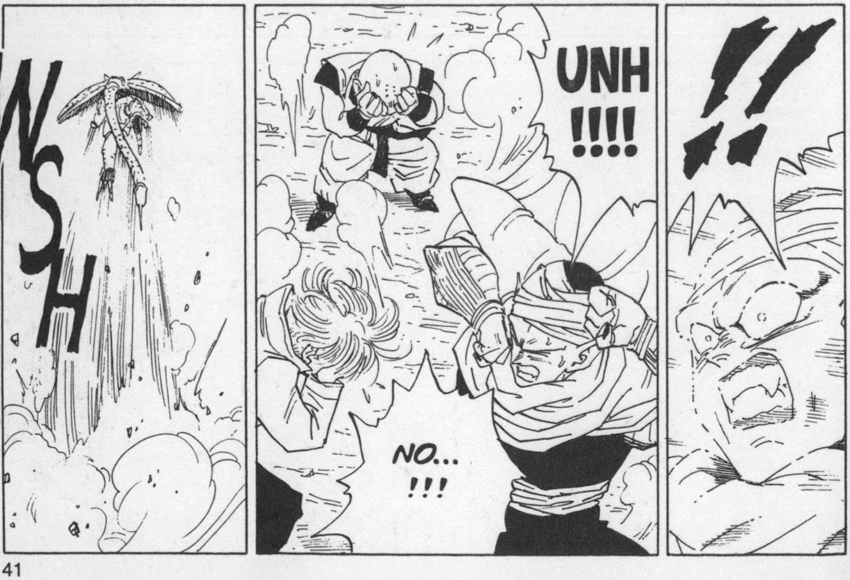
!!
UNH!!!!
NO...!!!
WSH

READ THIS WAY

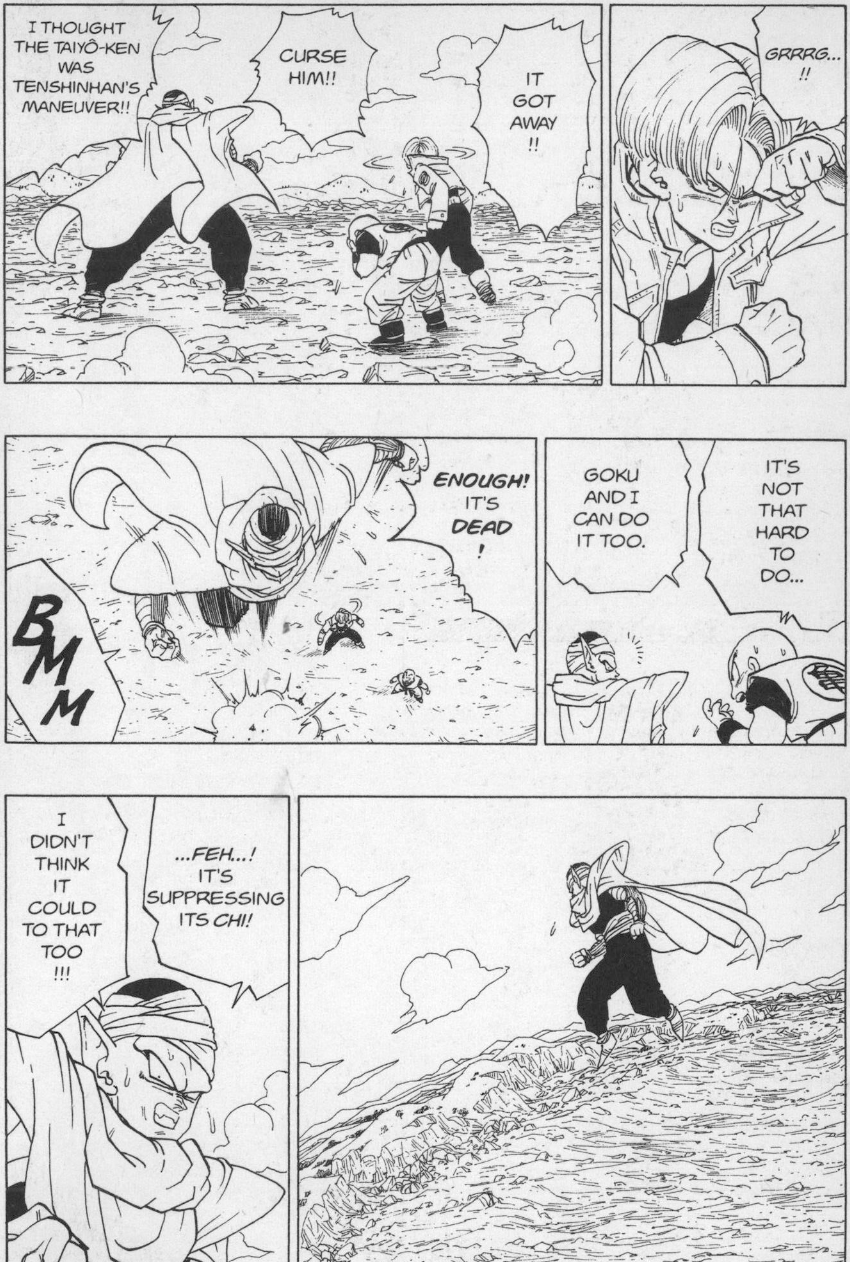
GRRRG... !!
IT GOT AWAY !!
CURSE HIM!!
I THOUGHT THE TAIYÔ-KEN WAS TENSHINHAN'S MANEUVER!!
IT'S NOT THAT HARD TO DO...
GOKU AND I CAN DO IT TOO.
ENOUGH! IT'S DEAD !
BMM
...FEH...! IT'S SUPPRESSING ITS CHI!
I DIDN'T THINK IT COULD TO THAT TOO !!!

READ THIS WAY

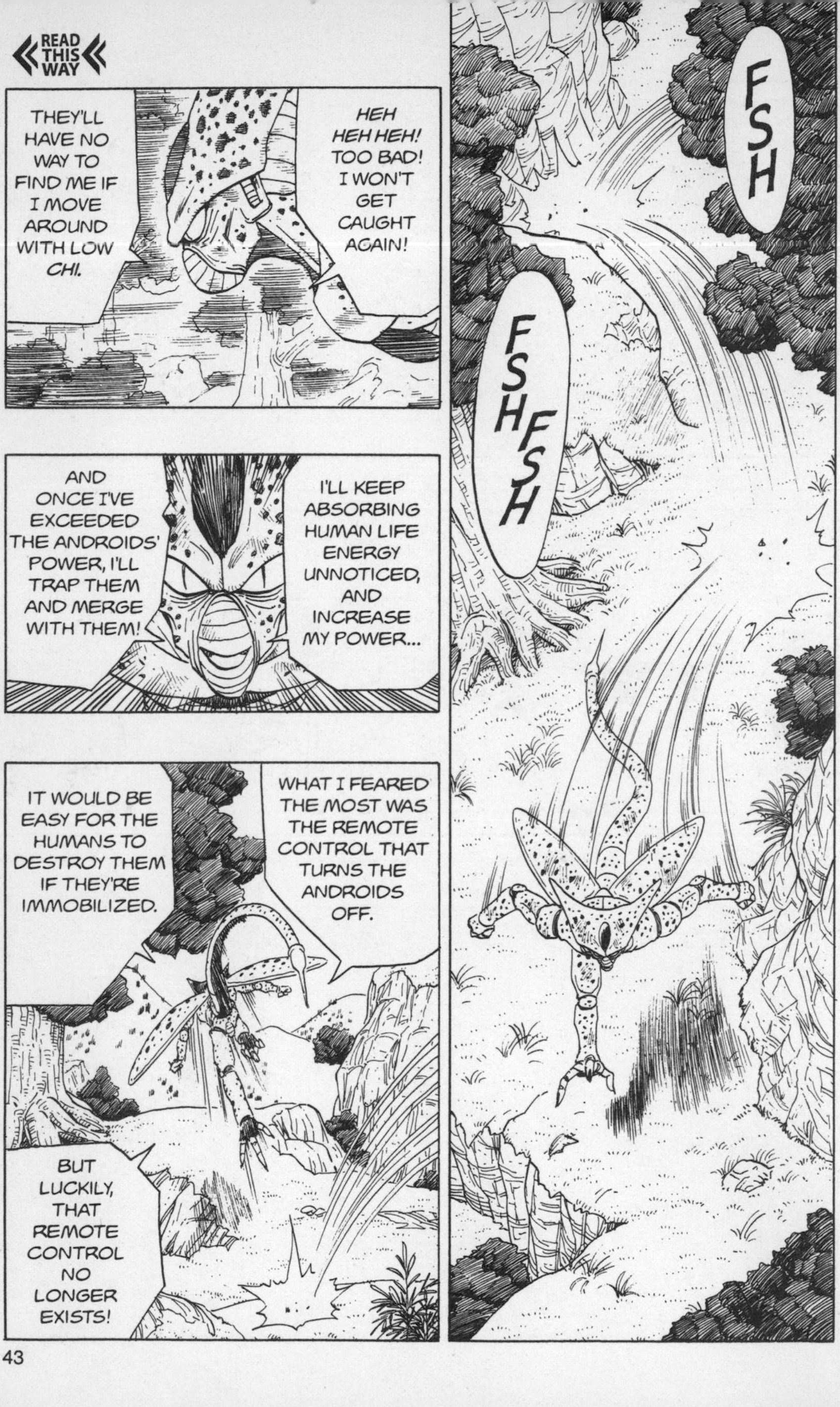
FSH
FSHFSH
HEH HEH HEH! TOO BAD! I WON'T GET CAUGHT AGAIN!
THEY'LL HAVE NO WAY TO FIND ME IF I MOVE AROUND WITH LOW CHI.
I'LL KEEP ABSORBING HUMAN LIFE ENERGY UNNOTICED, AND INCREASE MY POWER...
AND ONCE I'VE EXCEEDED THE ANDROIDS' POWER, I'LL TRAP THEM AND MERGE WITH THEM!
WHAT I FEARED THE MOST WAS THE REMOTE CONTROL THAT TURNS THE ANDROIDS OFF.
IT WOULD BE EASY FOR THE HUMANS TO DESTROY THEM IF THEY'RE IMMOBILIZED.
BUT LUCKILY, THAT REMOTE CONTROL NO LONGER EXISTS!

READ THIS WAY

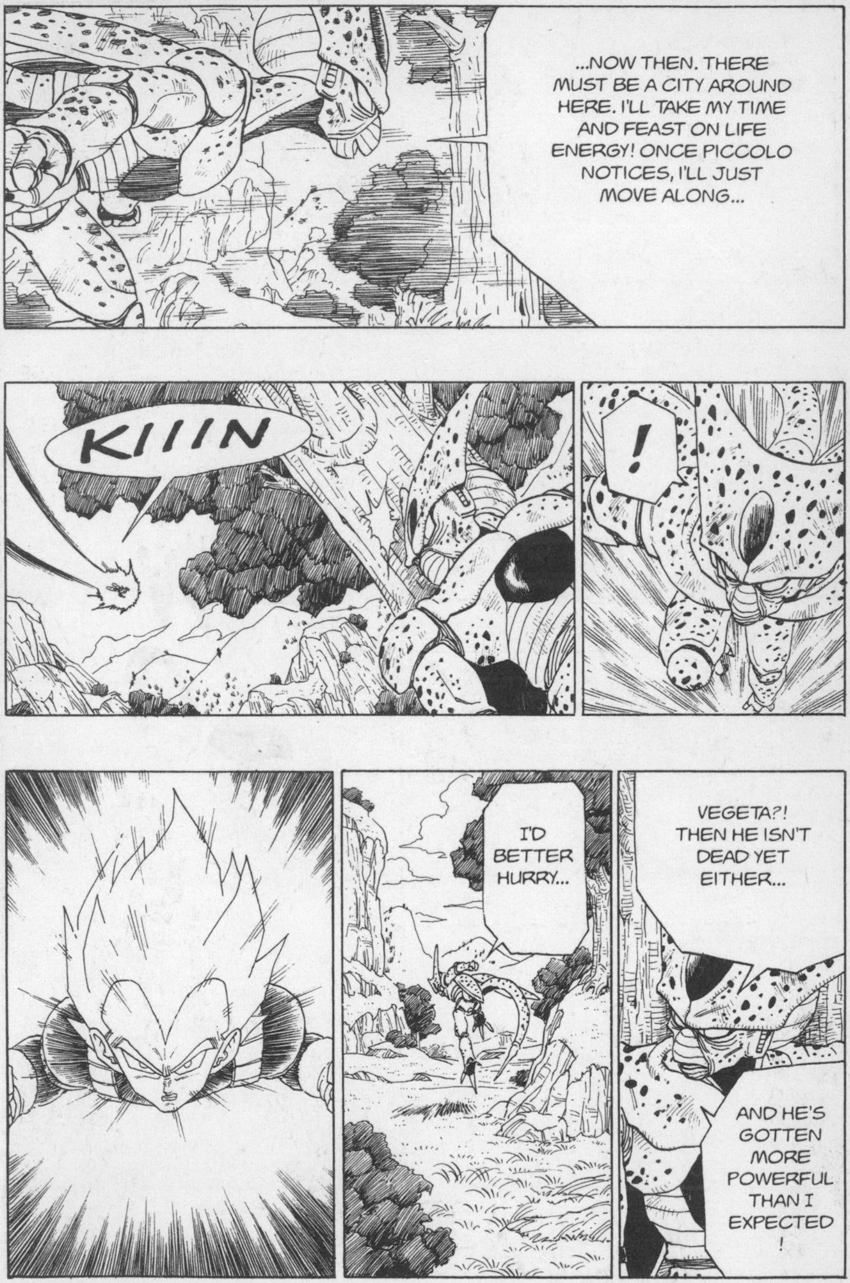
...NOW THEN. THERE MUST BE A CITY AROUND HERE. I'LL TAKE MY TIME AND FEAST ON LIFE ENERGY! ONCE PICCOLO NOTICES, I'LL JUST MOVE ALONG...
!
KIIIN
VEGETA?! THEN HE ISN'T DEAD YET EITHER...
AND HE'S GOTTEN MORE POWERFUL THAN I EXPECTED!
I'D BETTER HURRY...

READ THIS WAY

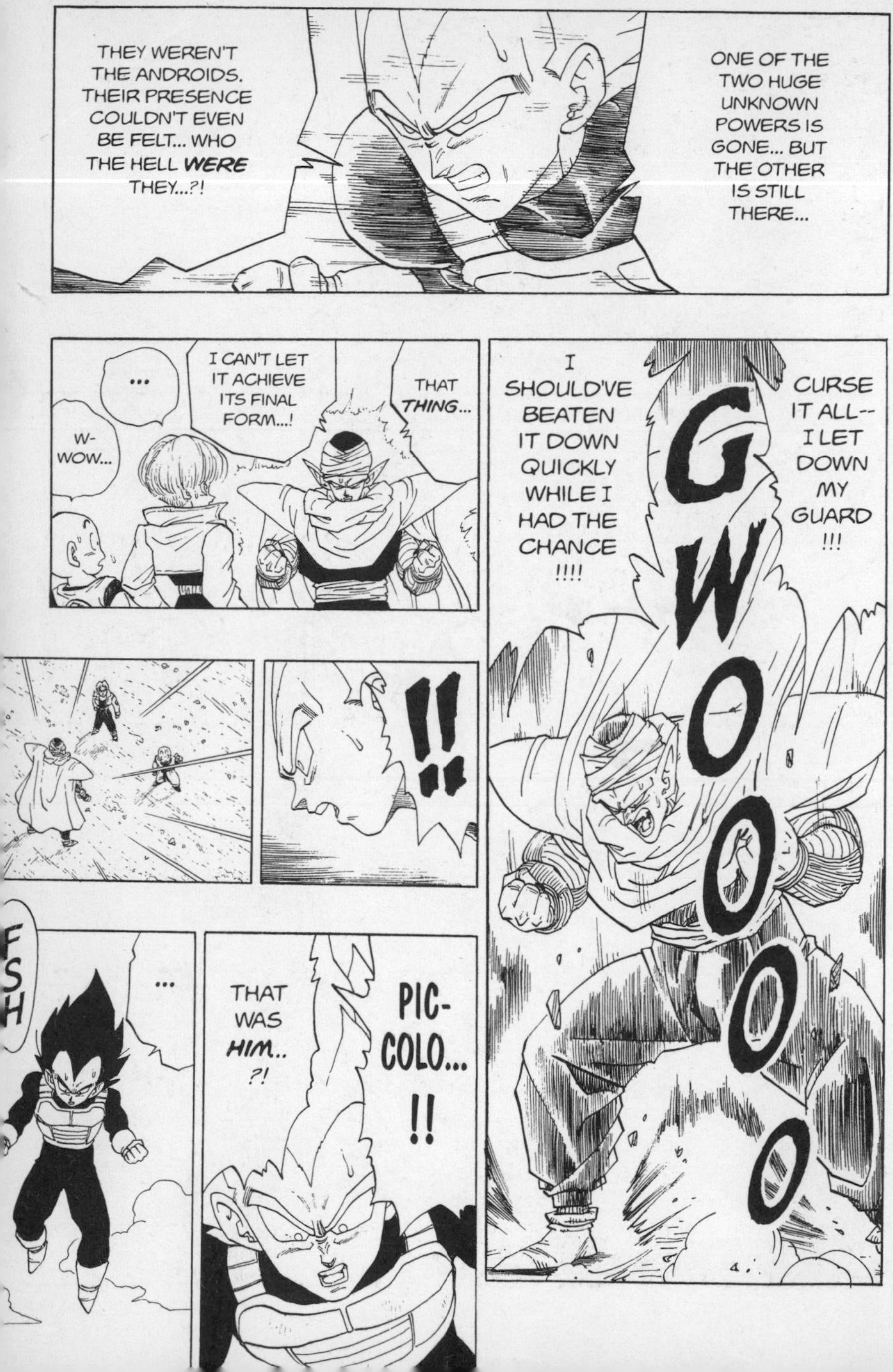

ONE OF THE TWO HUGE UNKNOWN POWERS IS GONE... BUT THE OTHER IS STILL THERE...
THEY WEREN'T THE ANDROIDS. THEIR PRESENCE COULDN'T EVEN BE FELT... WHO THE HELL *WERE* THEY...?!
CURSE IT ALL-- I LET DOWN MY GUARD!!!
I SHOULD'VE BEATEN IT DOWN QUICKLY WHILE I HAD THE CHANCE!!!!
GWOOOOO
THAT *THING*...
I CAN'T LET IT ACHIEVE ITS FINAL FORM...!
...
W-WOW...
!!
PIC-COLO...!!
THAT WAS *HIM*..?!
...
FSH

READ THIS WAY

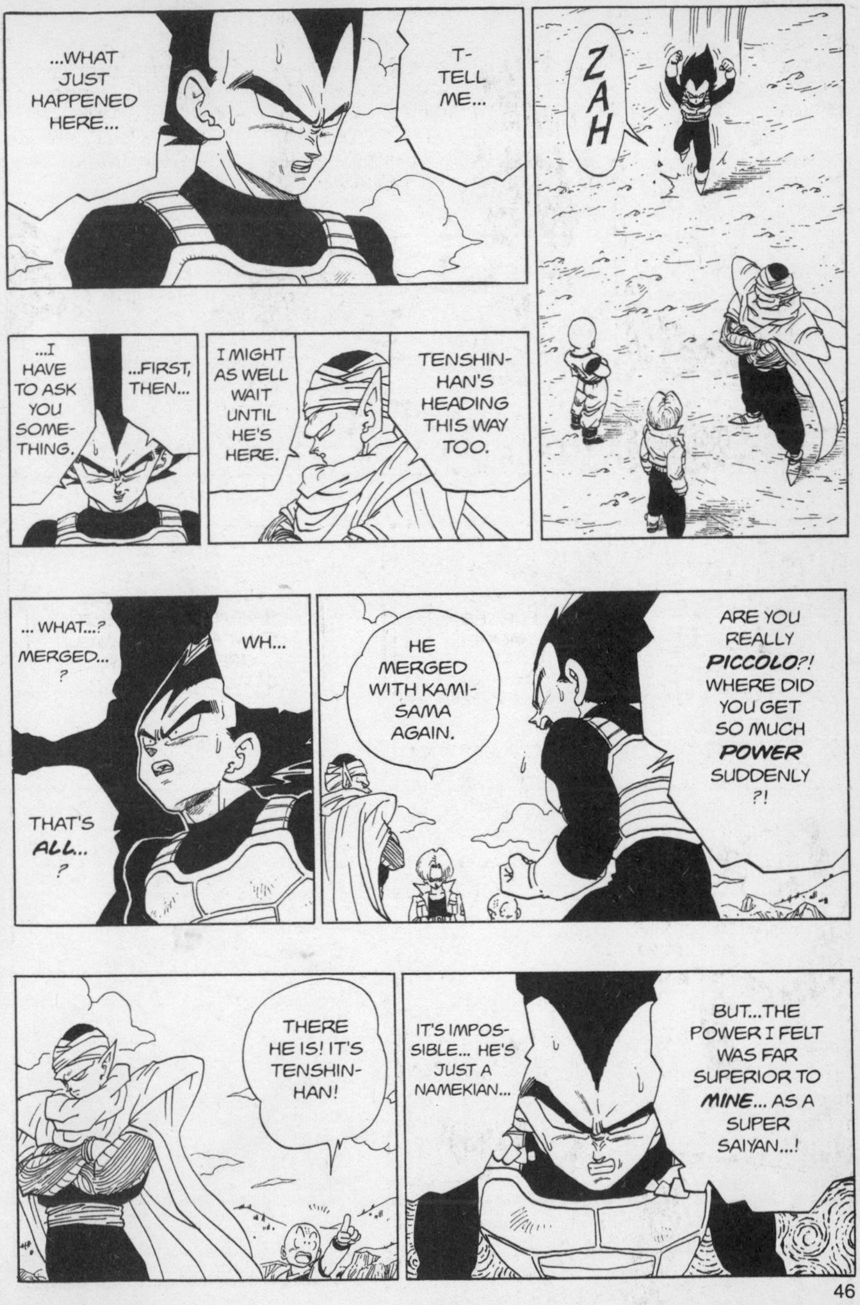

ZAH
T-TELL ME...
...WHAT JUST HAPPENED HERE...
TENSHIN-HAN'S HEADING THIS WAY TOO.
I MIGHT AS WELL WAIT UNTIL HE'S HERE.
...FIRST, THEN...
...I HAVE TO ASK YOU SOMETHING.
ARE YOU REALLY **PICCOLO**?! WHERE DID YOU GET SO MUCH **POWER** SUDDENLY?!
HE MERGED WITH KAMI-SAMA AGAIN.
WH...
... WHAT...? MERGED...?
THAT'S **ALL**...?
BUT...THE POWER I FELT WAS FAR SUPERIOR TO **MINE**... AS A SUPER SAIYAN...!
IT'S IMPOSSIBLE... HE'S JUST A NAMEKIAN...
THERE HE IS! IT'S TENSHIN-HAN!

READ THIS WAY

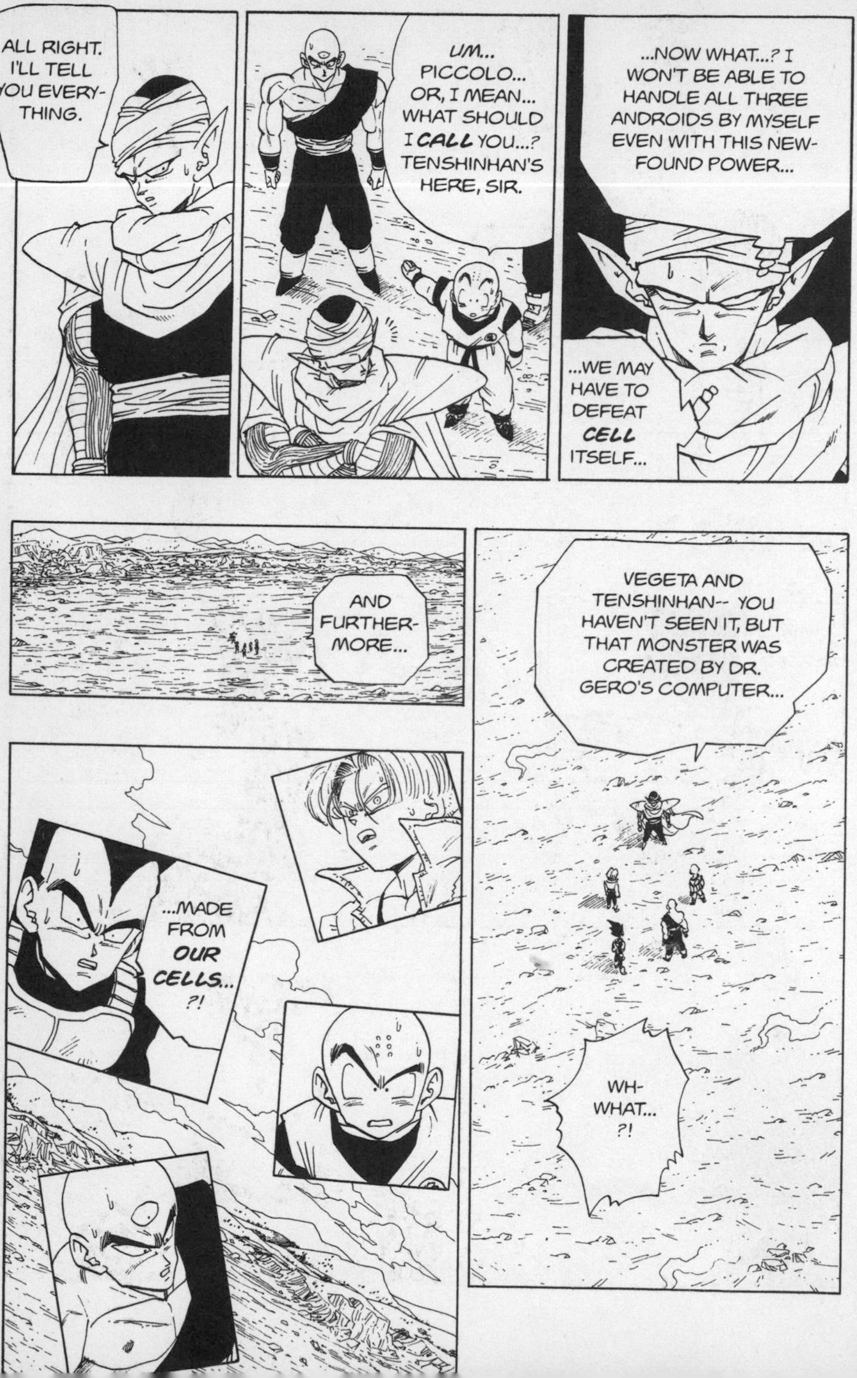
...NOW WHAT...? I WON'T BE ABLE TO HANDLE ALL THREE ANDROIDS BY MYSELF EVEN WITH THIS NEW-FOUND POWER...
...WE MAY HAVE TO DEFEAT **CELL** ITSELF...
UM... PICCOLO... OR, I MEAN... WHAT SHOULD I **CALL** YOU...? TENSHINHAN'S HERE, SIR.
ALL RIGHT. I'LL TELL YOU EVERY-THING.
VEGETA AND TENSHINHAN-- YOU HAVEN'T SEEN IT, BUT THAT MONSTER WAS CREATED BY DR. GERO'S COMPUTER...
WH-WHAT... ?!
AND FURTHER-MORE...
...MADE FROM **OUR CELLS**... ?!

READ THIS WAY

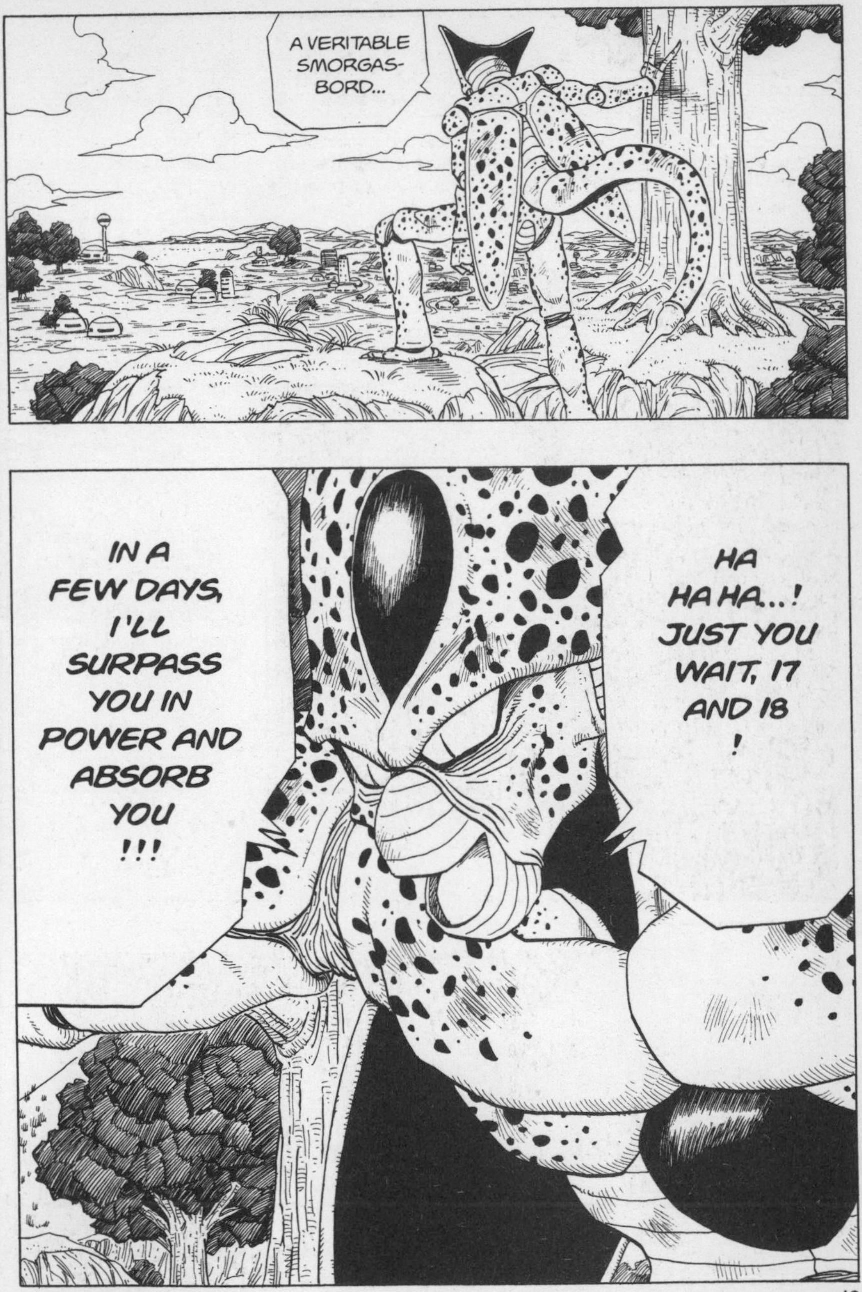
A VERITABLE SMORGAS-BORD...
HA HA HA...! JUST YOU WAIT, 17 AND 18!
IN A FEW DAYS, I'LL SURPASS YOU IN POWER AND ABSORB YOU!!!

READ THIS WAY

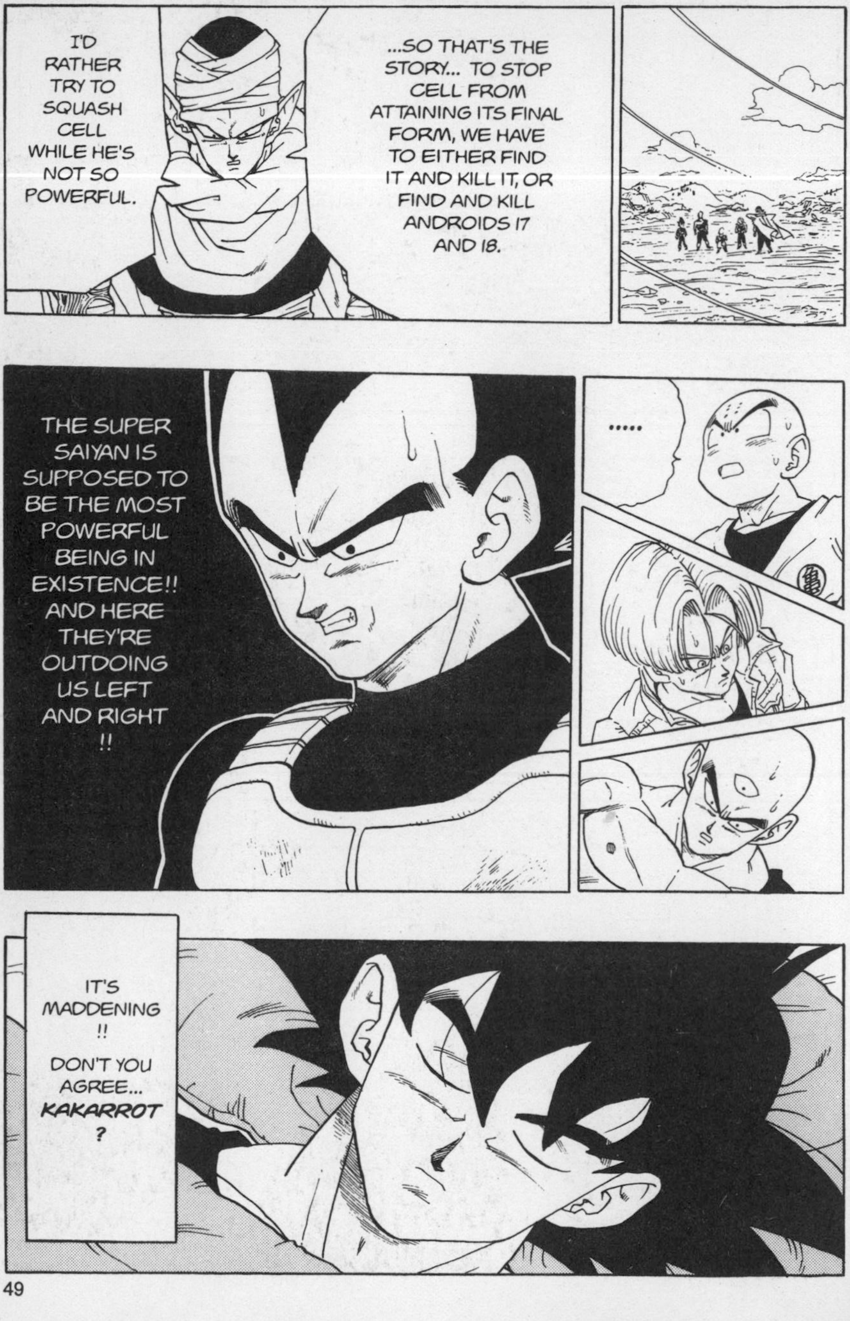
...SO THAT'S THE STORY... TO STOP CELL FROM ATTAINING ITS FINAL FORM, WE HAVE TO EITHER FIND IT AND KILL IT, OR FIND AND KILL ANDROIDS 17 AND 18.
I'D RATHER TRY TO SQUASH CELL WHILE HE'S NOT SO POWERFUL.
.....
THE SUPER SAIYAN IS SUPPOSED TO BE THE MOST POWERFUL BEING IN EXISTENCE!! AND HERE THEY'RE OUTDOING US LEFT AND RIGHT !!
IT'S MADDENING !!
DON'T YOU AGREE... ***KAKARROT*** ?

Tale 171 • Son Goku Awakens

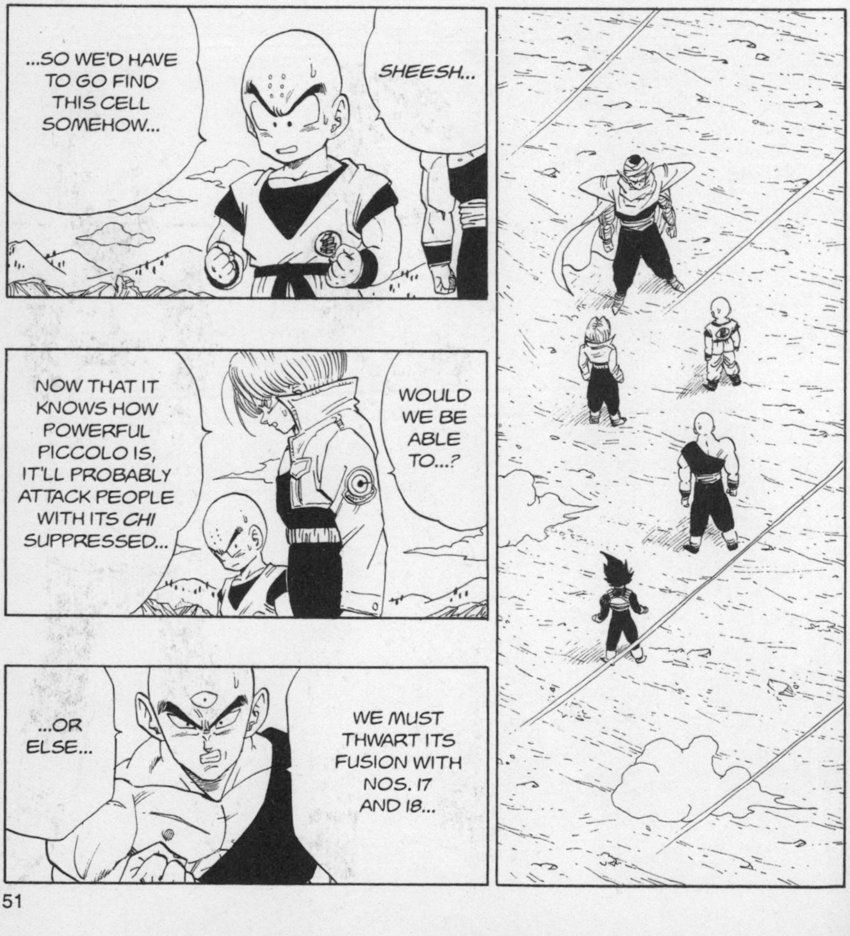
SHEESH...
...SO WE'D HAVE TO GO FIND THIS CELL SOMEHOW...
WOULD WE BE ABLE TO...?
NOW THAT IT KNOWS HOW POWERFUL PICCOLO IS, IT'LL PROBABLY ATTACK PEOPLE WITH ITS *CHI* SUPPRESSED...
WE MUST THWART ITS FUSION WITH NOS. 17 AND 18...
...OR ELSE...

READ THIS WAY

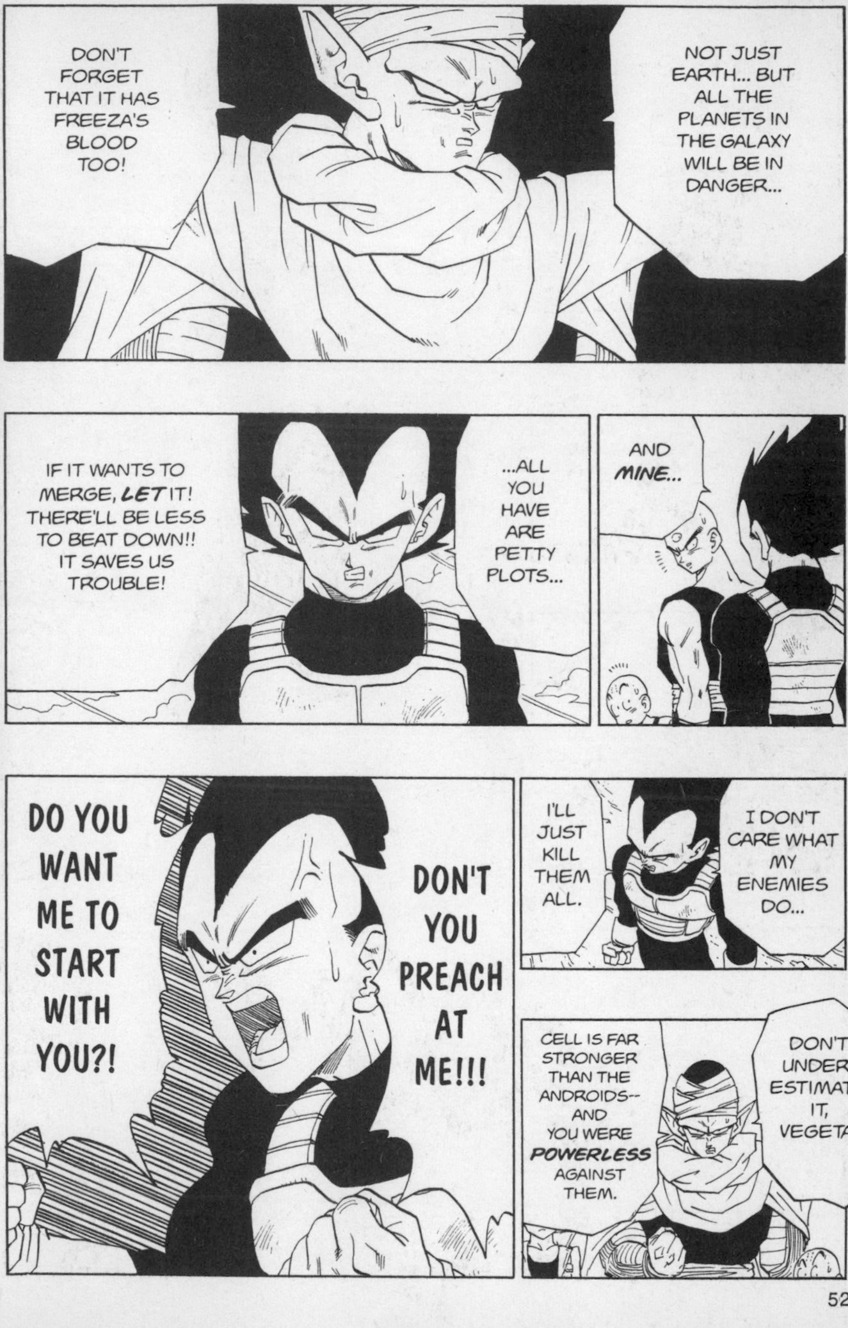

NOT JUST EARTH... BUT ALL THE PLANETS IN THE GALAXY WILL BE IN DANGER...
DON'T FORGET THAT IT HAS FREEZA'S BLOOD TOO!
AND MINE...
...ALL YOU HAVE ARE PETTY PLOTS...
IF IT WANTS TO MERGE, LET IT! THERE'LL BE LESS TO BEAT DOWN!! IT SAVES US TROUBLE!
I DON'T CARE WHAT MY ENEMIES DO...
I'LL JUST KILL THEM ALL.
DON'T UNDER-ESTIMATE IT, VEGETA.
CELL IS FAR STRONGER THAN THE ANDROIDS-- AND YOU WERE POWERLESS AGAINST THEM.
DON'T YOU PREACH AT ME!!!
DO YOU WANT ME TO START WITH YOU?!

READ THIS WAY

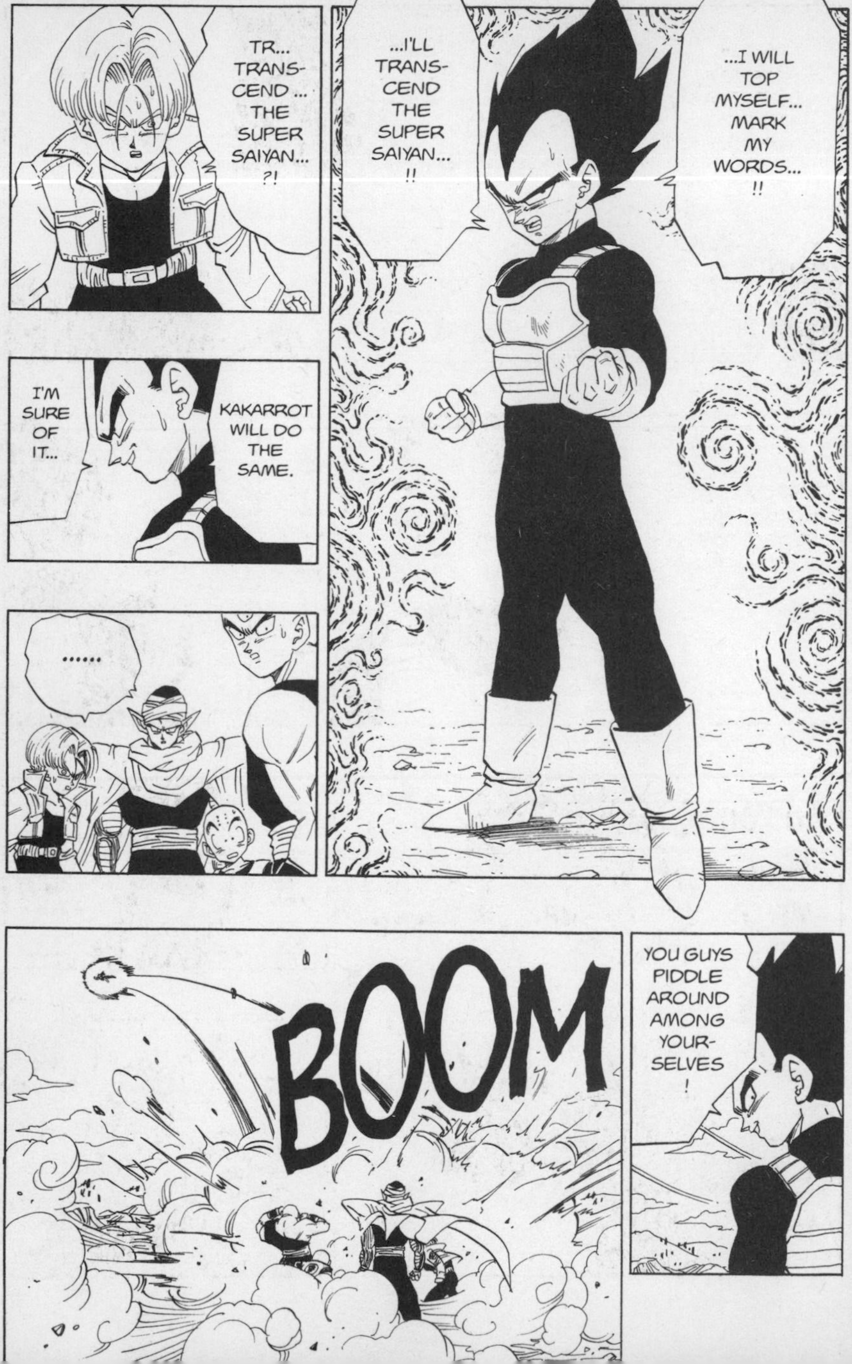
...I WILL TOP MYSELF... MARK MY WORDS...!!
...I'LL TRANSCEND THE SUPER SAIYAN...!!
TR... TRANSCEND... THE SUPER SAIYAN...?!
KAKARROT WILL DO THE SAME.
I'M SURE OF IT...
......
YOU GUYS PIDDLE AROUND AMONG YOURSELVES!
BOOM

READ THIS WAY

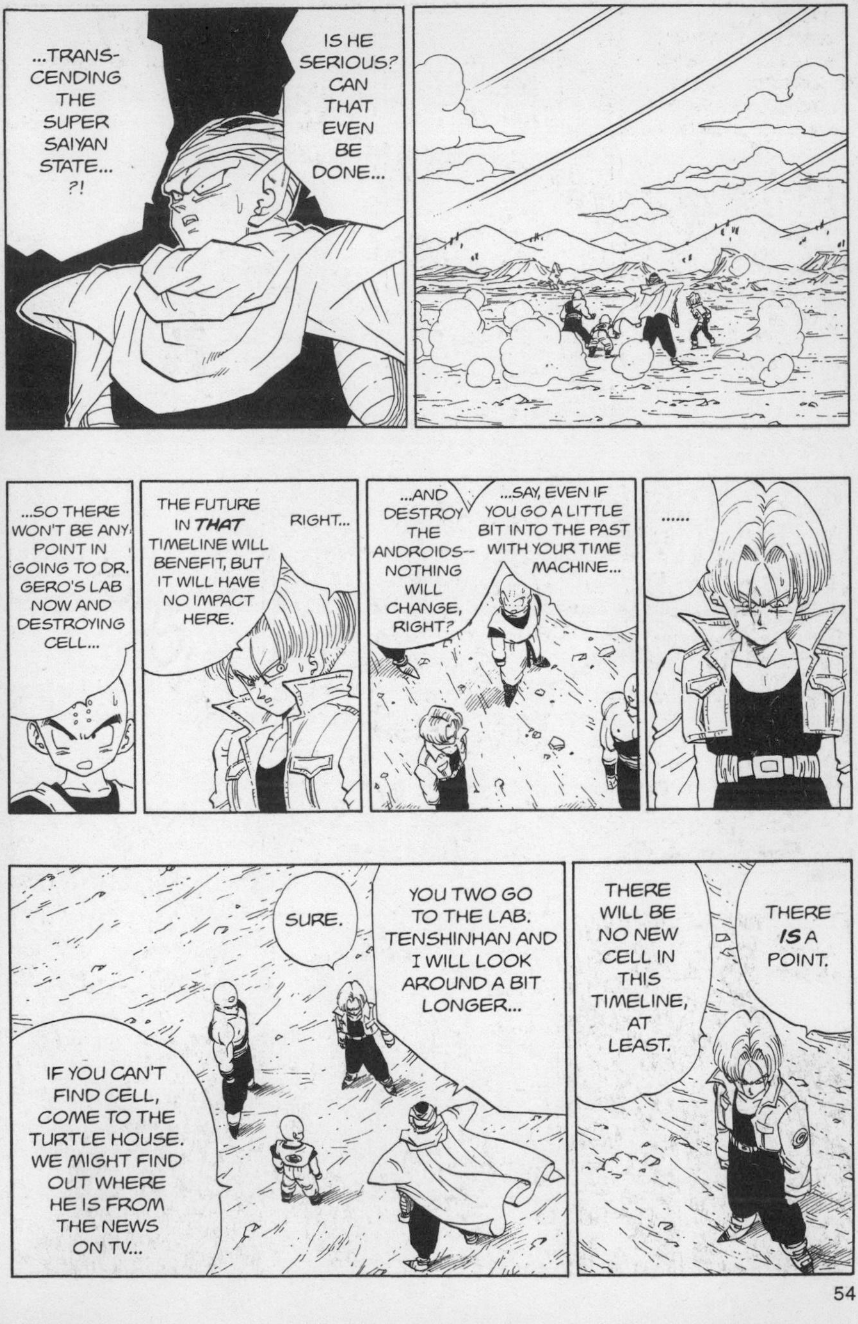
IS HE SERIOUS? CAN THAT EVEN BE DONE...
...TRANS-CENDING THE SUPER SAIYAN STATE... ?!
......
...SAY, EVEN IF YOU GO A LITTLE BIT INTO THE PAST WITH YOUR TIME MACHINE...
...AND DESTROY THE ANDROIDS--NOTHING WILL CHANGE, RIGHT?
RIGHT...
THE FUTURE IN *THAT* TIMELINE WILL BENEFIT, BUT IT WILL HAVE NO IMPACT HERE.
...SO THERE WON'T BE ANY POINT IN GOING TO DR. GERO'S LAB NOW AND DESTROYING CELL...
THERE *IS* A POINT.
THERE WILL BE NO NEW CELL IN THIS TIMELINE, AT LEAST.
YOU TWO GO TO THE LAB. TENSHINHAN AND I WILL LOOK AROUND A BIT LONGER...
SURE.
IF YOU CAN'T FIND CELL, COME TO THE TURTLE HOUSE. WE MIGHT FIND OUT WHERE HE IS FROM THE NEWS ON TV...

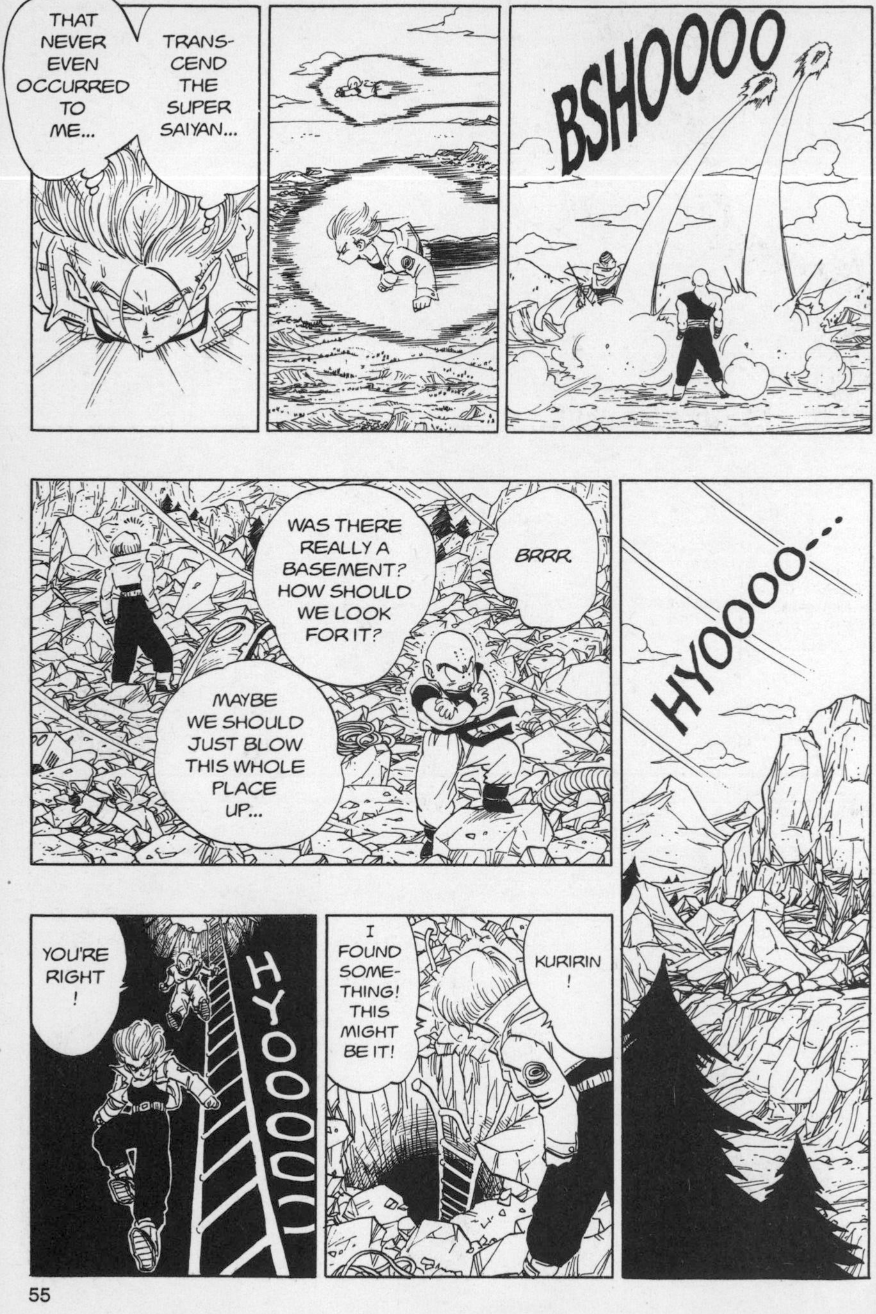
BSHOOOO
TRANSCEND THE SUPER SAIYAN...
THAT NEVER EVEN OCCURRED TO ME...
HYOOOO...
BRRR.
WAS THERE REALLY A BASEMENT? HOW SHOULD WE LOOK FOR IT?
MAYBE WE SHOULD JUST BLOW THIS WHOLE PLACE UP...
KURIRIN!
I FOUND SOMETHING! THIS MIGHT BE IT!
HYOOOO
YOU'RE RIGHT!

READ THIS WAY

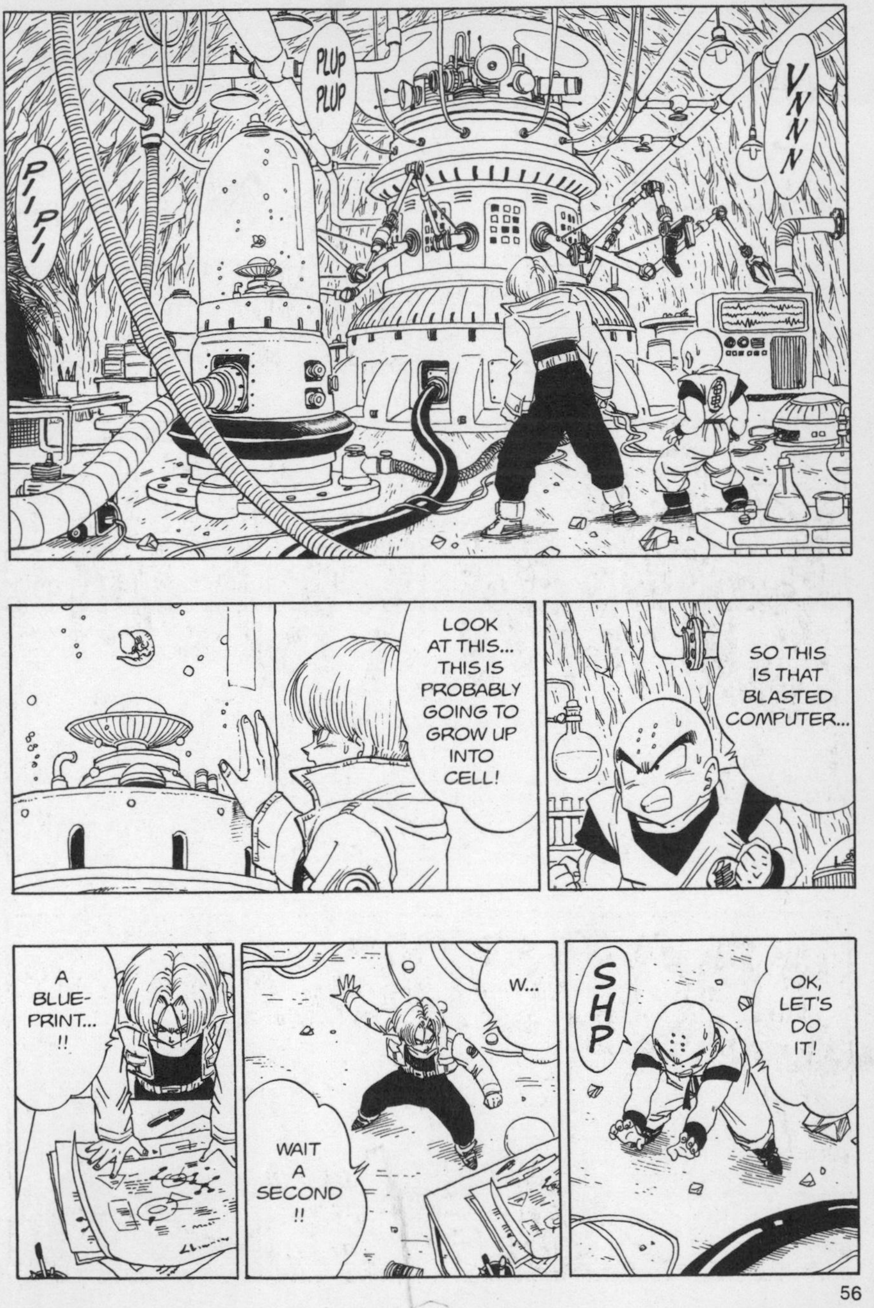
VNNN
PLUP PLUP
PII PII
SO THIS IS THAT BLASTED COMPUTER...
LOOK AT THIS... THIS IS PROBABLY GOING TO GROW UP INTO CELL!
OK, LET'S DO IT!
SHP
W...
WAIT A SECOND !!
A BLUE-PRINT... !!

READ THIS WAY

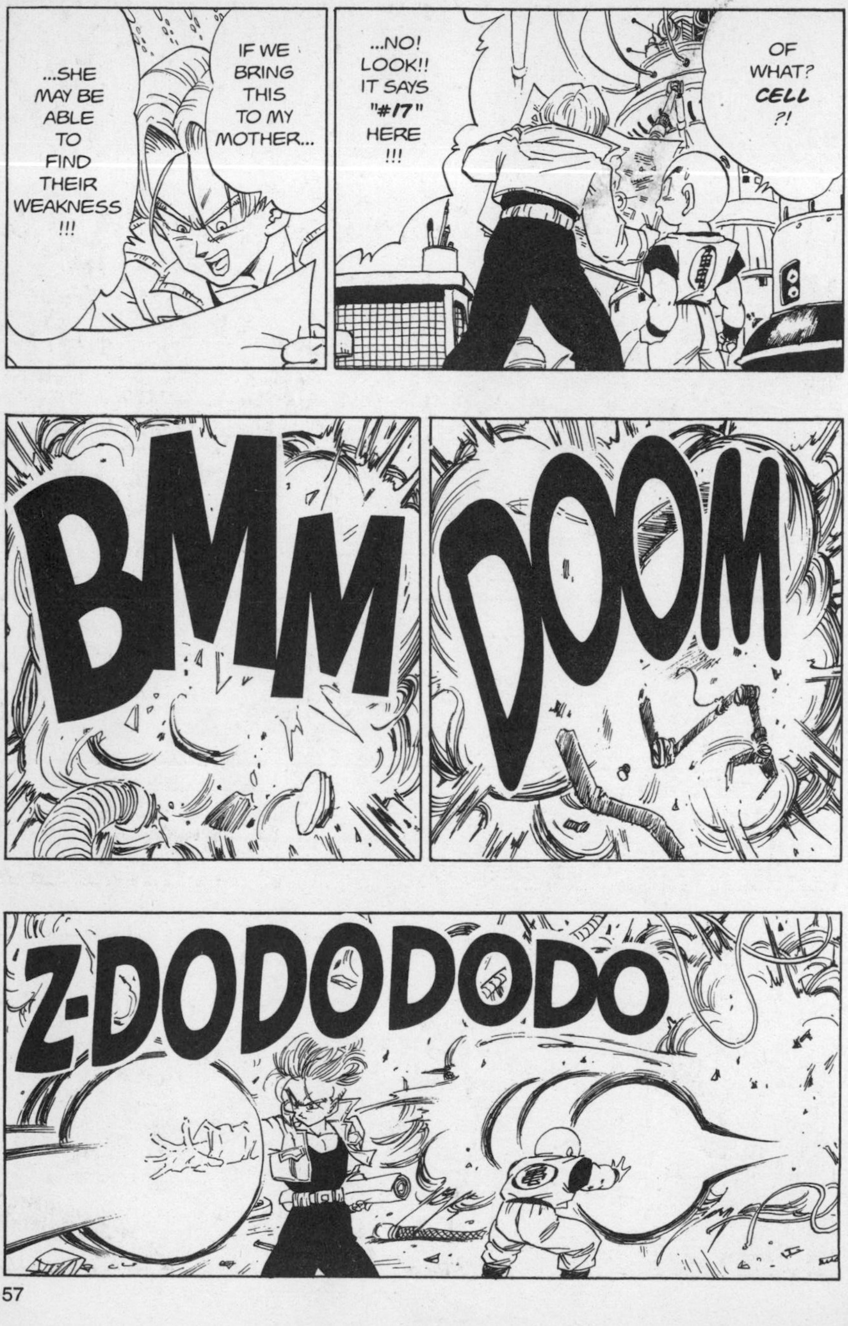
OF WHAT? CELL ?!
...NO! LOOK!! IT SAYS "#17" HERE !!!
IF WE BRING THIS TO MY MOTHER...
...SHE MAY BE ABLE TO FIND THEIR WEAKNESS !!!
BMM DOOM
Z-DODODODO

READ THIS WAY

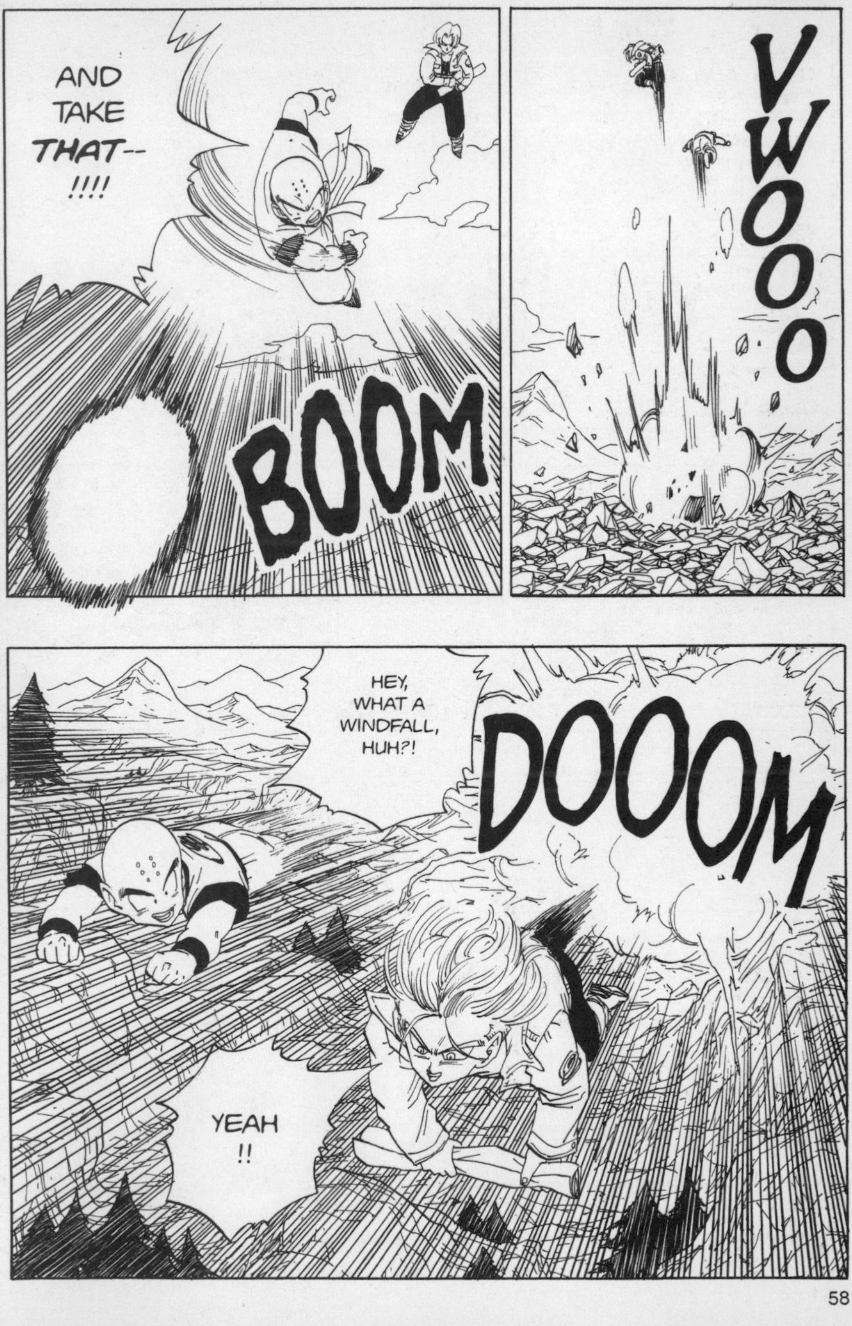
VWOOO
AND TAKE THAT--!!!!
BOOM
HEY, WHAT A WINDFALL, HUH?!
DOOOM
YEAH !!

READ THIS WAY

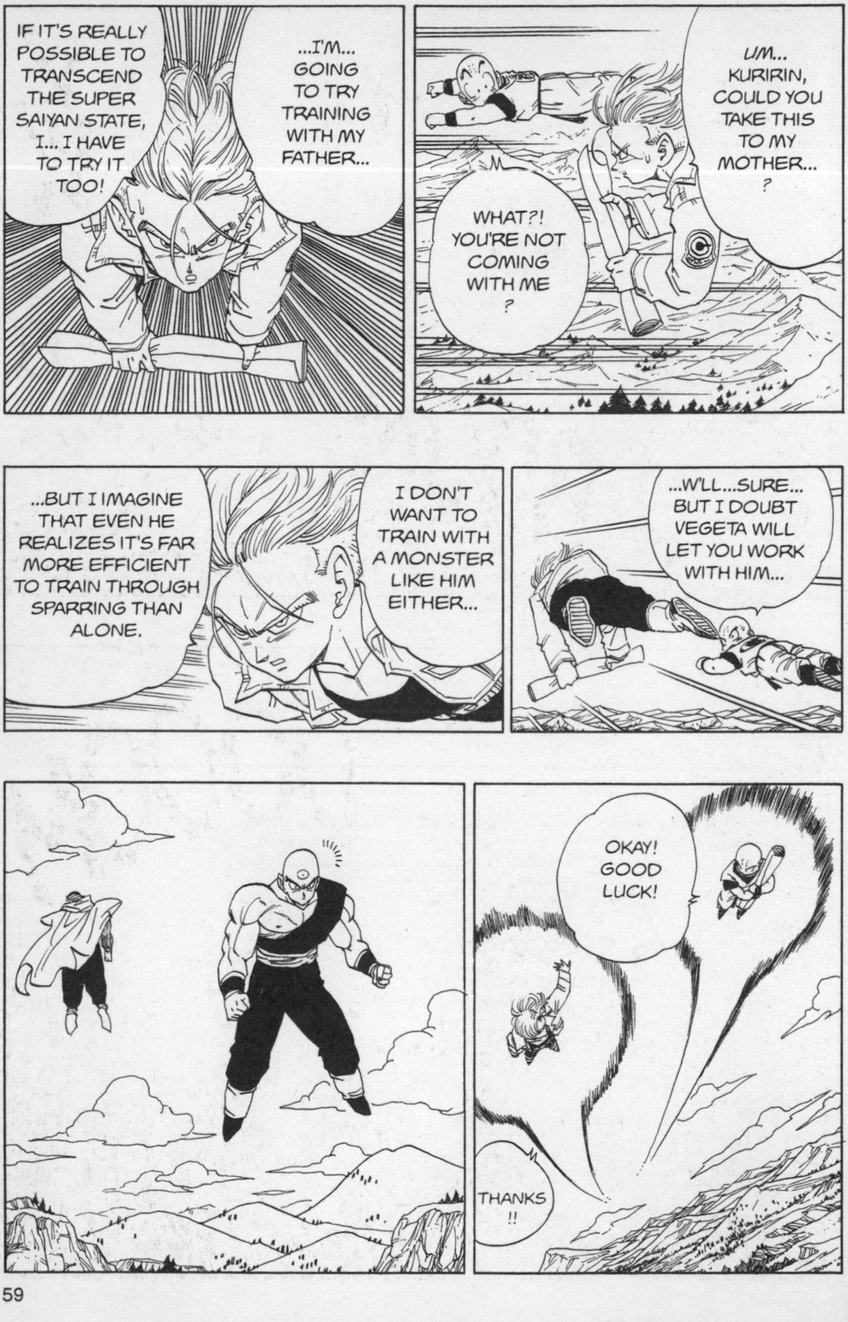
UM... KURIRIN, COULD YOU TAKE THIS TO MY MOTHER...?
WHAT?! YOU'RE NOT COMING WITH ME?
...I'M... GOING TO TRY TRAINING WITH MY FATHER...
IF IT'S REALLY POSSIBLE TO TRANSCEND THE SUPER SAIYAN STATE, I... I HAVE TO TRY IT TOO!
...W'LL...SURE... BUT I DOUBT VEGETA WILL LET YOU WORK WITH HIM...
I DON'T WANT TO TRAIN WITH A MONSTER LIKE HIM EITHER...
...BUT I IMAGINE THAT EVEN HE REALIZES IT'S FAR MORE EFFICIENT TO TRAIN THROUGH SPARRING THAN ALONE.
OKAY! GOOD LUCK!
THANKS!!

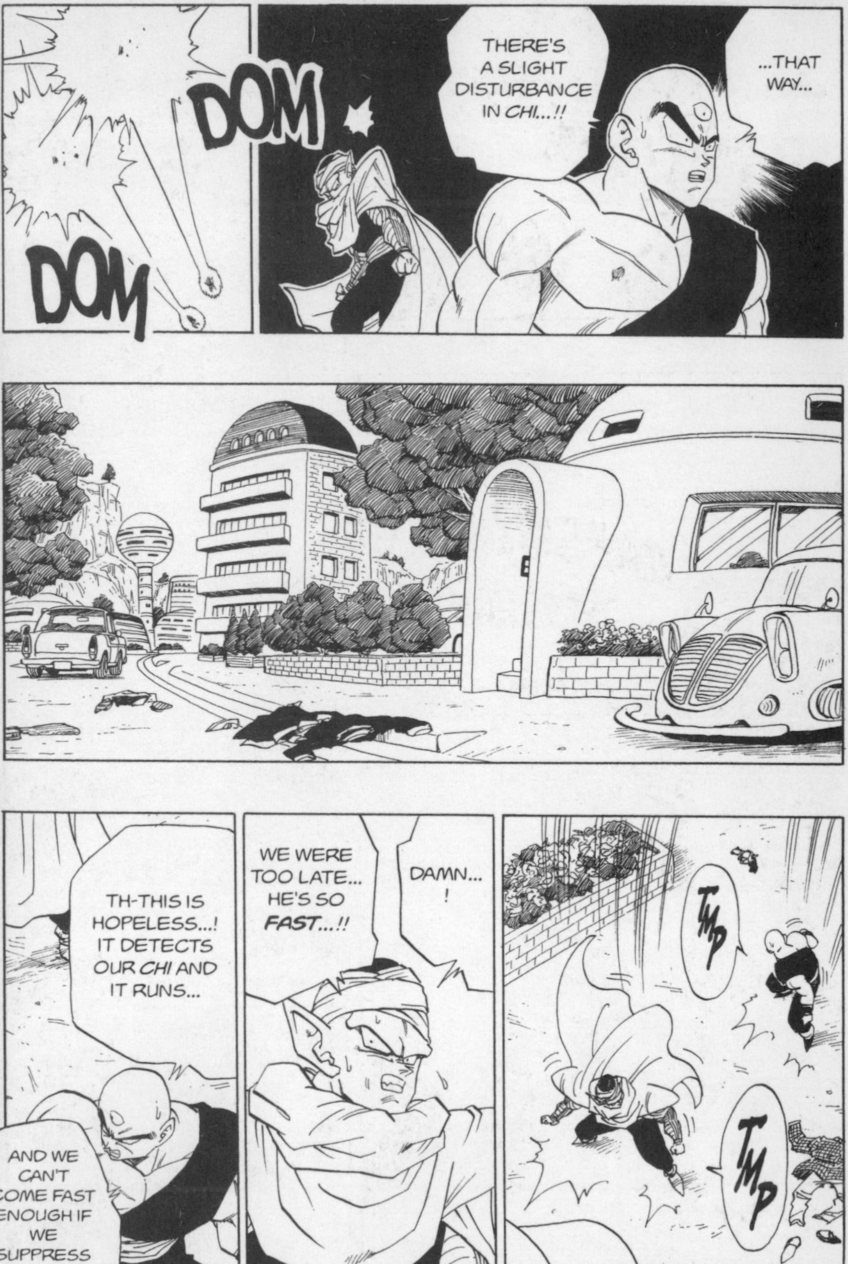
THERE'S A SLIGHT DISTURBANCE IN *CHI*...!!
...THAT WAY...
DOM
DOM
TMP
TMP
DAMN... !
WE WERE TOO LATE... HE'S SO ***FAST***...!!
TH-THIS IS HOPELESS...! IT DETECTS OUR *CHI* AND IT RUNS...
AND WE CAN'T COME FAST ENOUGH IF WE SUPPRESS OUR *CHI*!

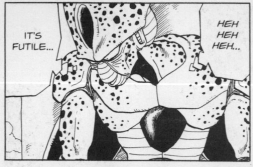

IT'S
FUTILE...

HEH
HEH
HEH...

...SO WE HAVE
TO FIND THE
ANDROIDS'
WEAKNESS FROM
THIS BLUEPRINT
AND THWART
THEIR MERGE
WITH
CELL...

...WHOA...

CAPSULE CO

CAPSULE CO.

READ THIS WAY

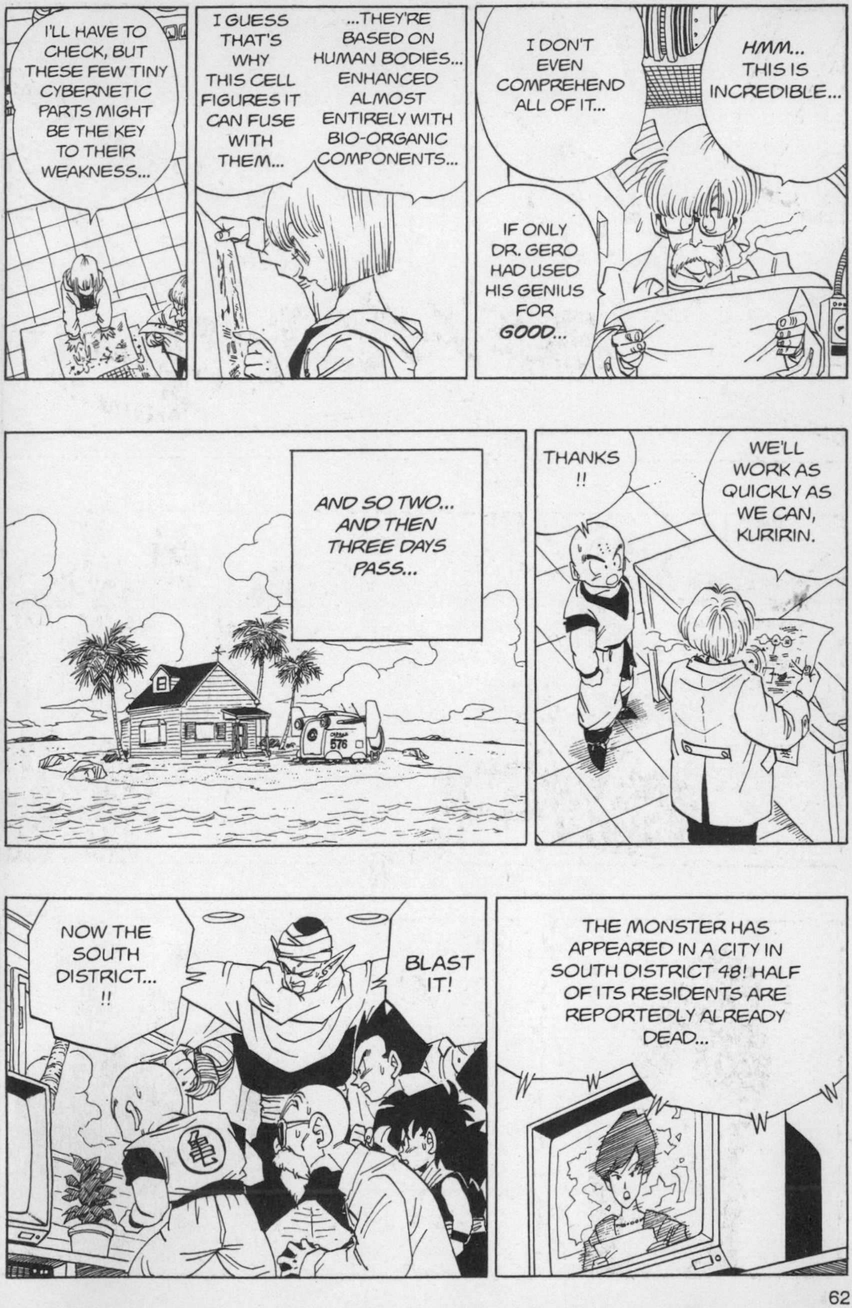
HMM... THIS IS INCREDIBLE...
I DON'T EVEN COMPREHEND ALL OF IT...
IF ONLY DR. GERO HAD USED HIS GENIUS FOR GOOD...
...THEY'RE BASED ON HUMAN BODIES... ENHANCED ALMOST ENTIRELY WITH BIO-ORGANIC COMPONENTS...
I GUESS THAT'S WHY THIS CELL FIGURES IT CAN FUSE WITH THEM...
I'LL HAVE TO CHECK, BUT THESE FEW TINY CYBERNETIC PARTS MIGHT BE THE KEY TO THEIR WEAKNESS...
WE'LL WORK AS QUICKLY AS WE CAN, KURIRIN.
THANKS !!
AND SO TWO... AND THEN THREE DAYS PASS...
THE MONSTER HAS APPEARED IN A CITY IN SOUTH DISTRICT 48! HALF OF ITS RESIDENTS ARE REPORTEDLY ALREADY DEAD...
BLAST IT!
NOW THE SOUTH DISTRICT... !!

READ THIS WAY

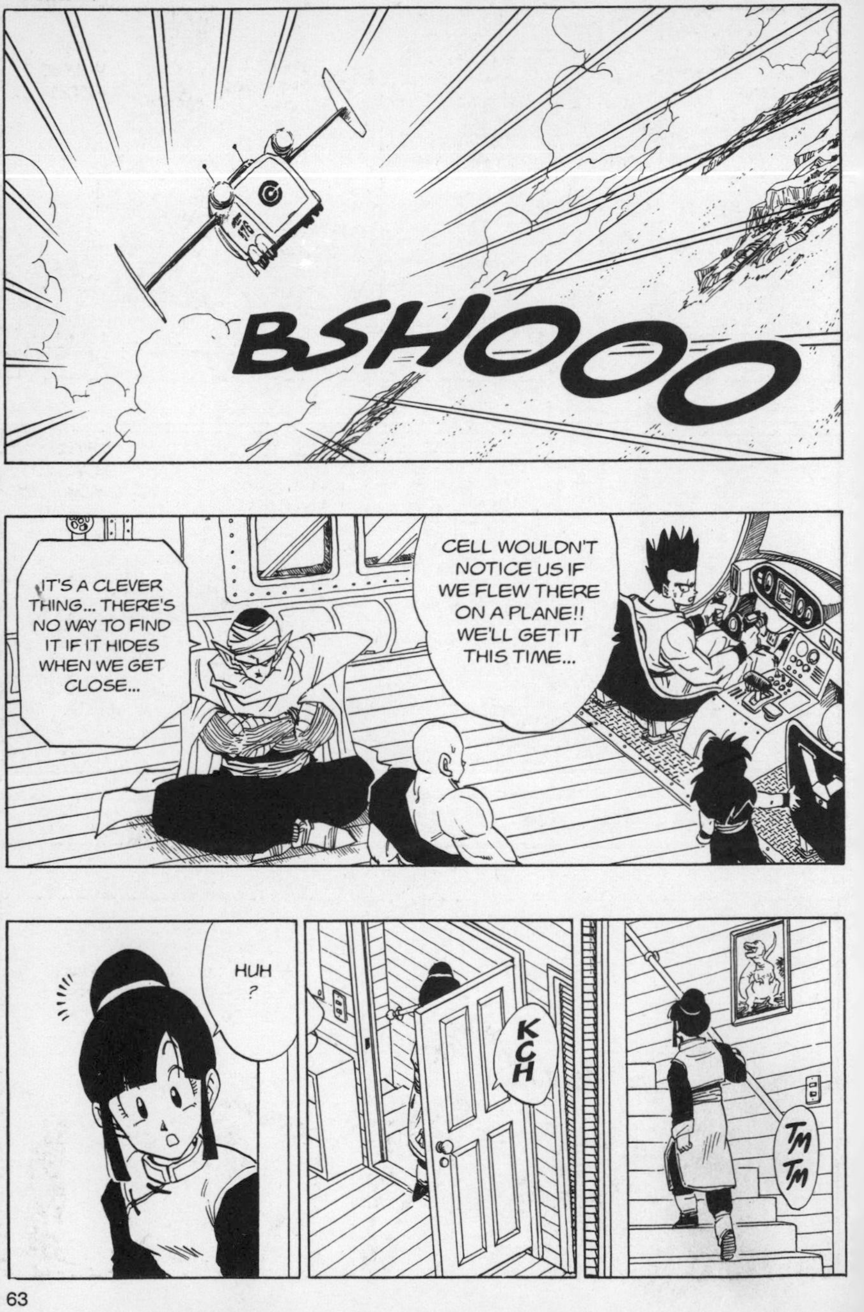
BSHOOO
CELL WOULDN'T NOTICE US IF WE FLEW THERE ON A PLANE!! WE'LL GET IT THIS TIME...
IT'S A CLEVER THING... THERE'S NO WAY TO FIND IT IF IT HIDES WHEN WE GET CLOSE...
TM TM
KCH
HUH ?

READ THIS WAY

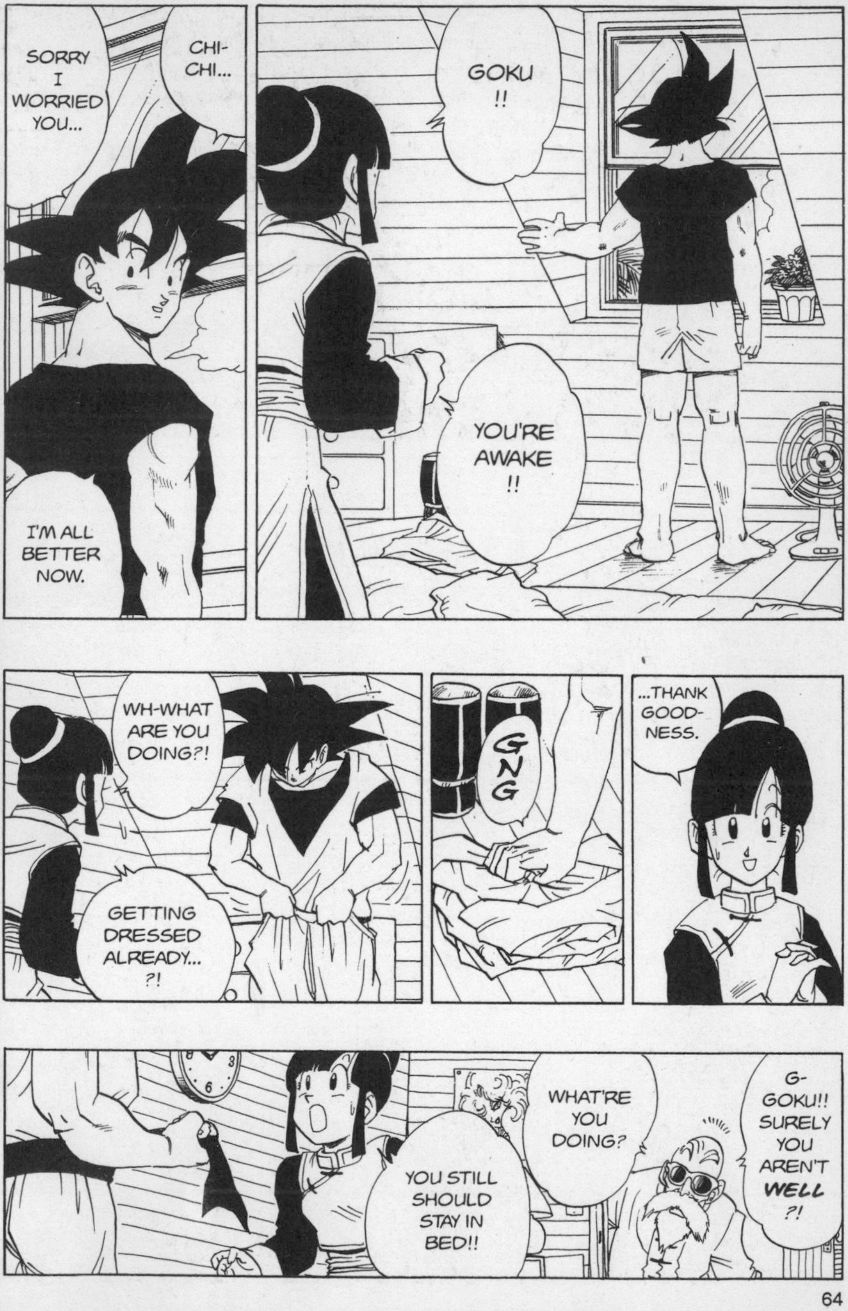

GOKU !!
YOU'RE AWAKE !!
CHI-CHI...
SORRY I WORRIED YOU...
I'M ALL BETTER NOW.
...THANK GOOD-NESS.
GNG
WH-WHAT ARE YOU DOING?!
GETTING DRESSED ALREADY... ?!
G-GOKU!! SURELY YOU AREN'T **WELL** ?!
WHAT'RE YOU DOING?
YOU STILL SHOULD STAY IN BED!!

READ THIS WAY

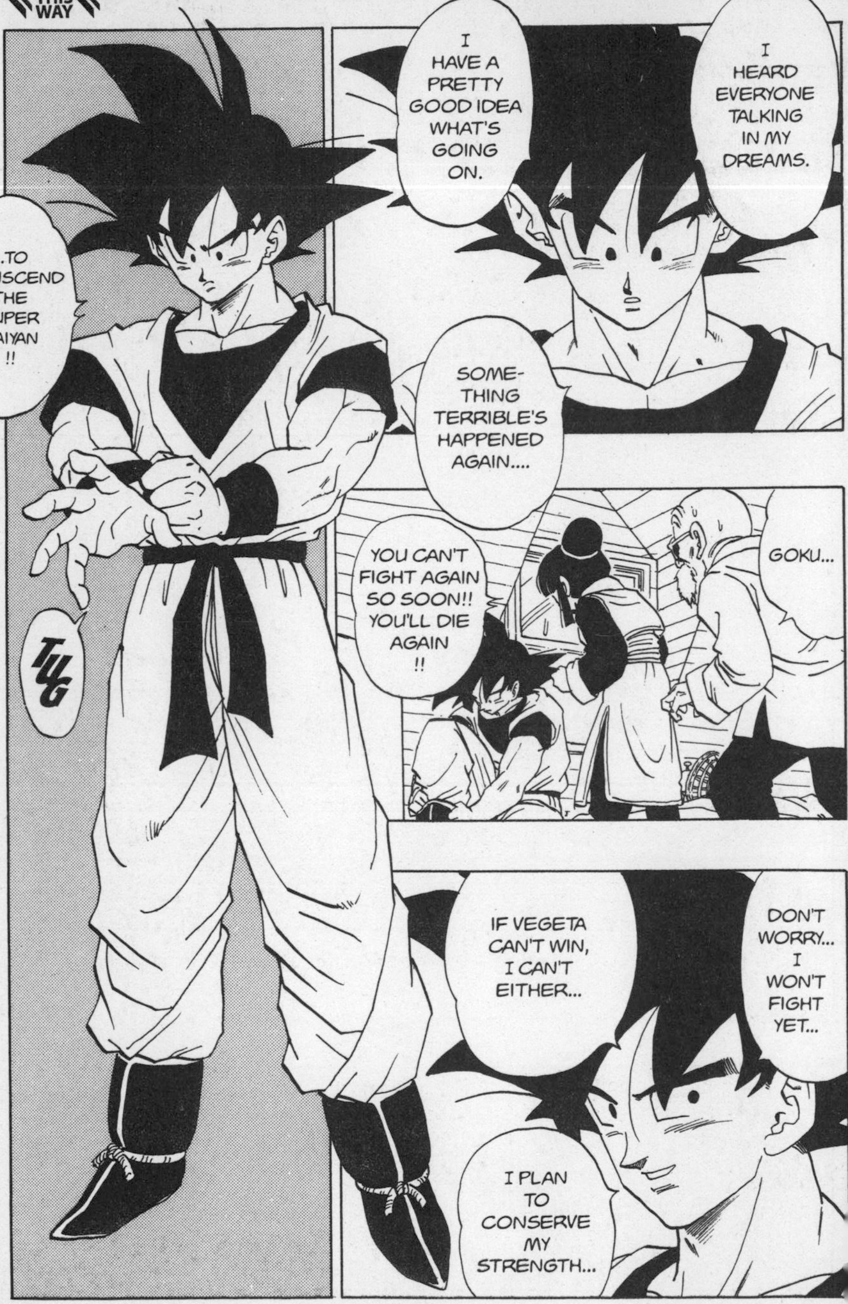
I HEARD EVERYONE TALKING IN MY DREAMS.
I HAVE A PRETTY GOOD IDEA WHAT'S GOING ON.
SOME-THING TERRIBLE'S HAPPENED AGAIN....
GOKU...
YOU CAN'T FIGHT AGAIN SO SOON!! YOU'LL DIE AGAIN!!
DON'T WORRY... I WON'T FIGHT YET...
IF VEGETA CAN'T WIN, I CAN'T EITHER...
I PLAN TO CONSERVE MY STRENGTH...
...TO TRANSCEND THE SUPER SAIYAN!!
TUG

READ THIS WAY

DBZ : 172 • The Super Saiyans' Training

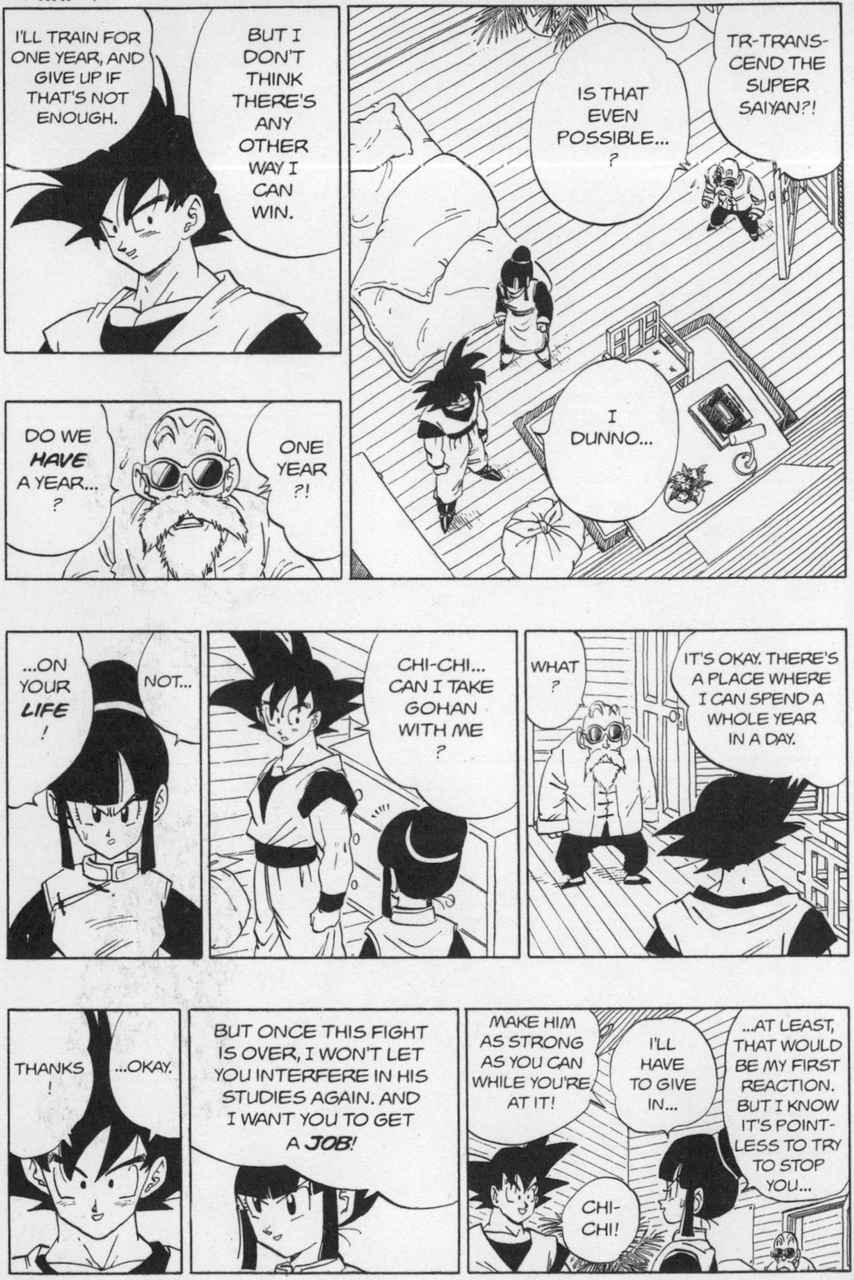
TR-TRANSCEND THE SUPER SAIYAN?!
IS THAT EVEN POSSIBLE...?
I DUNNO...
BUT I DON'T THINK THERE'S ANY OTHER WAY I CAN WIN.
I'LL TRAIN FOR ONE YEAR, AND GIVE UP IF THAT'S NOT ENOUGH.
ONE YEAR?!
DO WE HAVE A YEAR...?
IT'S OKAY. THERE'S A PLACE WHERE I CAN SPEND A WHOLE YEAR IN A DAY.
WHAT?
CHI-CHI... CAN I TAKE GOHAN WITH ME?
NOT...
...ON YOUR LIFE!
...AT LEAST, THAT WOULD BE MY FIRST REACTION. BUT I KNOW IT'S POINTLESS TO TRY TO STOP YOU...
I'LL HAVE TO GIVE IN...
MAKE HIM AS STRONG AS YOU CAN WHILE YOU'RE AT IT!
CHI-CHI!
BUT ONCE THIS FIGHT IS OVER, I WON'T LET YOU INTERFERE IN HIS STUDIES AGAIN. AND I WANT YOU TO GET A JOB!
...OKAY.
THANKS!

READ THIS WAY

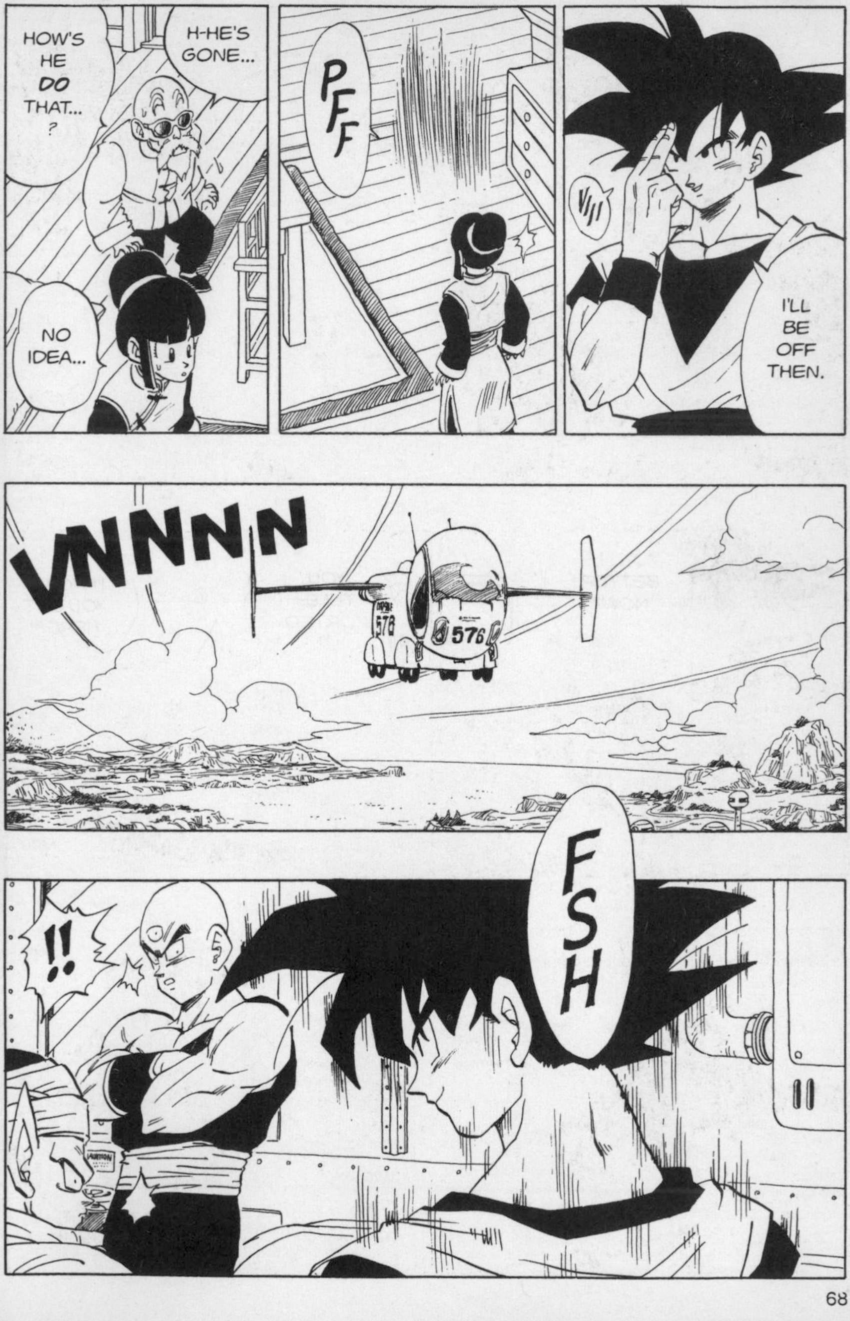
I'LL BE OFF THEN.
PFF
H-HE'S GONE...
HOW'S HE *DO* THAT... ?
NO IDEA...
VNNNN
FSH
!!

READ THIS WAY

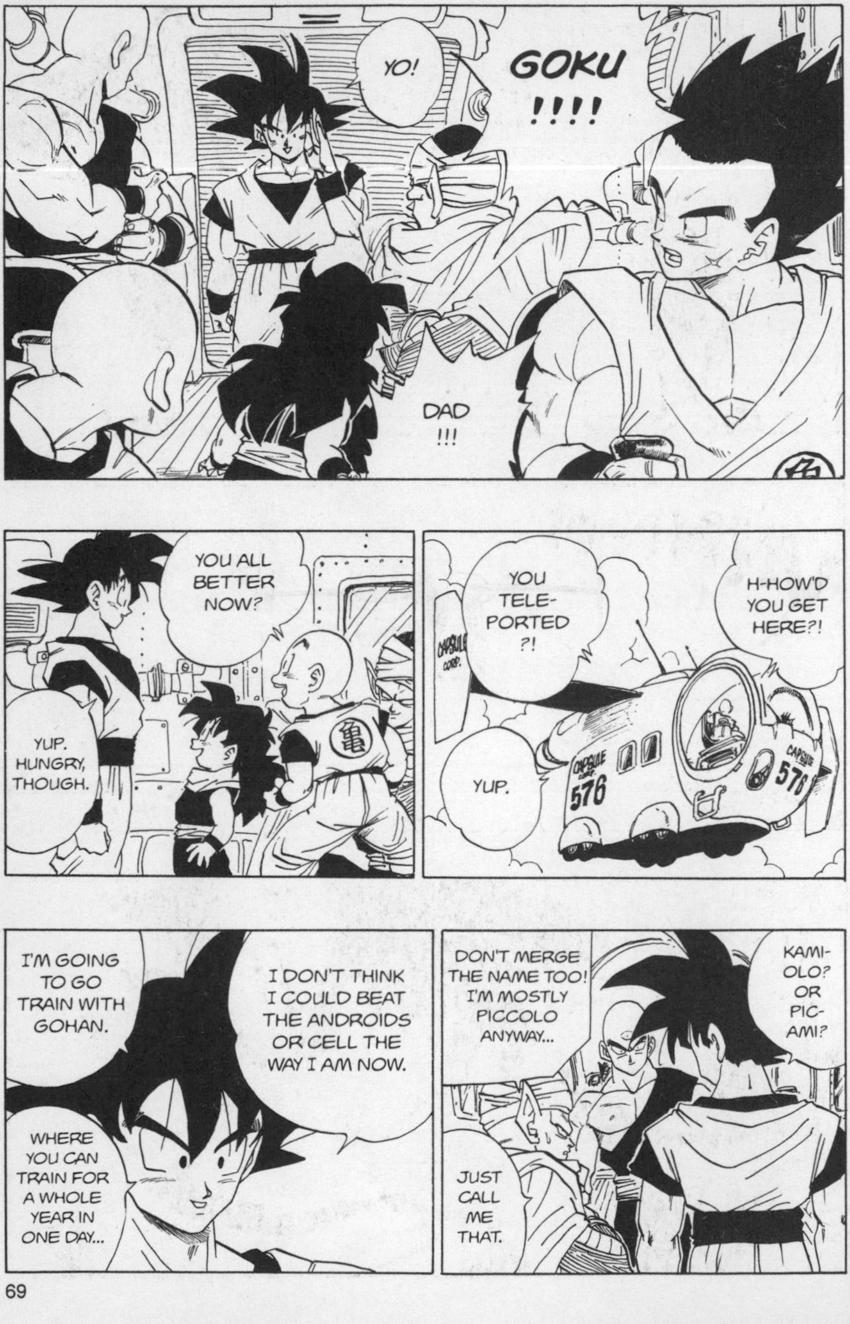
GOKU !!!!
YO!
DAD !!!
H-HOW'D YOU GET HERE?!
YOU TELE-PORTED ?!
YUP.
YOU ALL BETTER NOW?
YUP. HUNGRY, THOUGH.
KAMI-OLO? OR PIC-AMI?
DON'T MERGE THE NAME TOO! I'M MOSTLY PICCOLO ANYWAY...
JUST CALL ME THAT.
I DON'T THINK I COULD BEAT THE ANDROIDS OR CELL THE WAY I AM NOW.
I'M GOING TO GO TRAIN WITH GOHAN.
WHERE YOU CAN TRAIN FOR A WHOLE YEAR IN ONE DAY...

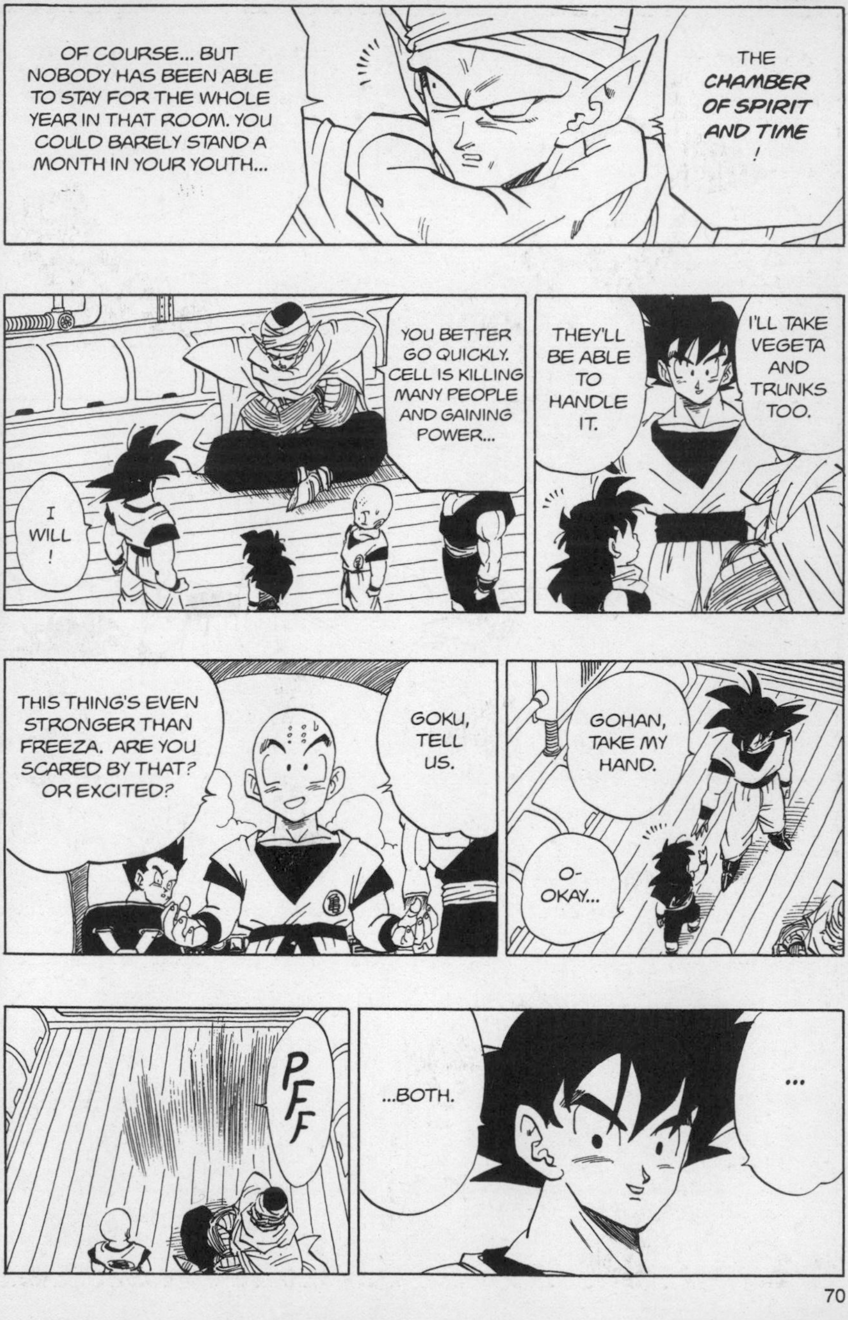
THE CHAMBER OF SPIRIT AND TIME!
OF COURSE... BUT NOBODY HAS BEEN ABLE TO STAY FOR THE WHOLE YEAR IN THAT ROOM. YOU COULD BARELY STAND A MONTH IN YOUR YOUTH...
I'LL TAKE VEGETA AND TRUNKS TOO.
THEY'LL BE ABLE TO HANDLE IT.
YOU BETTER GO QUICKLY. CELL IS KILLING MANY PEOPLE AND GAINING POWER...
I WILL!
GOHAN, TAKE MY HAND.
O-OKAY...
GOKU, TELL US.
THIS THING'S EVEN STRONGER THAN FREEZA. ARE YOU SCARED BY THAT? OR EXCITED?
...
...BOTH.
PFF

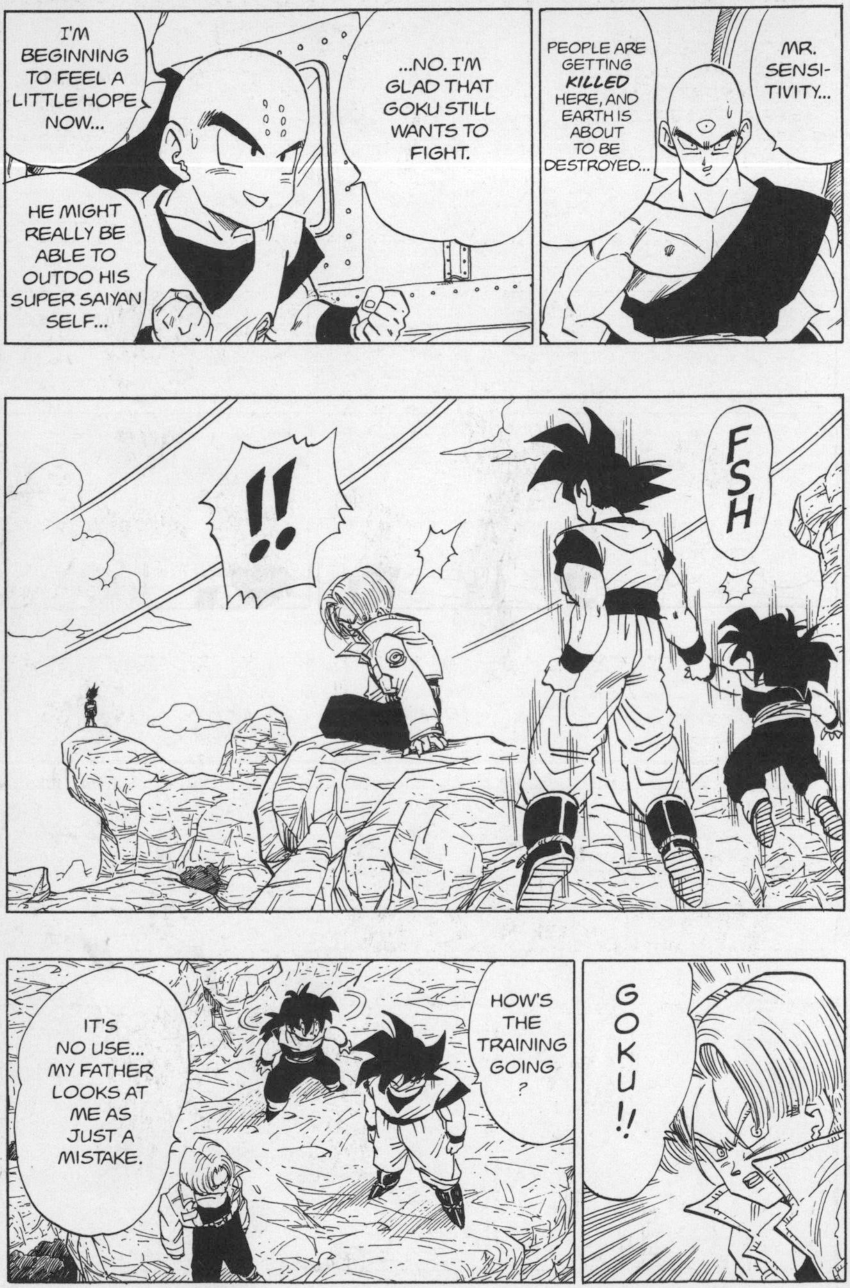
MR. SENSITIVITY...
PEOPLE ARE GETTING **KILLED** HERE, AND EARTH IS ABOUT TO BE DESTROYED...
...NO. I'M GLAD THAT GOKU STILL WANTS TO FIGHT.
I'M BEGINNING TO FEEL A LITTLE HOPE NOW...
HE MIGHT REALLY BE ABLE TO OUTDO HIS SUPER SAIYAN SELF...
FSH
!!
GOKU!!
HOW'S THE TRAINING GOING?
IT'S NO USE... MY FATHER LOOKS AT ME AS JUST A MISTAKE.

READ THIS WAY

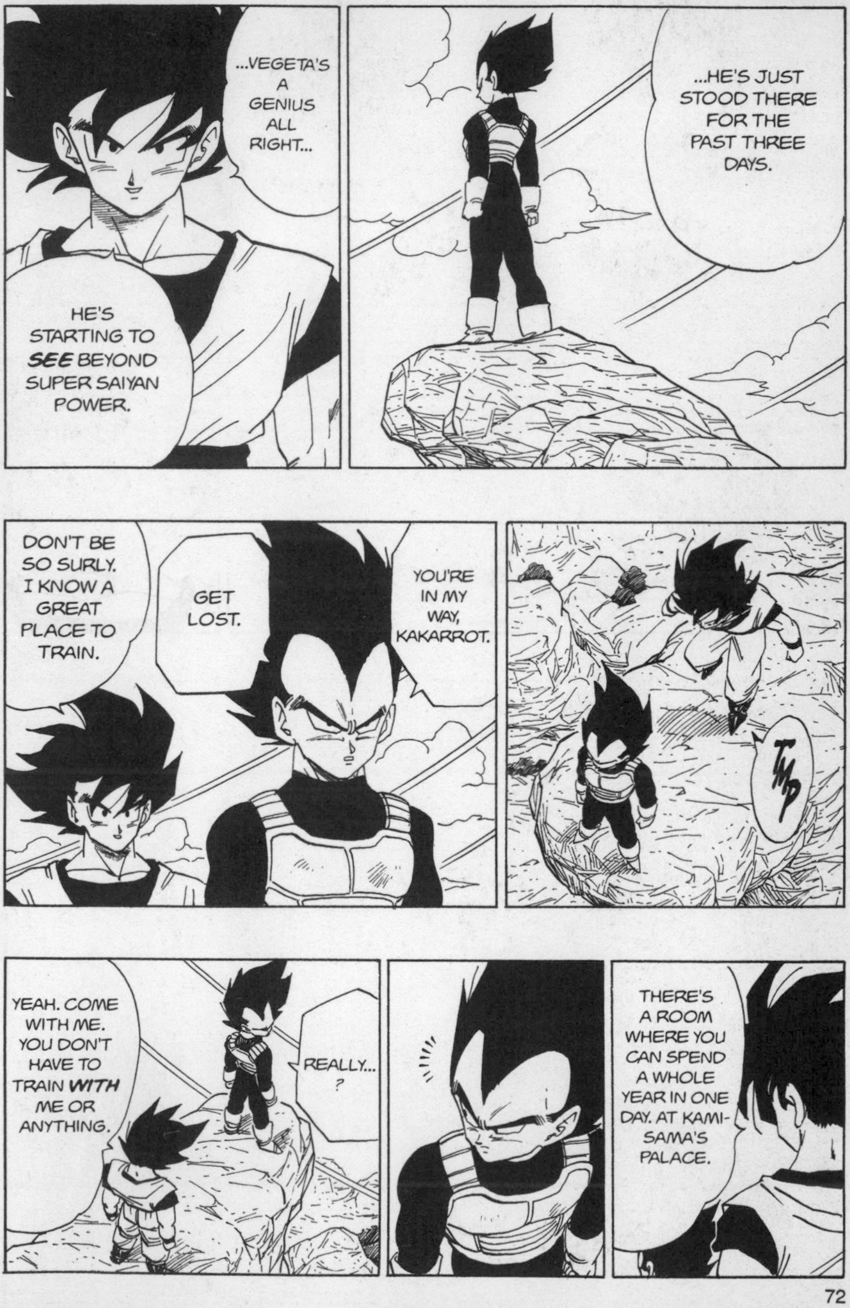
...HE'S JUST STOOD THERE FOR THE PAST THREE DAYS.
...VEGETA'S A GENIUS ALL RIGHT...
HE'S STARTING TO *SEE* BEYOND SUPER SAIYAN POWER.
TMP
YOU'RE IN MY WAY, KAKARROT.
GET LOST.
DON'T BE SO SURLY. I KNOW A GREAT PLACE TO TRAIN.
THERE'S A ROOM WHERE YOU CAN SPEND A WHOLE YEAR IN ONE DAY. AT KAMI-SAMA'S PALACE.
REALLY...?
YEAH. COME WITH ME. YOU DON'T HAVE TO TRAIN *WITH* ME OR ANYTHING.

READ THIS WAY

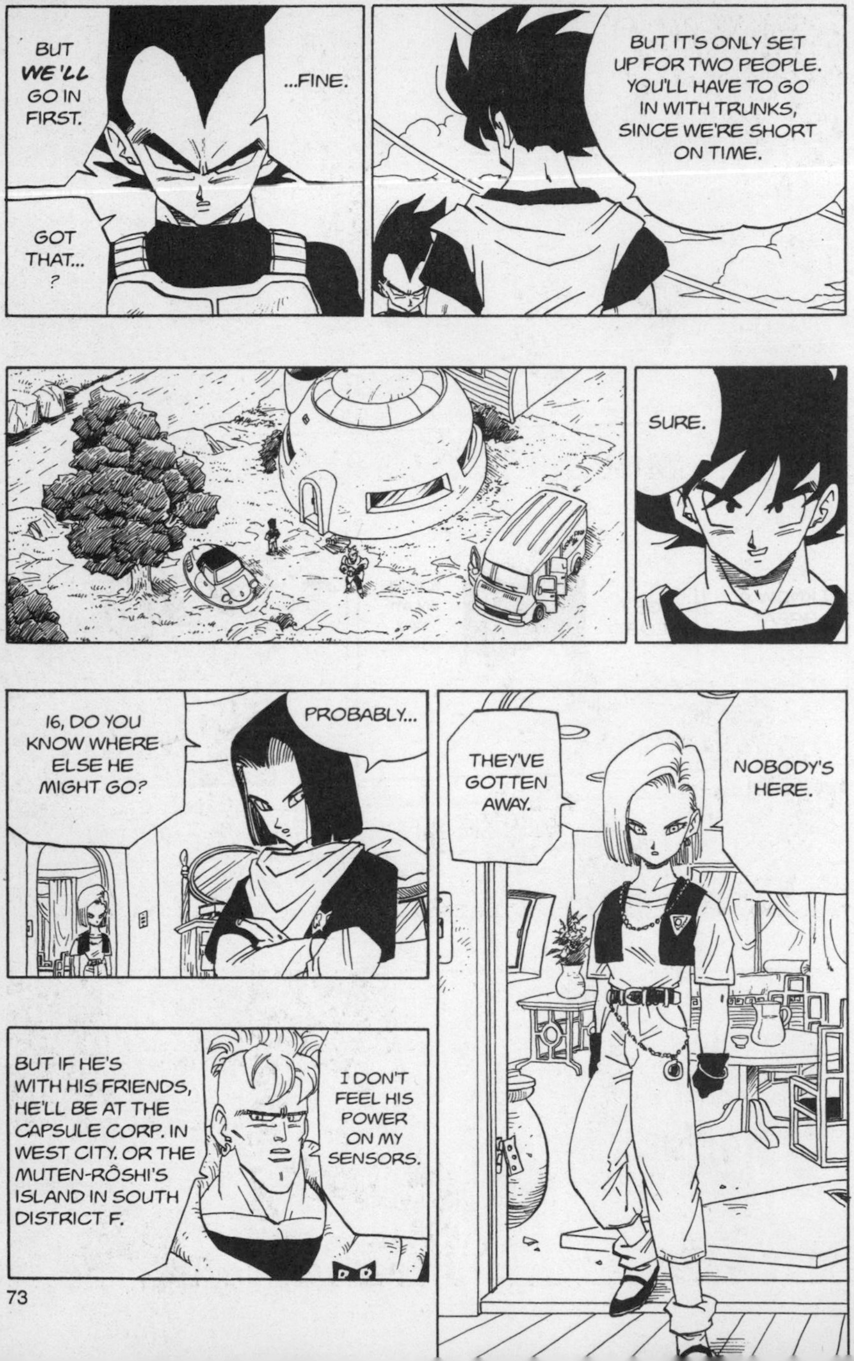
BUT IT'S ONLY SET UP FOR TWO PEOPLE. YOU'LL HAVE TO GO IN WITH TRUNKS, SINCE WE'RE SHORT ON TIME.
...FINE.
BUT WE'LL GO IN FIRST.
GOT THAT... ?
SURE.
NOBODY'S HERE.
THEY'VE GOTTEN AWAY.
PROBABLY...
16, DO YOU KNOW WHERE ELSE HE MIGHT GO?
I DON'T FEEL HIS POWER ON MY SENSORS.
BUT IF HE'S WITH HIS FRIENDS, HE'LL BE AT THE CAPSULE CORP. IN WEST CITY. OR THE MUTEN-RÔSHI'S ISLAND IN SOUTH DISTRICT F.

READ THIS WAY

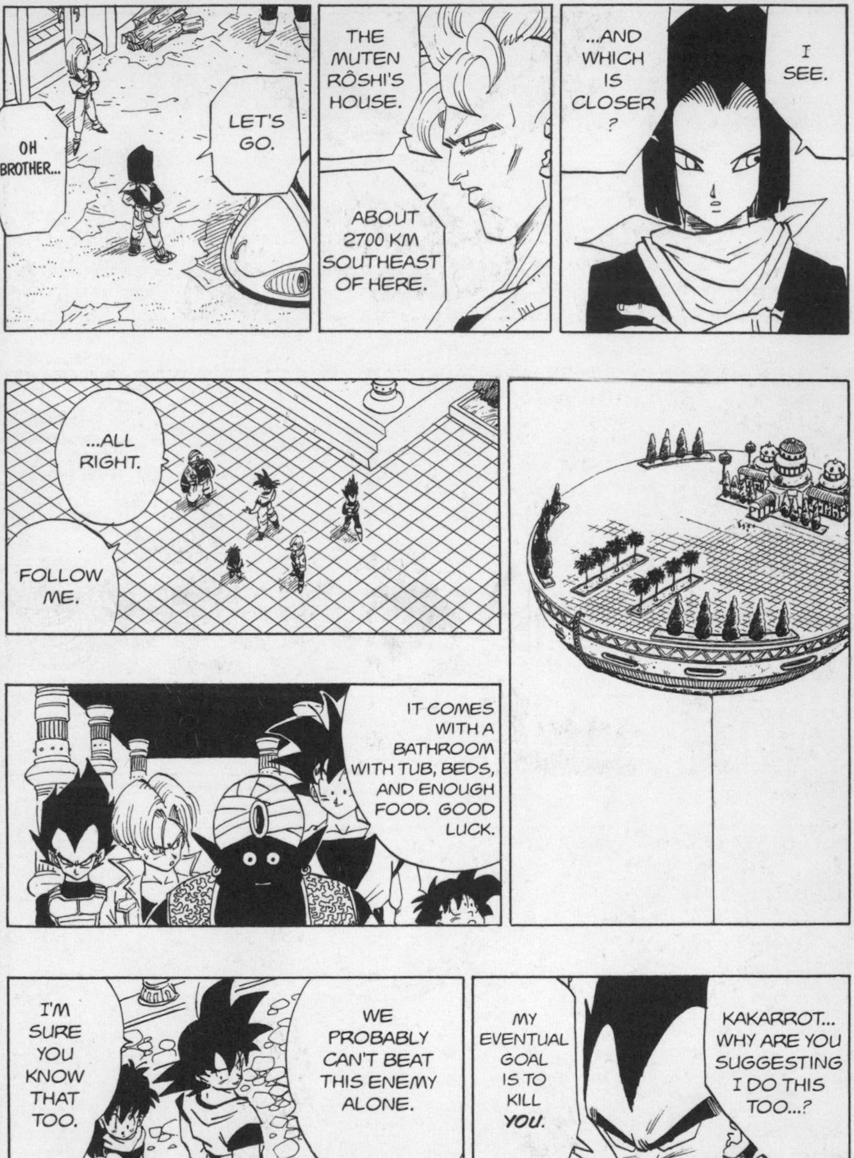

I SEE.
...AND WHICH IS CLOSER ?
THE MUTEN RÔSHI'S HOUSE.
ABOUT 2700 KM SOUTHEAST OF HERE.
LET'S GO.
OH BROTHER...
...ALL RIGHT.
FOLLOW ME.
IT COMES WITH A BATHROOM WITH TUB, BEDS, AND ENOUGH FOOD. GOOD LUCK.
KAKARROT... WHY ARE YOU SUGGESTING I DO THIS TOO...?
MY EVENTUAL GOAL IS TO KILL *YOU*.
WE PROBABLY CAN'T BEAT THIS ENEMY ALONE.
I'M SURE YOU KNOW THAT TOO.

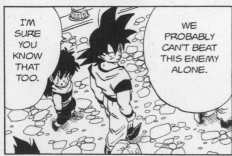

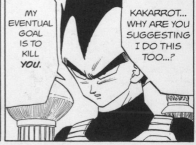

READ THIS WAY

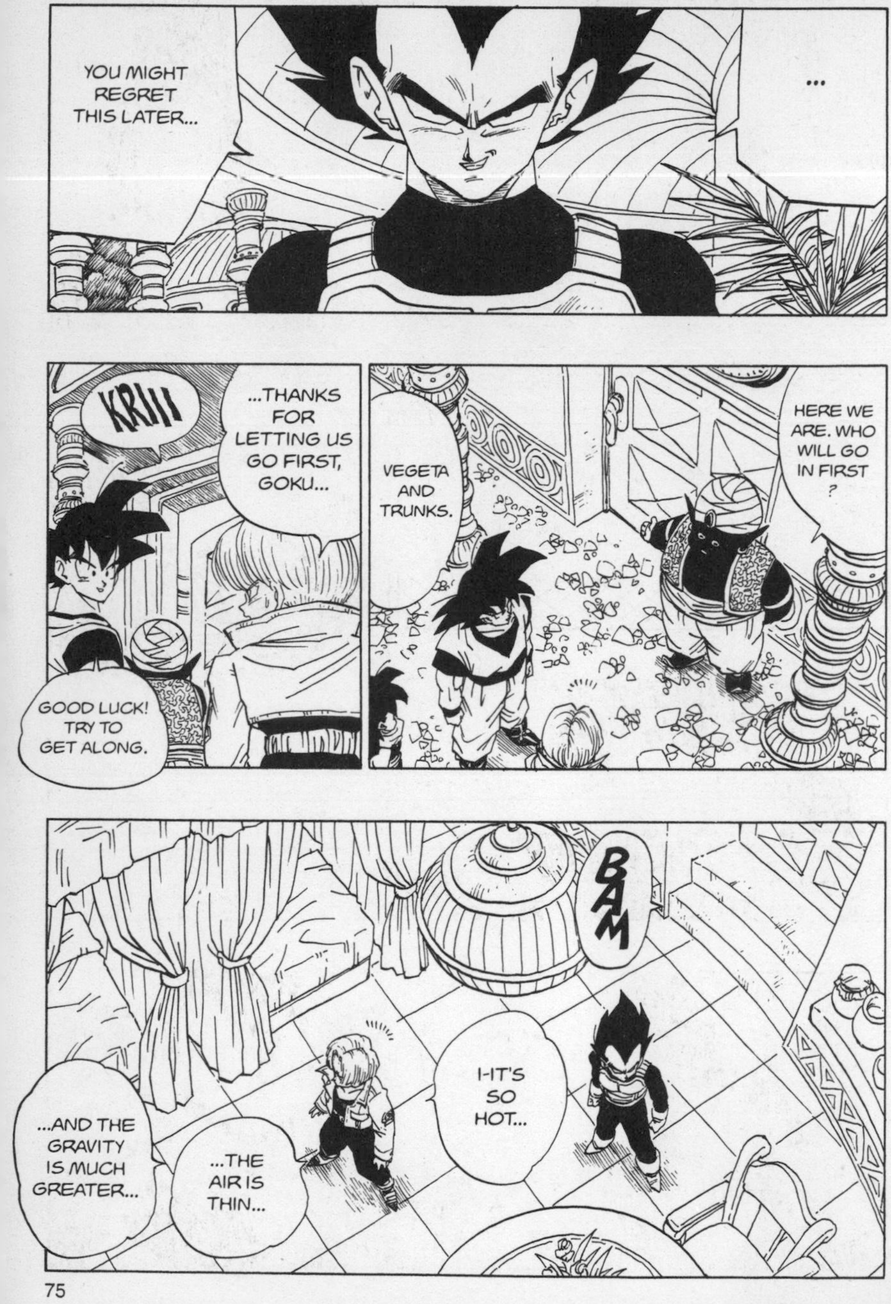
...
YOU MIGHT REGRET THIS LATER...
HERE WE ARE. WHO WILL GO IN FIRST ?
VEGETA AND TRUNKS.
...THANKS FOR LETTING US GO FIRST, GOKU...
KRIII
GOOD LUCK! TRY TO GET ALONG.
BAM
I-IT'S SO HOT...
...THE AIR IS THIN...
...AND THE GRAVITY IS MUCH GREATER...

READ THIS WAY

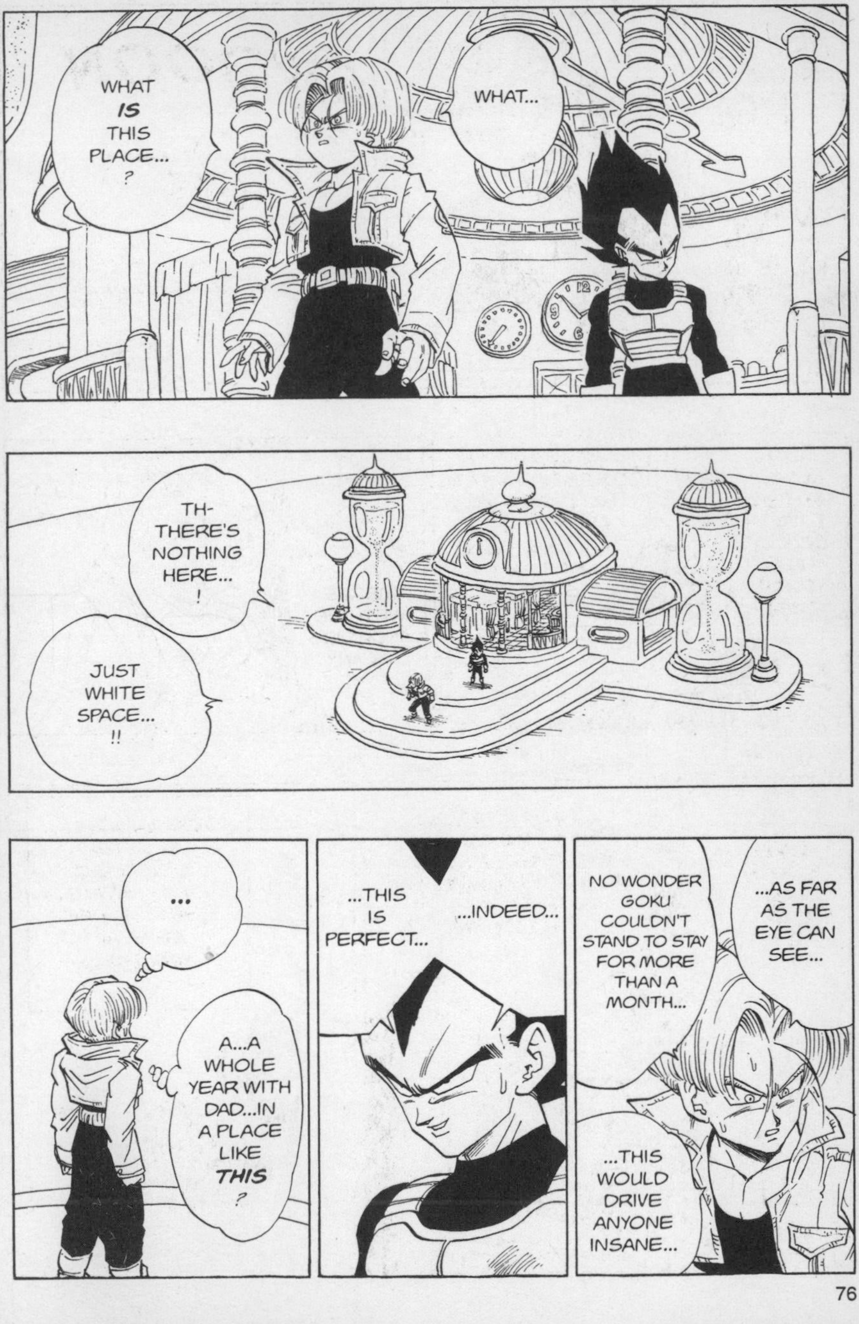
WHAT...
WHAT **IS** THIS PLACE...?
TH-THERE'S NOTHING HERE...!
JUST WHITE SPACE...!!
...AS FAR AS THE EYE CAN SEE...
NO WONDER GOKU COULDN'T STAND TO STAY FOR MORE THAN A MONTH...
...THIS WOULD DRIVE ANYONE INSANE...
...INDEED...
...THIS IS PERFECT...
...
A...A WHOLE YEAR WITH DAD...IN A PLACE LIKE **THIS**?

READ THIS WAY

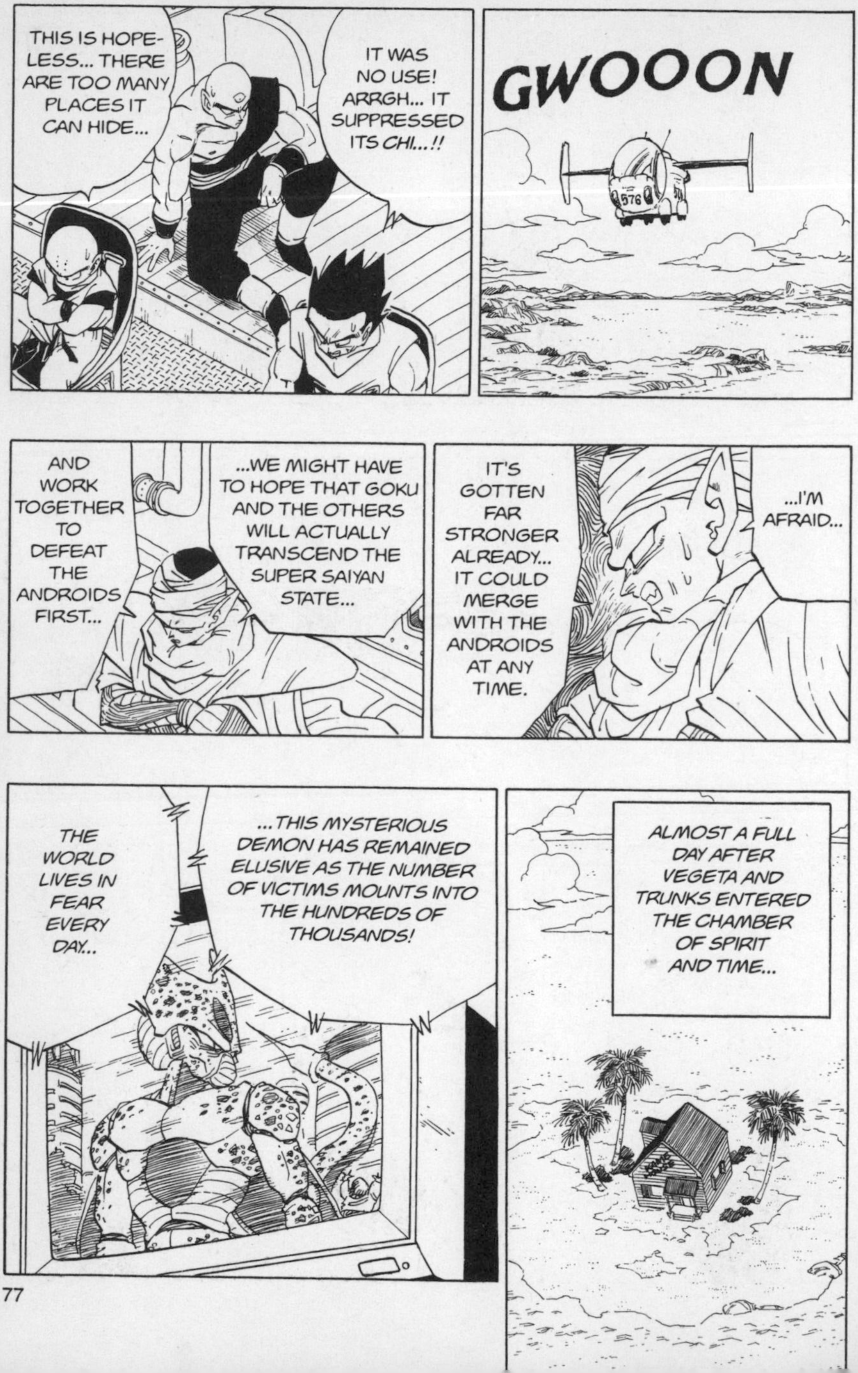
GWOOON
IT WAS NO USE! ARRGH... IT SUPPRESSED ITS CHI...!!
THIS IS HOPE-LESS... THERE ARE TOO MANY PLACES IT CAN HIDE...
...I'M AFRAID...
IT'S GOTTEN FAR STRONGER ALREADY... IT COULD MERGE WITH THE ANDROIDS AT ANY TIME.
...WE MIGHT HAVE TO HOPE THAT GOKU AND THE OTHERS WILL ACTUALLY TRANSCEND THE SUPER SAIYAN STATE...
AND WORK TOGETHER TO DEFEAT THE ANDROIDS FIRST...
ALMOST A FULL DAY AFTER VEGETA AND TRUNKS ENTERED THE CHAMBER OF SPIRIT AND TIME...
...THIS MYSTERIOUS DEMON HAS REMAINED ELUSIVE AS THE NUMBER OF VICTIMS MOUNTS INTO THE HUNDREDS OF THOUSANDS!
THE WORLD LIVES IN FEAR EVERY DAY...

READ THIS WAY

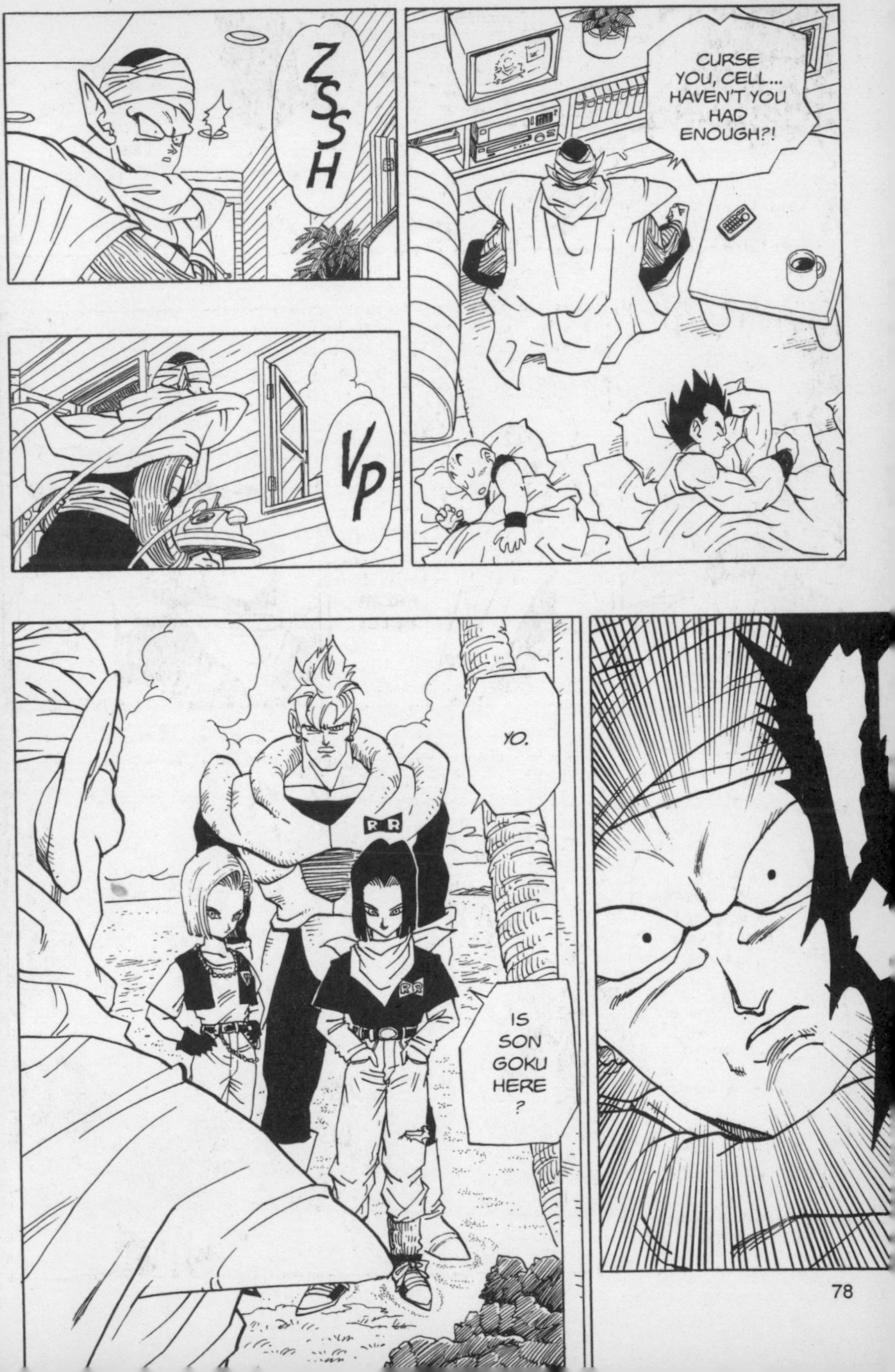
CURSE YOU, CELL... HAVEN'T YOU HAD ENOUGH?!
ZSSH
VP
YO.
IS SON GOKU HERE?

READ THIS WAY

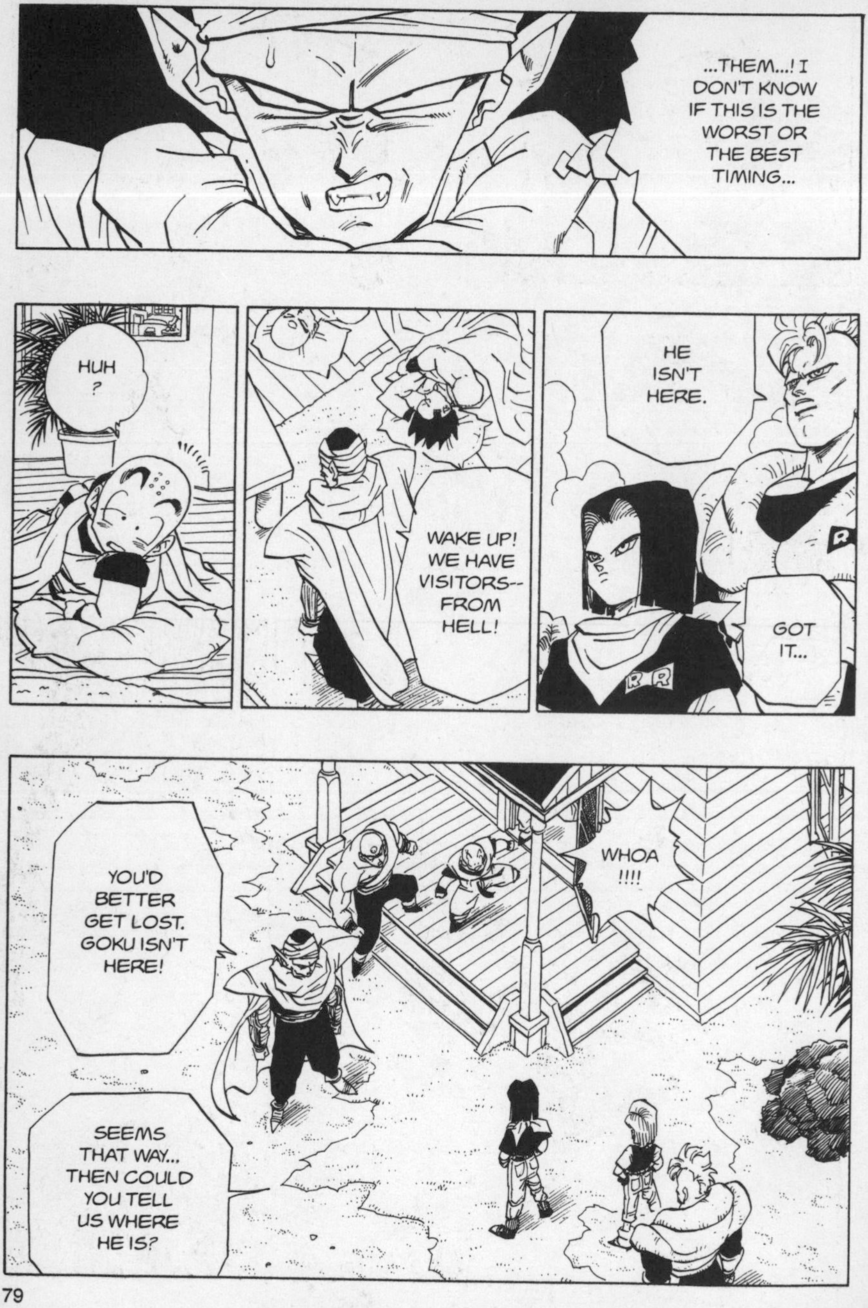
...THEM...! I DON'T KNOW IF THIS IS THE WORST OR THE BEST TIMING...
HE ISN'T HERE.
GOT IT...
WAKE UP! WE HAVE VISITORS--FROM HELL!
HUH?
WHOA!!!!
YOU'D BETTER GET LOST. GOKU ISN'T HERE!
SEEMS THAT WAY... THEN COULD YOU TELL US WHERE HE IS?

READ THIS WAY

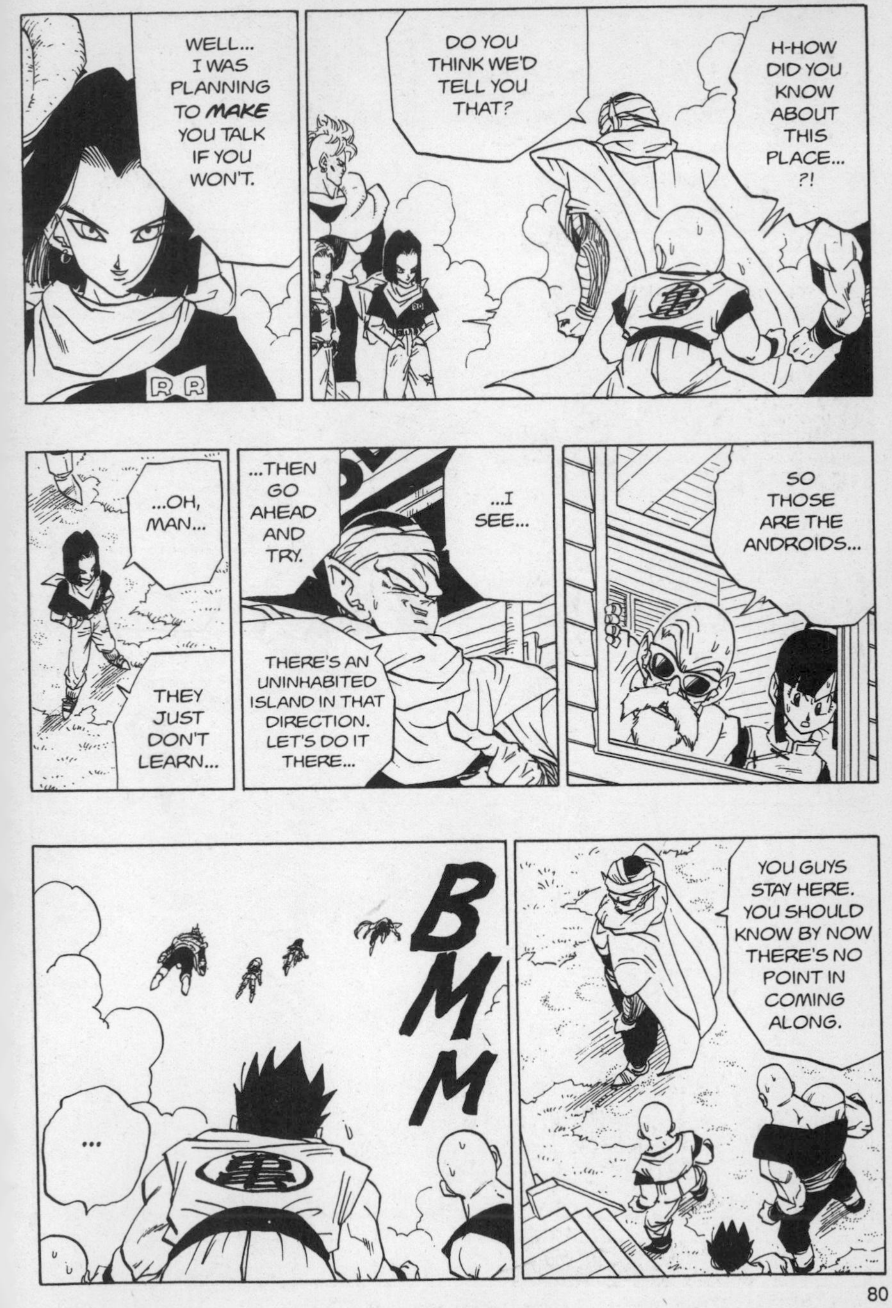
H-HOW DID YOU KNOW ABOUT THIS PLACE... ?!
DO YOU THINK WE'D TELL YOU THAT?
WELL... I WAS PLANNING TO *MAKE* YOU TALK IF YOU WON'T.
SO THOSE ARE THE ANDROIDS...
...I SEE...
...THEN GO AHEAD AND TRY.
THERE'S AN UNINHABITED ISLAND IN THAT DIRECTION. LET'S DO IT THERE...
...OH, MAN...
THEY JUST DON'T LEARN...
YOU GUYS STAY HERE. YOU SHOULD KNOW BY NOW THERE'S NO POINT IN COMING ALONG.
BMM
...

READ THIS WAY

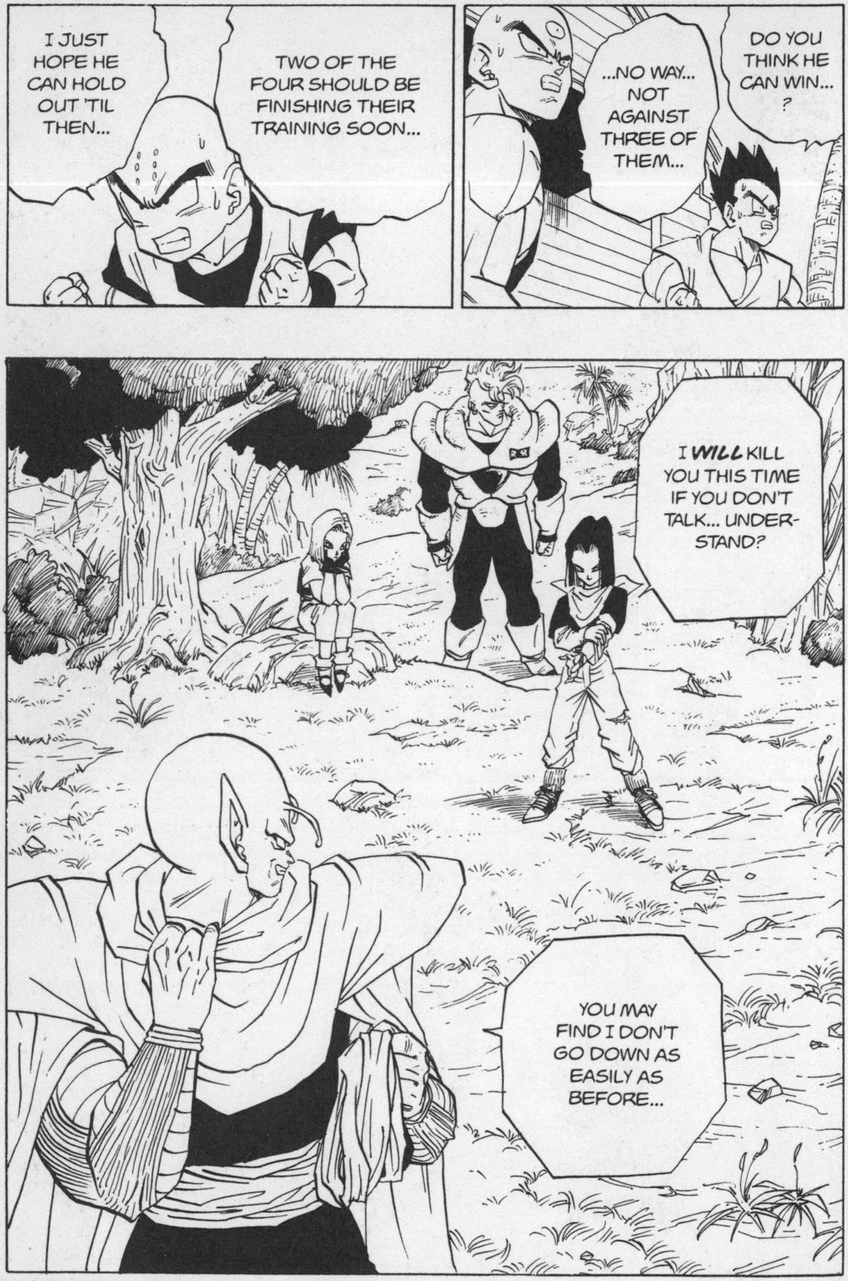
DO YOU THINK HE CAN WIN... ?
...NO WAY... NOT AGAINST THREE OF THEM...
TWO OF THE FOUR SHOULD BE FINISHING THEIR TRAINING SOON...
I JUST HOPE HE CAN HOLD OUT 'TIL THEN...
I **WILL** KILL YOU THIS TIME IF YOU DON'T TALK... UNDER-STAND?
YOU MAY FIND I DON'T GO DOWN AS EASILY AS BEFORE...

NEXT: The New Piccolo vs. #17

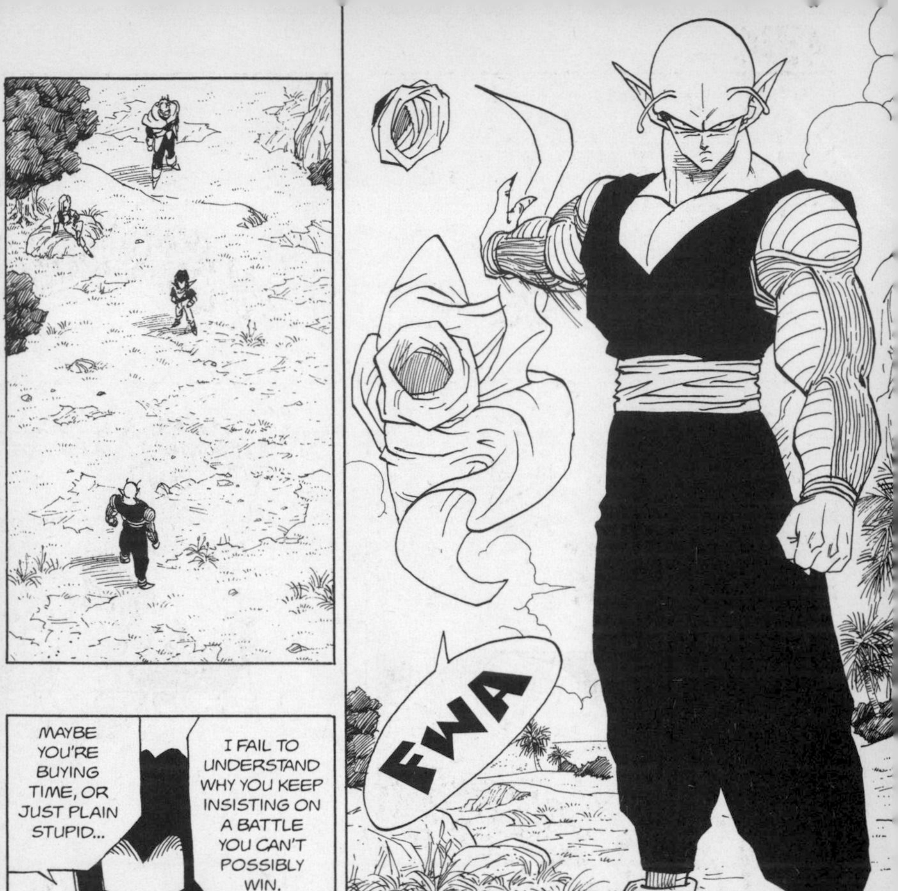
FWA
I FAIL TO UNDERSTAND WHY YOU KEEP INSISTING ON A BATTLE YOU CAN'T POSSIBLY WIN.
MAYBE YOU'RE BUYING TIME, OR JUST PLAIN STUPID...

DBZ : 173 • Piccolo vs. #17

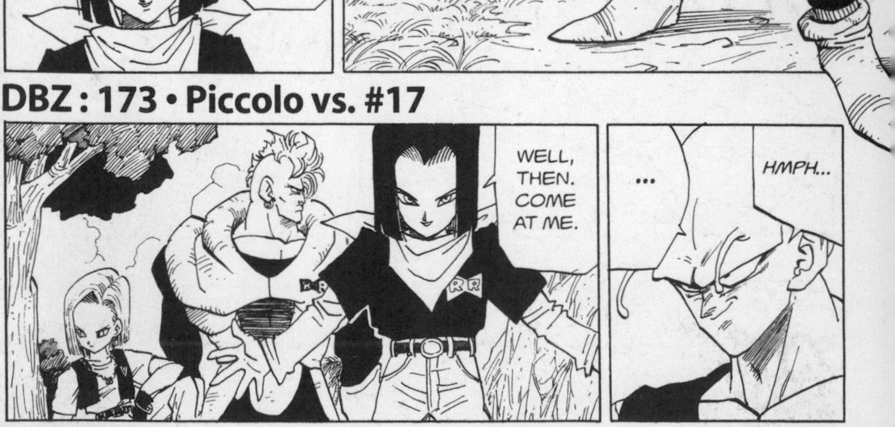
HMPH...
...
WELL, THEN. COME AT ME.

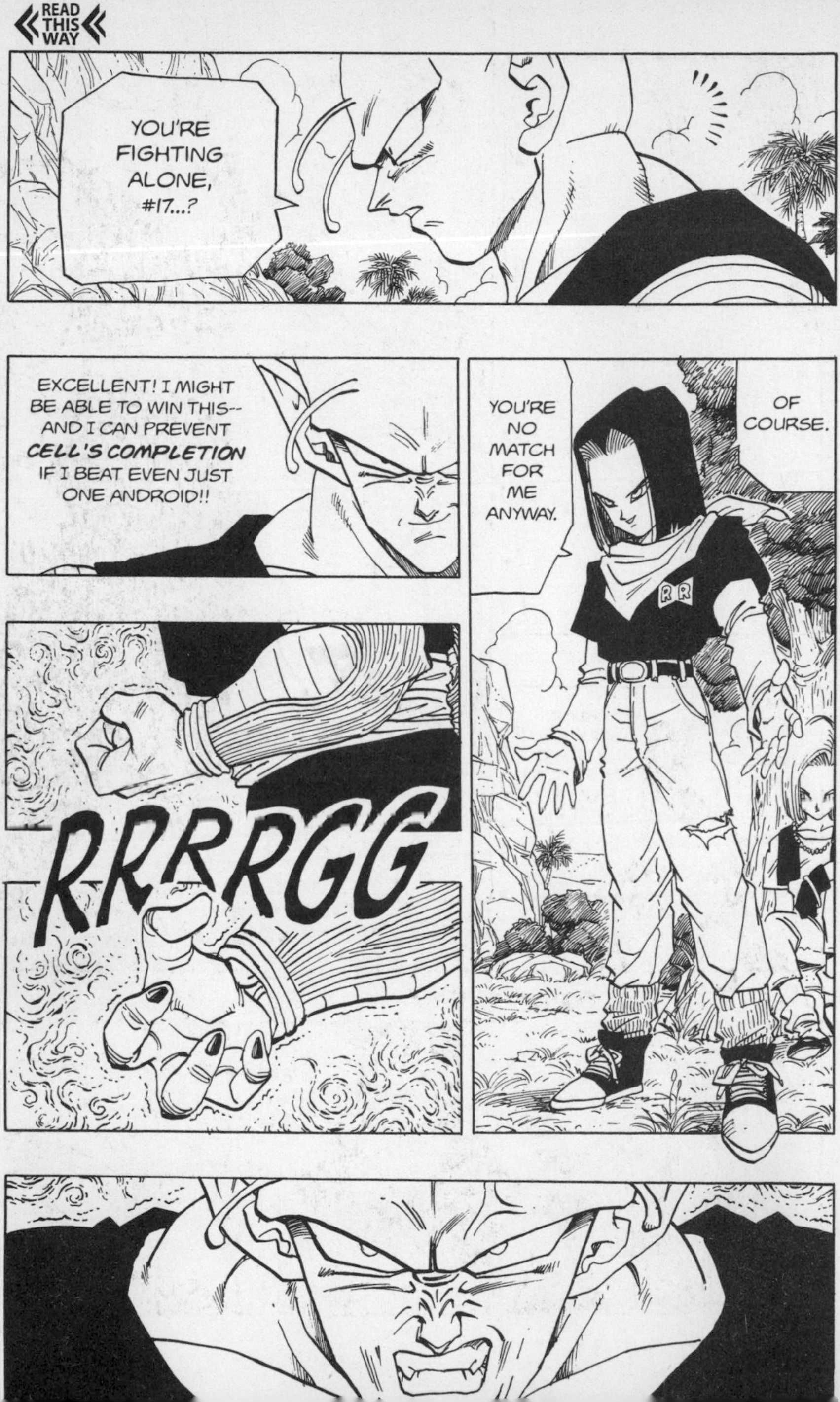
READ THIS WAY
YOU'RE FIGHTING ALONE, #17...?
OF COURSE.
YOU'RE NO MATCH FOR ME ANYWAY.
EXCELLENT! I MIGHT BE ABLE TO WIN THIS-- AND I CAN PREVENT **CELL'S COMPLETION** IF I BEAT EVEN JUST ONE ANDROID!!
RRRRGG

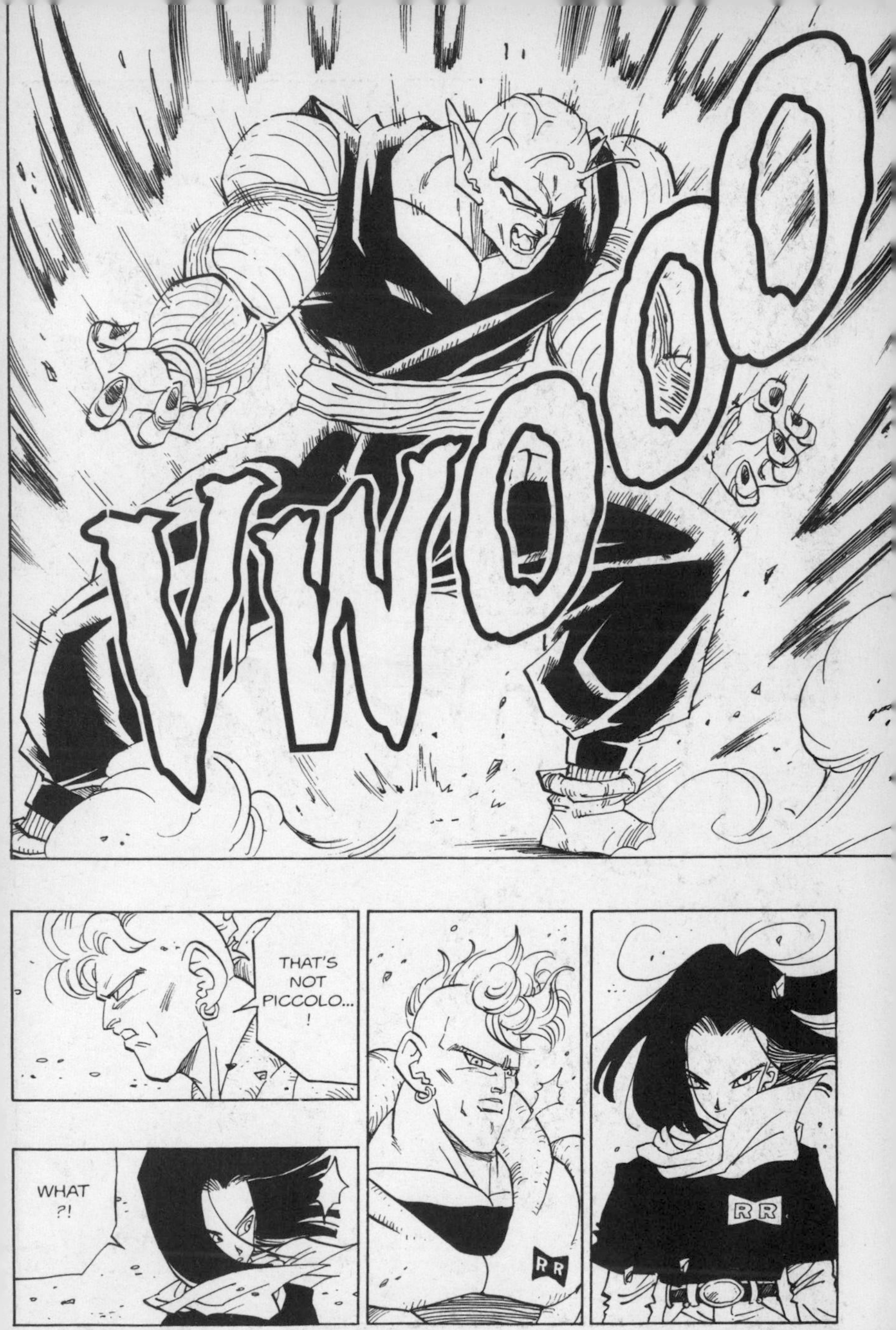
VWOOOOO
THAT'S NOT PICCOLO... !
WHAT ?!

READ THIS WAY

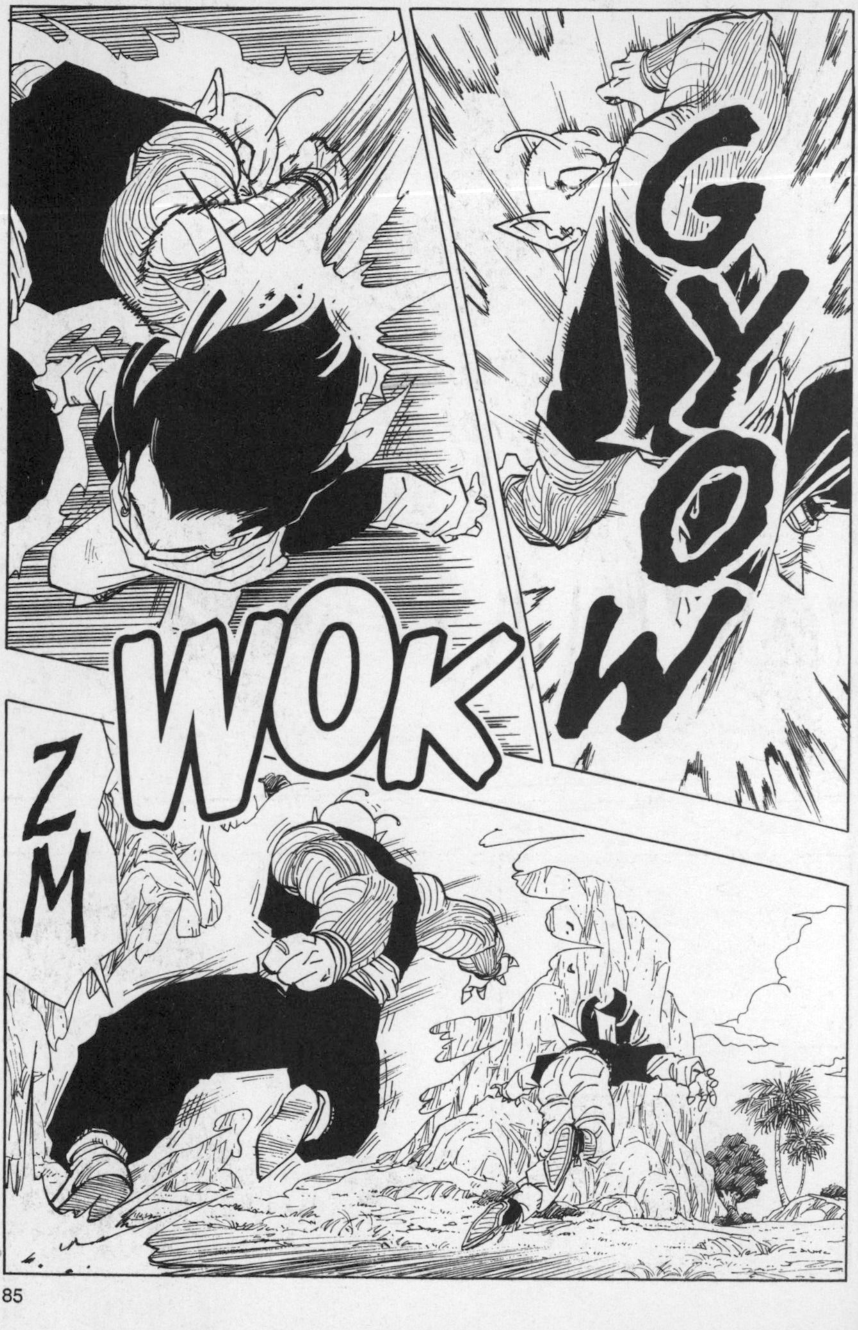
GYOW
WOK
ZM

READ THIS WAY

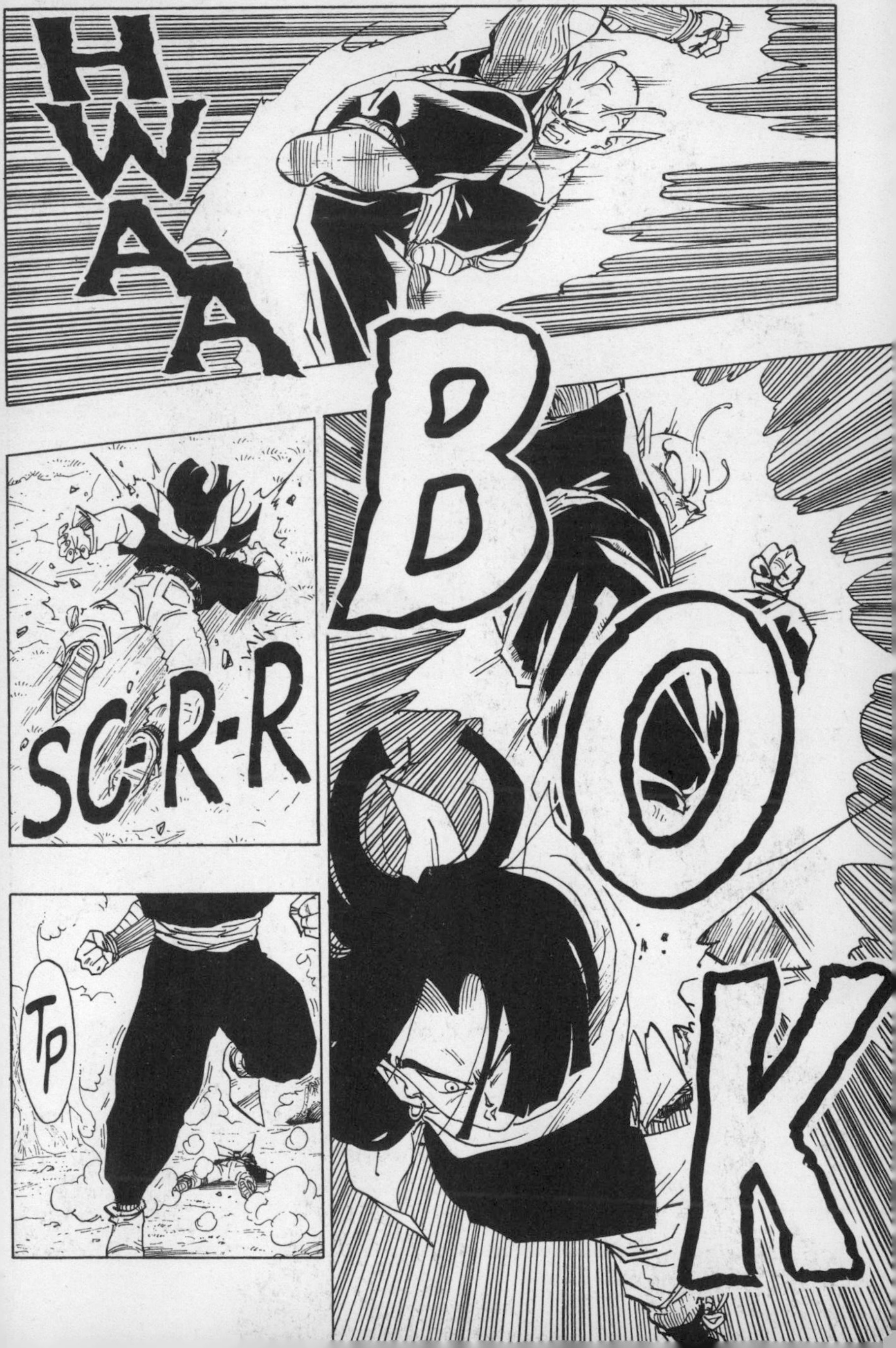
HWAA
BOK
SC-R-R
Tp

READ THIS WAY

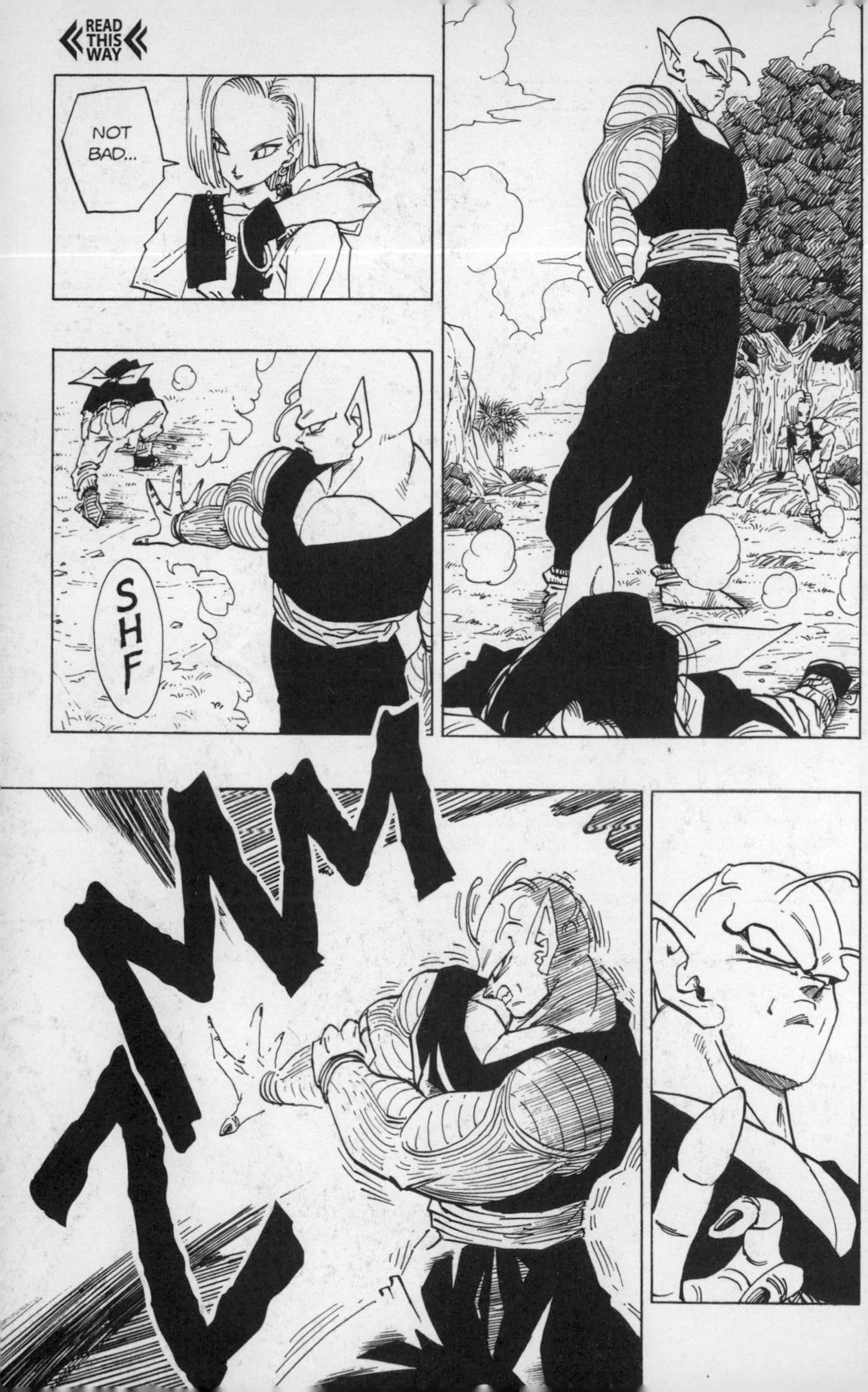
NOT BAD...
SHF

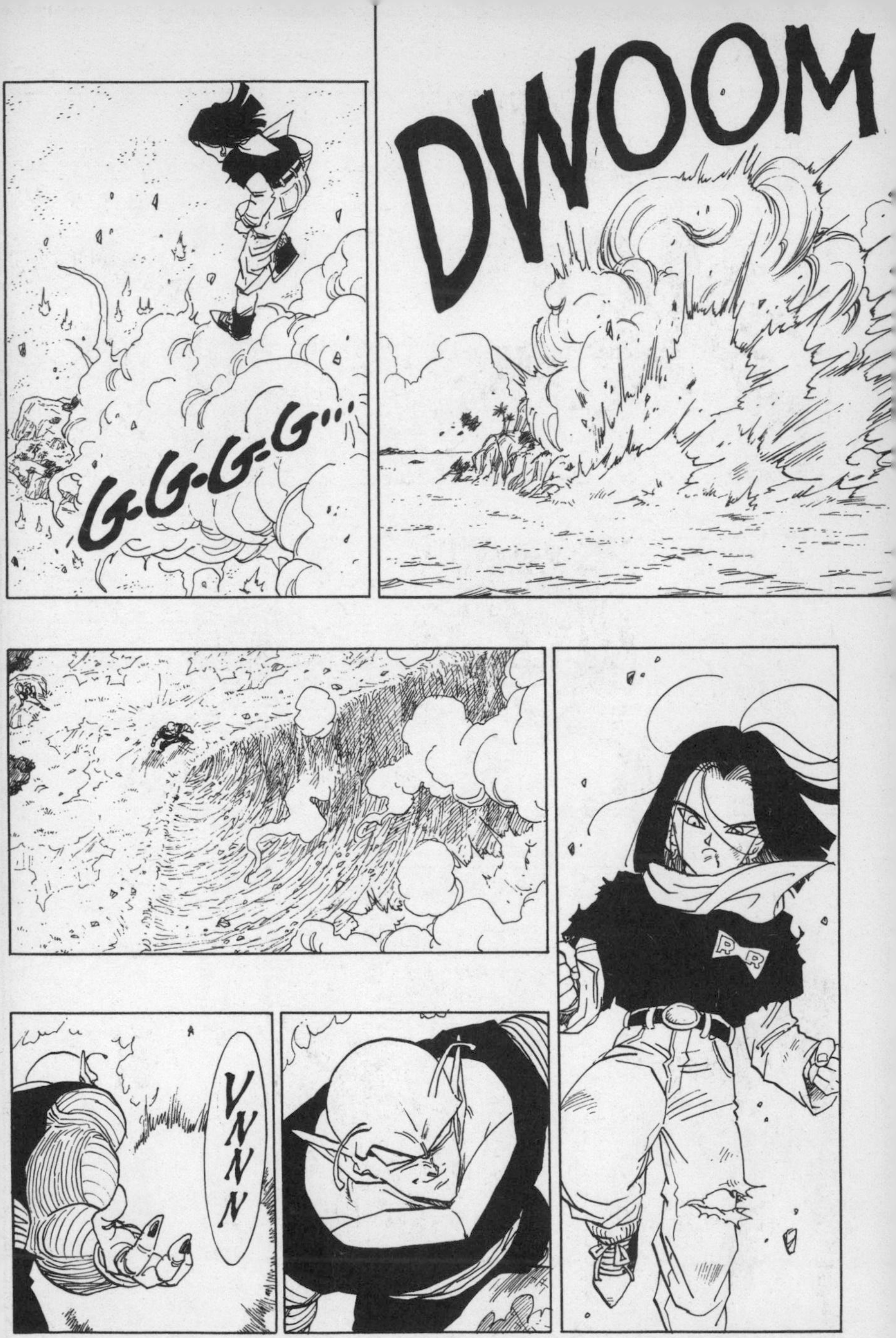
DWOOM
G-G-G-G...
VNNN

READ THIS WAY

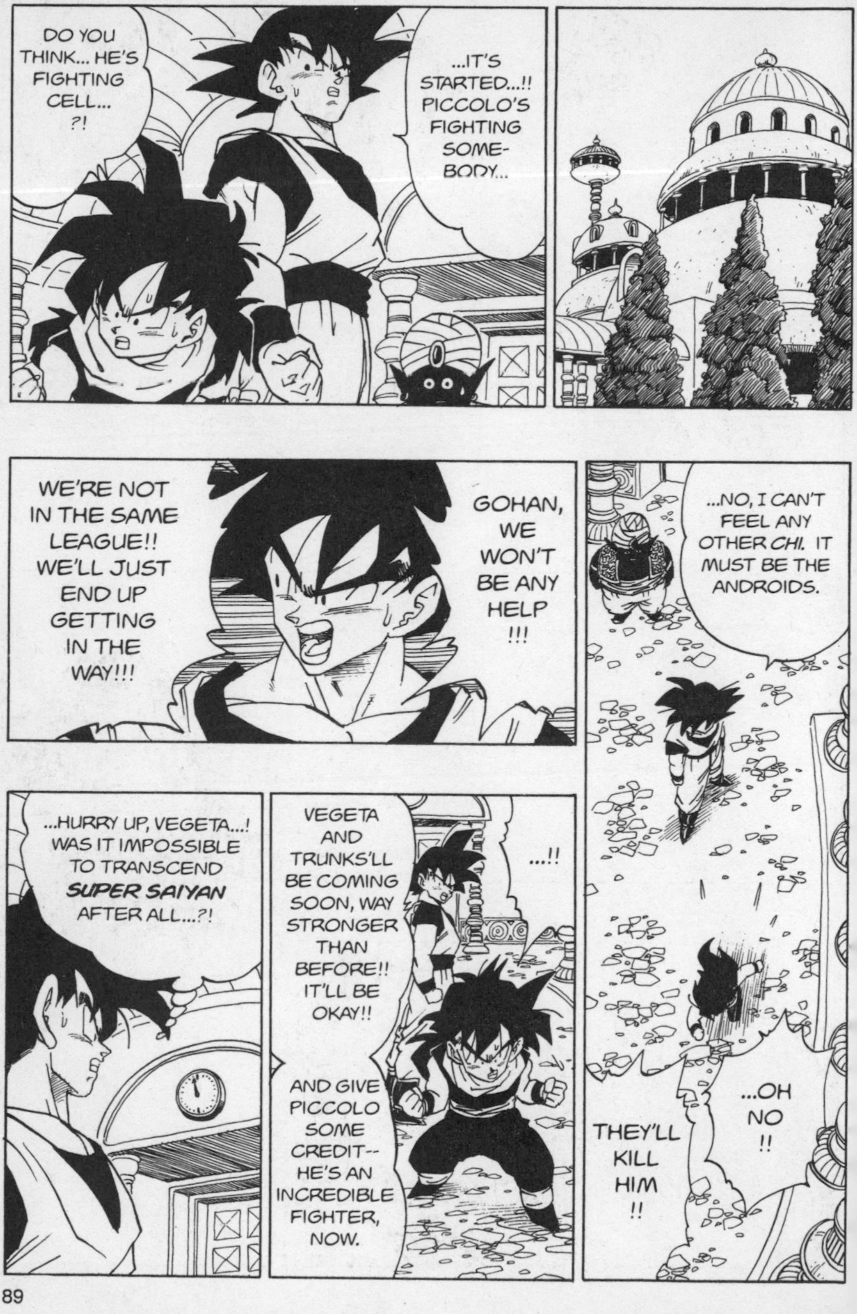
...IT'S STARTED...!! PICCOLO'S FIGHTING SOME-BODY...
DO YOU THINK... HE'S FIGHTING CELL... ?!
...NO, I CAN'T FEEL ANY OTHER *CHI.* IT MUST BE THE ANDROIDS.
...OH NO !!
THEY'LL KILL HIM !!
GOHAN, WE WON'T BE ANY HELP !!!
WE'RE NOT IN THE SAME LEAGUE!! WE'LL JUST END UP GETTING IN THE WAY!!!
...!!
VEGETA AND TRUNKS'LL BE COMING SOON, WAY STRONGER THAN BEFORE!! IT'LL BE OKAY!!
AND GIVE PICCOLO SOME CREDIT-- HE'S AN INCREDIBLE FIGHTER, NOW.
...HURRY UP, VEGETA...! WAS IT IMPOSSIBLE TO TRANSCEND ***SUPER SAIYAN*** AFTER ALL...?!

READ THIS WAY

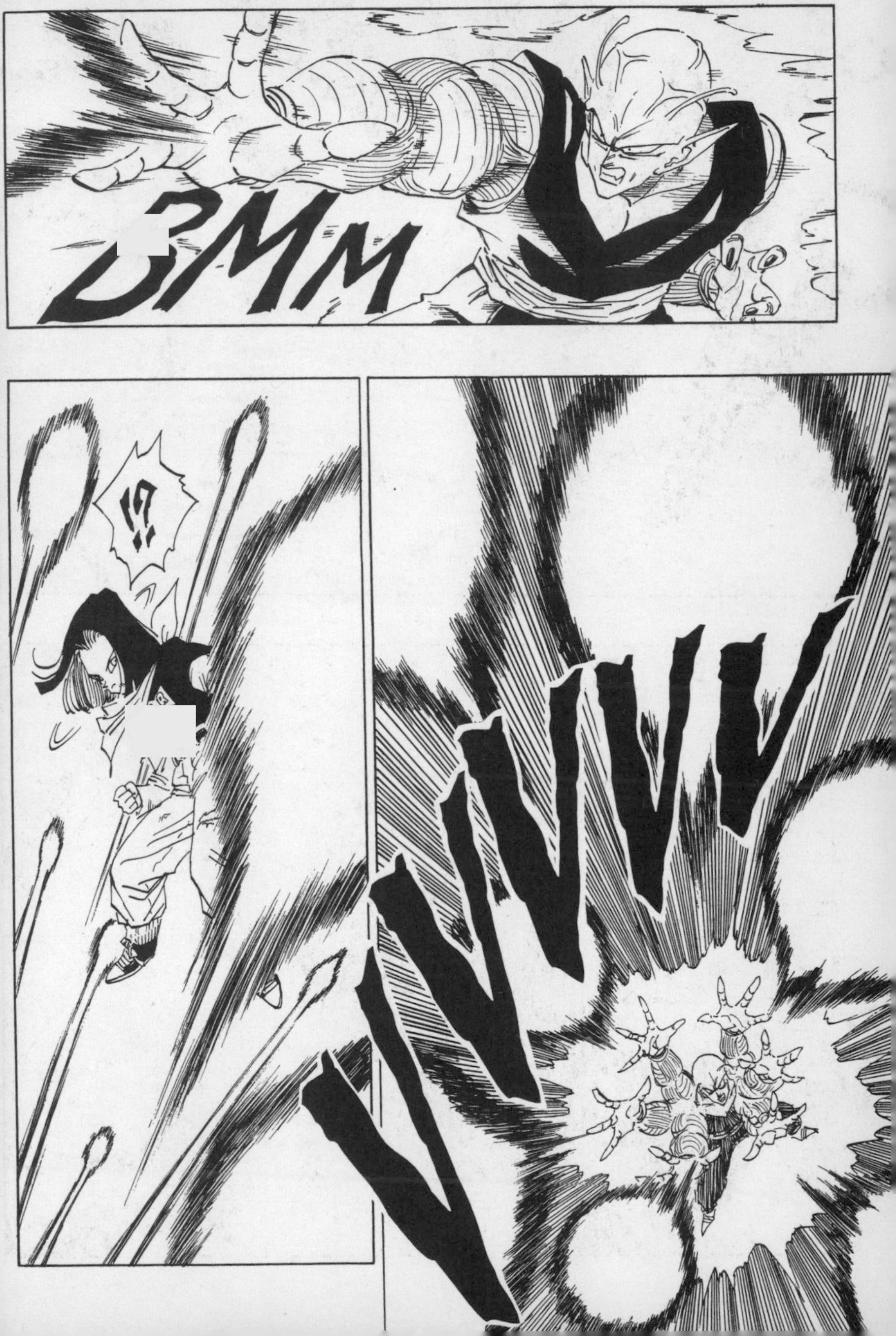
BMM
!?

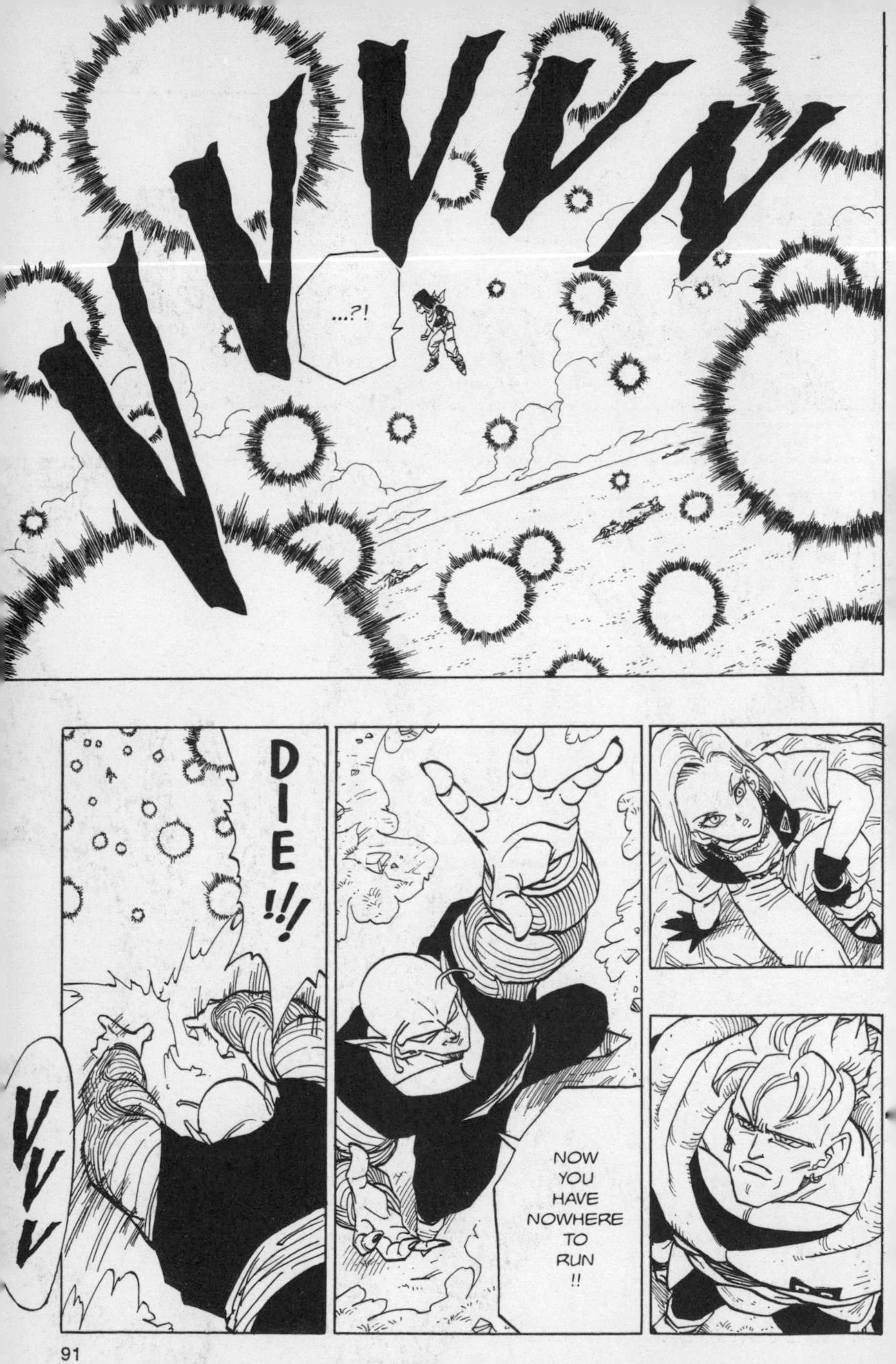
VVVVN
...?!
NOW YOU HAVE NOWHERE TO RUN !!
DIE !!!
VVVV

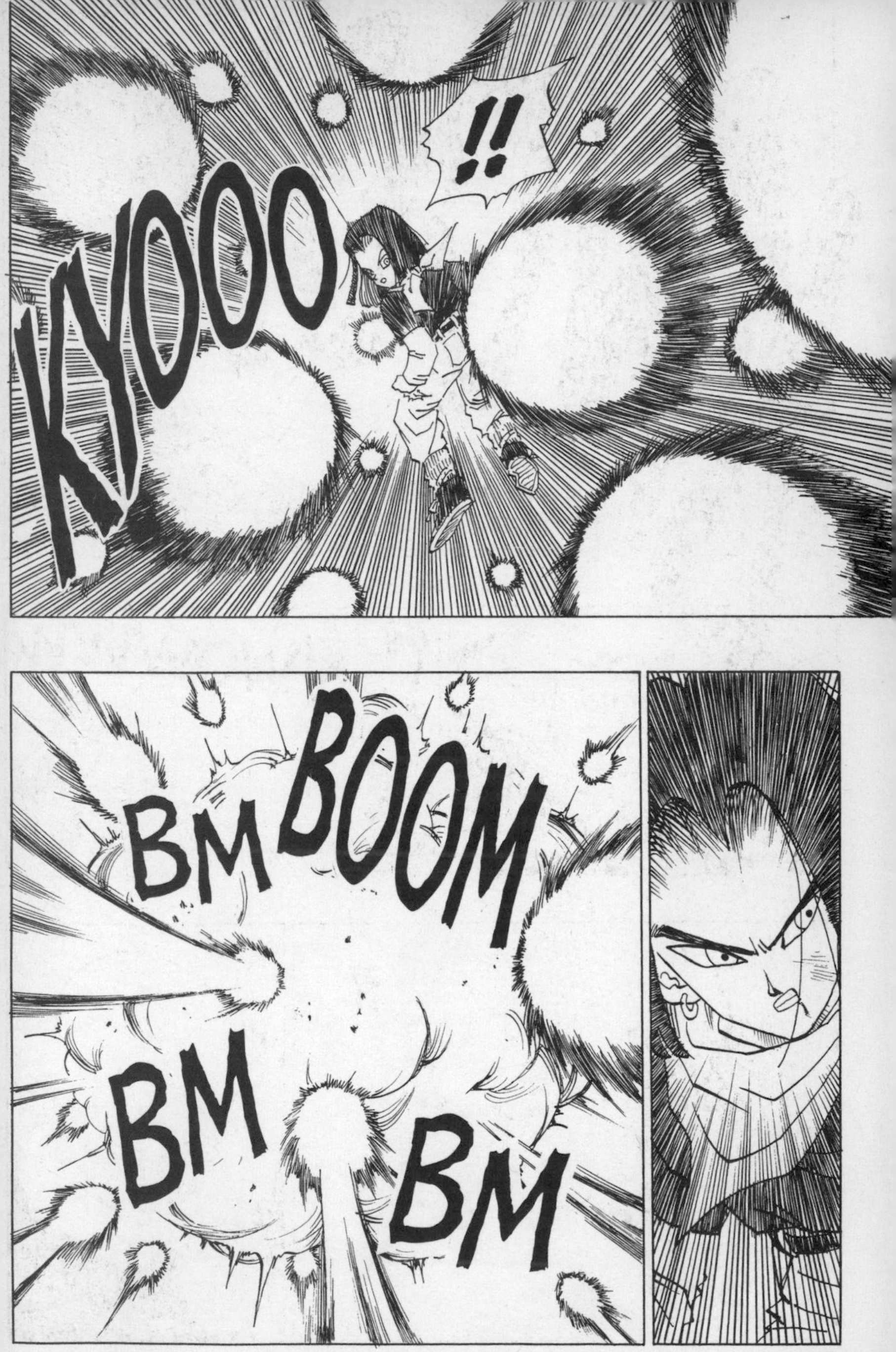
!!
KYOOO
BOOM
BM
BM
BM

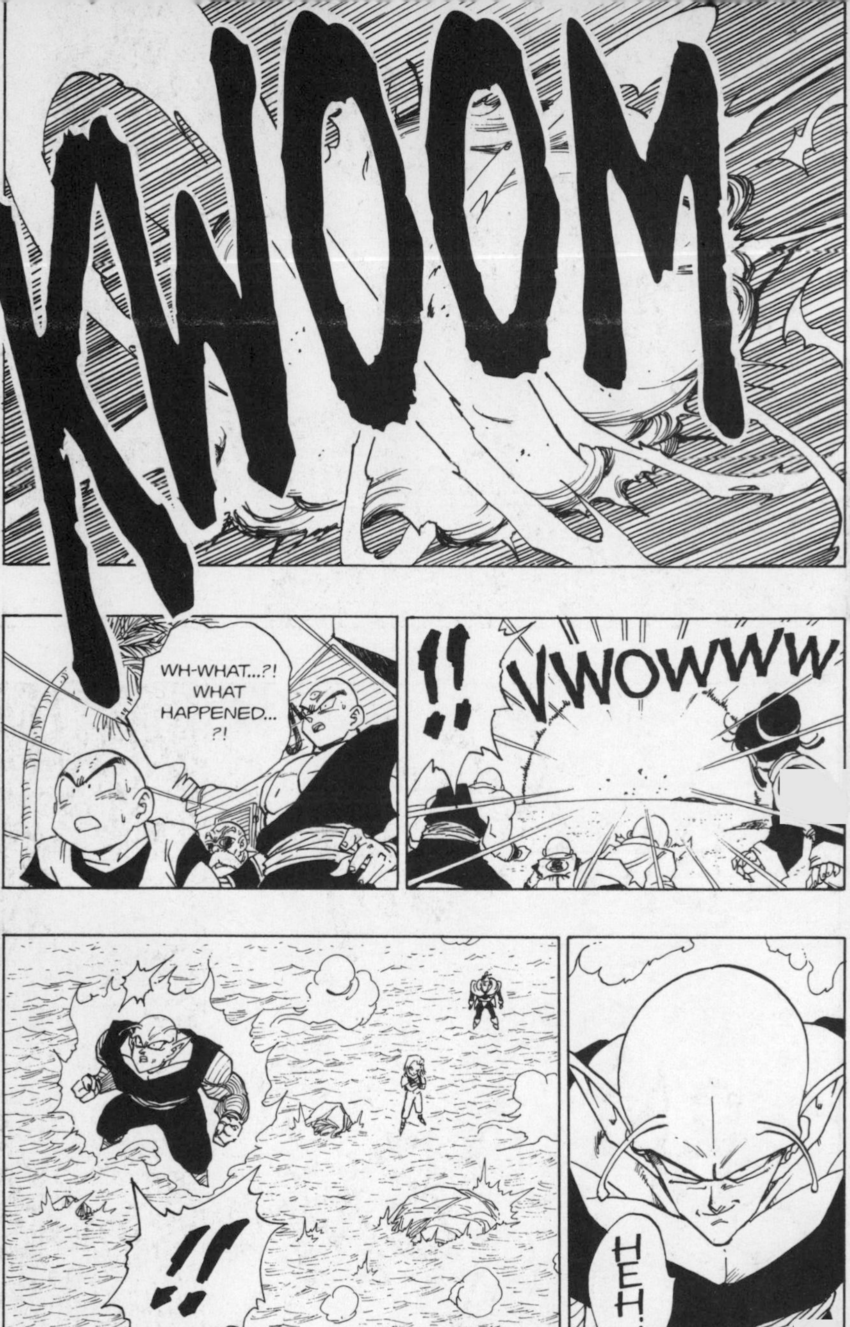
KWOOM
!!
VWOWWW
WH-WHAT...?! WHAT HAPPENED...?!
HEH...
!!

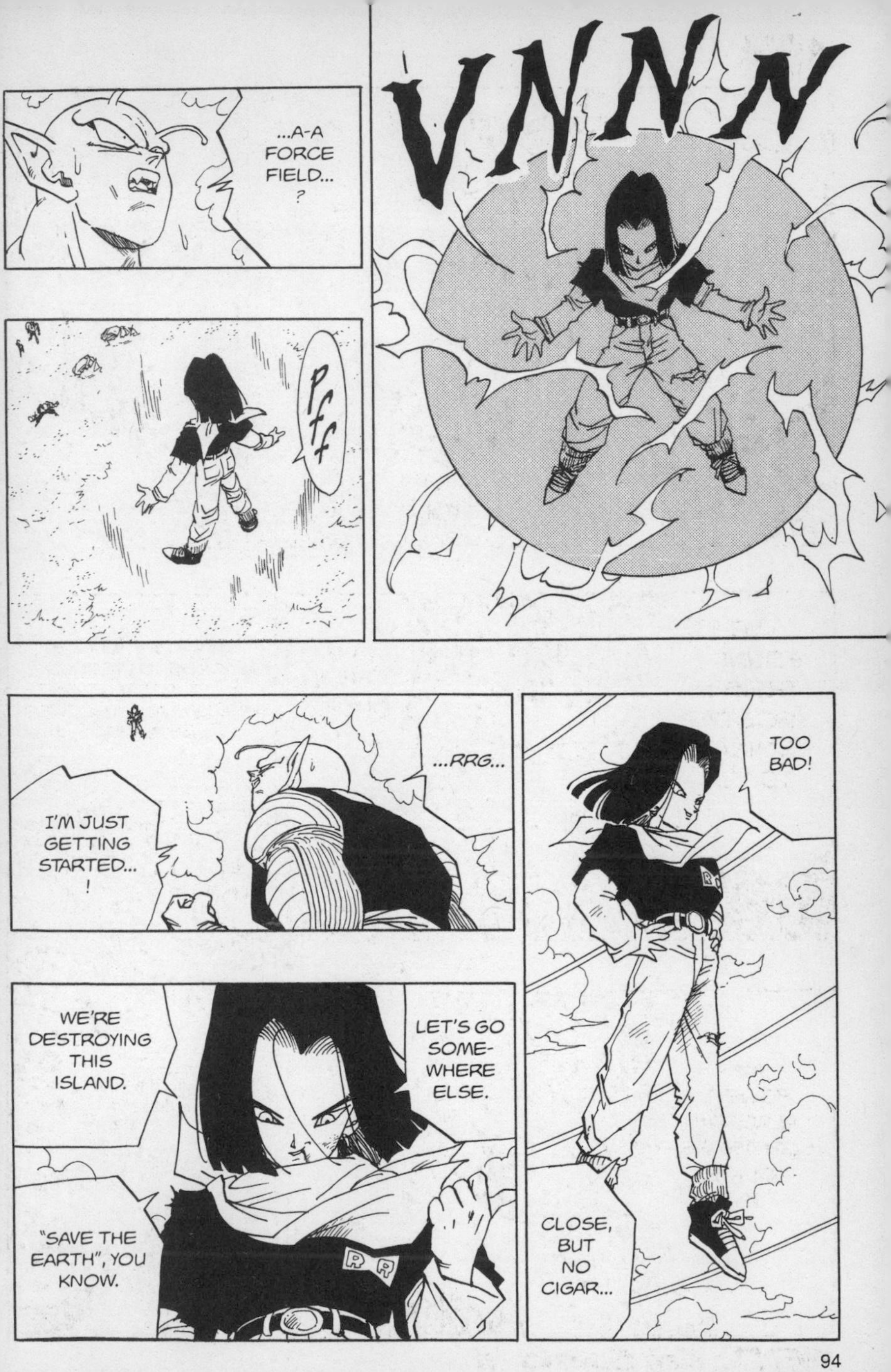
VNNN
...A-A FORCE FIELD...?
Pff
TOO BAD!
CLOSE, BUT NO CIGAR...
...RRG...
I'M JUST GETTING STARTED...!
LET'S GO SOMEWHERE ELSE.
WE'RE DESTROYING THIS ISLAND.
"SAVE THE EARTH", YOU KNOW.

READ THIS WAY

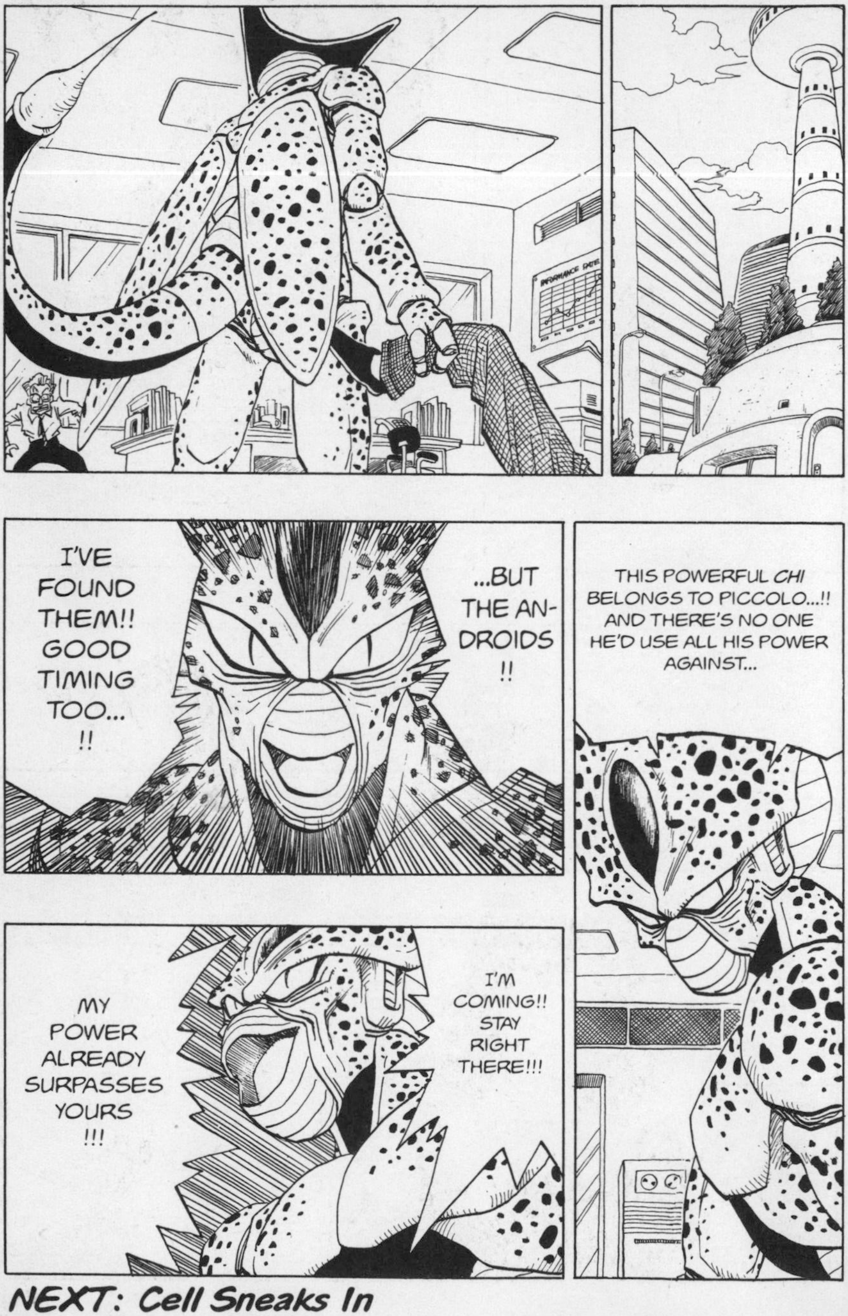
THIS POWERFUL CHI BELONGS TO PICCOLO...!! AND THERE'S NO ONE HE'D USE ALL HIS POWER AGAINST...
...BUT THE ANDROIDS !!
I'VE FOUND THEM!! GOOD TIMING TOO... !!
I'M COMING!! STAY RIGHT THERE!!!
MY POWER ALREADY SURPASSES YOURS !!!

NEXT: Cell Sneaks In

DBZ:174 • Waiting in the Wings

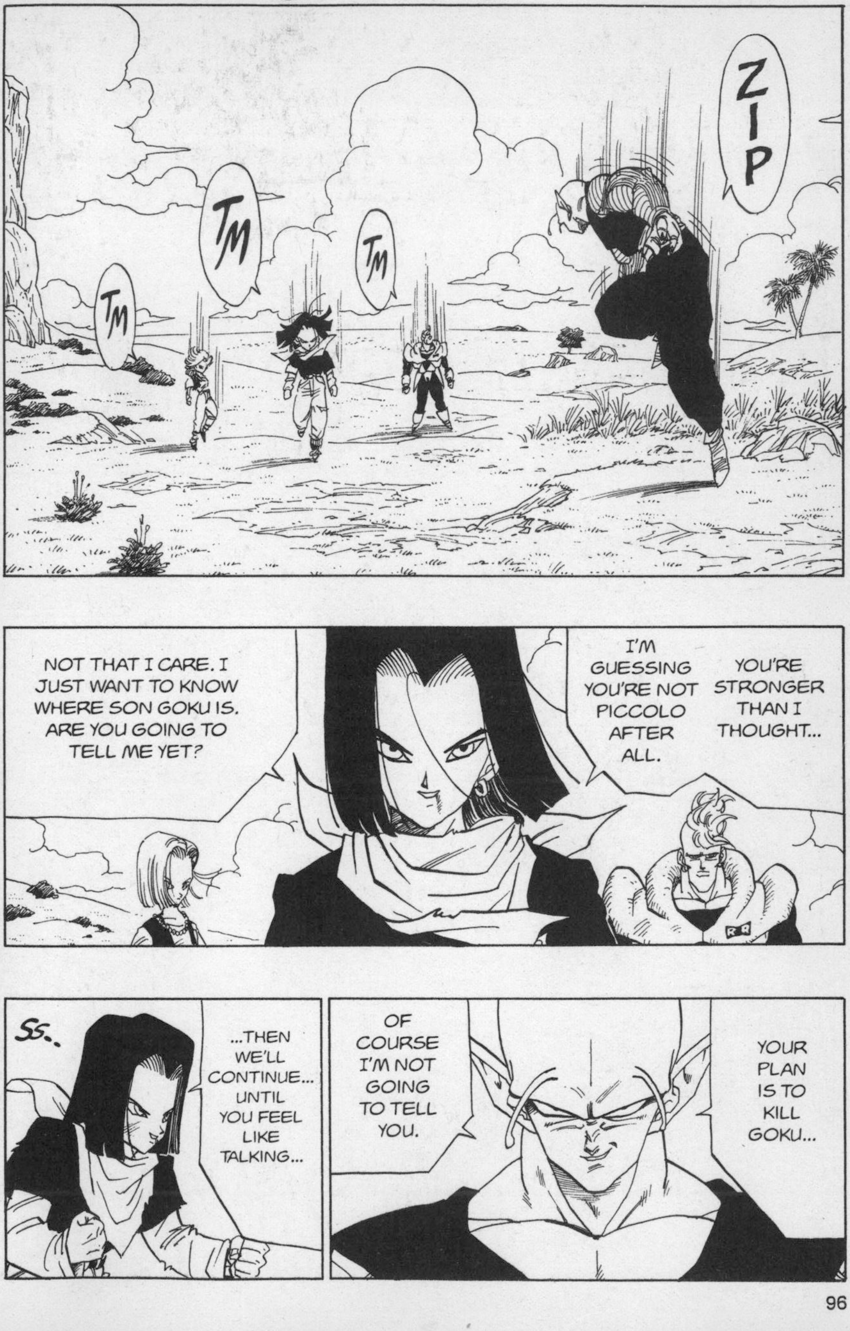
ZIP
TM
TM
TM
YOU'RE STRONGER THAN I THOUGHT...
I'M GUESSING YOU'RE NOT PICCOLO AFTER ALL.
NOT THAT I CARE. I JUST WANT TO KNOW WHERE SON GOKU IS. ARE YOU GOING TO TELL ME YET?
YOUR PLAN IS TO KILL GOKU...
OF COURSE I'M NOT GOING TO TELL YOU.
...THEN WE'LL CONTINUE... UNTIL YOU FEEL LIKE TALKING...
SS..

READ THIS WAY

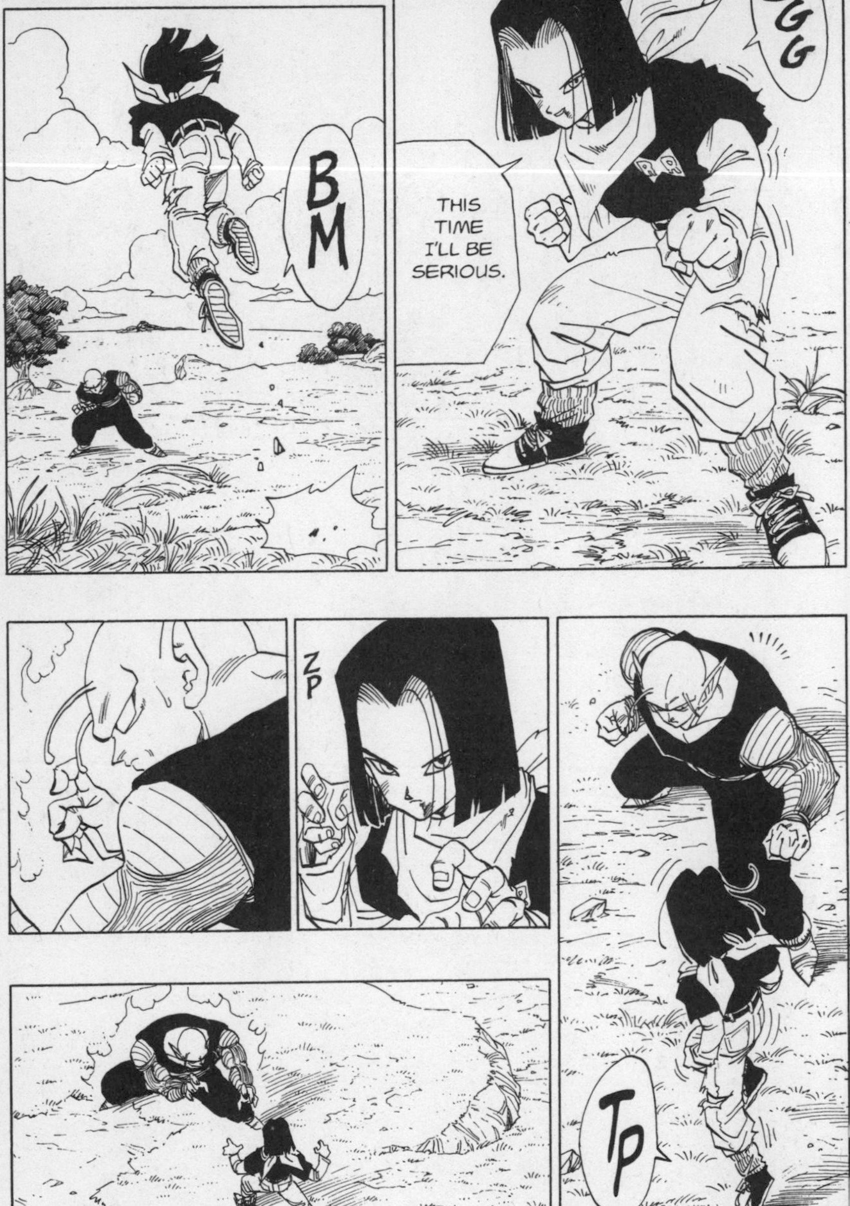
GGG
THIS TIME I'LL BE SERIOUS.
BM
TP
ZP

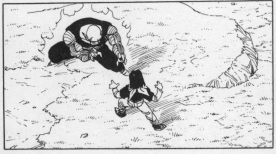

READ THIS WAY

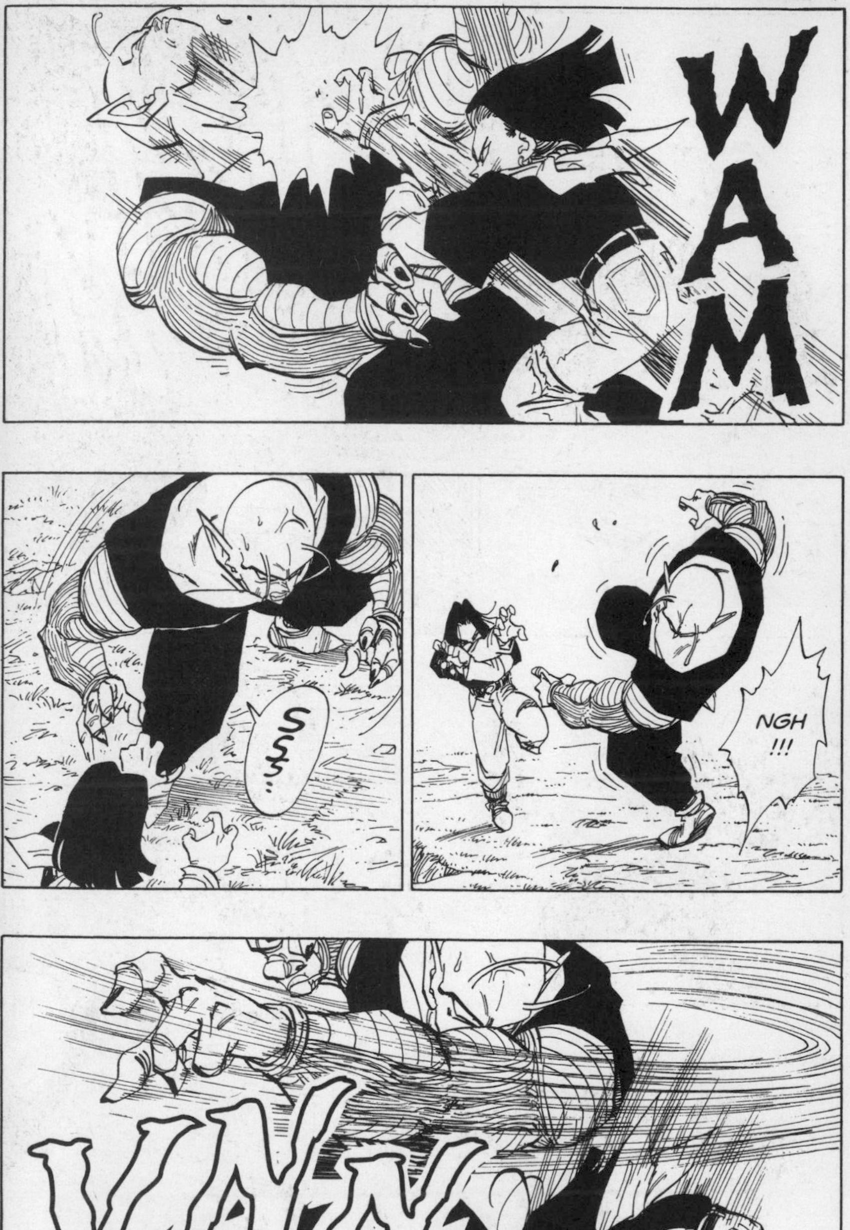
WAM
NGH !!!
Ssh..
VNN

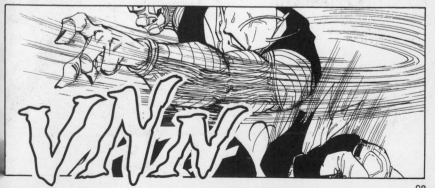

READ THIS WAY

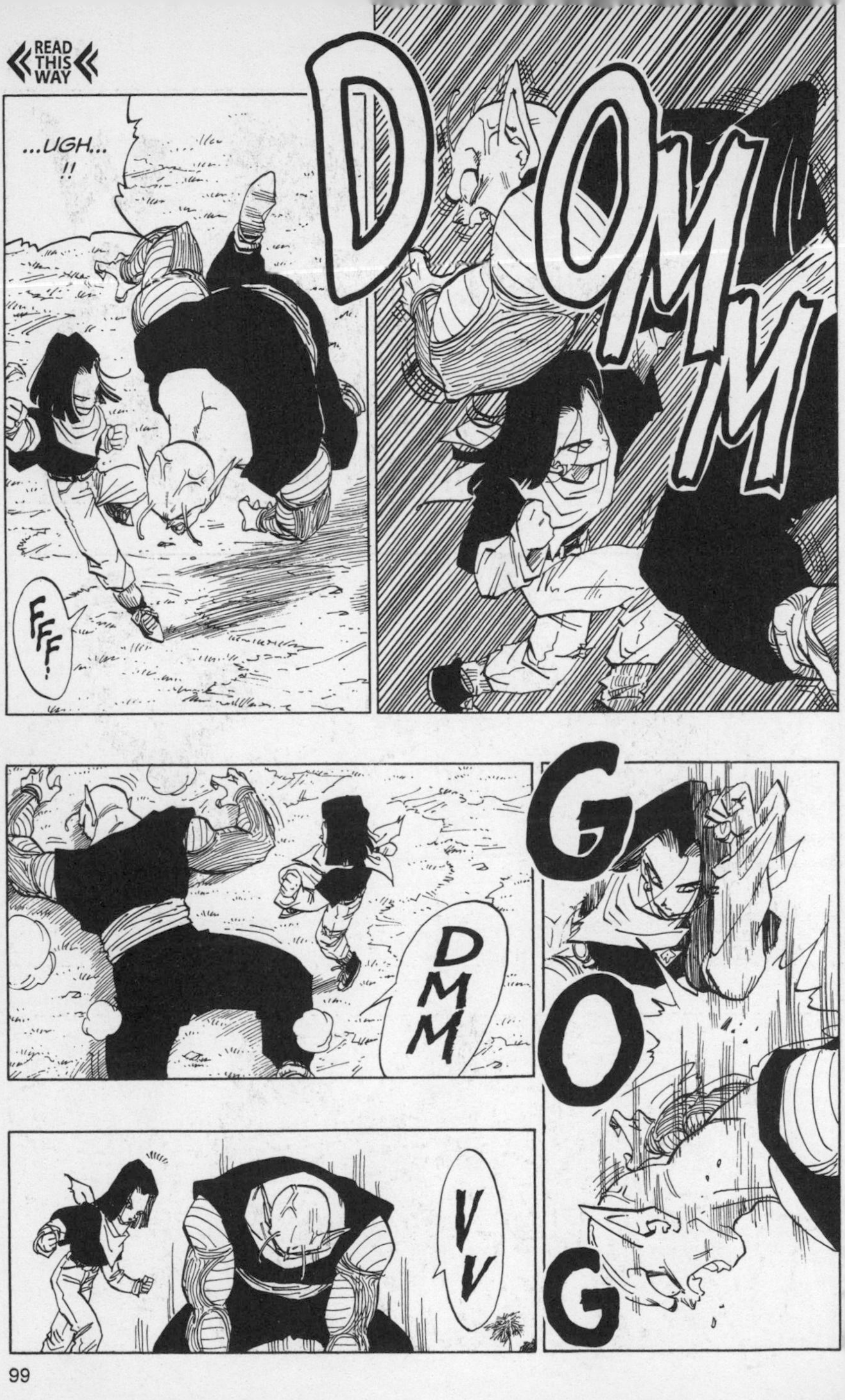

DOMM
...UGH... !!
FFF!
GOG
DMM
VV

READ THIS WAY

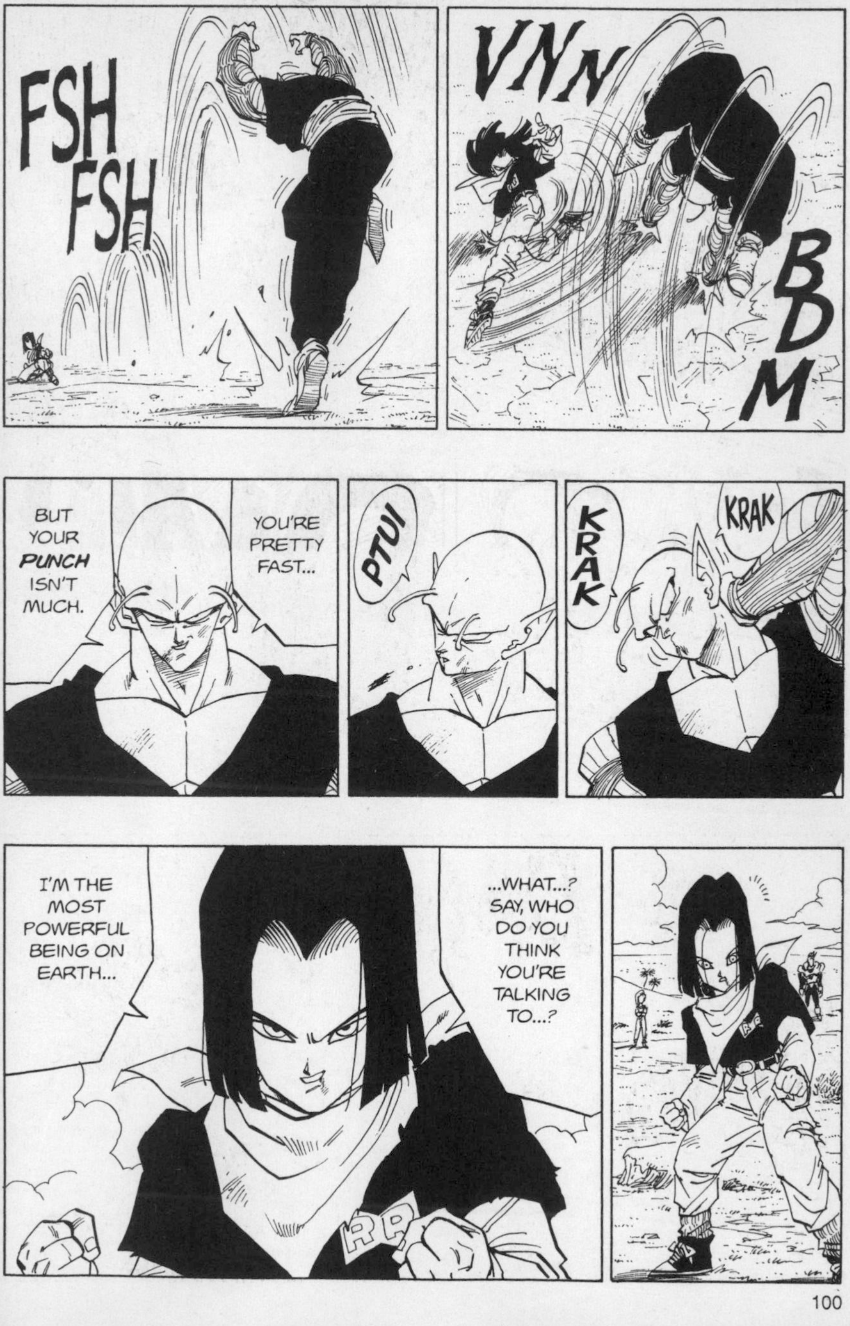
VNN
BDM
FSH FSH
KRAK
KRAK
PTUI
YOU'RE PRETTY FAST...
BUT YOUR PUNCH ISN'T MUCH.
...WHAT...? SAY, WHO DO YOU THINK YOU'RE TALKING TO...?
I'M THE MOST POWERFUL BEING ON EARTH...

READ THIS WAY

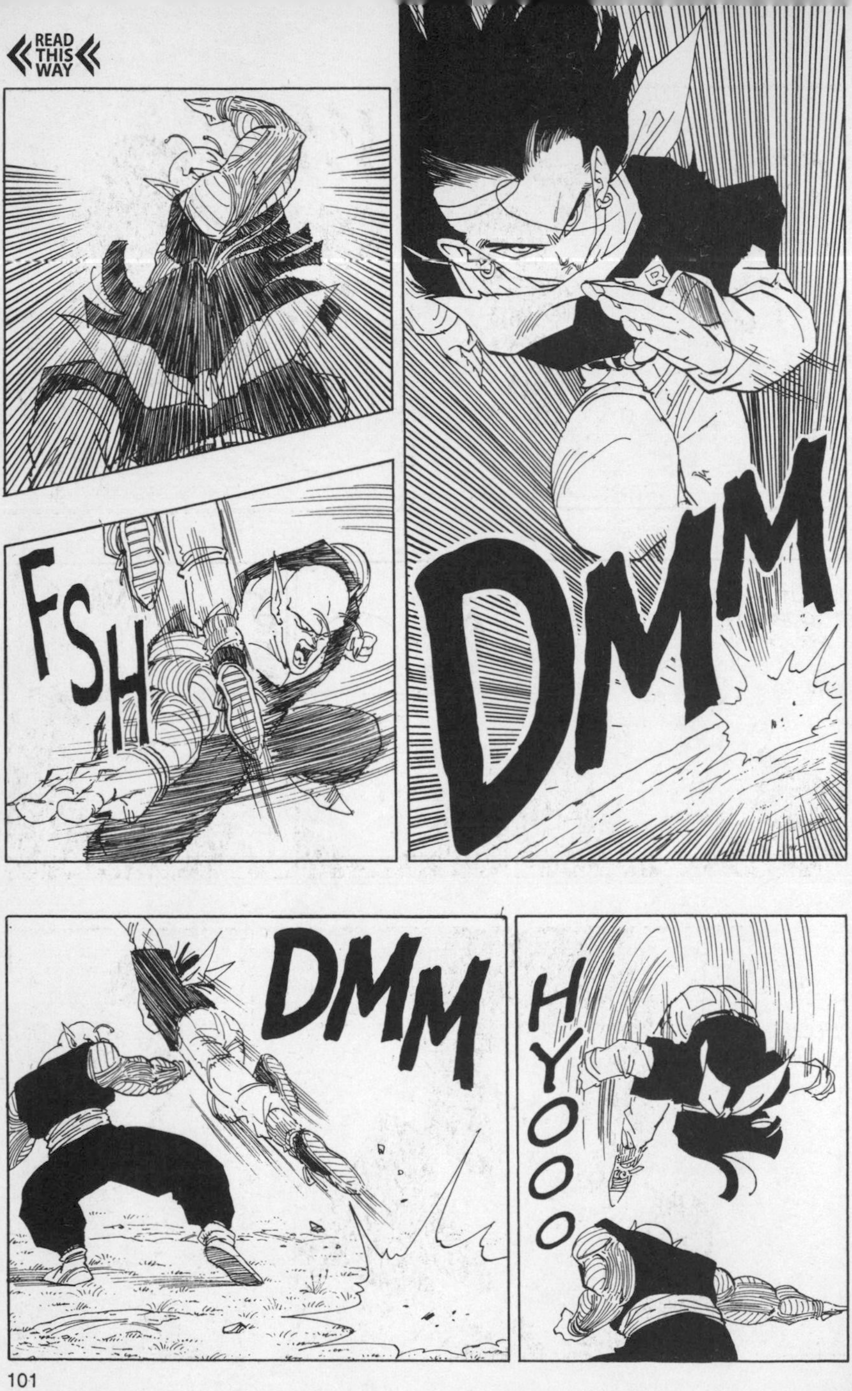
DMM
FSH
HYOOO
DMM

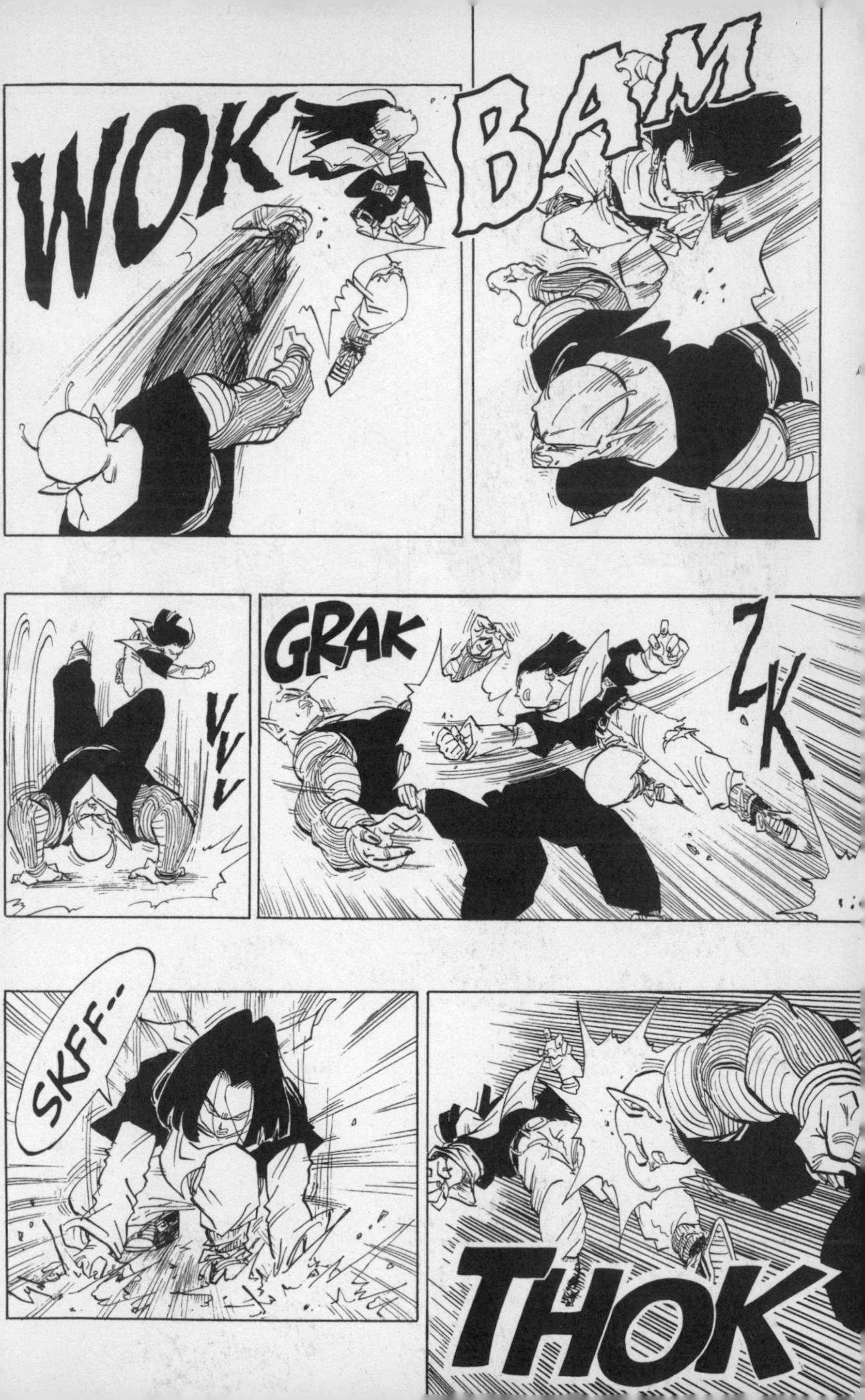
BAM
WOK
ZK
GRAK
VVV
THOK
SKFF..

READ THIS WAY

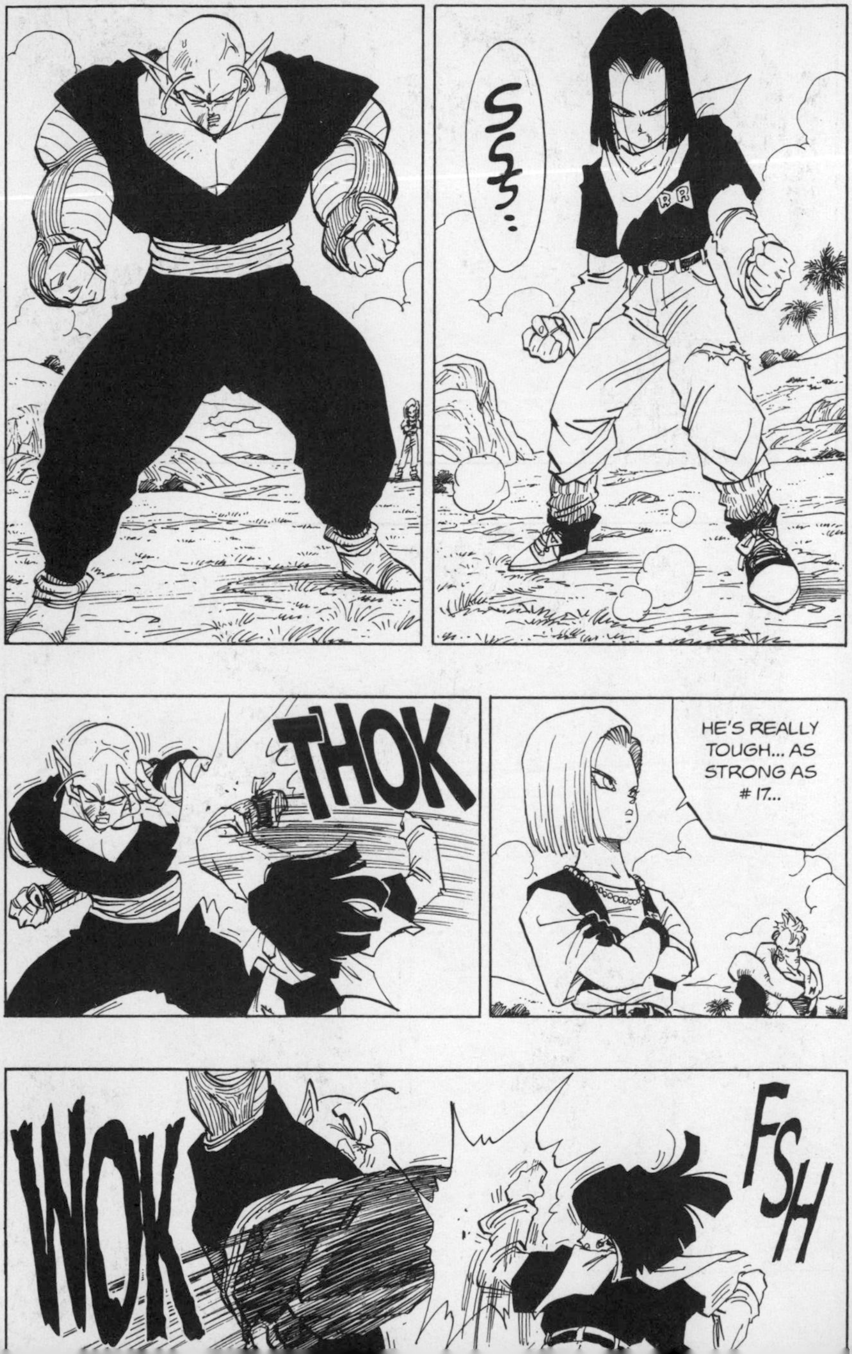

SSS...
HE'S REALLY TOUGH... AS STRONG AS # 17...
THOK
FSH
WOK

READ THIS WAY

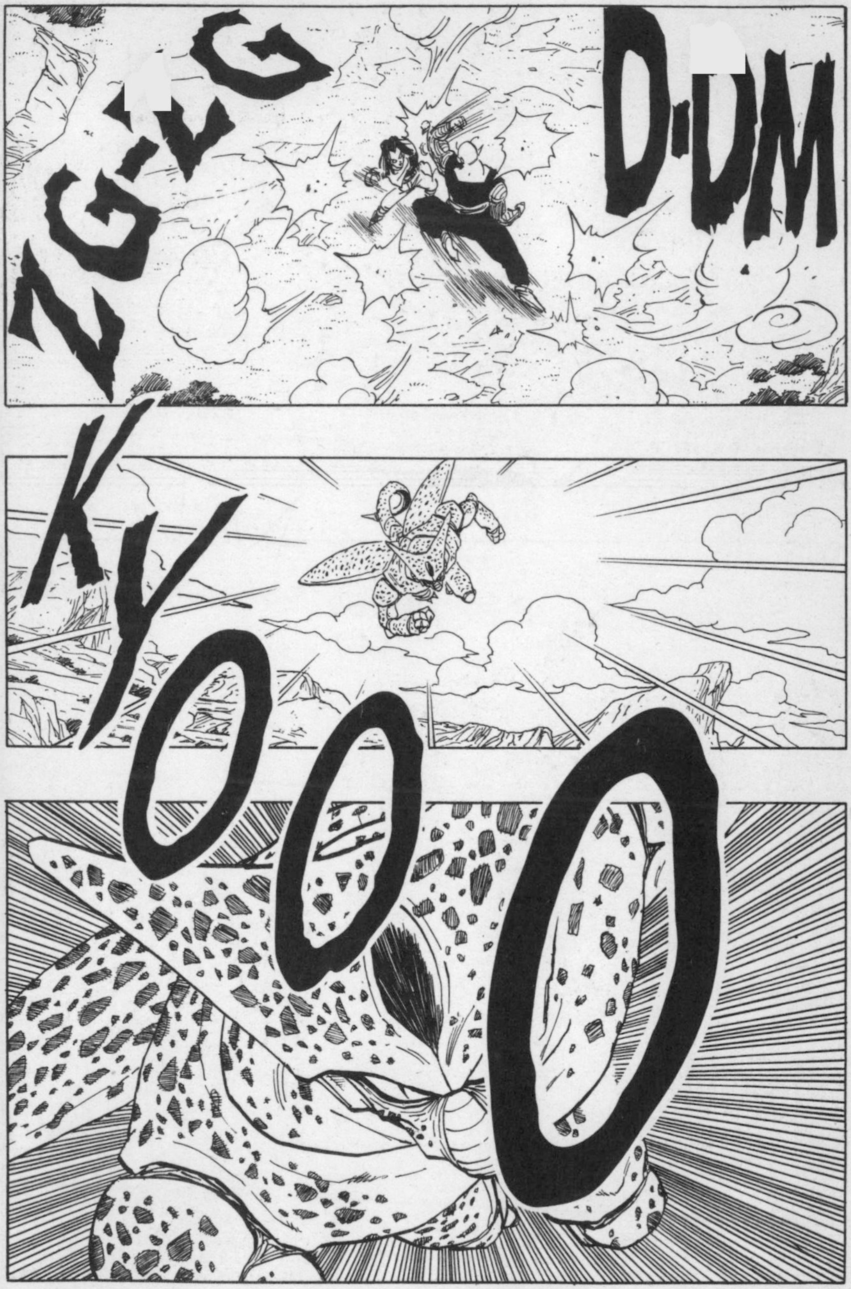
D-DM
ZG-ZG
KYOOOO

READ THIS WAY

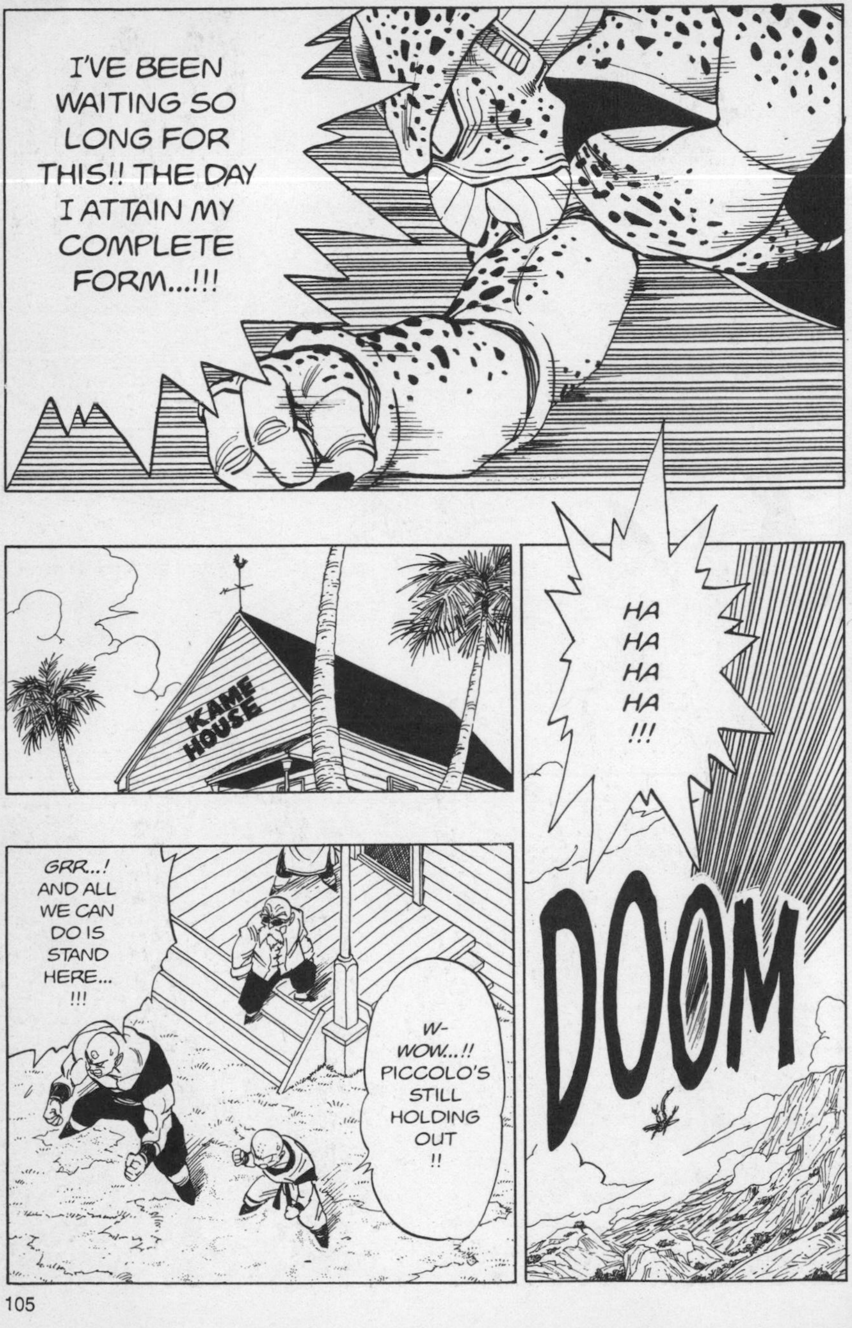
I'VE BEEN WAITING SO LONG FOR THIS!! THE DAY I ATTAIN MY COMPLETE FORM...!!!
HA HA HA HA !!!
DOOM
KAME HOUSE
W-WOW...!! PICCOLO'S STILL HOLDING OUT !!
GRR...! AND ALL WE CAN DO IS STAND HERE... !!!

READ THIS WAY

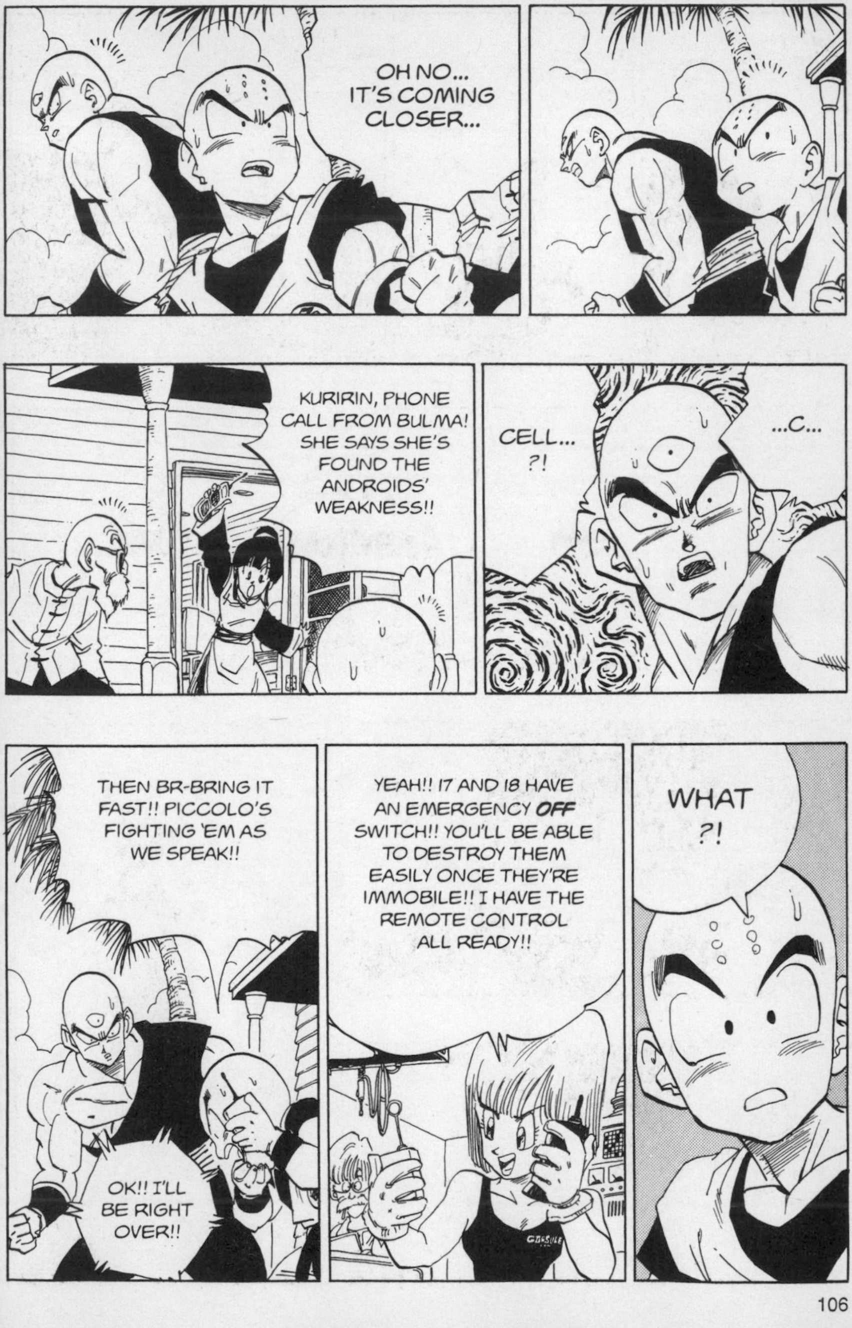
OH NO... IT'S COMING CLOSER...
...C...
CELL... ?!
KURIRIN, PHONE CALL FROM BULMA! SHE SAYS SHE'S FOUND THE ANDROIDS' WEAKNESS!!
WHAT ?!
YEAH!! 17 AND 18 HAVE AN EMERGENCY OFF SWITCH!! YOU'LL BE ABLE TO DESTROY THEM EASILY ONCE THEY'RE IMMOBILE!! I HAVE THE REMOTE CONTROL ALL READY!!
THEN BR-BRING IT FAST!! PICCOLO'S FIGHTING 'EM AS WE SPEAK!!
OK!! I'LL BE RIGHT OVER!!

READ THIS WAY

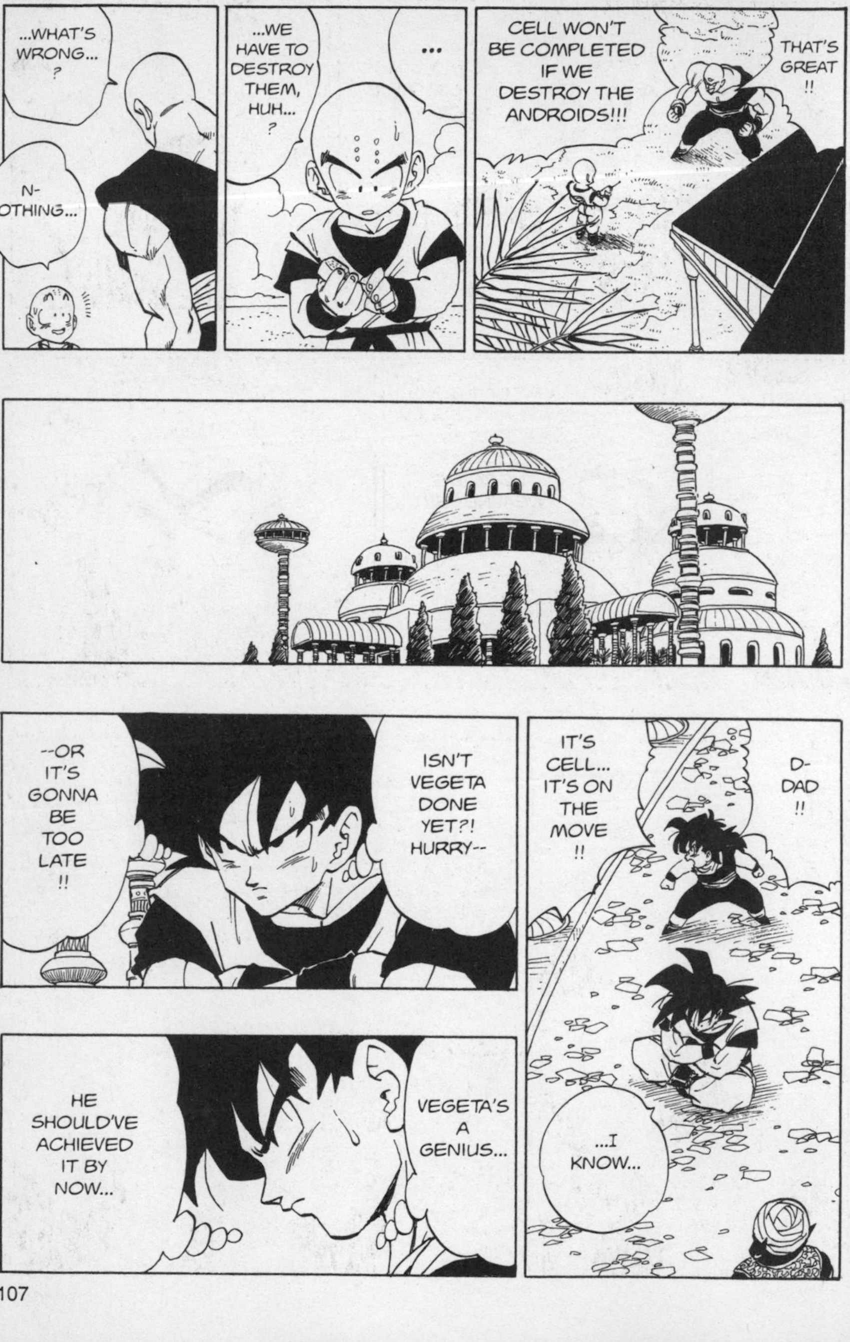

THAT'S GREAT !!
CELL WON'T BE COMPLETED IF WE DESTROY THE ANDROIDS!!!
...
...WE HAVE TO DESTROY THEM, HUH... ?
...WHAT'S WRONG... ?
N- NOTHING...
D- DAD !!
IT'S CELL... IT'S ON THE MOVE !!
...I KNOW...
ISN'T VEGETA DONE YET?! HURRY--
--OR IT'S GONNA BE TOO LATE !!
VEGETA'S A GENIUS...
HE SHOULD'VE ACHIEVED IT BY NOW...

READ THIS WAY

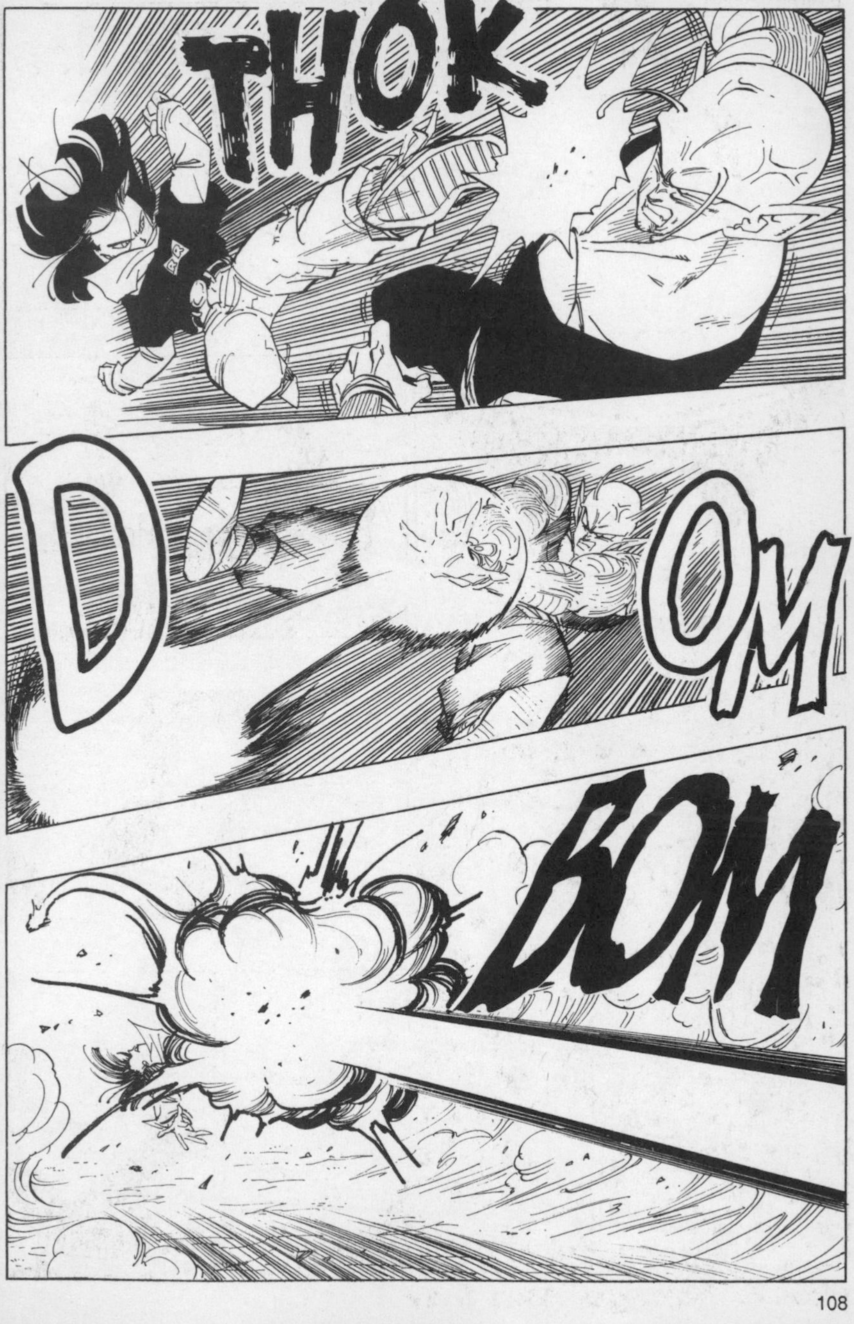
THOK
DOM
BOM

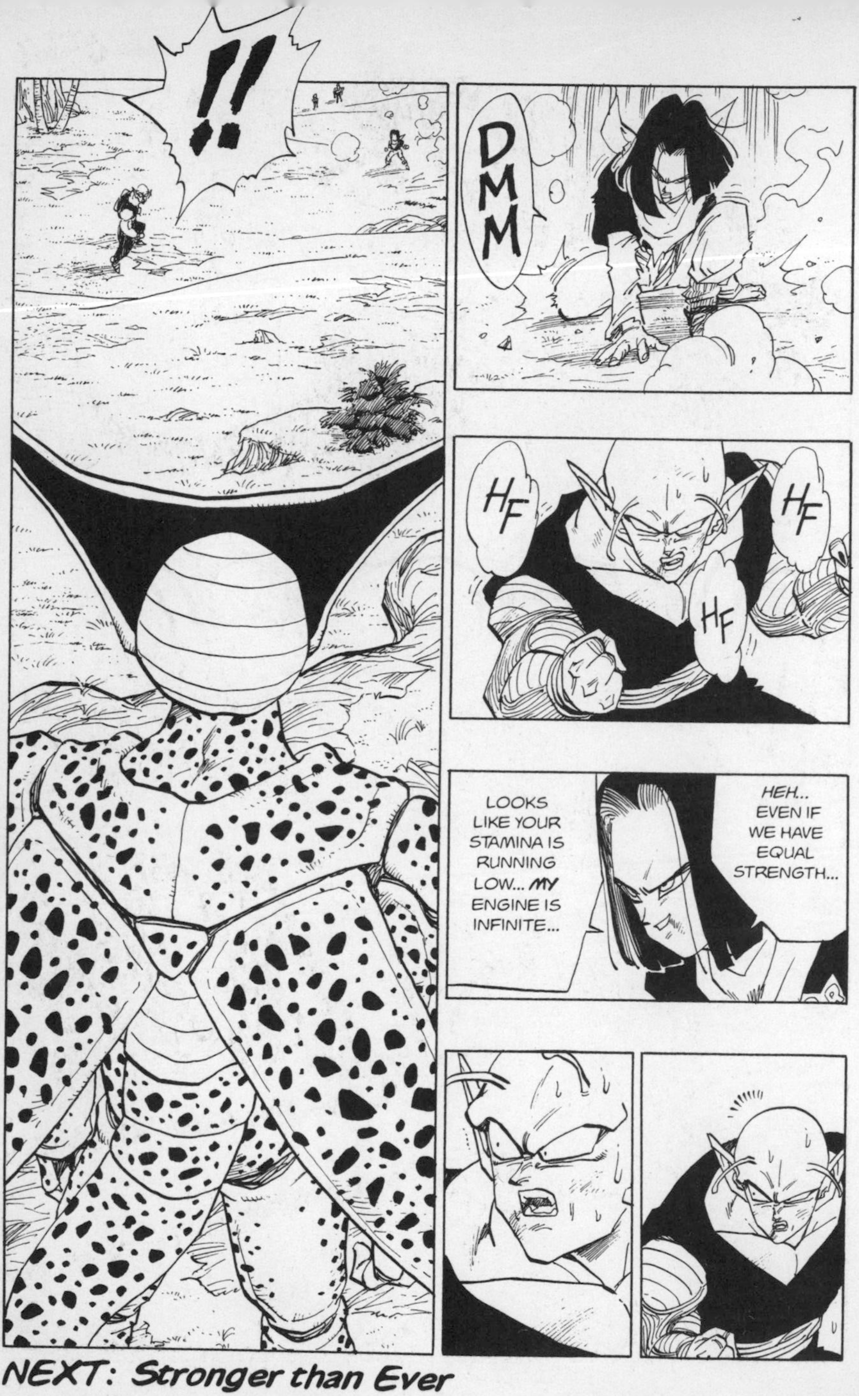
DMM
HF
HF
HF
HEH... EVEN IF WE HAVE EQUAL STRENGTH...
LOOKS LIKE YOUR STAMINA IS RUNNING LOW... MY ENGINE IS INFINITE...
!!

NEXT: Stronger than Ever

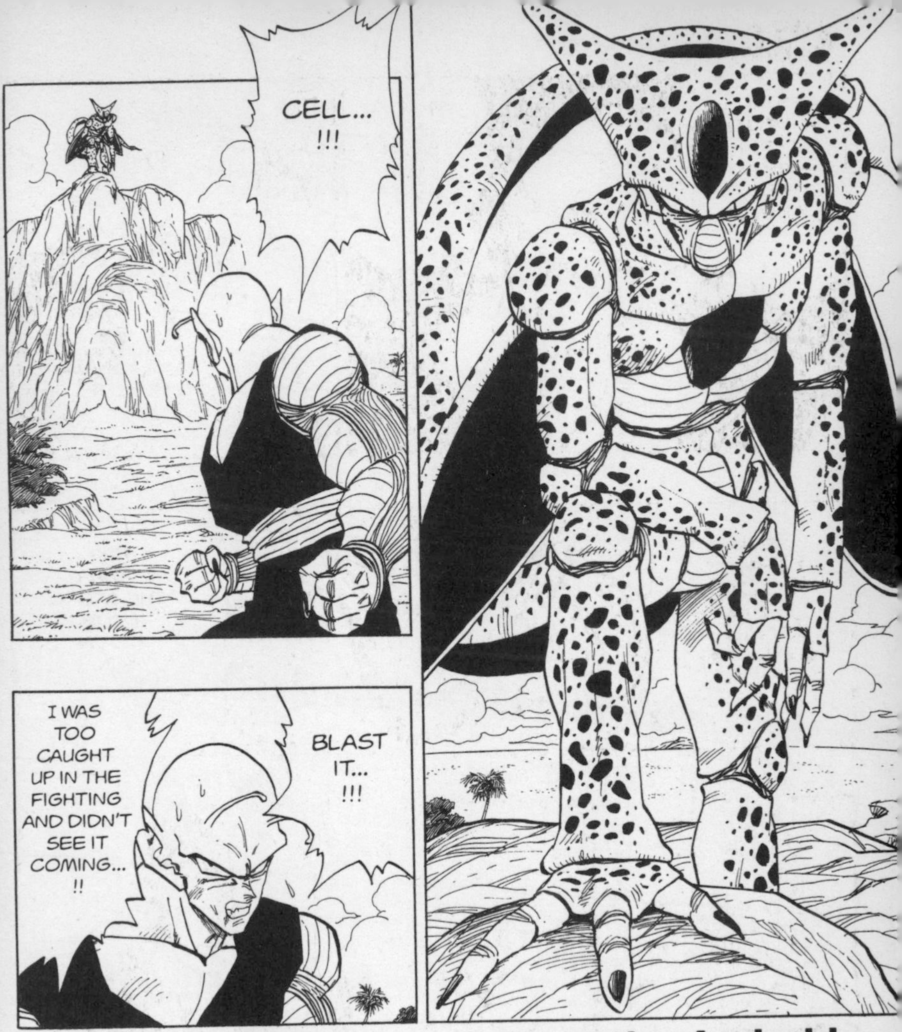
CELL... !!!
BLAST IT... !!!
I WAS TOO CAUGHT UP IN THE FIGHTING AND DIDN'T SEE IT COMING... !!

DBZ:175 • Cell vs. the Androids

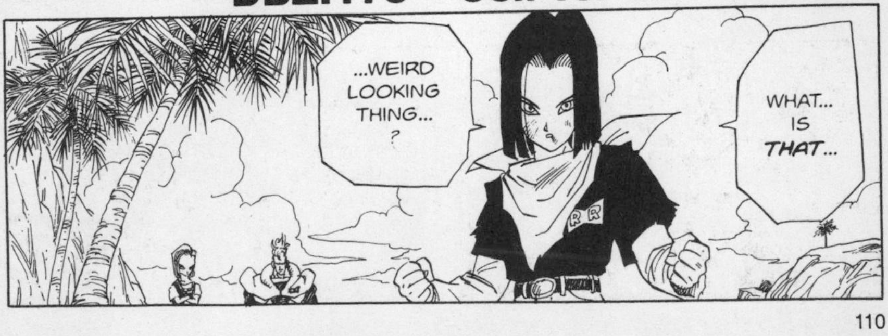
WHAT... IS THAT...
...WEIRD LOOKING THING... ?

READ THIS WAY

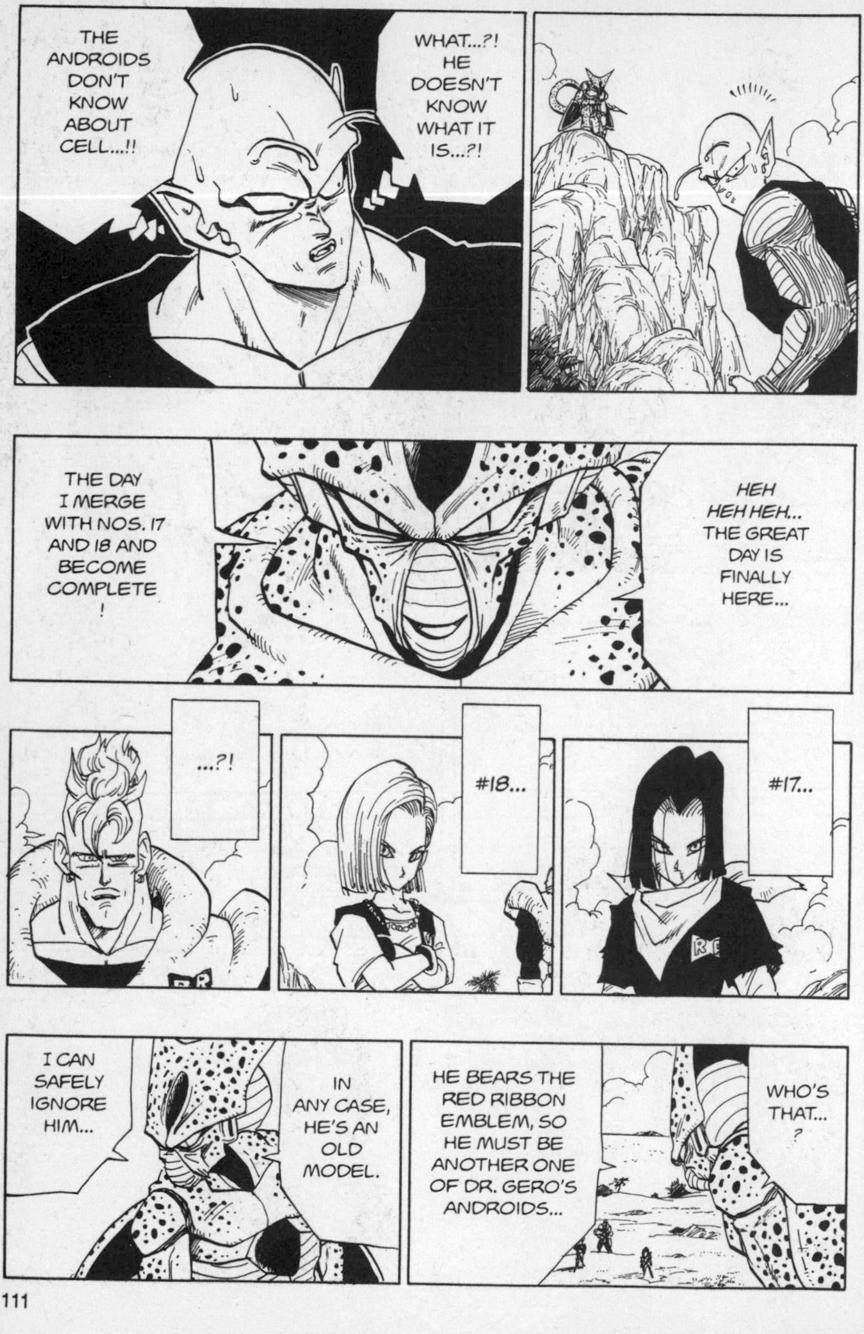
WHAT...?! HE DOESN'T KNOW WHAT IT IS...?!
THE ANDROIDS DON'T KNOW ABOUT CELL...!!
HEH HEH HEH... THE GREAT DAY IS FINALLY HERE...
THE DAY I MERGE WITH NOS. 17 AND 18 AND BECOME COMPLETE!
#17...
#18...
...?!
WHO'S THAT...?
HE BEARS THE RED RIBBON EMBLEM, SO HE MUST BE ANOTHER ONE OF DR. GERO'S ANDROIDS...
IN ANY CASE, HE'S AN OLD MODEL.
I CAN SAFELY IGNORE HIM...

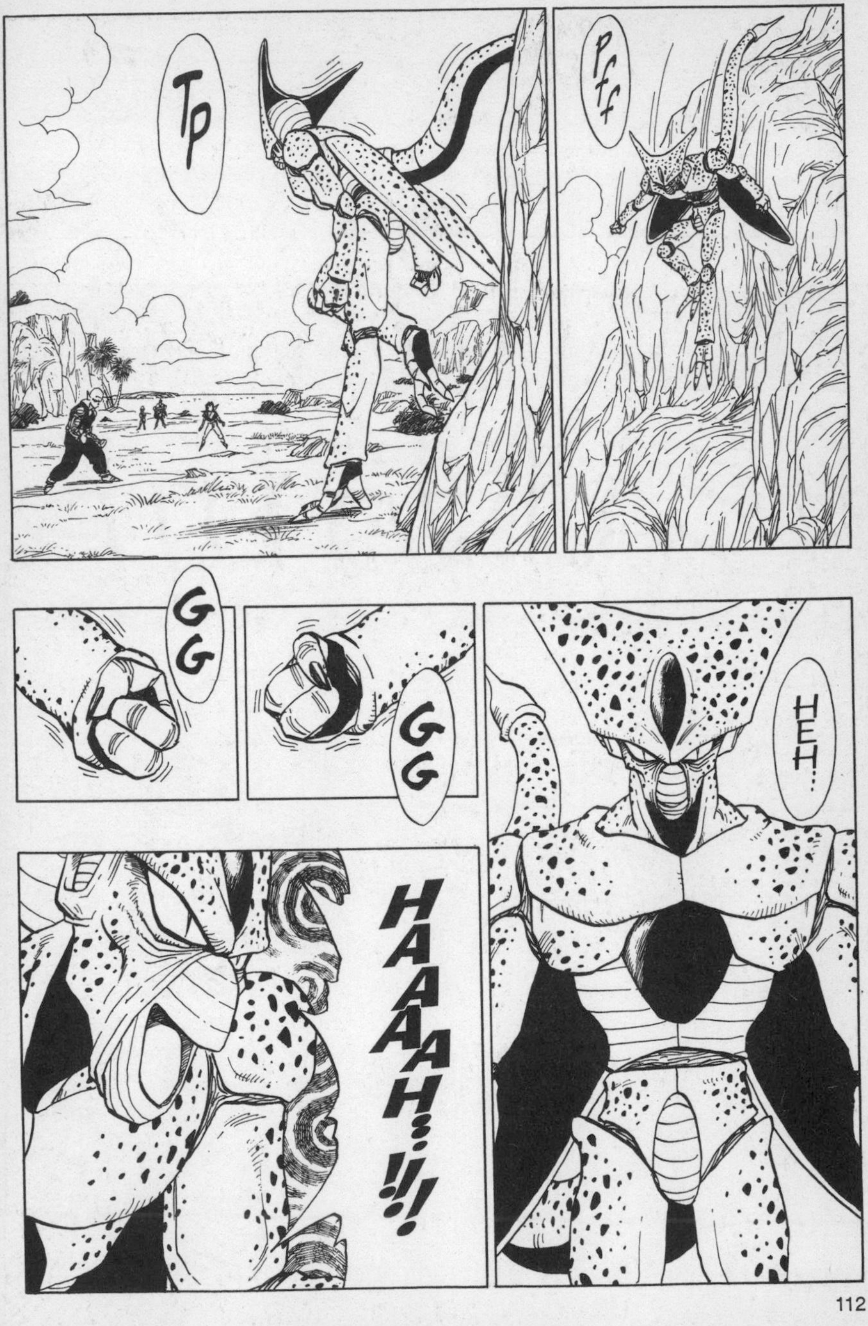
Pff
Tp
HEH!
GG
GG
HAAAAH!!!!

READ THIS WAY

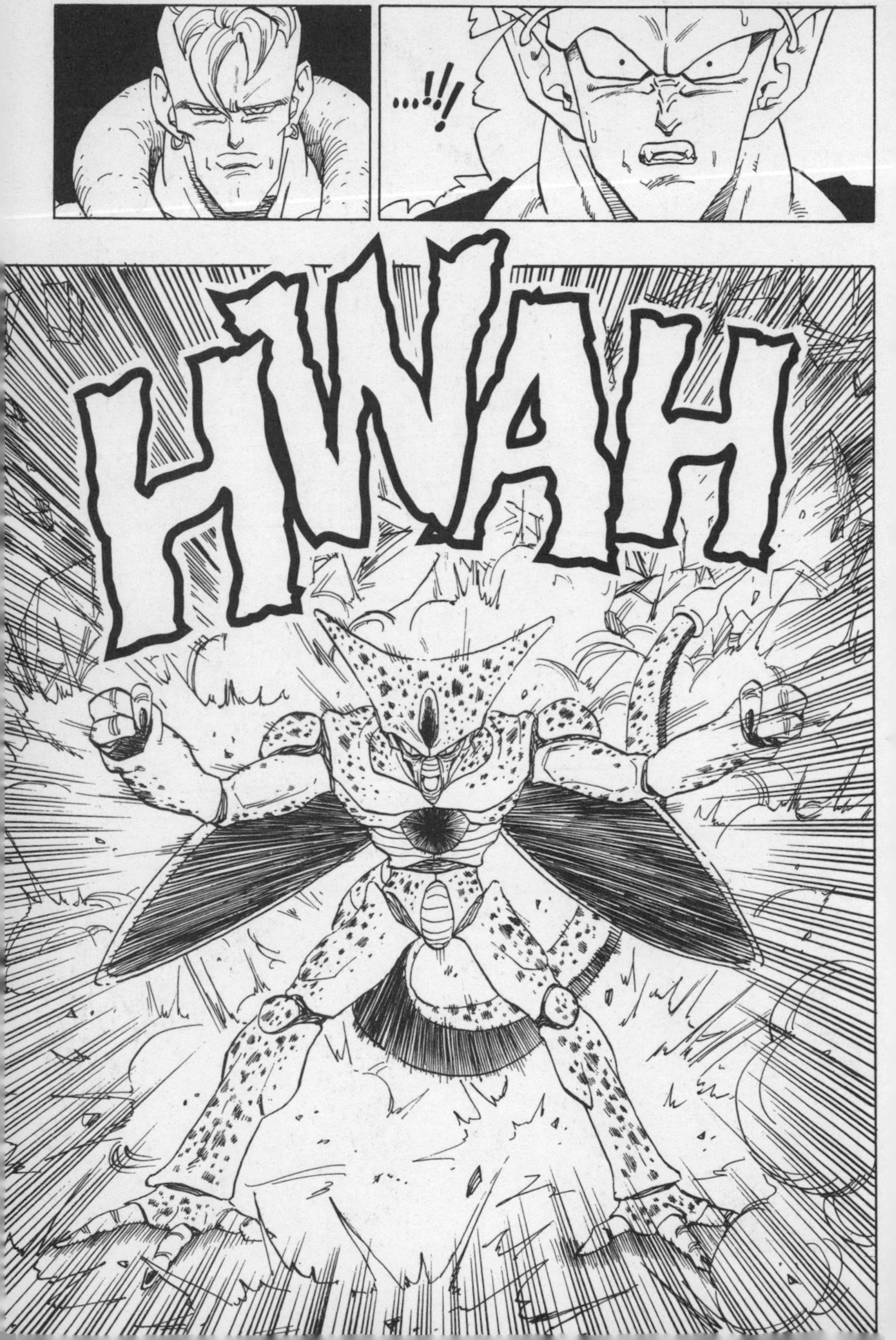
...!!
HWAH

READ THIS WAY

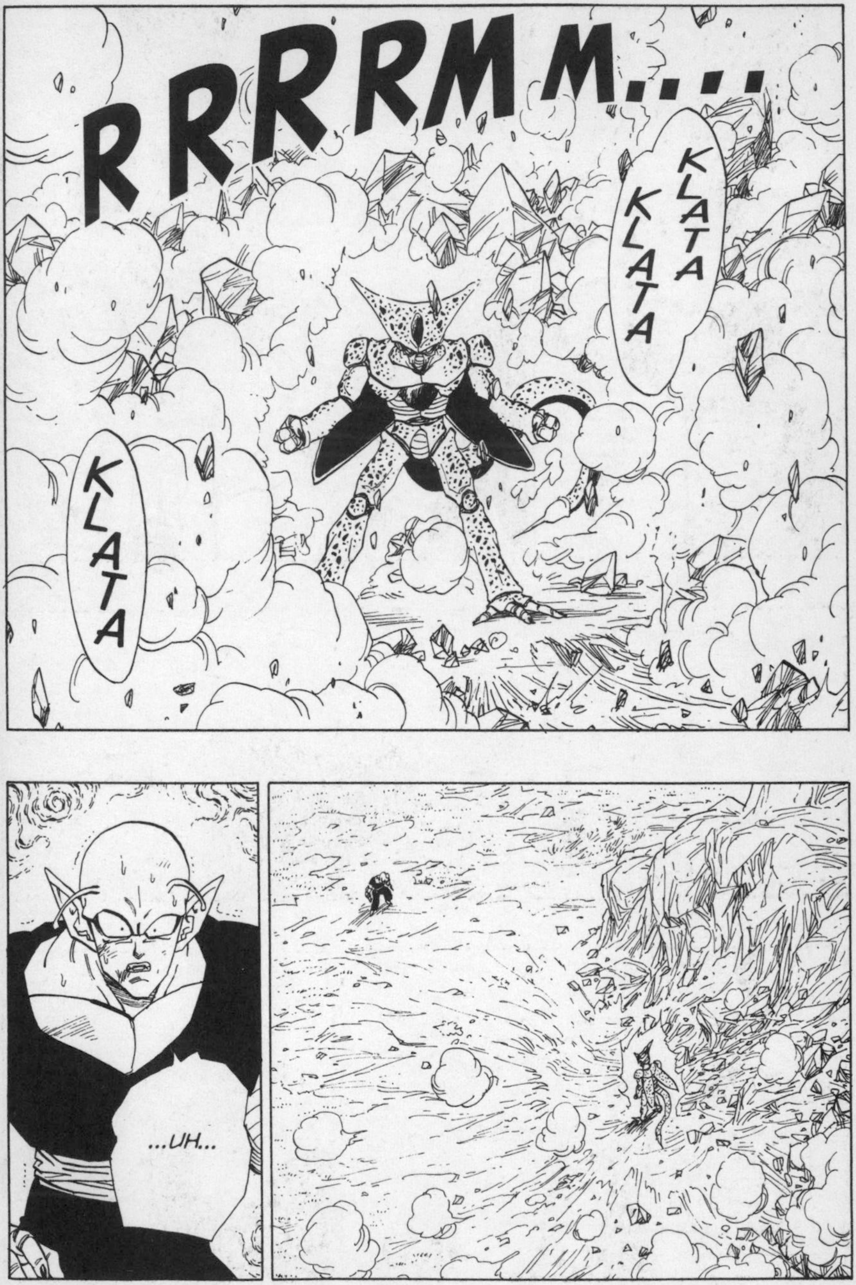
RRRRRM....
KLATA KLATA
KLATA
...UH...

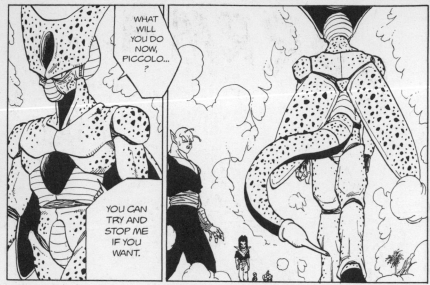

WHAT WILL YOU DO NOW, PICCOLO...?

YOU CAN TRY AND STOP ME IF YOU WANT.

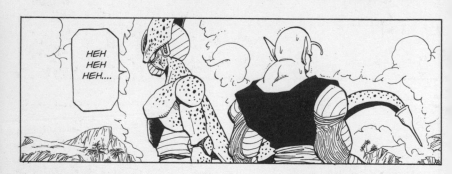

HEH HEH HEH....

I...I DIDN'T THINK YOU'D GOTTEN SO FAR... H-HOW MANY VICTIMS DID YOU KILL...?!

VICTIMS? THEY SHOULD CONSIDER IT AN HONOR TO BECOME PART OF ME!

...

READ THIS WAY

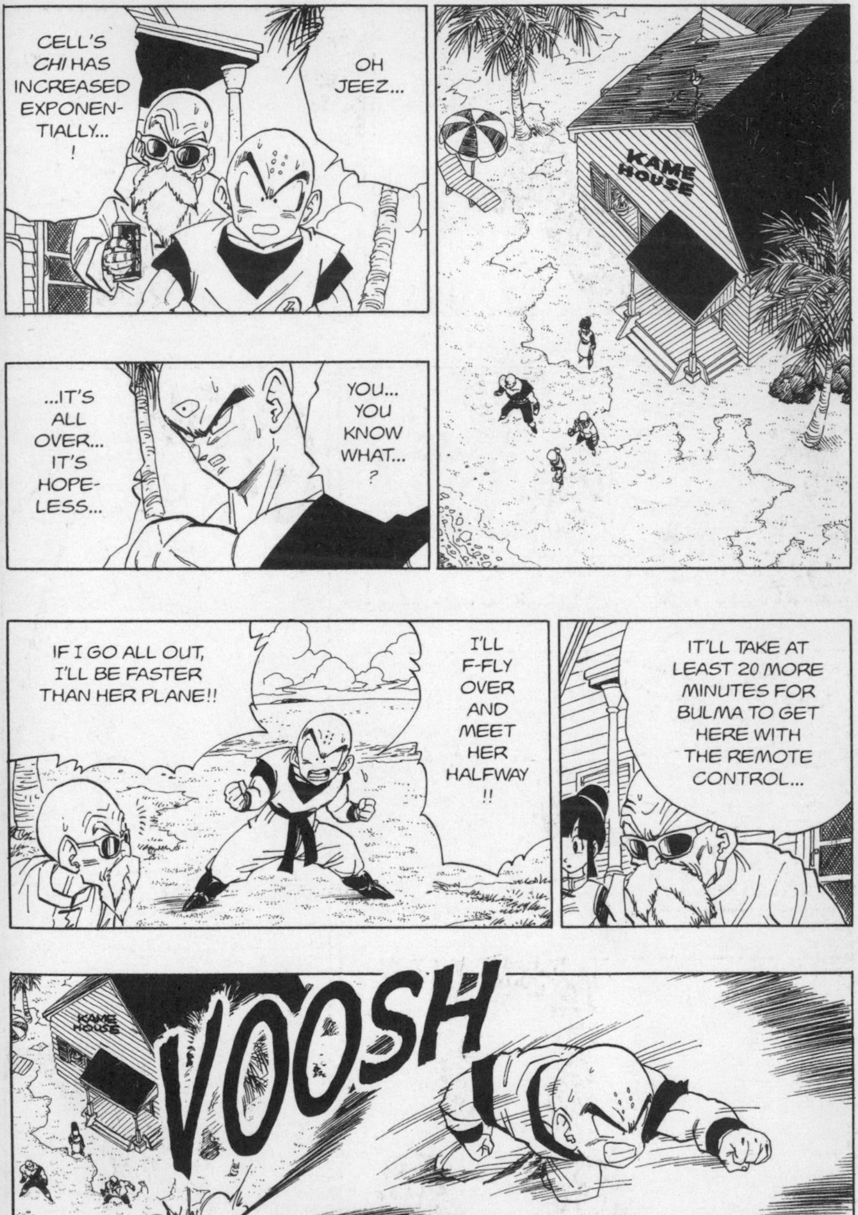
KAME HOUSE
OH JEEZ...
CELL'S CHI HAS INCREASED EXPONEN-TIALLY... !
YOU... YOU KNOW WHAT... ?
...IT'S ALL OVER... IT'S HOPE-LESS...
IT'LL TAKE AT LEAST 20 MORE MINUTES FOR BULMA TO GET HERE WITH THE REMOTE CONTROL...
I'LL F-FLY OVER AND MEET HER HALFWAY !!
IF I GO ALL OUT, I'LL BE FASTER THAN HER PLANE!!
VOOSH
KAME HOUSE

READ THIS WAY

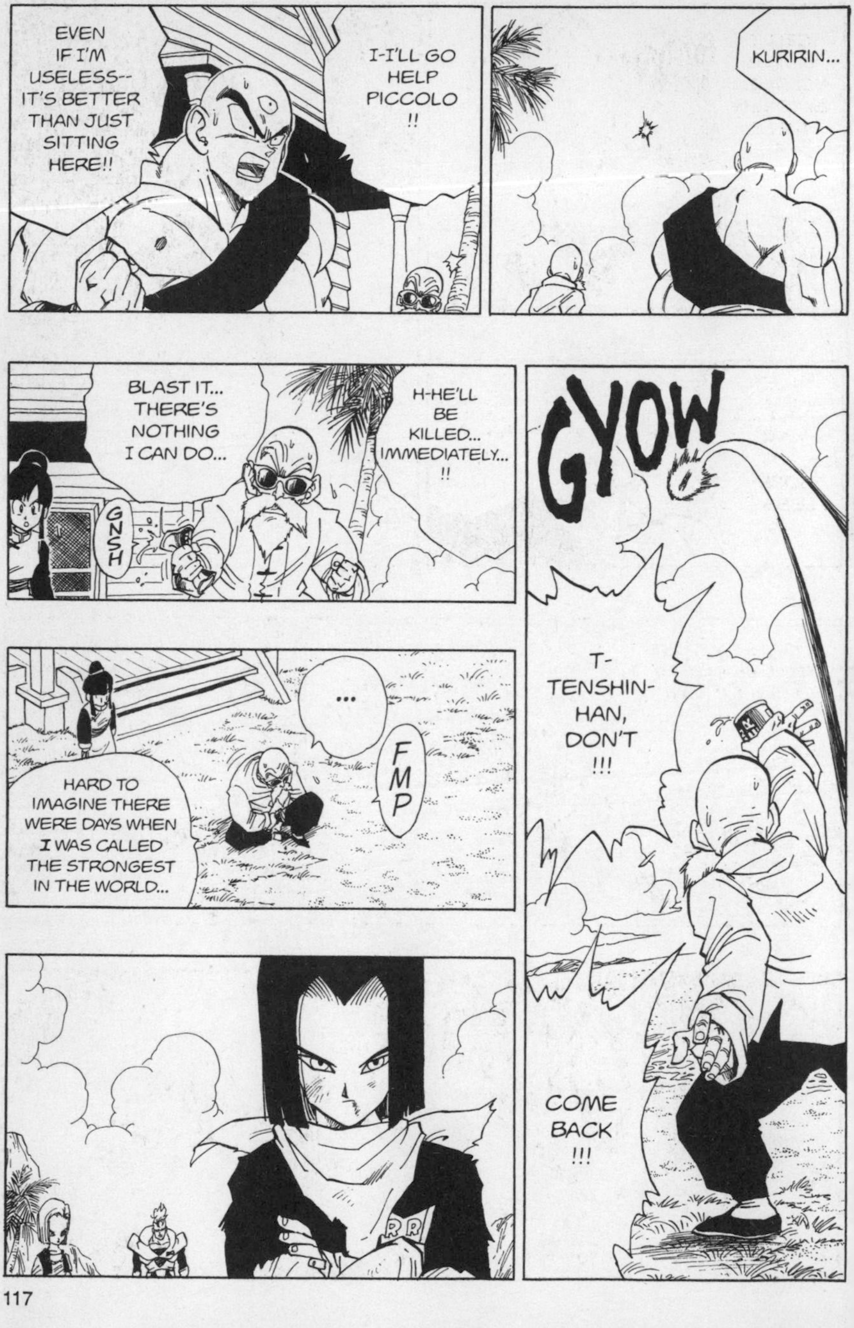
KURIRIN...
I-I'LL GO HELP PICCOLO !!
EVEN IF I'M USELESS-- IT'S BETTER THAN JUST SITTING HERE!!
GYOW
T- TENSHIN-HAN, DON'T !!!
COME BACK !!!
H-HE'LL BE KILLED... IMMEDIATELY... !!
BLAST IT... THERE'S NOTHING I CAN DO...
GNSH
...
FMP
HARD TO IMAGINE THERE WERE DAYS WHEN I WAS CALLED THE STRONGEST IN THE WORLD...
RR

READ THIS WAY

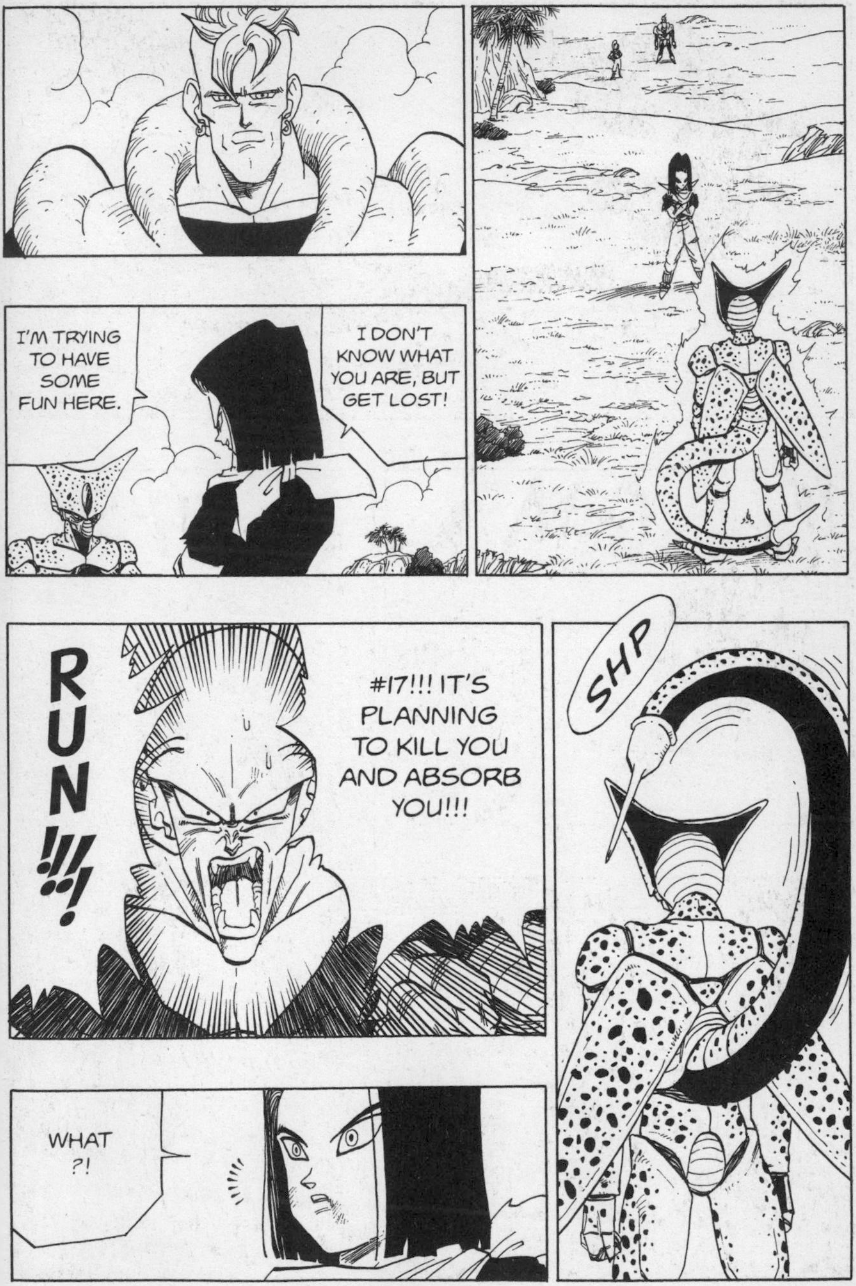
I DON'T KNOW WHAT YOU ARE, BUT GET LOST!
I'M TRYING TO HAVE SOME FUN HERE.
SHP
#17!!! IT'S PLANNING TO KILL YOU AND ABSORB YOU!!!
RUN!!!!
WHAT?!

READ THIS WAY

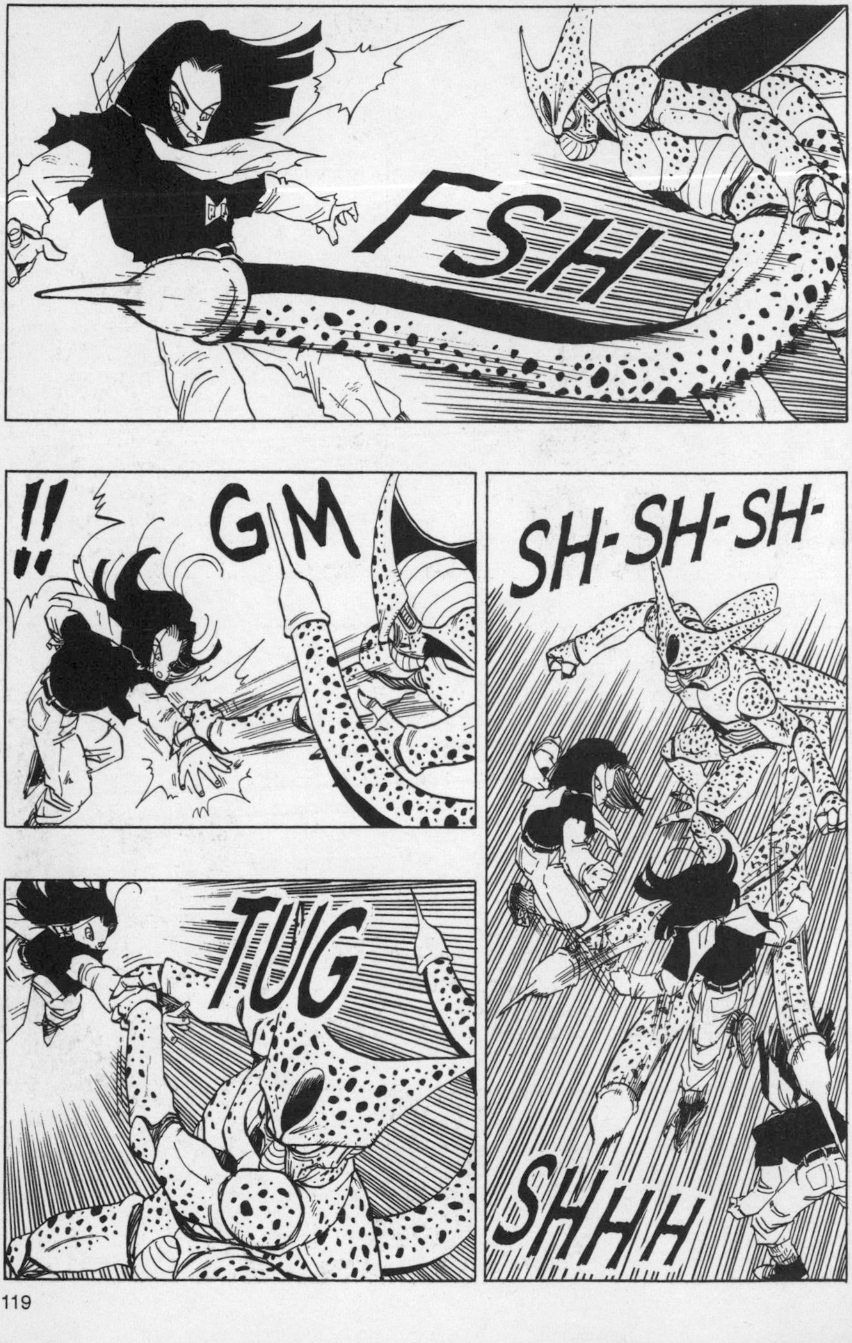
FSH
SH-SH-SH-
SHHH
!!
GM
TUG

READ THIS WAY

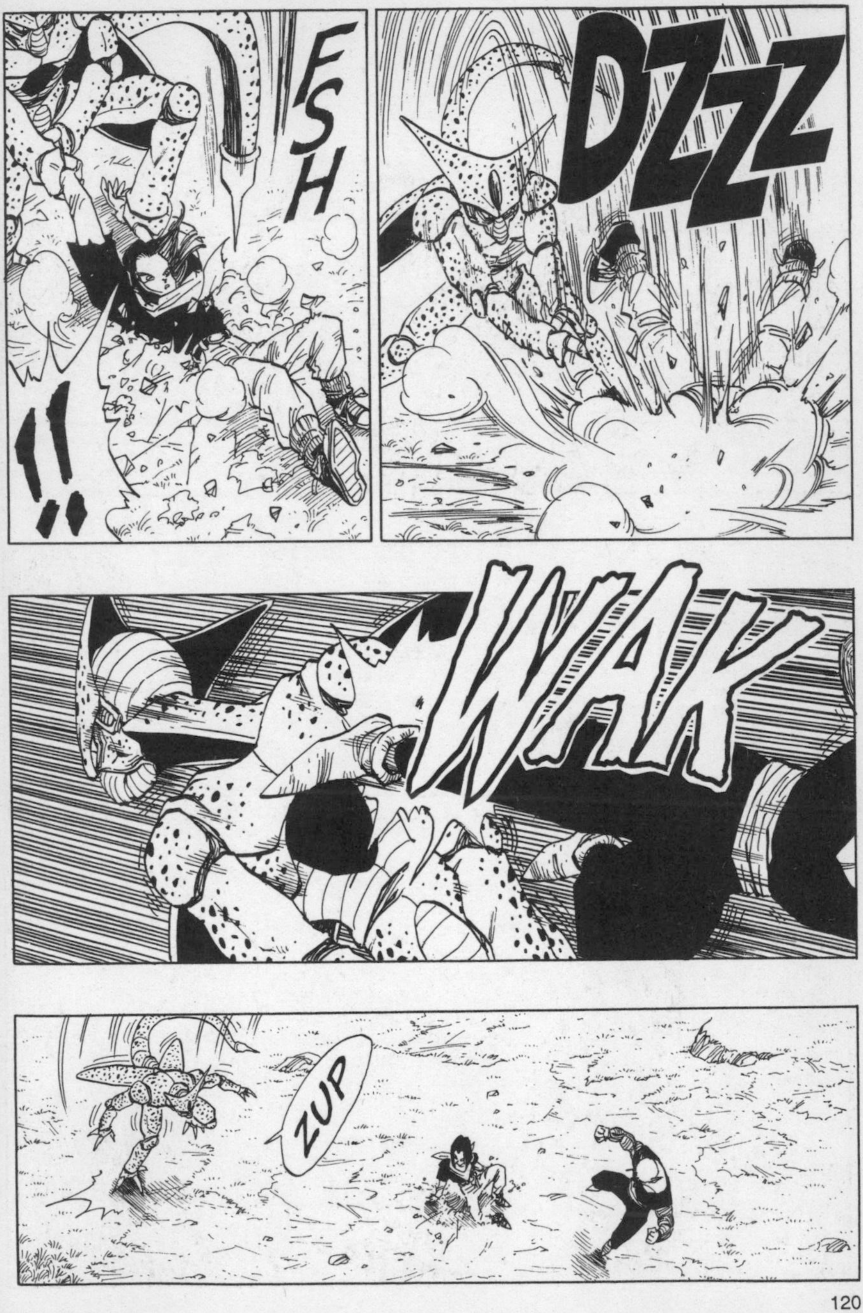
DZZ
FSH
!!
WAK
ZUP

READ THIS WAY

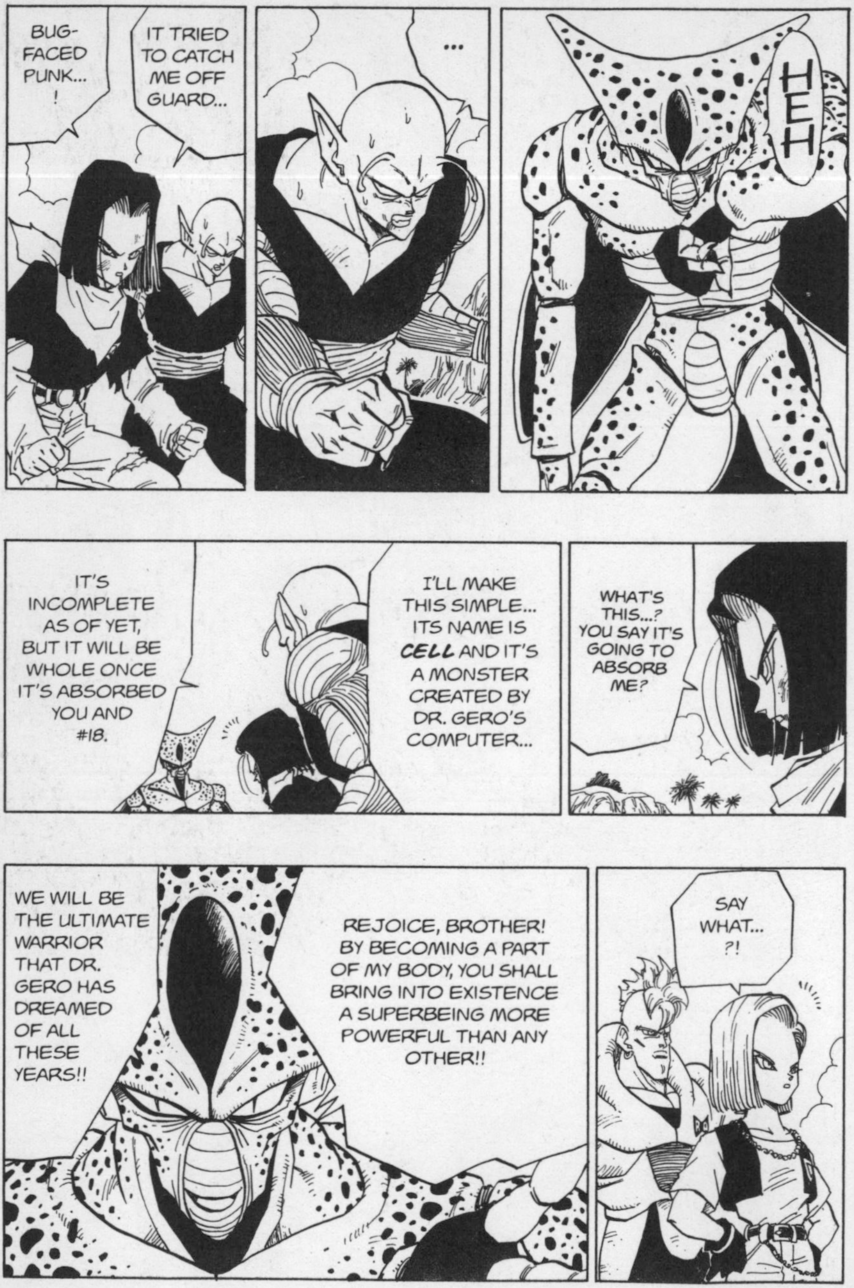
HEH
...
IT TRIED TO CATCH ME OFF GUARD...
BUG-FACED PUNK... !
WHAT'S THIS...? YOU SAY IT'S GOING TO ABSORB ME?
I'LL MAKE THIS SIMPLE... ITS NAME IS **CELL** AND IT'S A MONSTER CREATED BY DR. GERO'S COMPUTER...
IT'S INCOMPLETE AS OF YET, BUT IT WILL BE WHOLE ONCE IT'S ABSORBED YOU AND #18.
SAY WHAT... ?!
REJOICE, BROTHER! BY BECOMING A PART OF MY BODY, YOU SHALL BRING INTO EXISTENCE A SUPERBEING MORE POWERFUL THAN ANY OTHER!!
WE WILL BE THE ULTIMATE WARRIOR THAT DR. GERO HAS DREAMED OF ALL THESE YEARS!!

READ THIS WAY

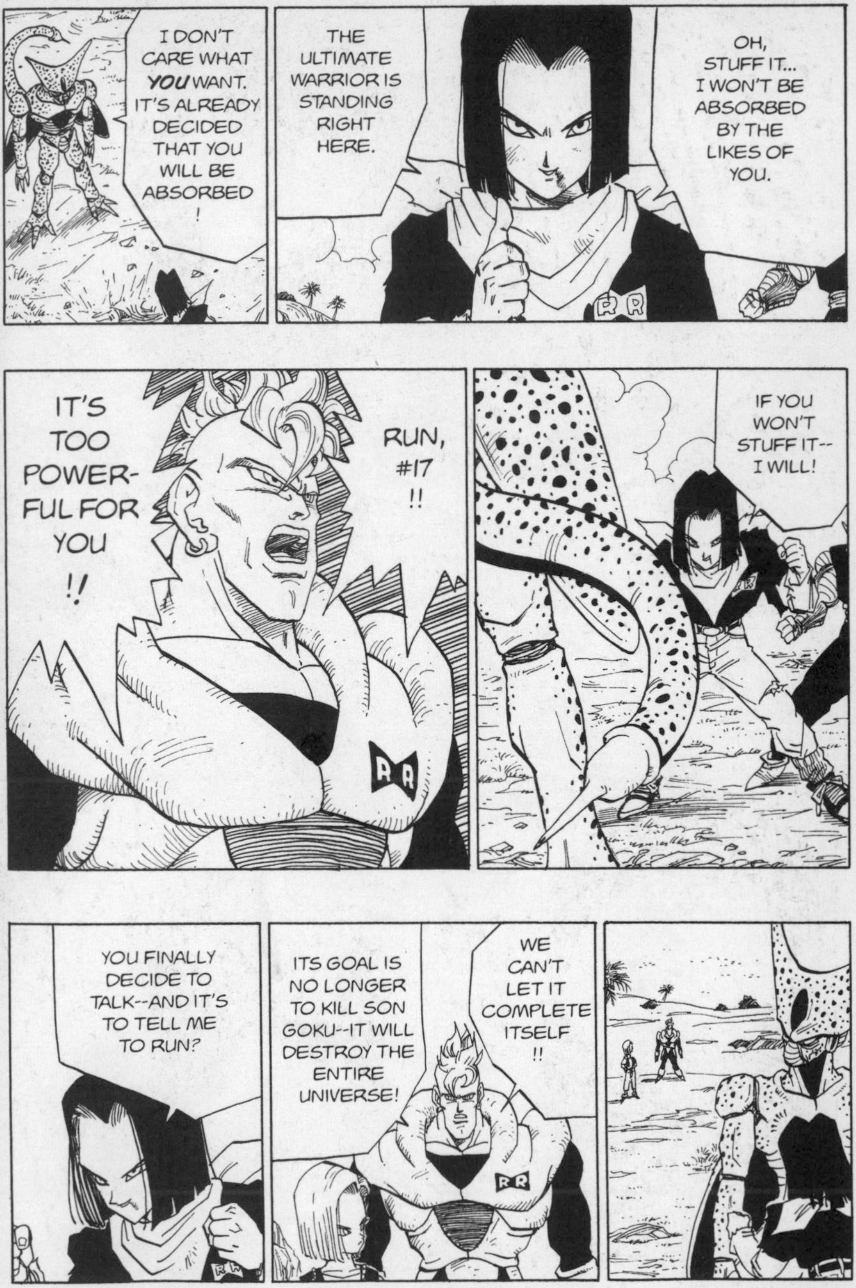
OH, STUFF IT... I WON'T BE ABSORBED BY THE LIKES OF YOU.
THE ULTIMATE WARRIOR IS STANDING RIGHT HERE.
I DON'T CARE WHAT YOU WANT. IT'S ALREADY DECIDED THAT YOU WILL BE ABSORBED!
IF YOU WON'T STUFF IT-- I WILL!
RUN, #17 !!
IT'S TOO POWERFUL FOR YOU !!
WE CAN'T LET IT COMPLETE ITSELF !!
ITS GOAL IS NO LONGER TO KILL SON GOKU--IT WILL DESTROY THE ENTIRE UNIVERSE!
YOU FINALLY DECIDE TO TALK--AND IT'S TO TELL ME TO RUN?

READ THIS WAY

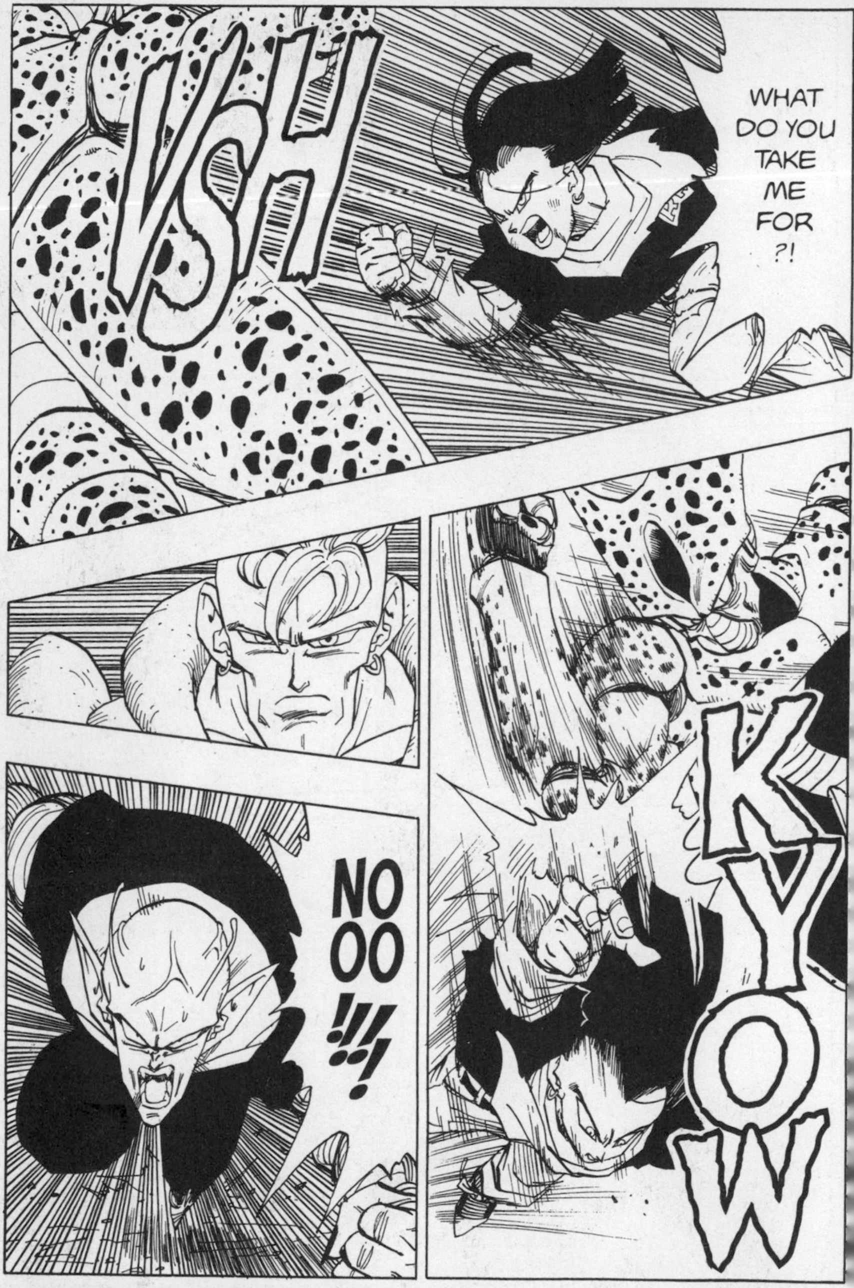
VSH
WHAT DO YOU TAKE ME FOR ?!
KYOW
NOOO!!!!

NEXT: The Bio-organic Horror

DBZ: 176 • New Piccolo... Last Piccolo?

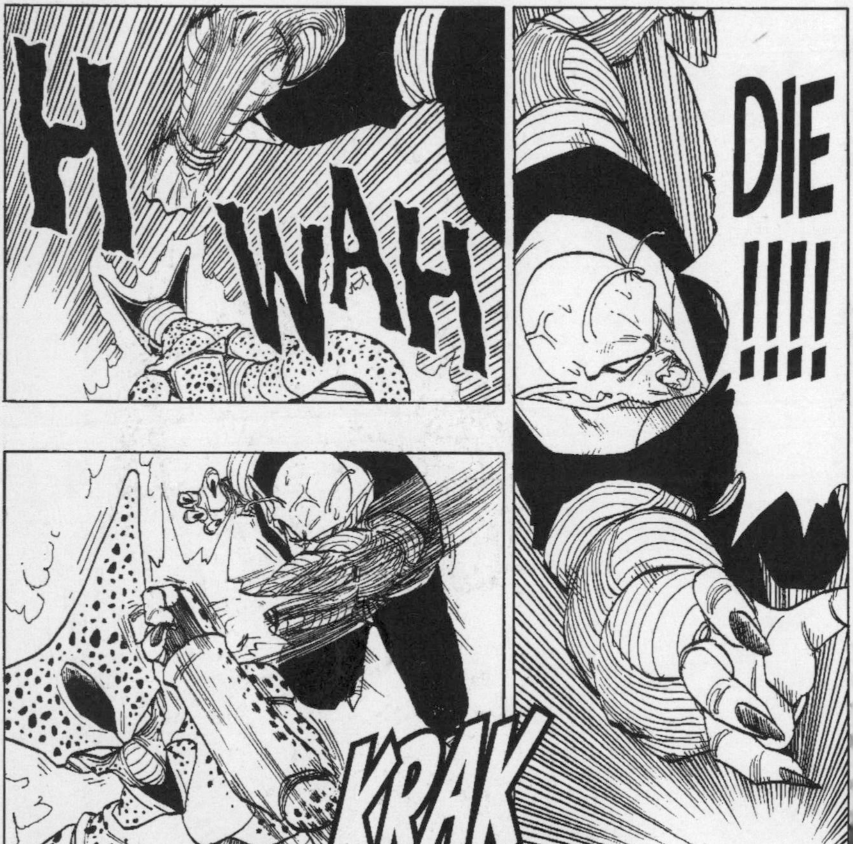
DIE !!!!
HWAH
KRAK

READ THIS WAY

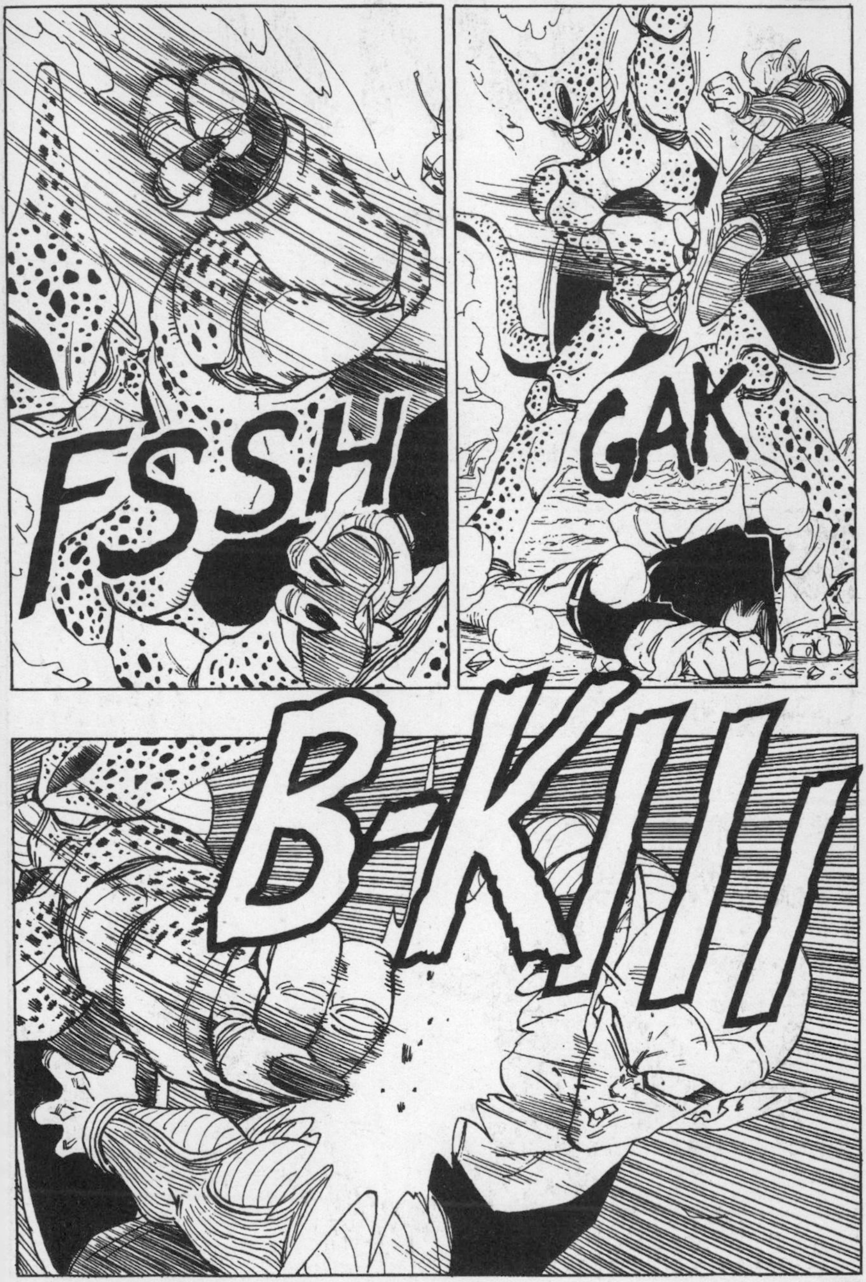

GAK
FSSH
B-KIII

READ THIS WAY

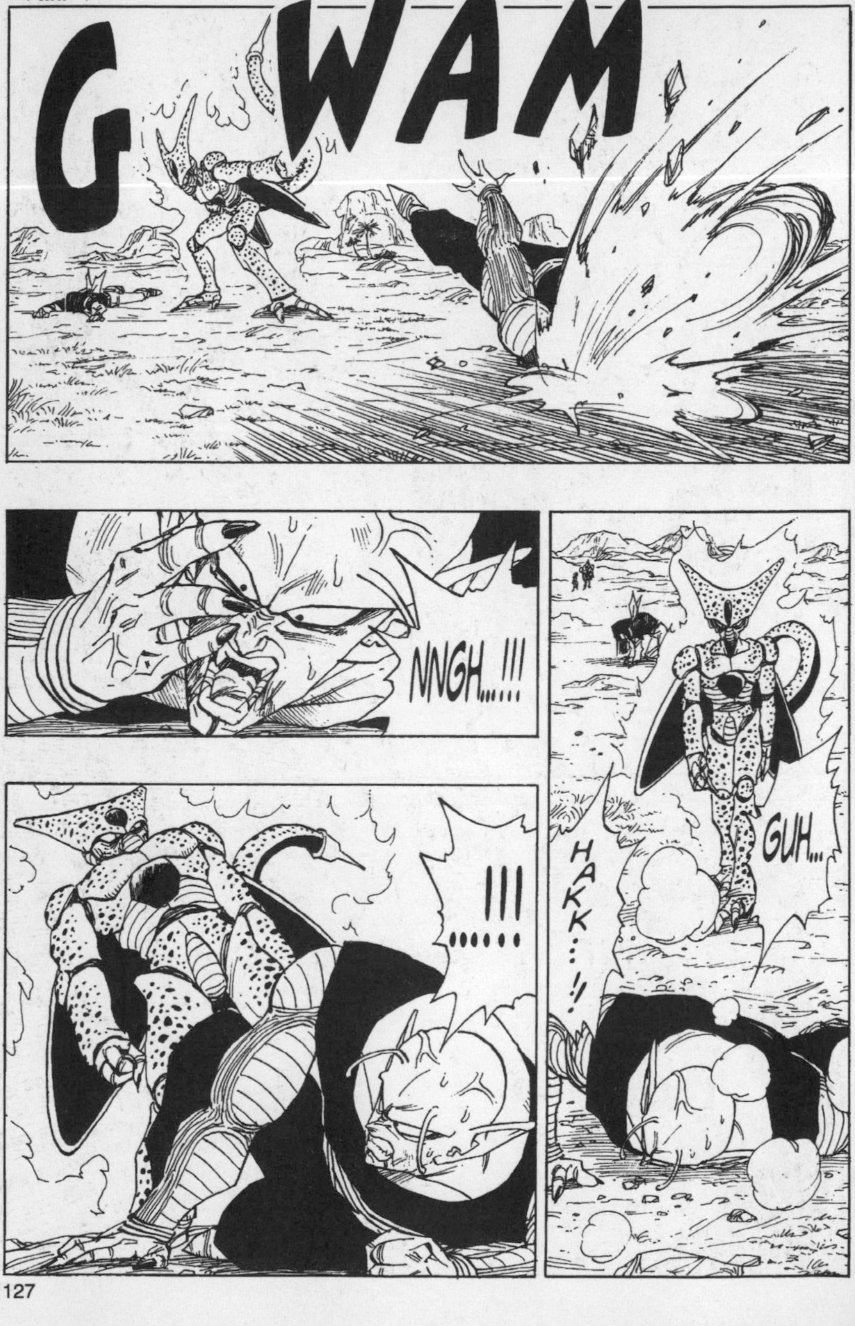
GWAM
GUH...
HAKK...!!
NNGH...!!!
......!!!

READ THIS WAY

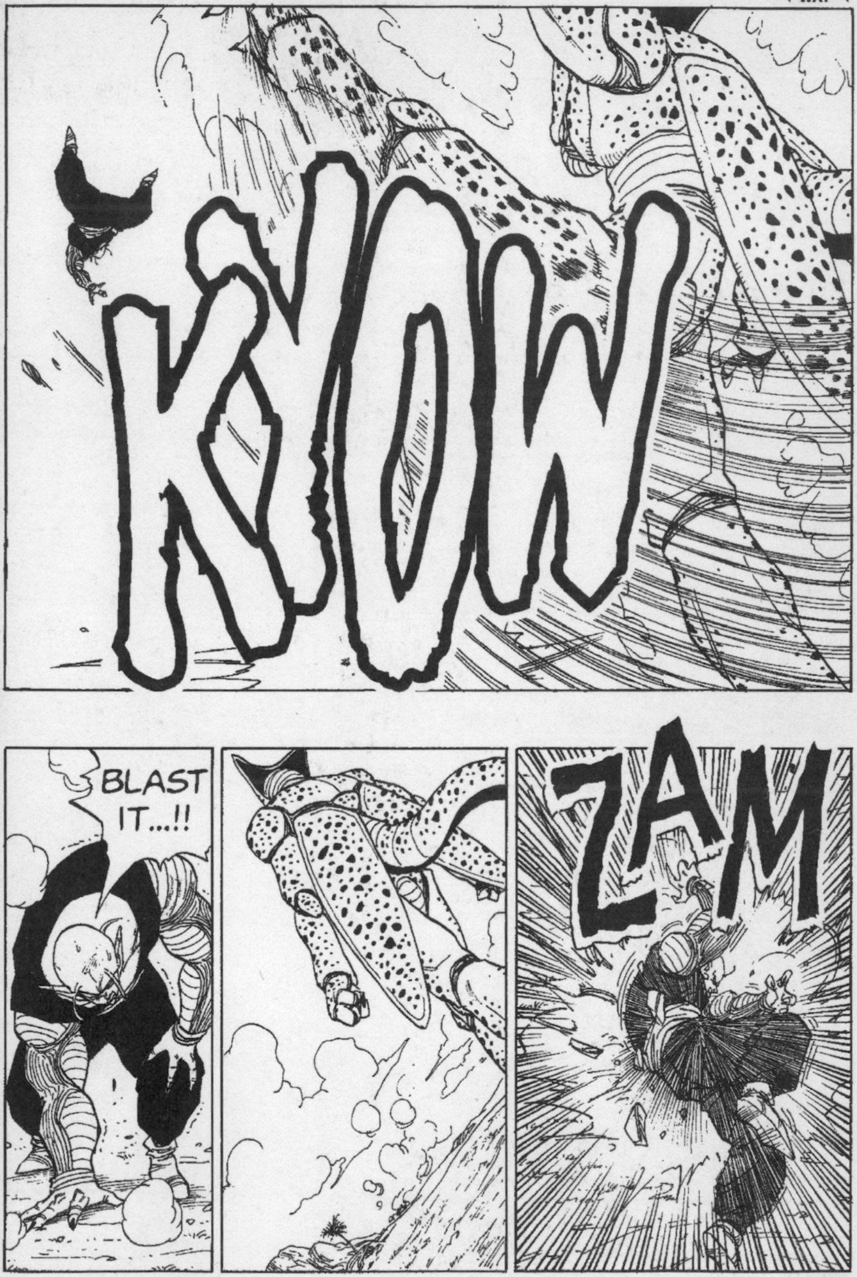
KYOW
ZAM
BLAST IT...!!

READ THIS WAY

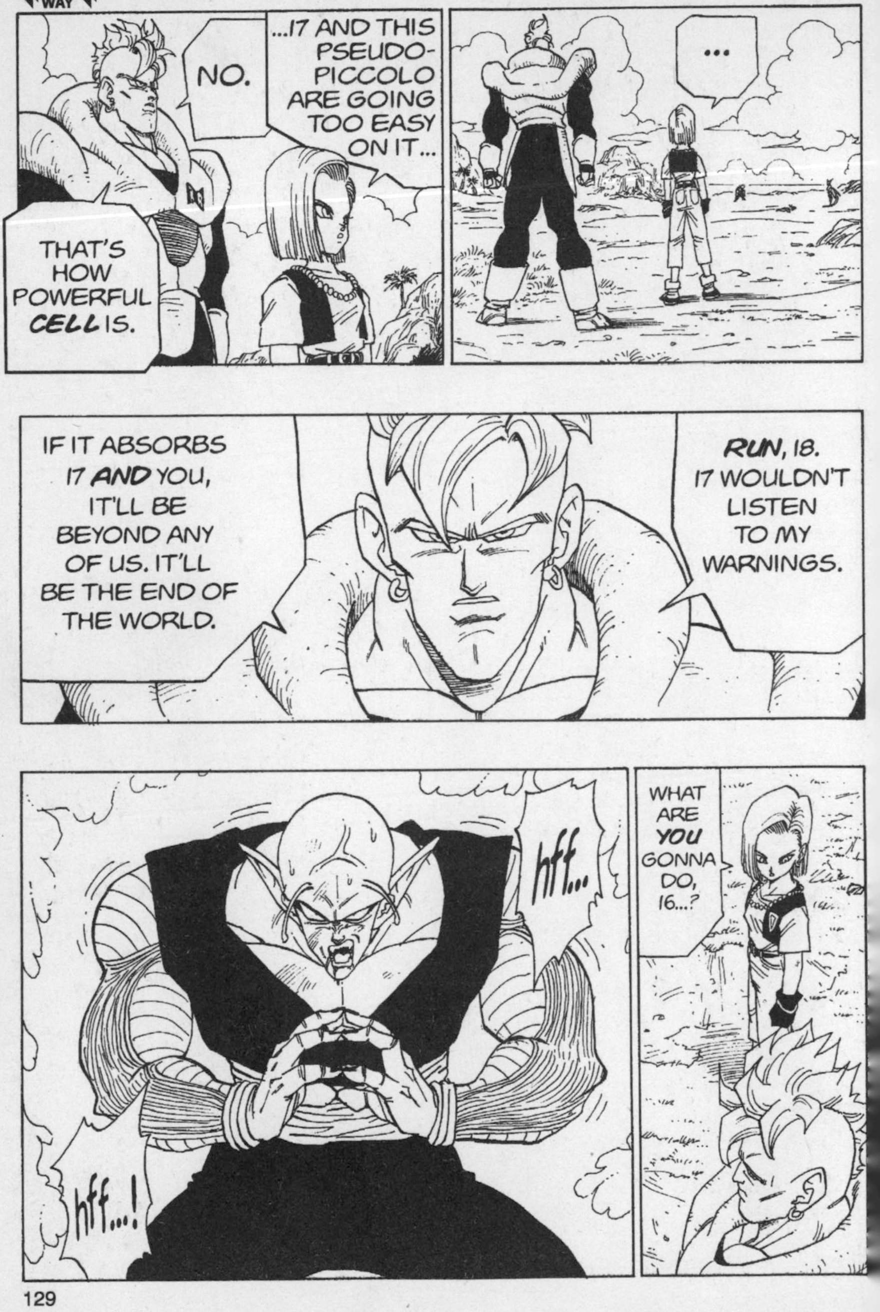
...
...17 AND THIS PSEUDO-PICCOLO ARE GOING TOO EASY ON IT...
NO.
THAT'S HOW POWERFUL CELL IS.
RUN, 18. 17 WOULDN'T LISTEN TO MY WARNINGS.
IF IT ABSORBS 17 AND YOU, IT'LL BE BEYOND ANY OF US. IT'LL BE THE END OF THE WORLD.
WHAT ARE YOU GONNA DO, 16...?
hff...
hff...!

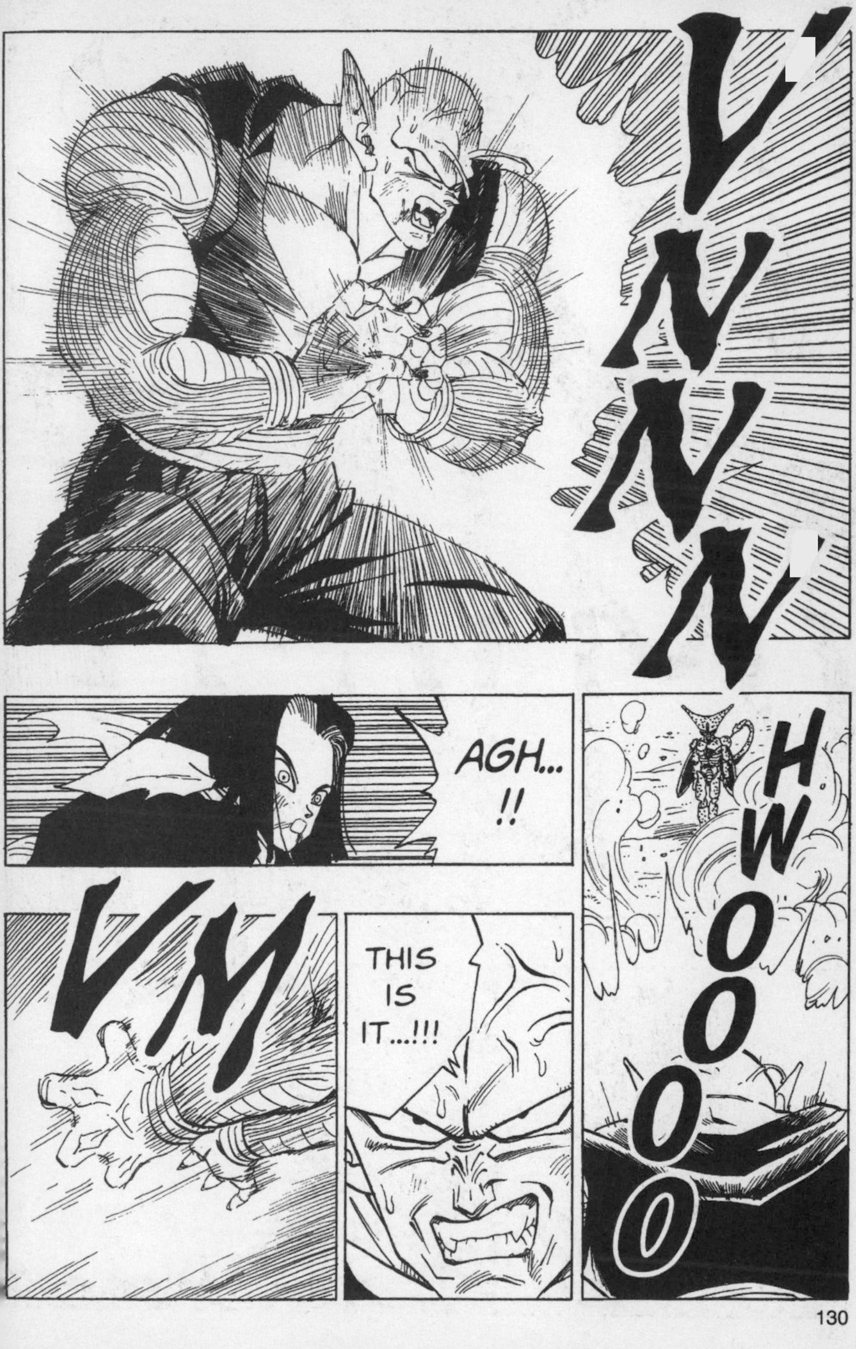
VNNN
HWOOOO
AGH... !!
THIS IS IT...!!!
VM

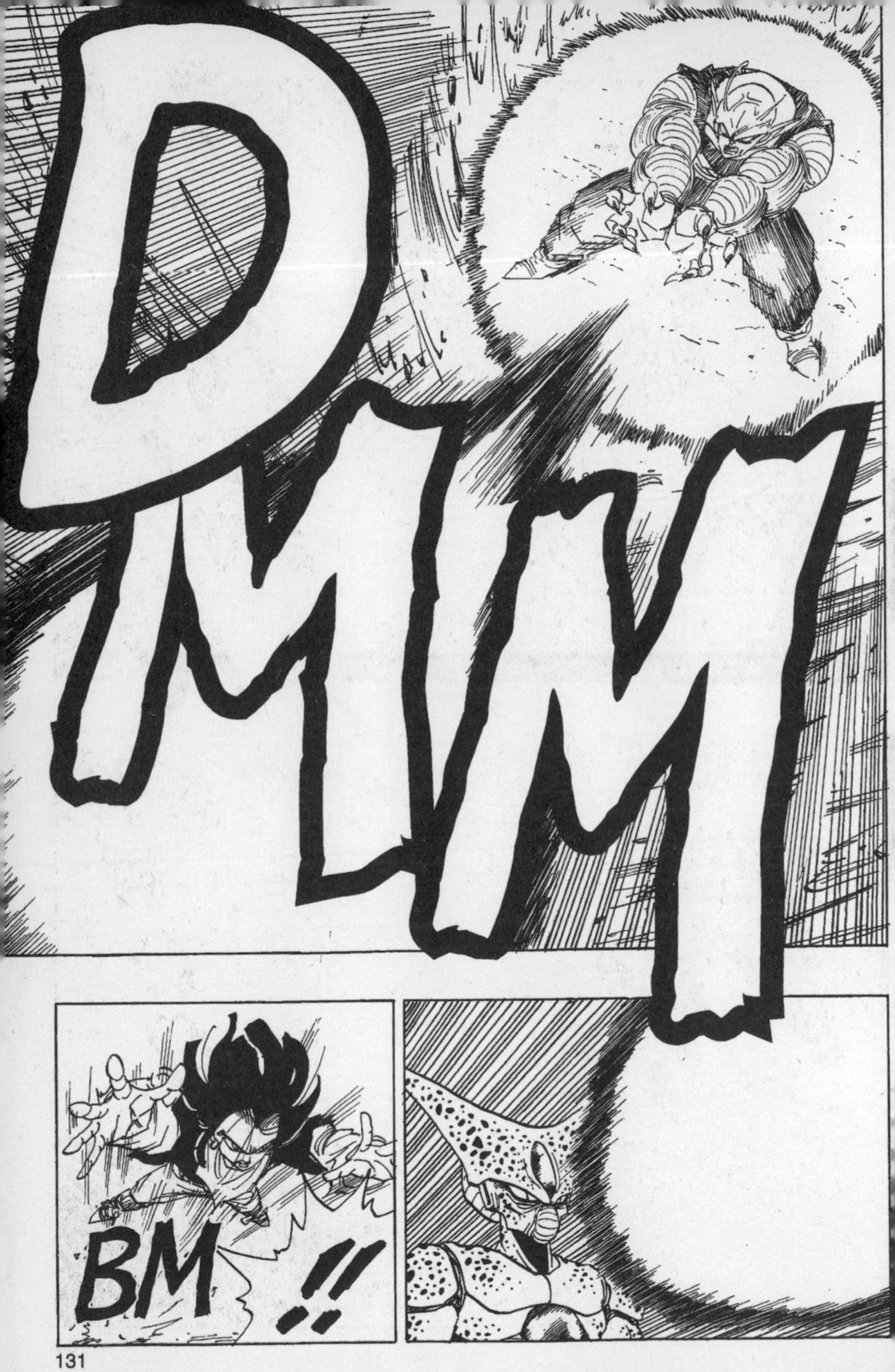
DMM
BM!!

READ THIS WAY

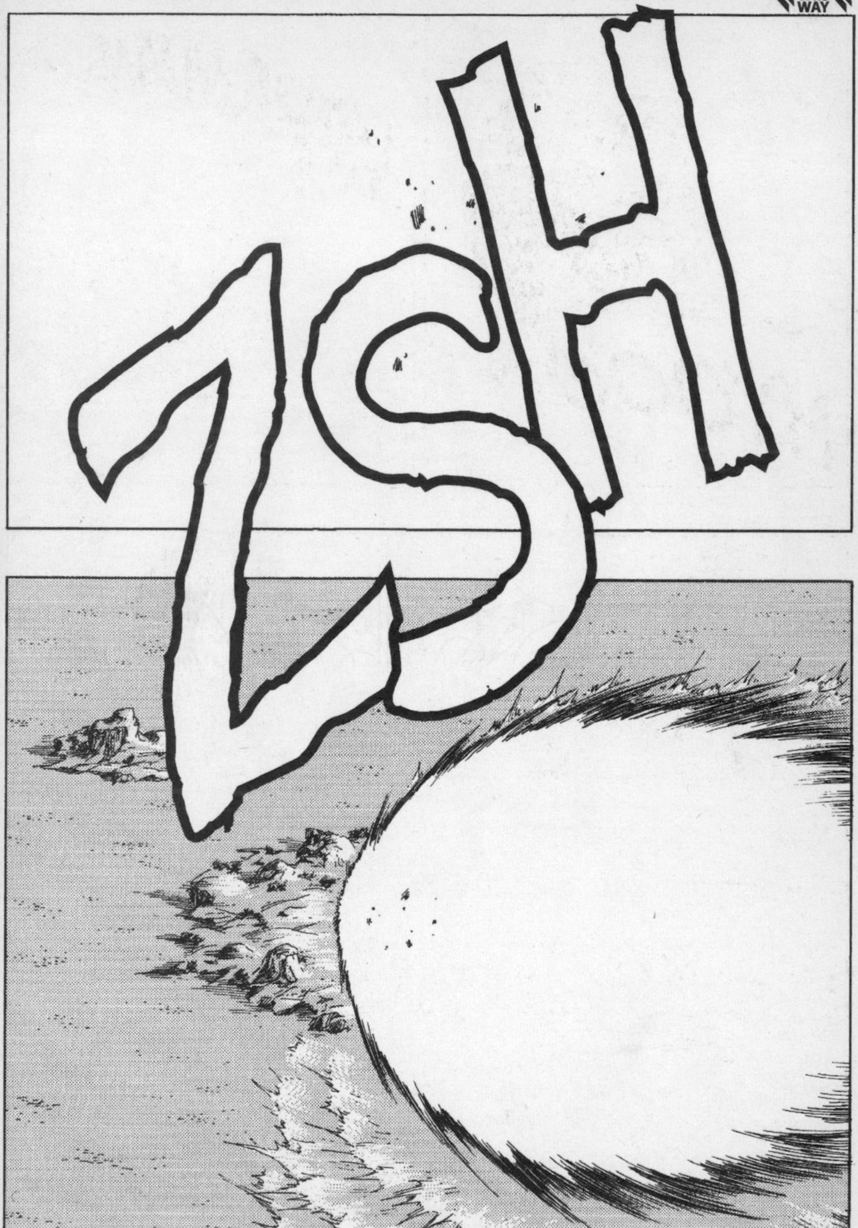
ZSH

READ THIS WAY

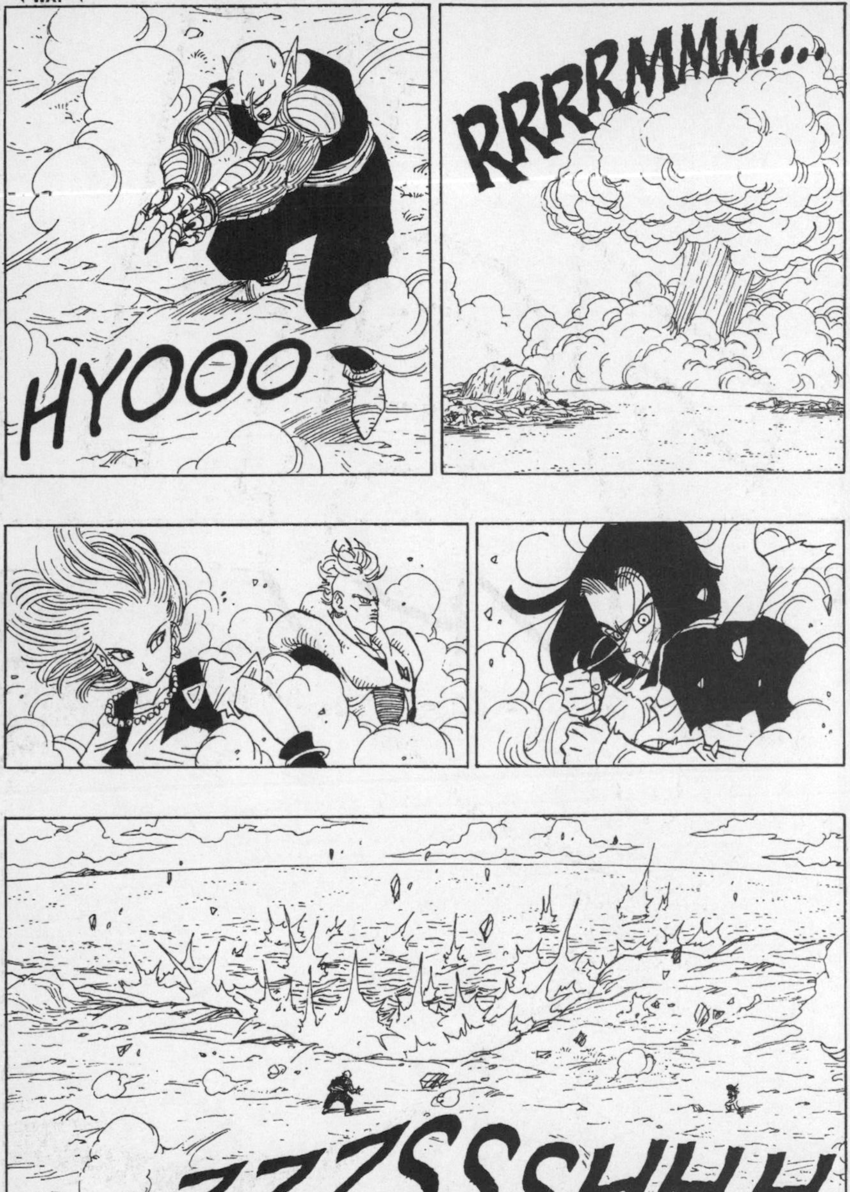
RRRRMMM....
HYOOO
ZZZSSSHHH

READ THIS WAY

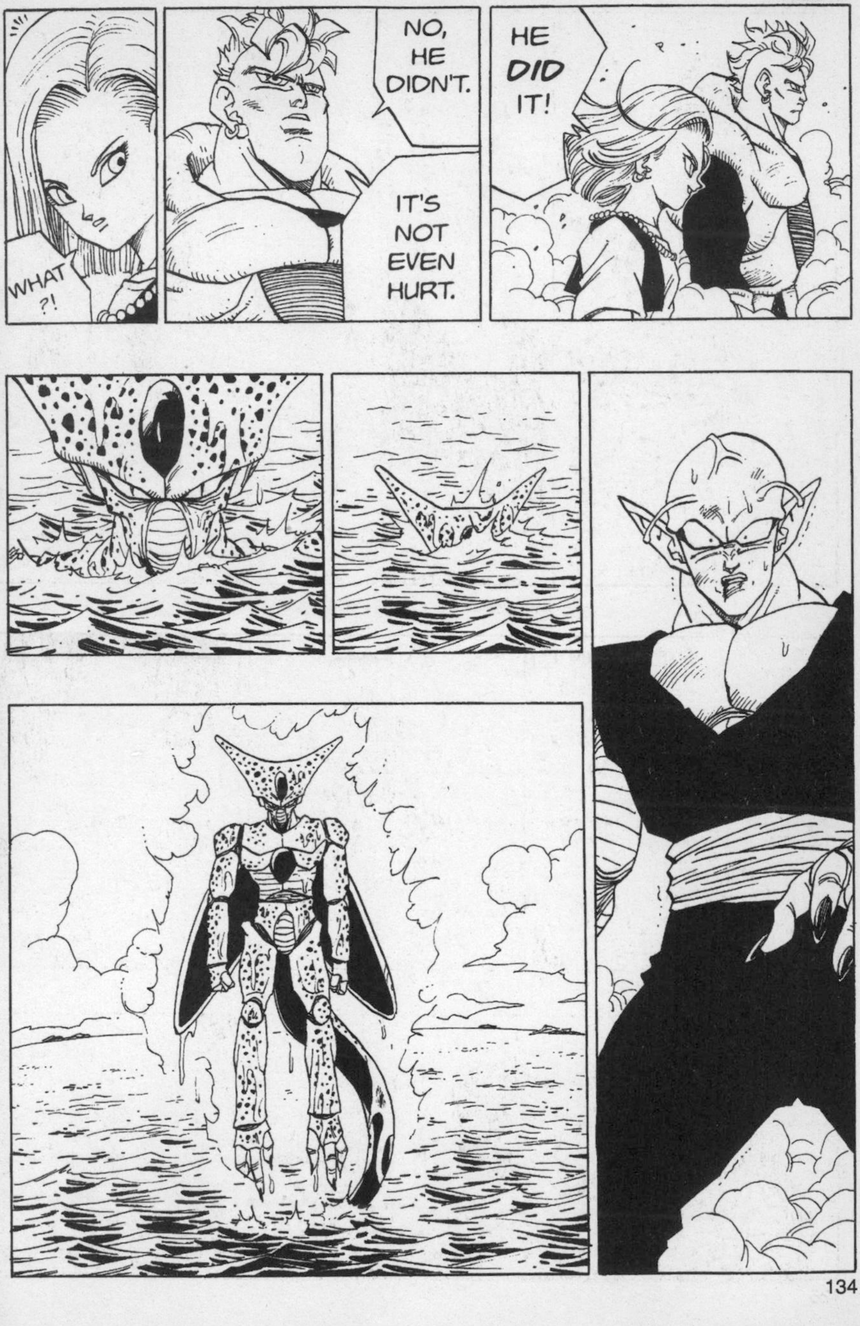
HE DID IT!
NO, HE DIDN'T.
IT'S NOT EVEN HURT.
WHAT ?!

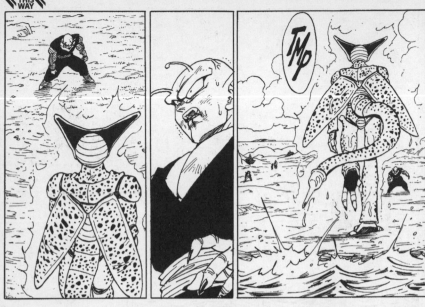

...IT'S HOPE-LESS...

I...I CAN'T BELIEVE THIS... IF *THEY* CAN'T DO IT...

READ THIS WAY

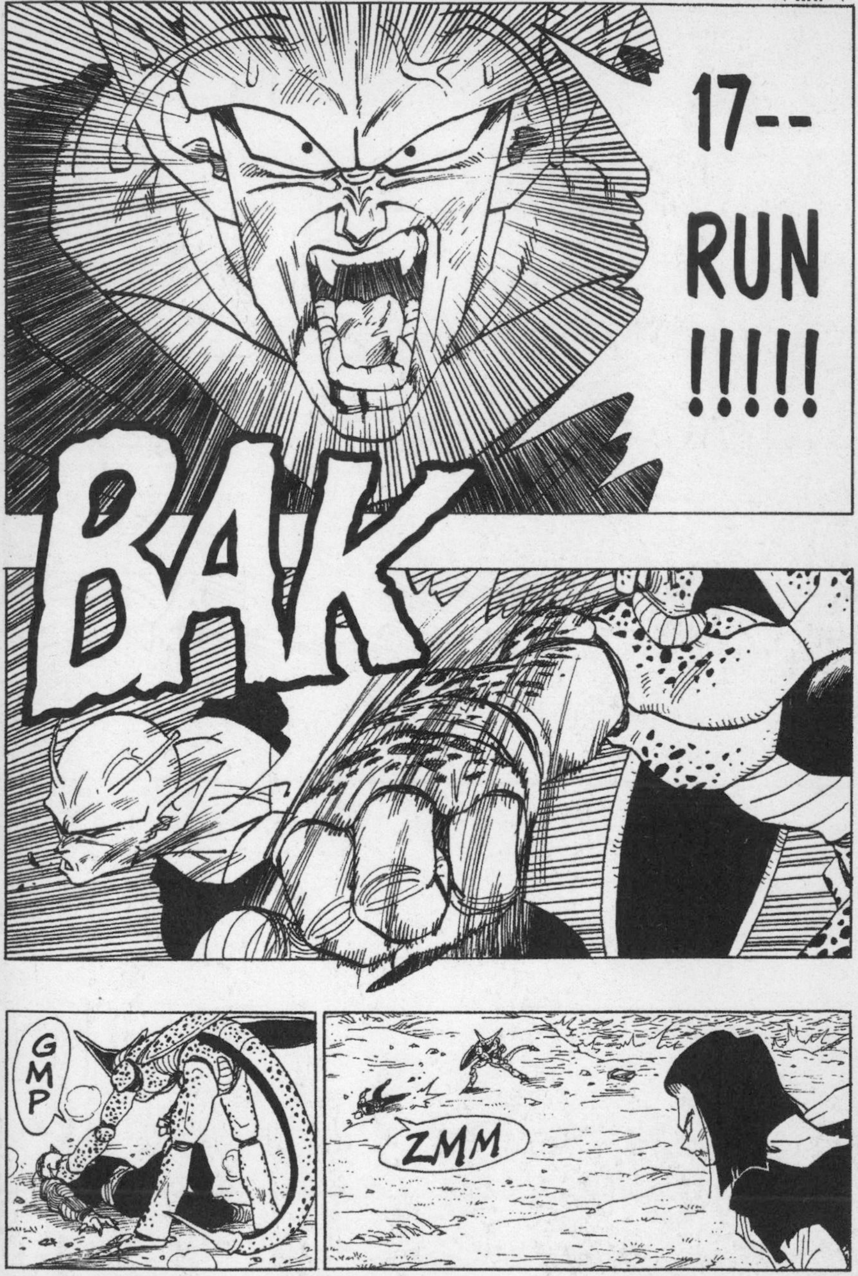

17-- RUN !!!!!
BAK
ZMM
GMP

READ THIS WAY

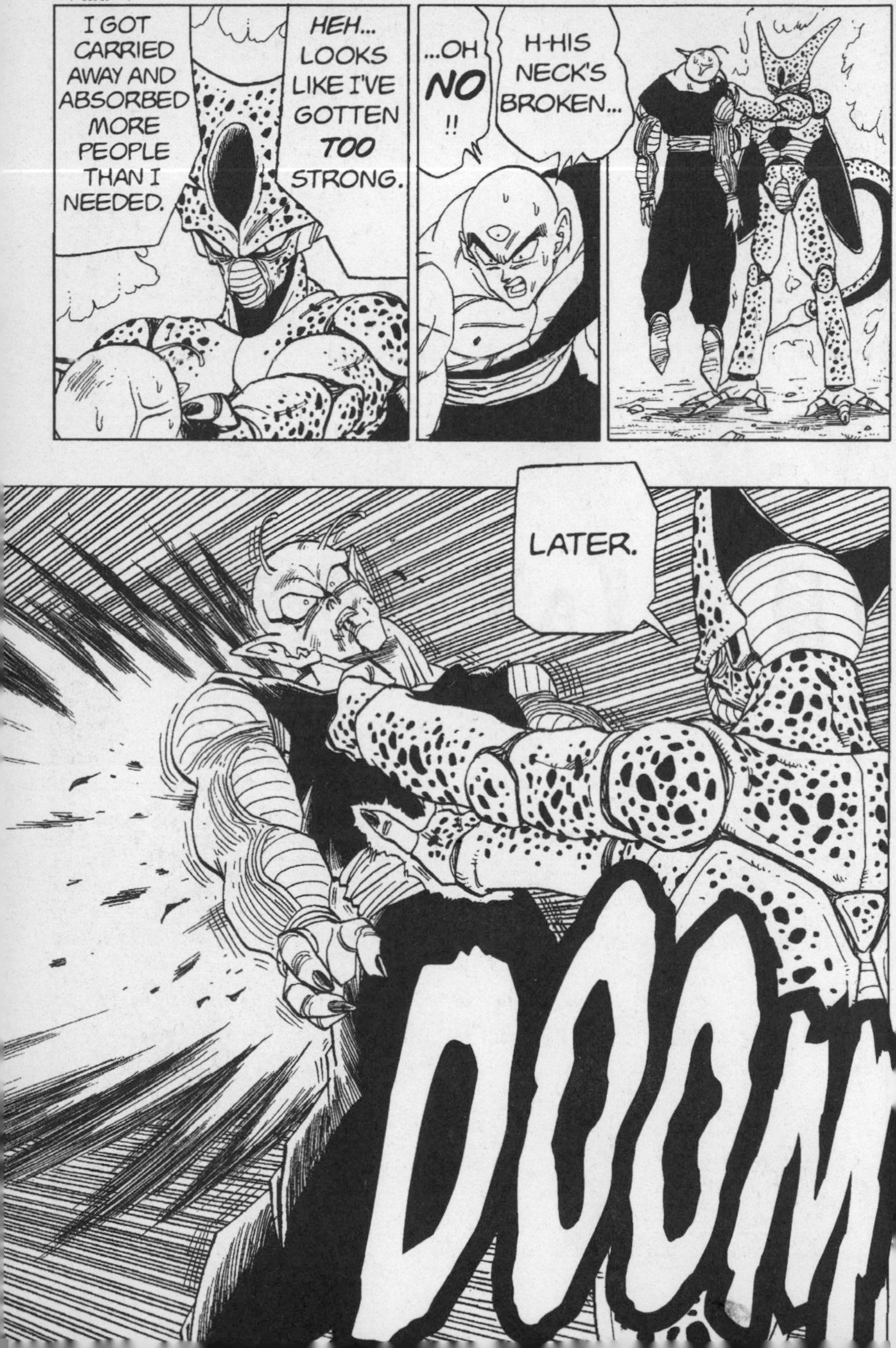
H-HIS NECK'S BROKEN...
...OH NO !!
HEH... LOOKS LIKE I'VE GOTTEN TOO STRONG.
I GOT CARRIED AWAY AND ABSORBED MORE PEOPLE THAN I NEEDED.
LATER.
DOOM

READ THIS WAY

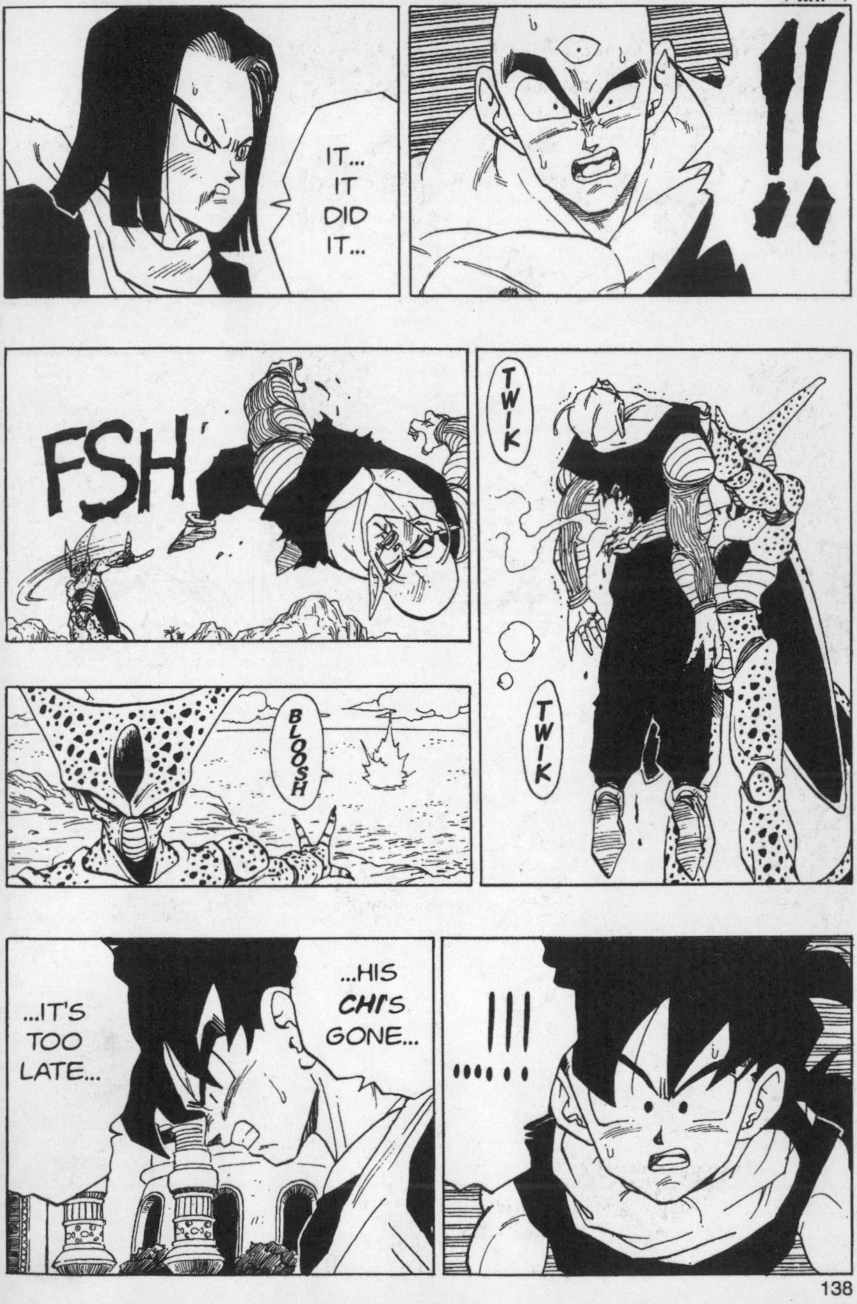

!!
IT... IT DID IT...
TWIK
TWIK
FSH
BLOOSH
!!!
......!!
...HIS CHI'S GONE...
...IT'S TOO LATE...

READ THIS WAY

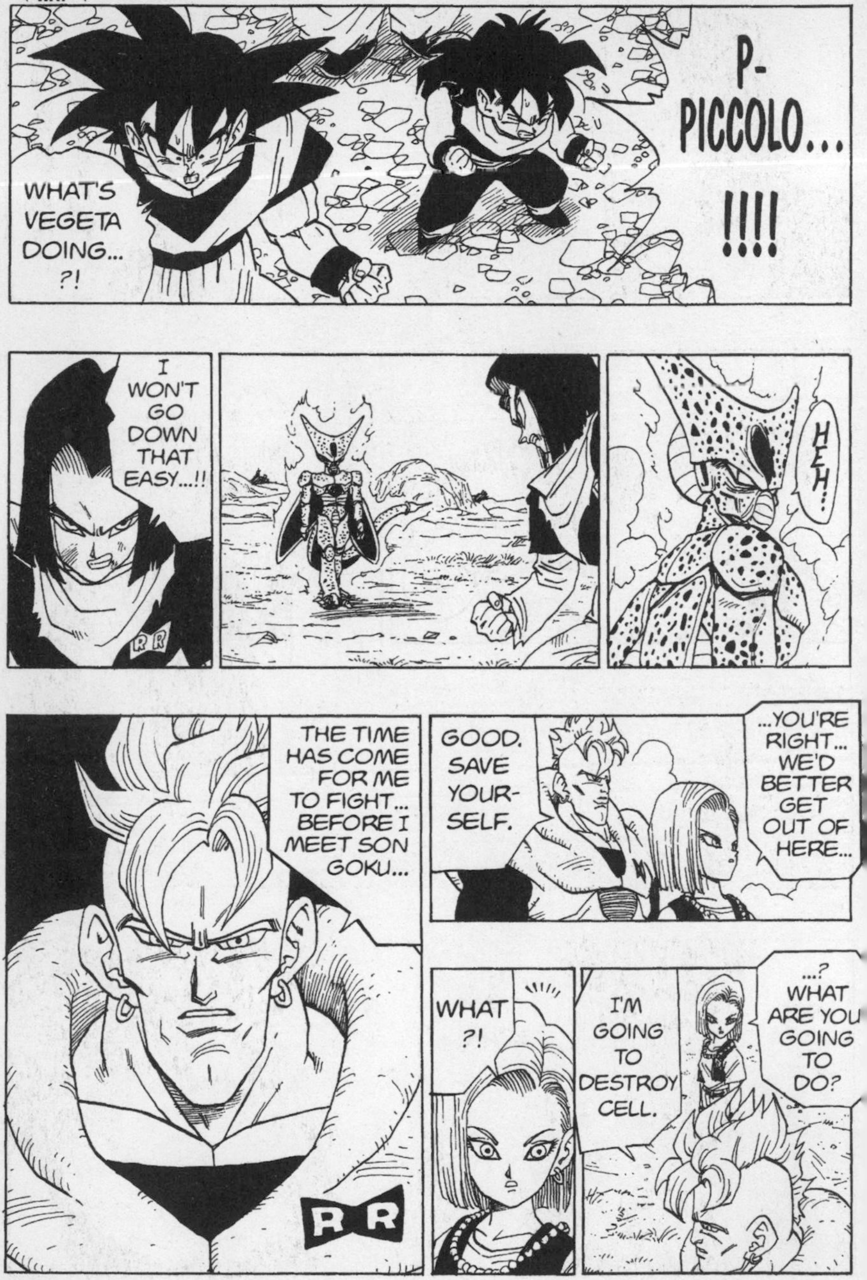
P-PICCOLO...!!!!
WHAT'S VEGETA DOING...?!
HEH!
I WON'T GO DOWN THAT EASY...!!
...YOU'RE RIGHT... WE'D BETTER GET OUT OF HERE...
GOOD. SAVE YOURSELF.
...? WHAT ARE YOU GOING TO DO?
I'M GOING TO DESTROY CELL.
WHAT?!
THE TIME HAS COME FOR ME TO FIGHT... BEFORE I MEET SON GOKU...

DBZ:177 • CELL VS. #16

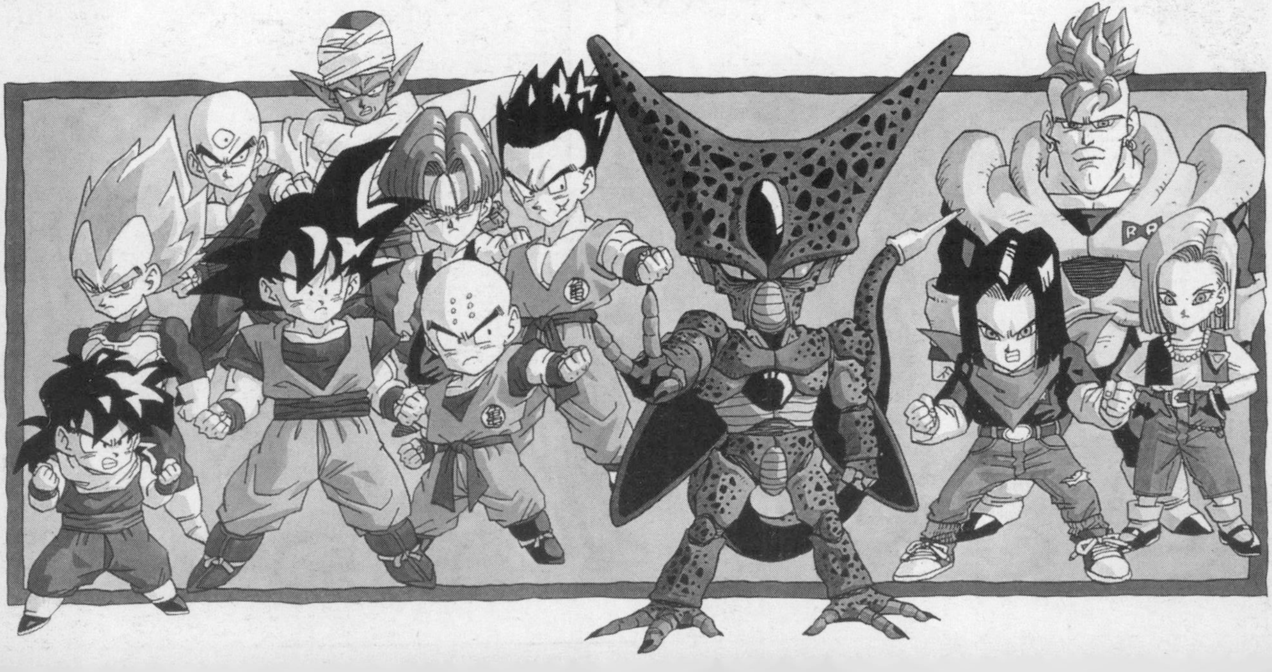

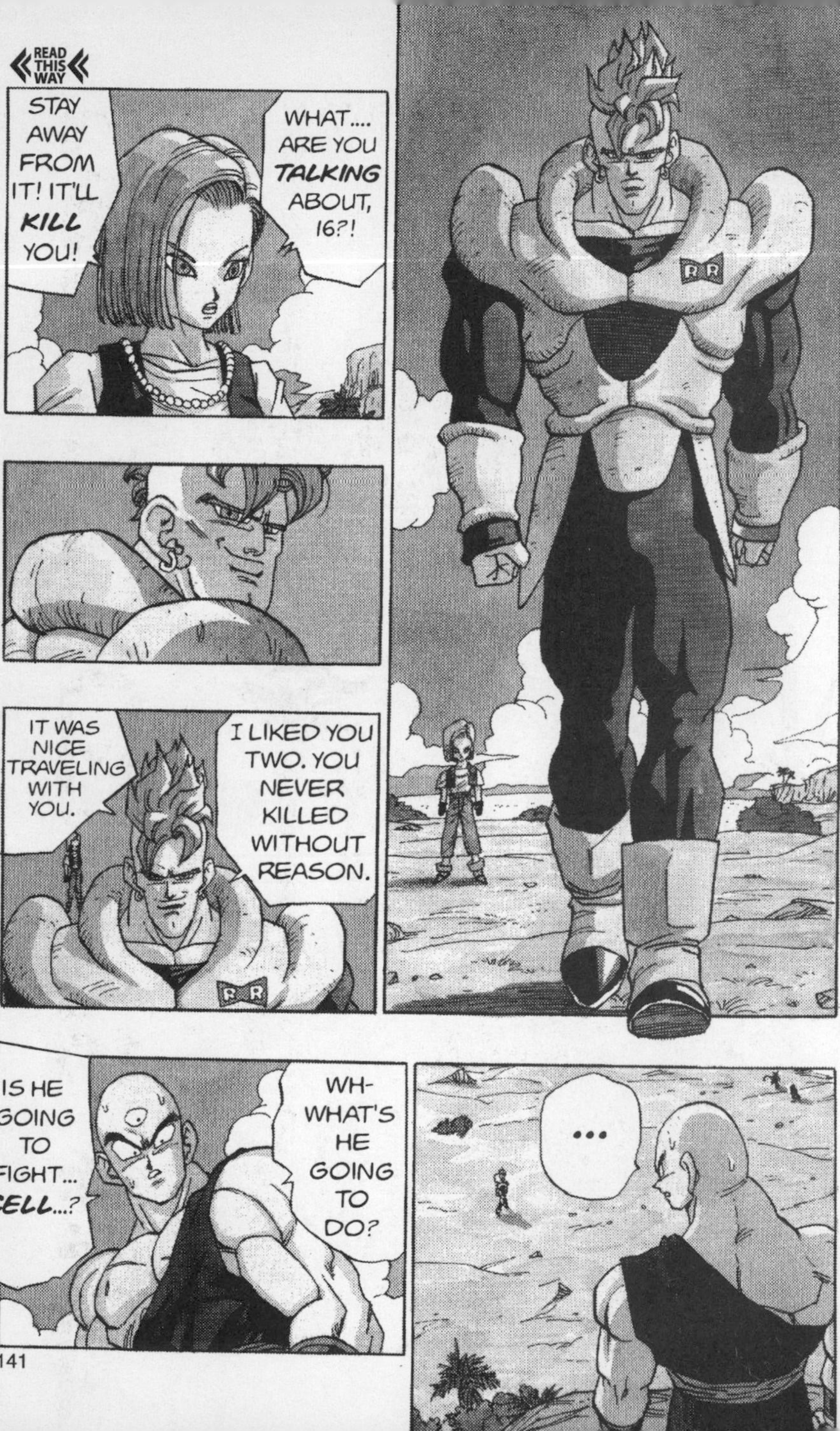
READ THIS WAY
WHAT.... ARE YOU **TALKING** ABOUT, 16?!
STAY AWAY FROM IT! IT'LL **KILL** YOU!
I LIKED YOU TWO. YOU NEVER KILLED WITHOUT REASON.
IT WAS NICE TRAVELING WITH YOU.
...
WH- WHAT'S HE GOING TO DO?
IS HE GOING TO FIGHT... **CELL**...?

READ THIS WAY

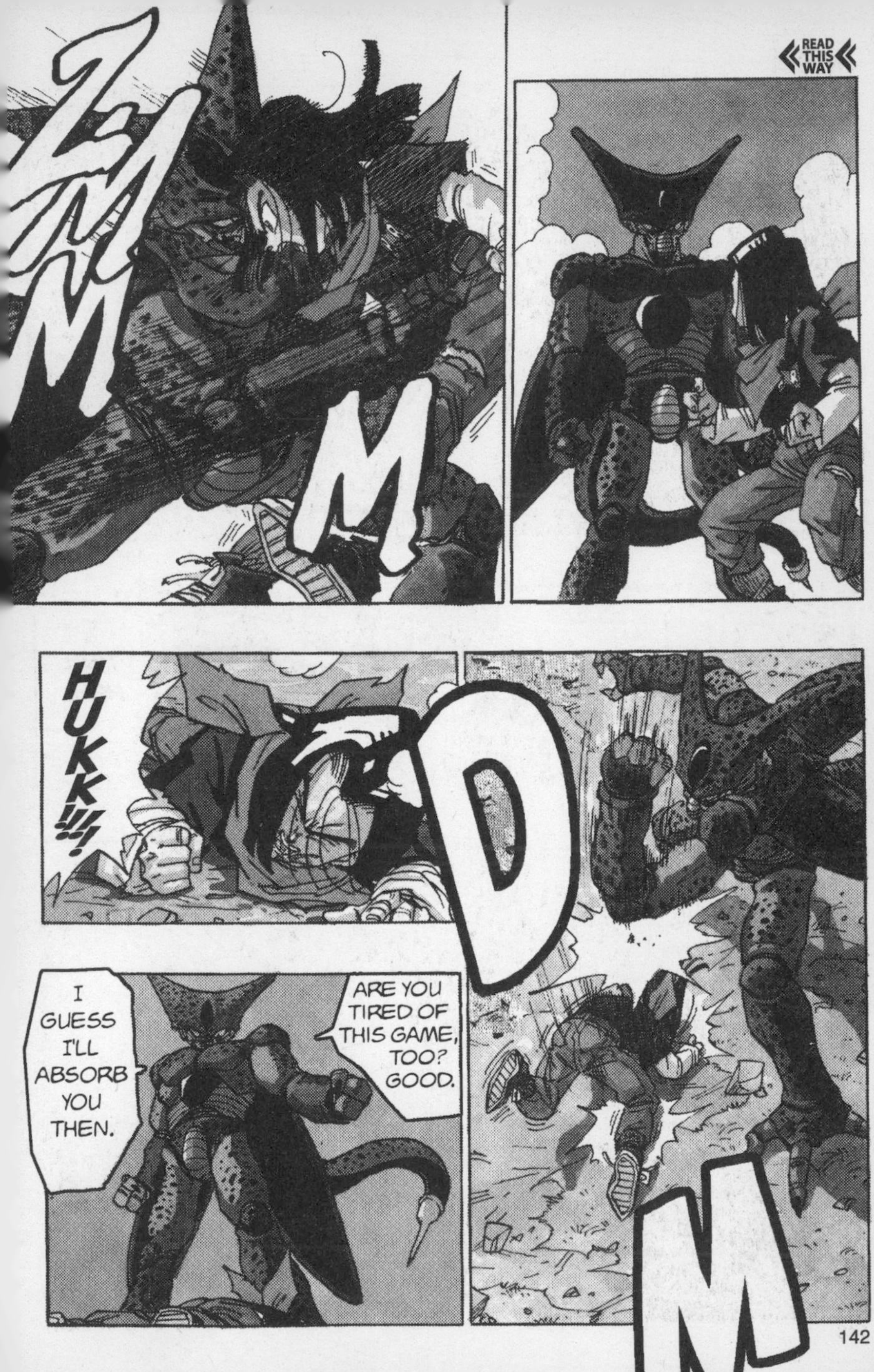
ZMM
M
D
M
HUKK!!!
ARE YOU TIRED OF THIS GAME, TOO? GOOD.
I GUESS I'LL ABSORB YOU THEN.

READ THIS WAY

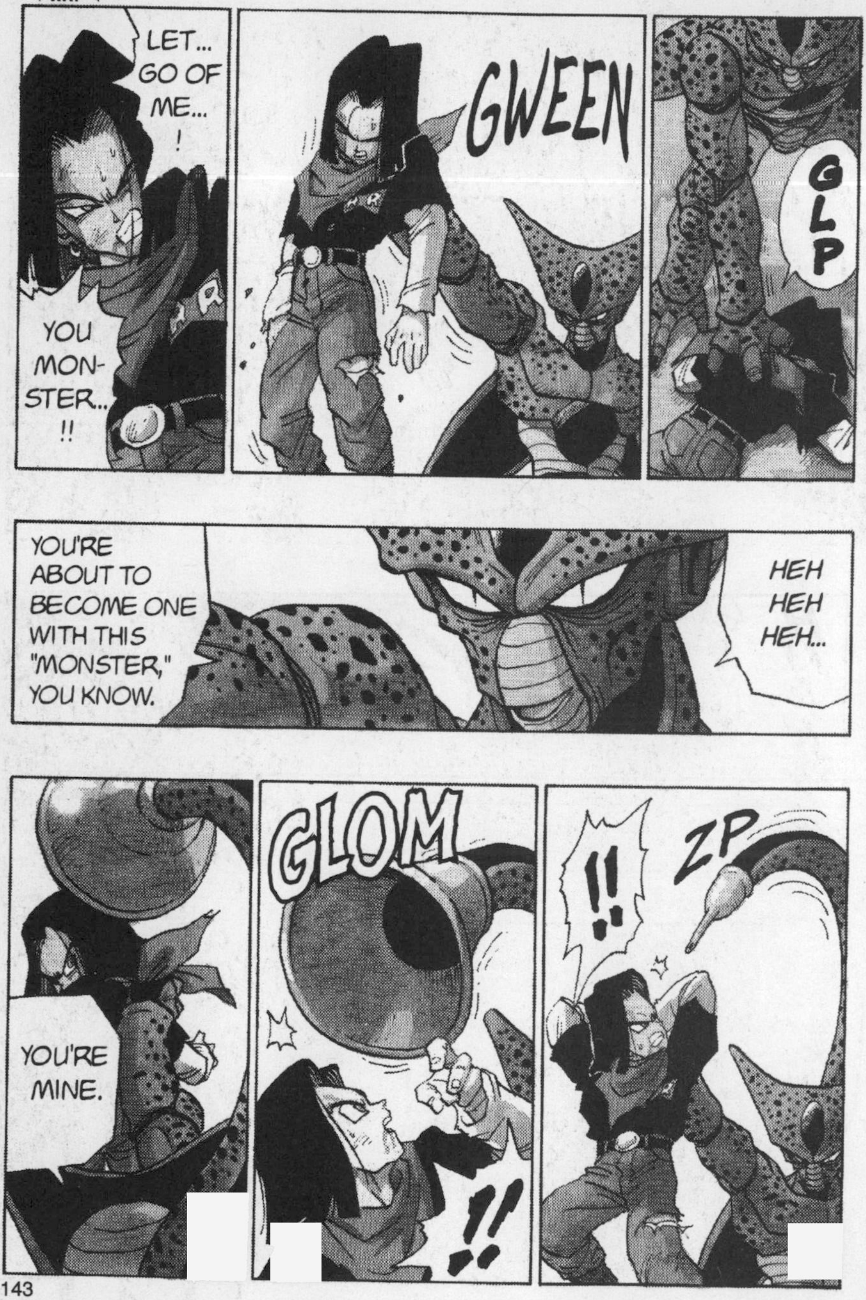

GLP
GWEEN
LET... GO OF ME... !
YOU MONSTER... !!
HEH HEH HEH...
YOU'RE ABOUT TO BECOME ONE WITH THIS "MONSTER," YOU KNOW.
ZP
!!
GLOM
!!
YOU'RE MINE.

READ THIS WAY

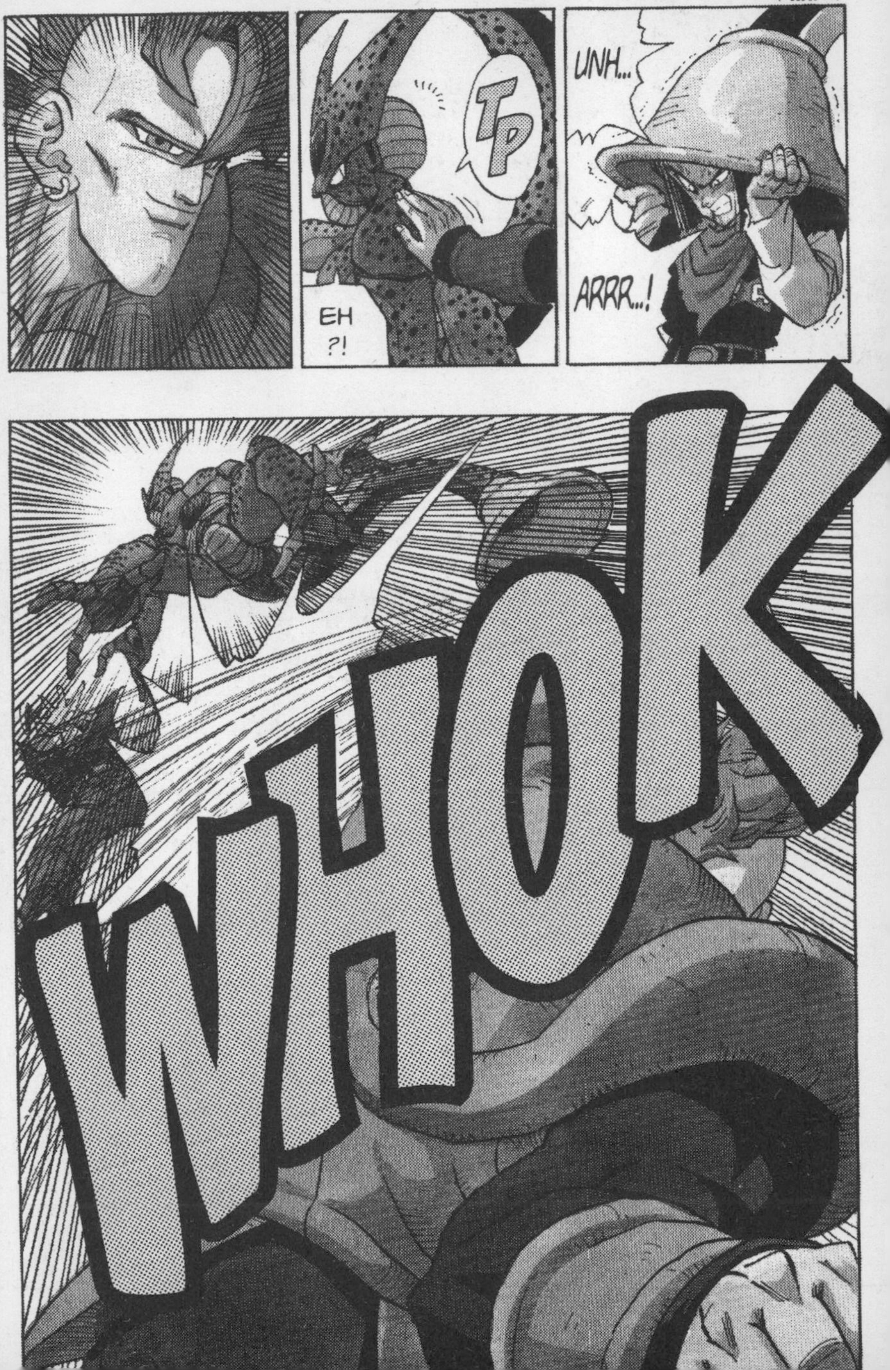
UNH...
ARRR...!
TP
EH ?!
WHOK

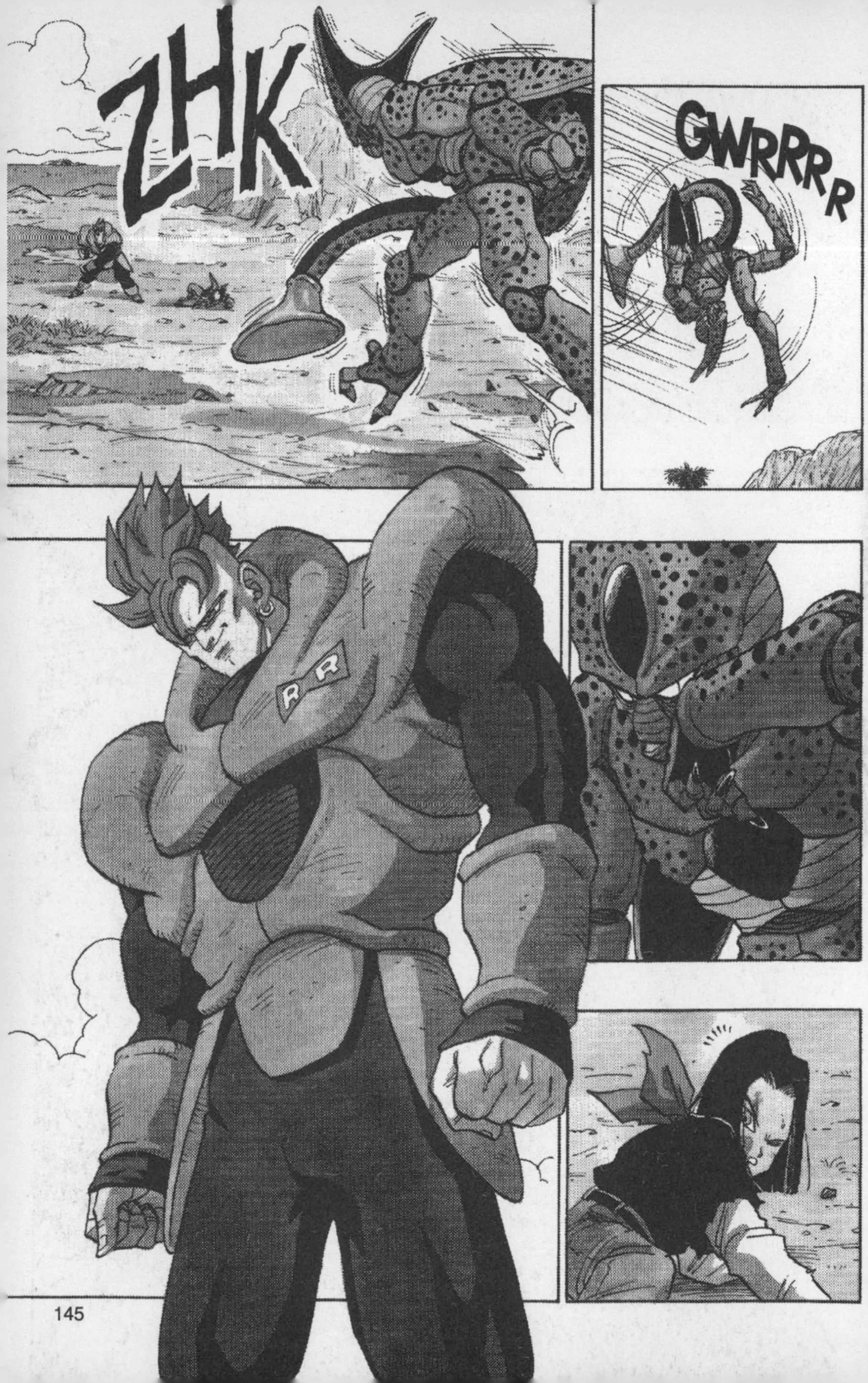
GWRRRR
ZHK

READ THIS WAY

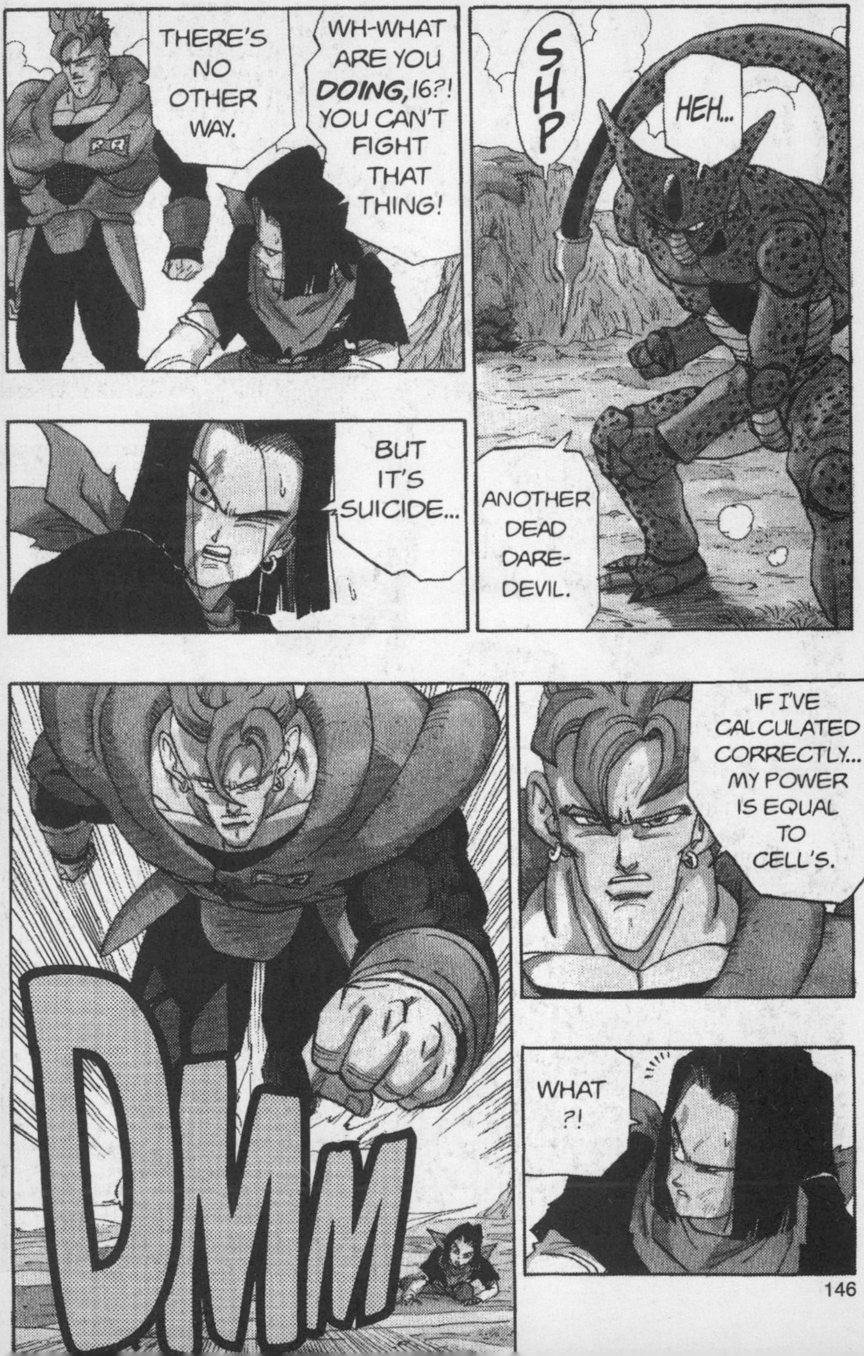
SHP
HEH...
ANOTHER DEAD DARE-DEVIL.
WH-WHAT ARE YOU **DOING,** 16?! YOU CAN'T FIGHT THAT THING!
THERE'S NO OTHER WAY.
BUT IT'S SUICIDE...
IF I'VE CALCULATED CORRECTLY... MY POWER IS EQUAL TO CELL'S.
WHAT ?!
DMM

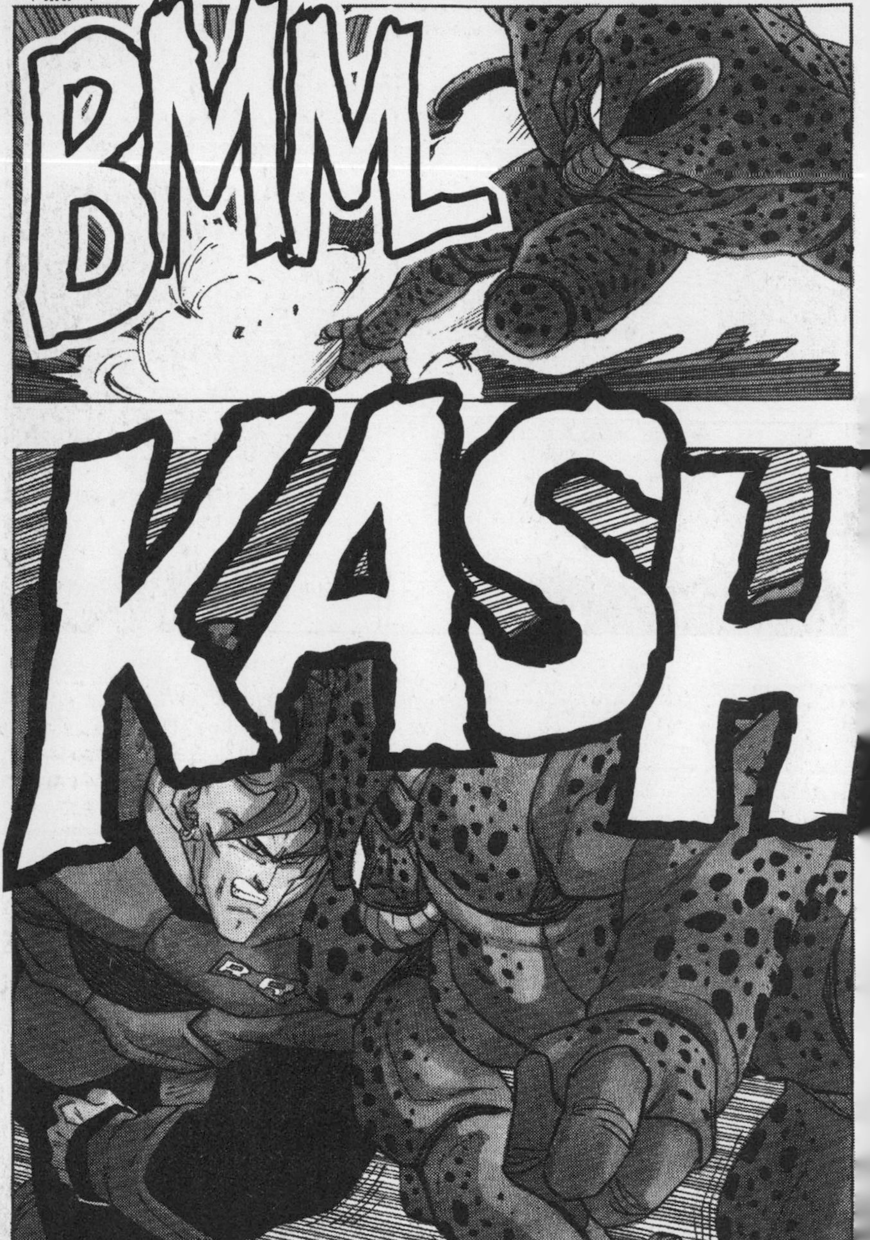
BMML
KASH

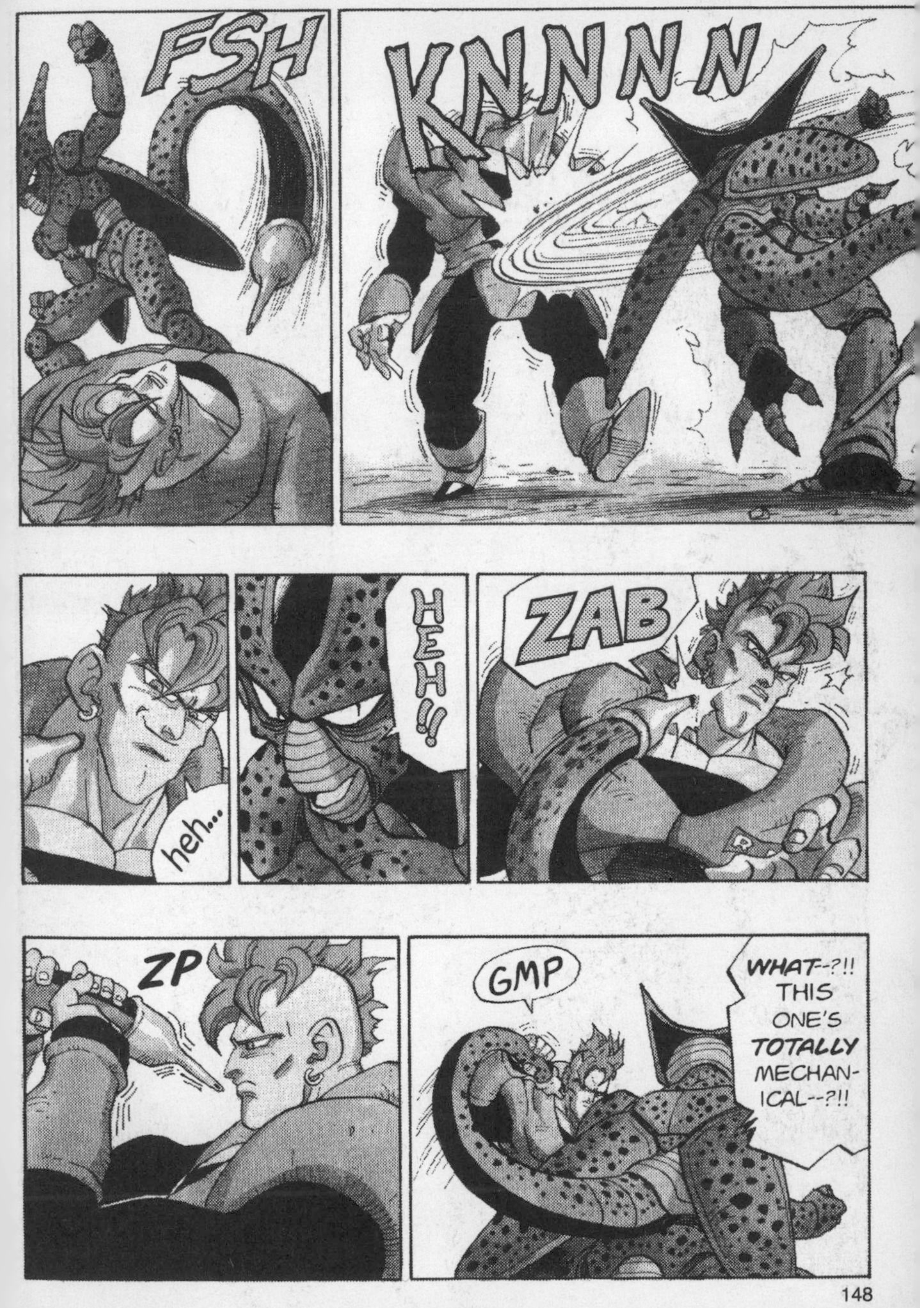
KNNNN
FSH
ZAB
HEH!!
heh...
GMP
WHAT--?!! THIS ONE'S TOTALLY MECHANICAL--?!!
ZP

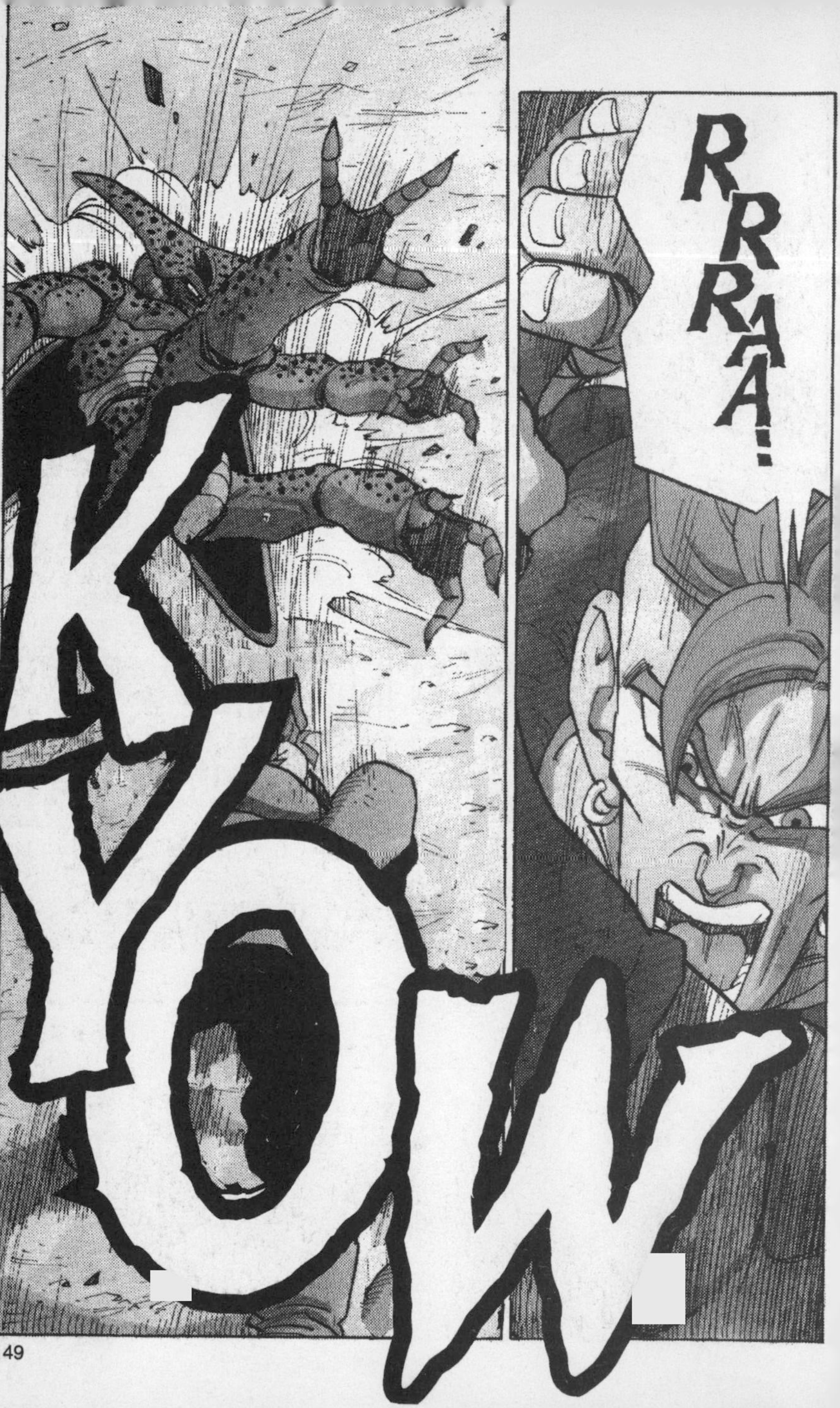
RRRAA!
KYOW

READ THIS WAY

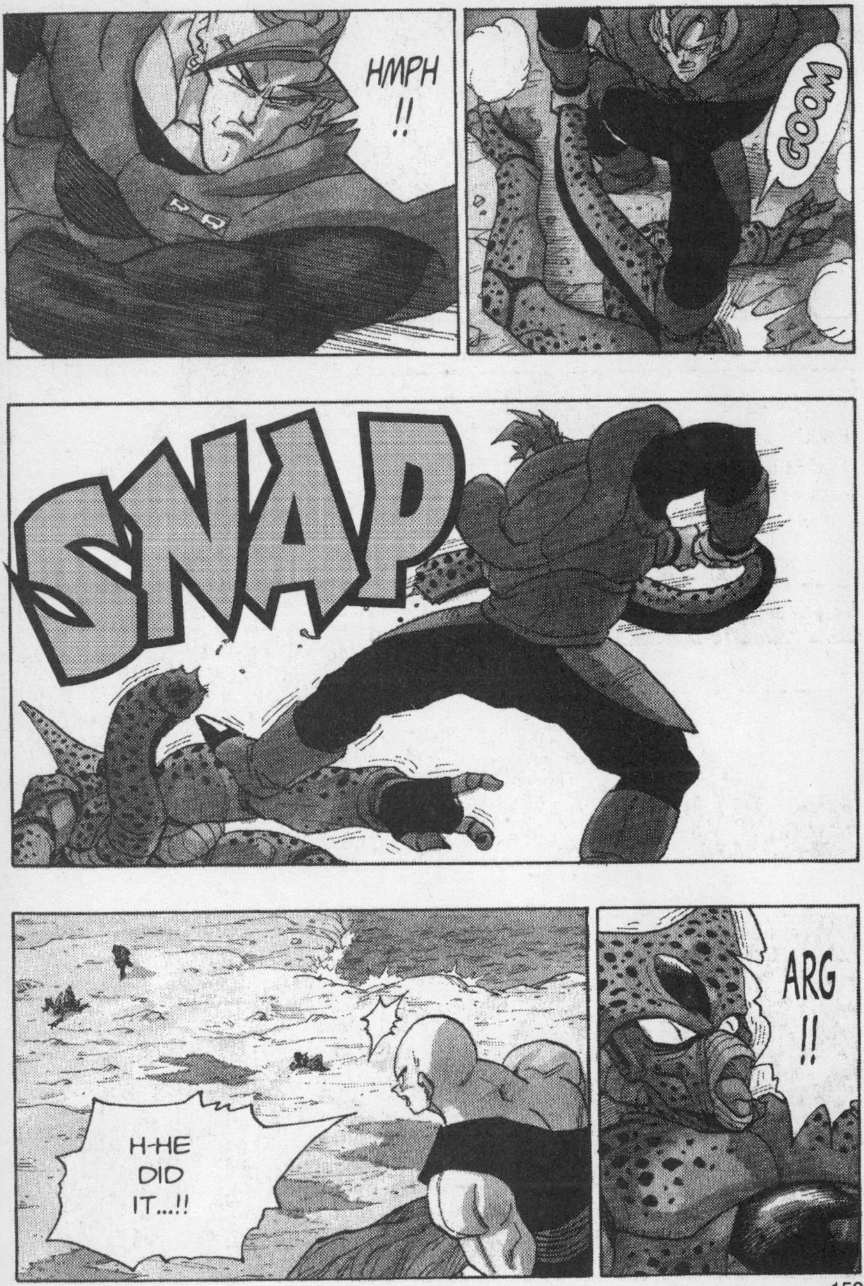
GOOM
HMPH !!
SNAP
ARG !!
H-HE DID IT...!!

TOSS

NOW YOU CAN'T ABSORB *THEM* ANYMORE.

I HAVE PICCOLO'S CELLS IN ME TOO.

YOU FOR- GET...

?

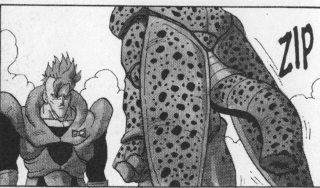

ZIP

READ THIS WAY

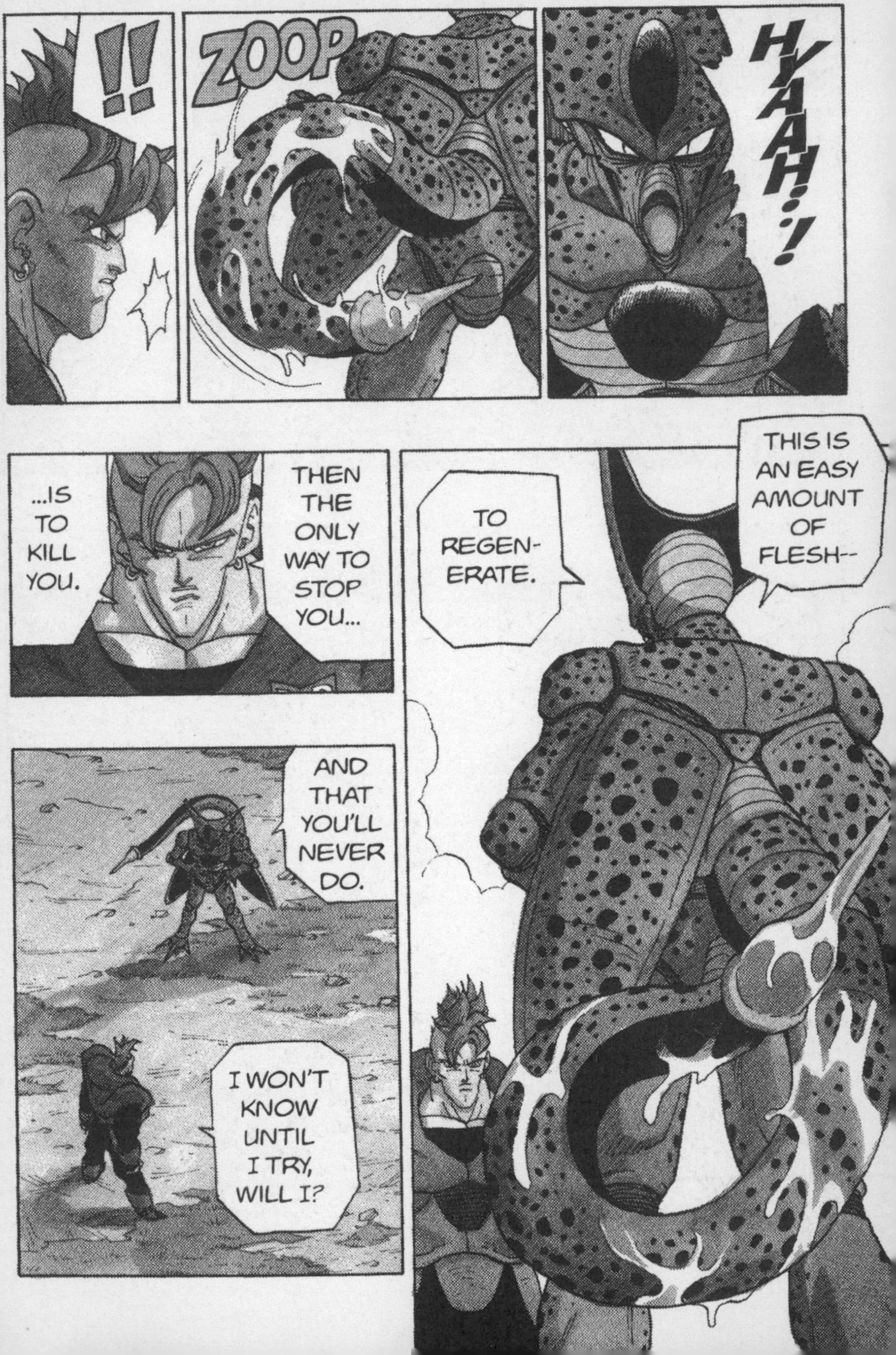
HYAAH!!
ZOOP
!!
THIS IS AN EASY AMOUNT OF FLESH--
TO REGEN-ERATE.
THEN THE ONLY WAY TO STOP YOU...
...IS TO KILL YOU.
AND THAT YOU'LL NEVER DO.
I WON'T KNOW UNTIL I TRY, WILL I?

READ THIS WAY

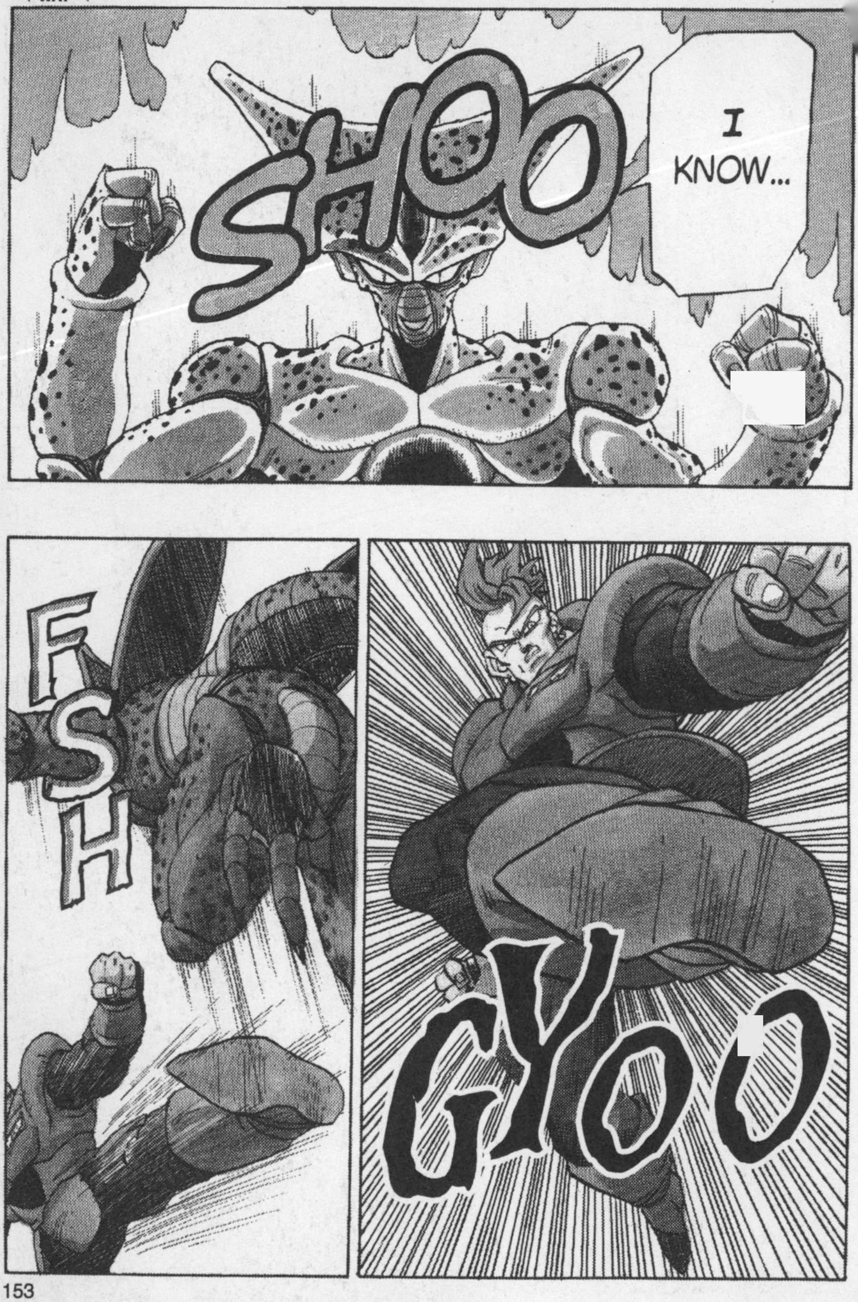
I KNOW...
SHOO
GYOO
FSH

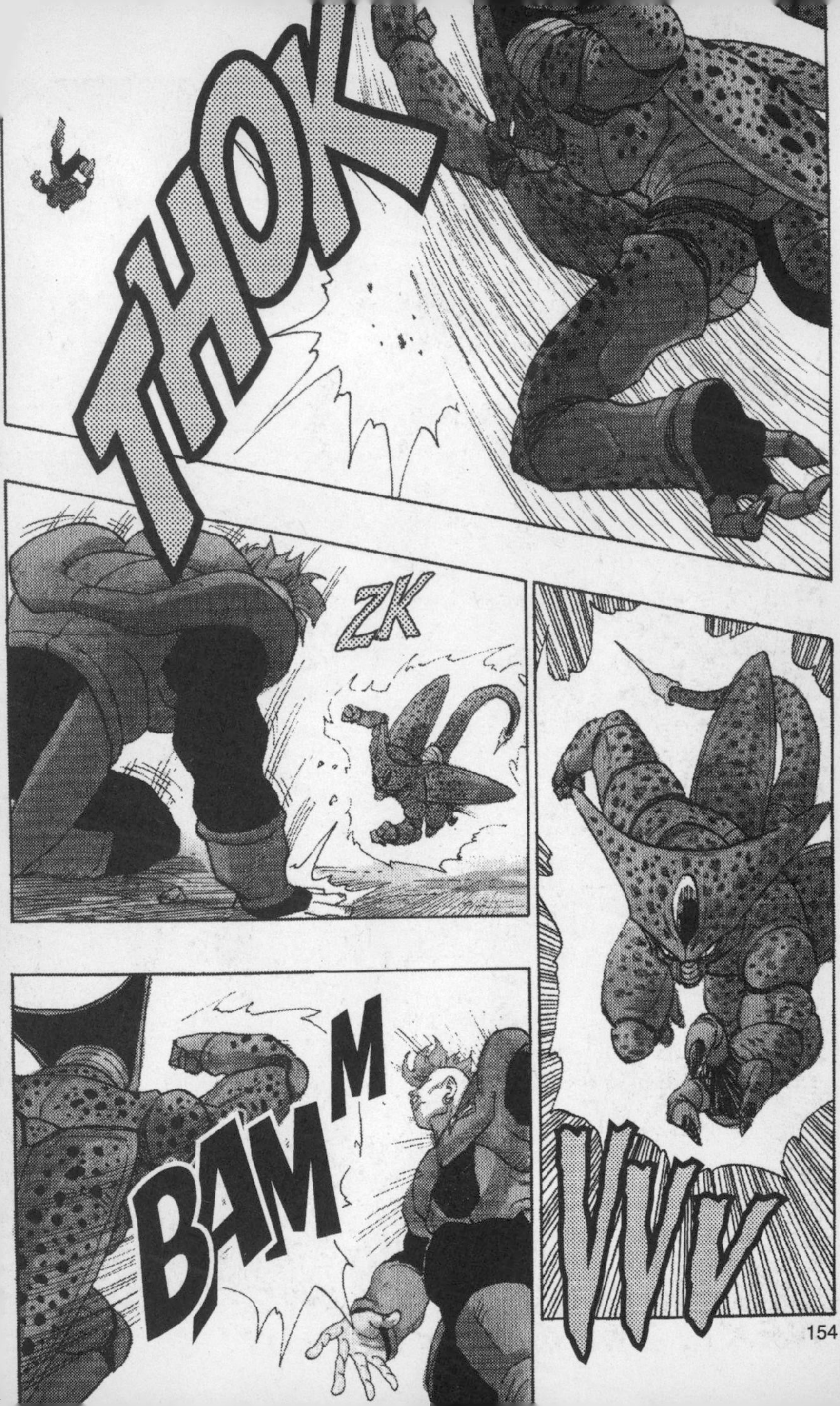
THOK
VVV
ZK
BAMM

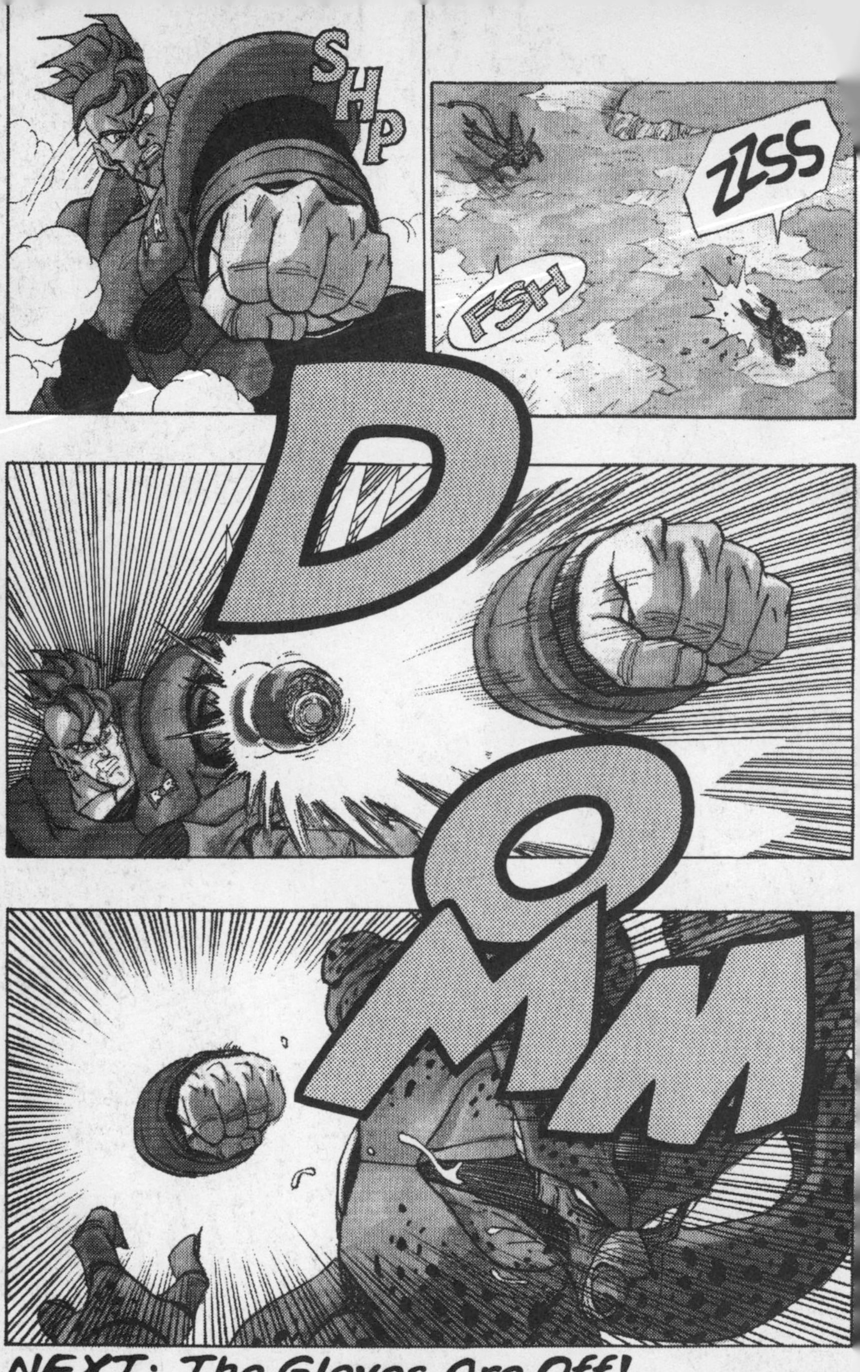
ZZSS
FSH
SHP
DOOM

NEXT: The Gloves Are Off!

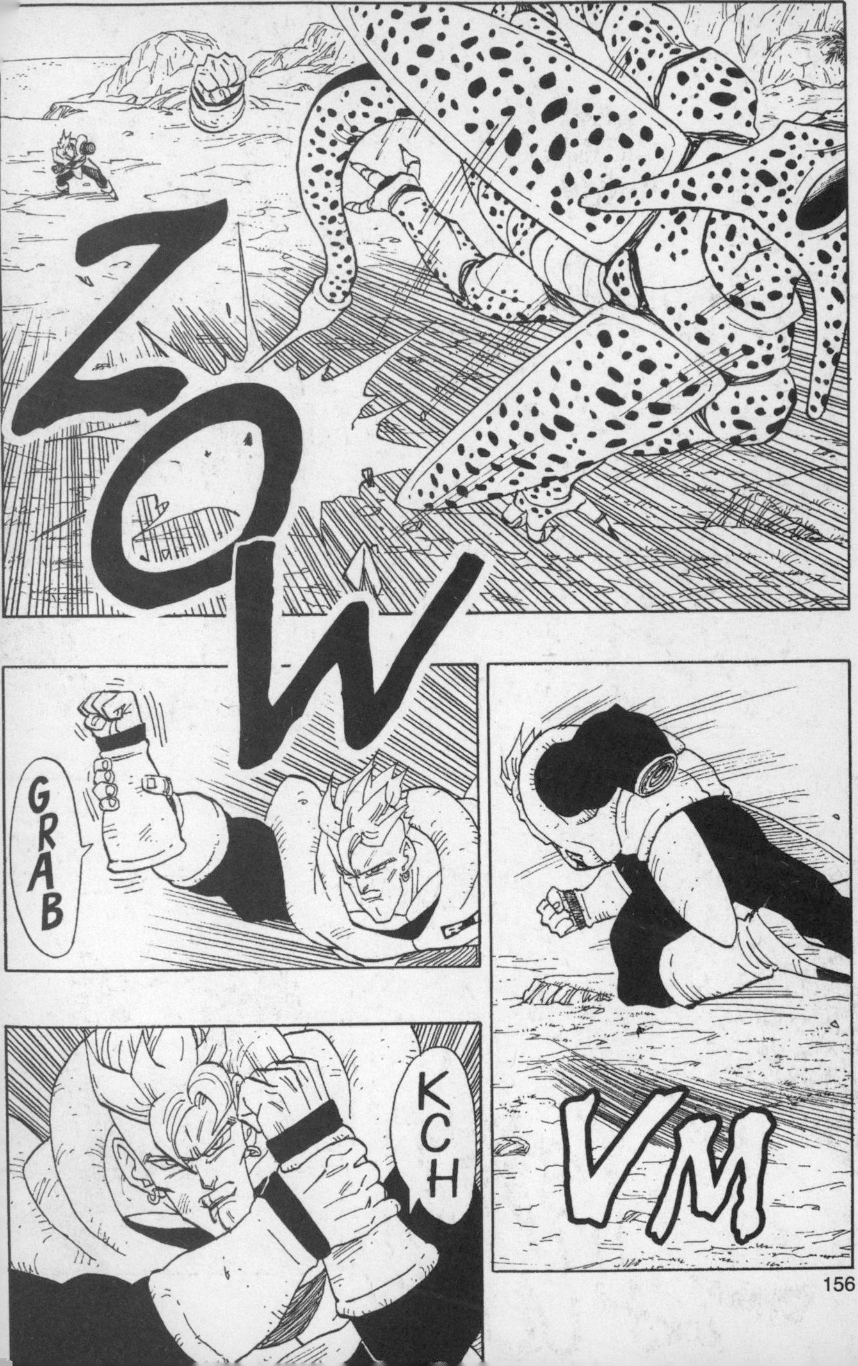
ZOW
VM
GRAB
KCH

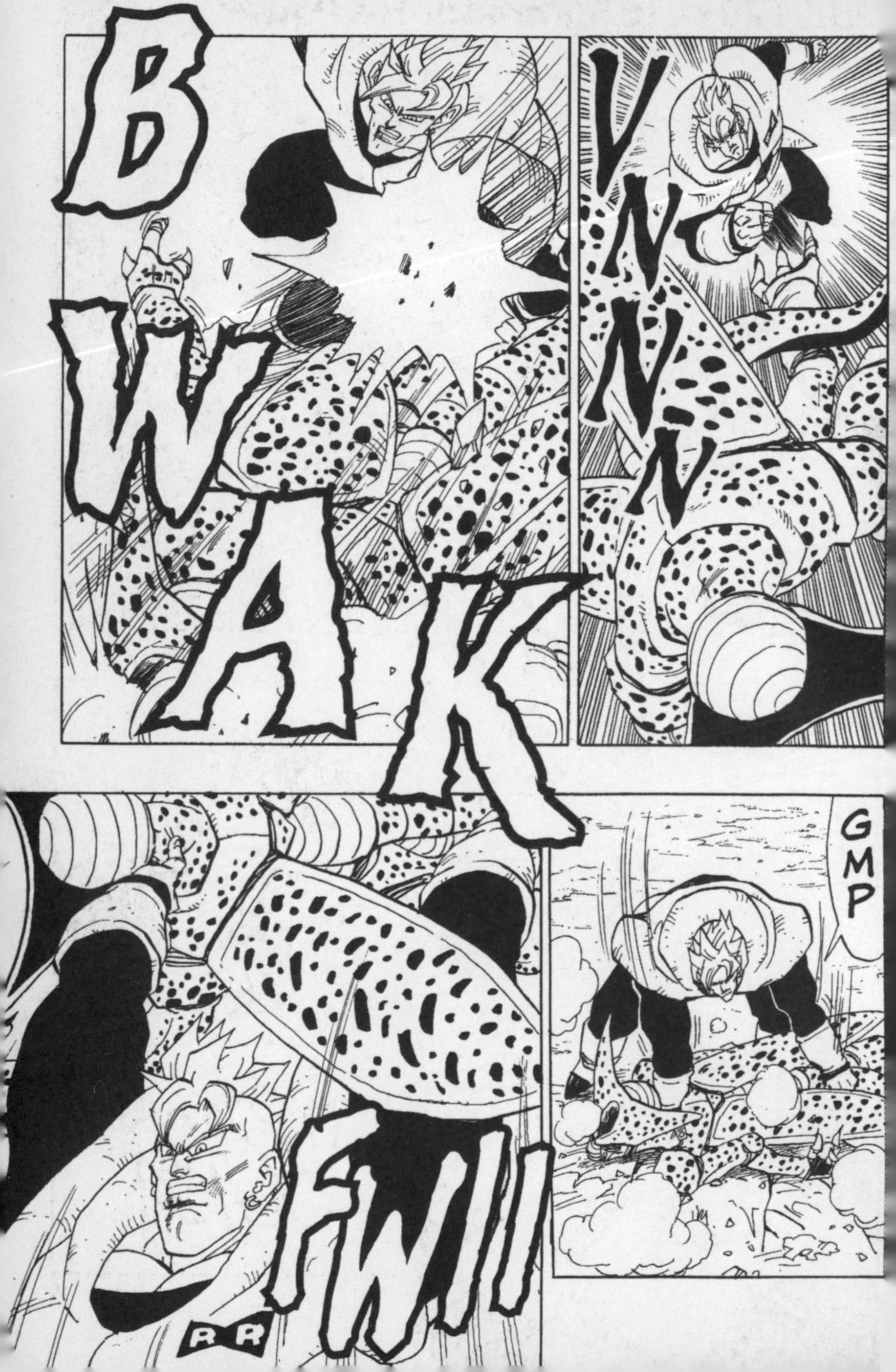
VNNN
BWAK
GMP
FWI!

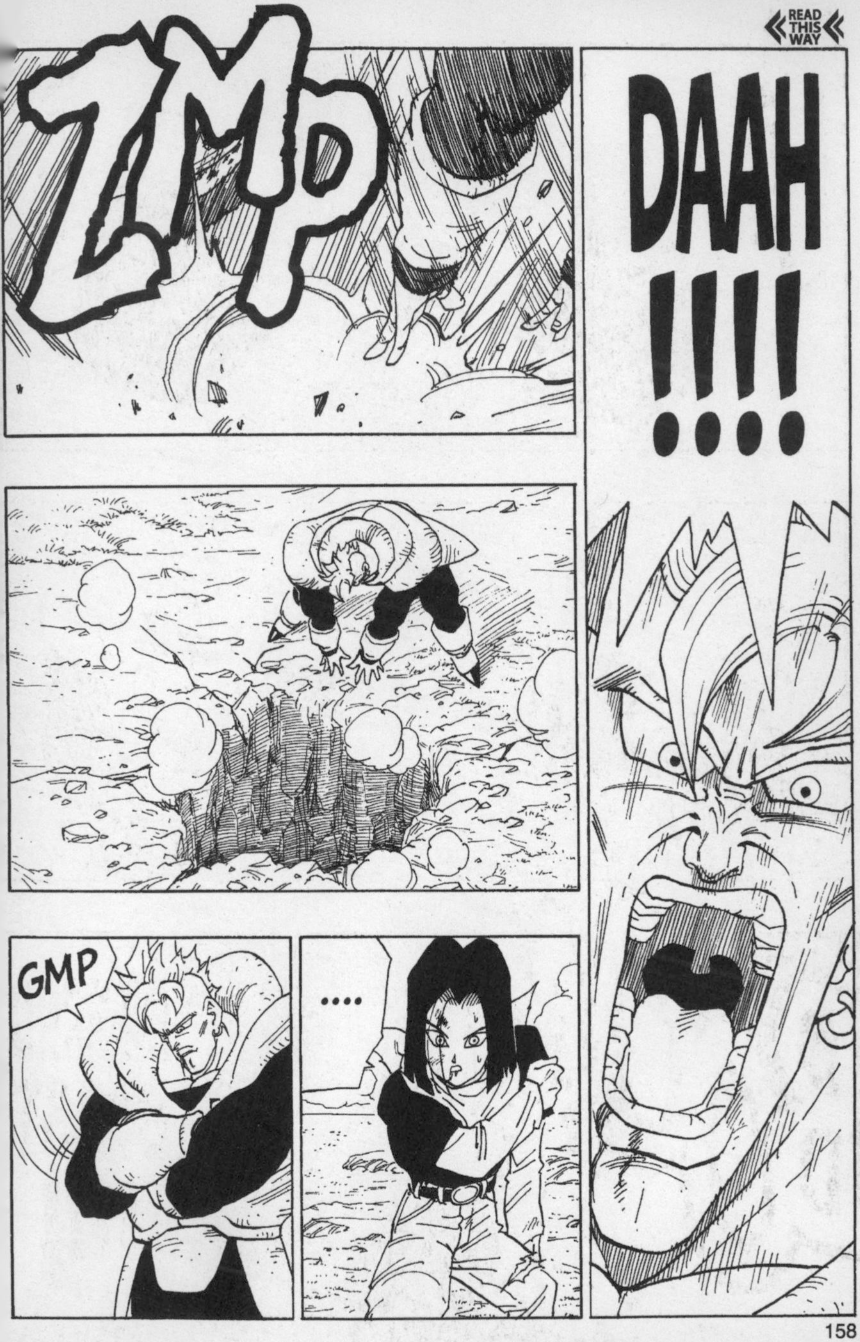
DAAH!!!!....
ZMP
....
GMP

READ THIS WAY

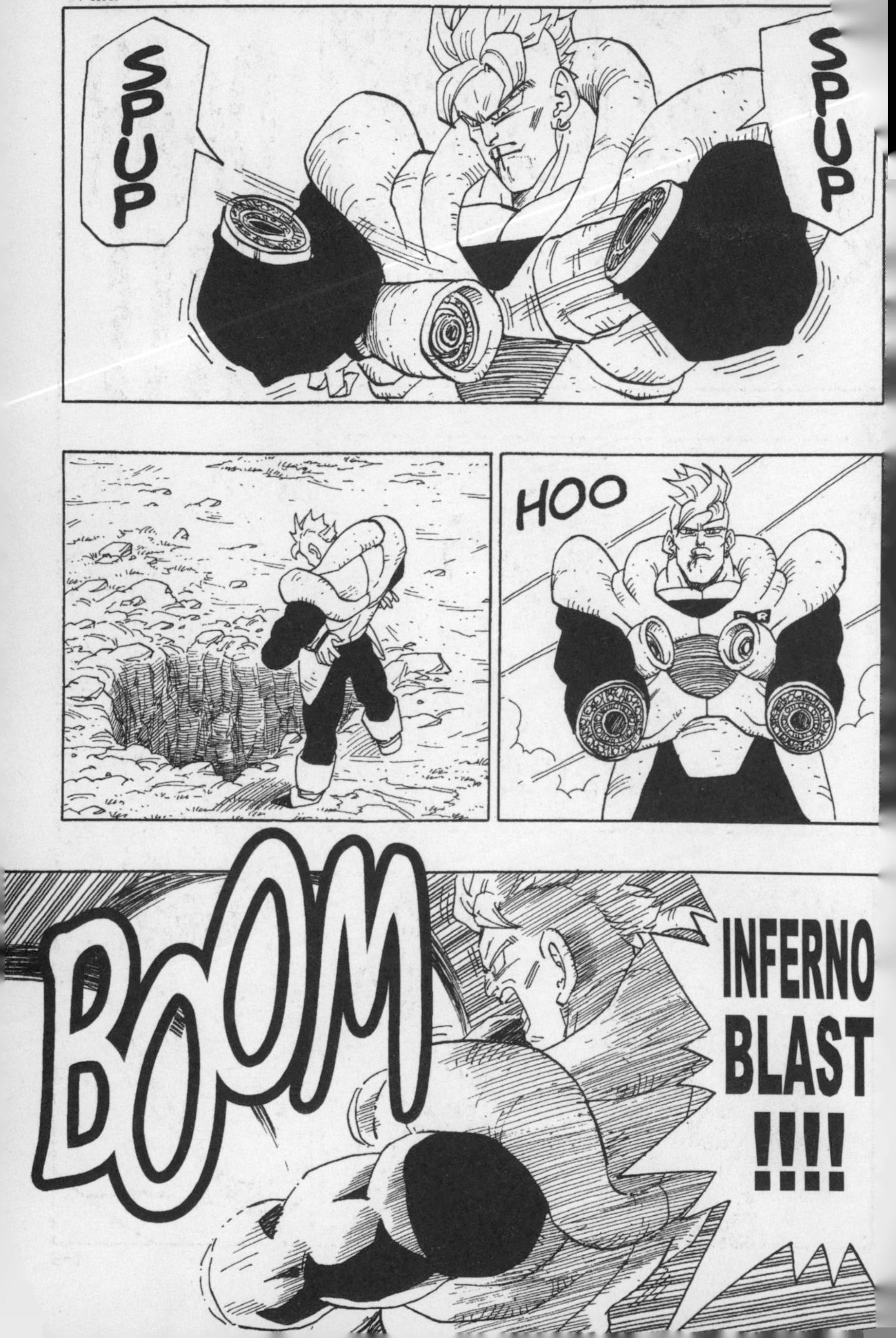
SPUP
SPUP
HOO
INFERNO BLAST!!!!
BOOM

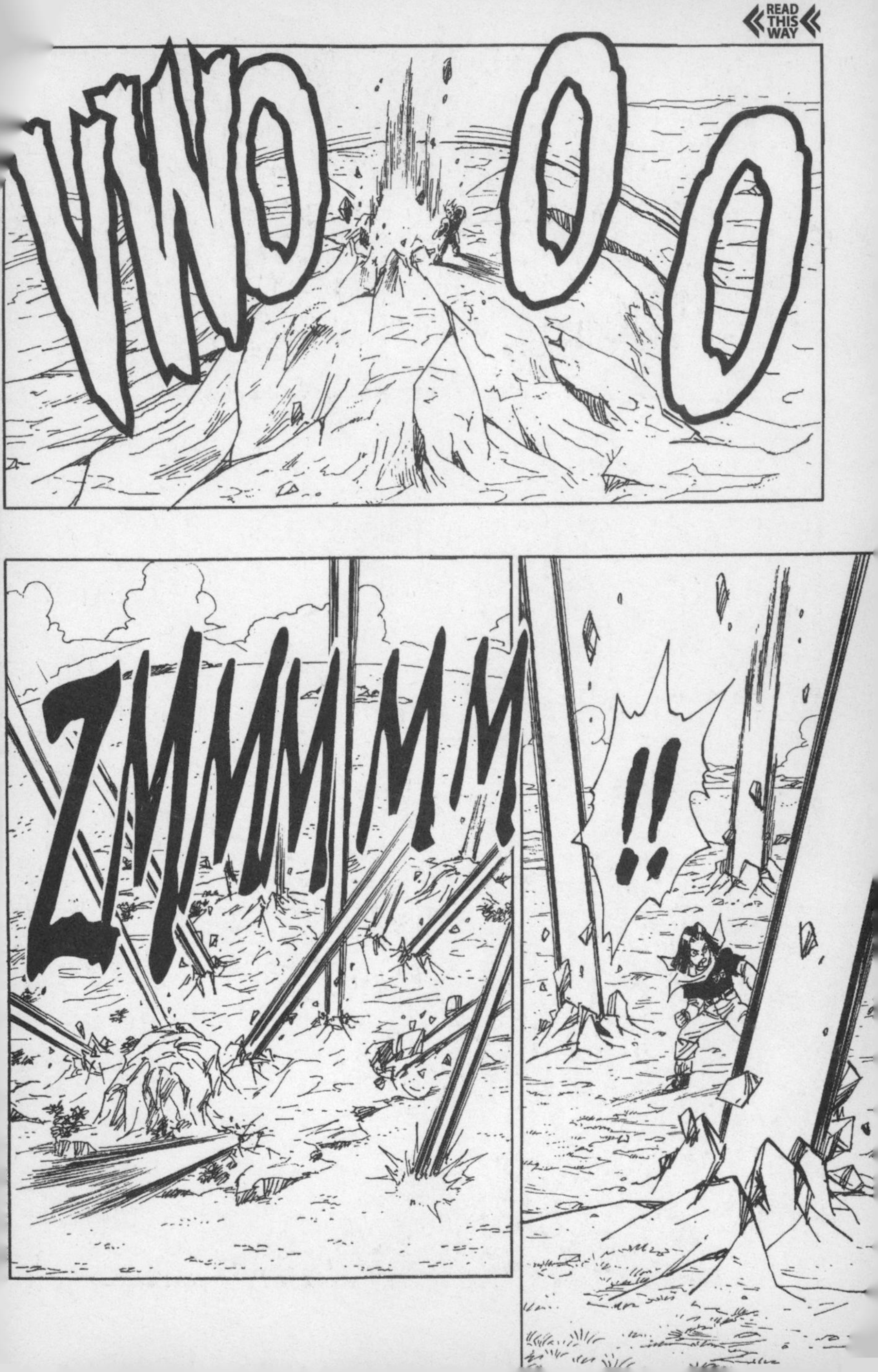
READ THIS WAY
VWOOO
ZMMMMM!!

READ THIS WAY

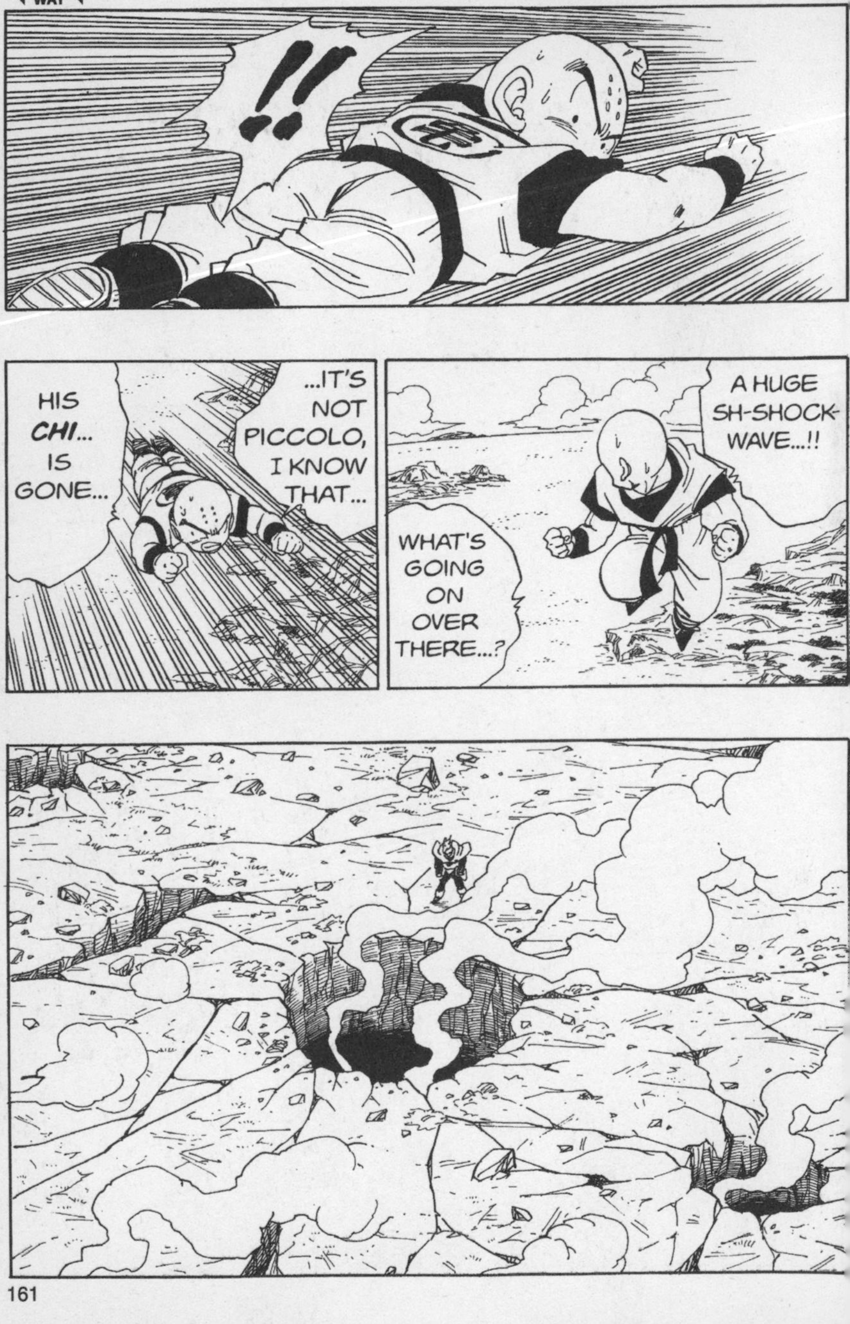
!!
A HUGE SH-SHOCK-WAVE...!!
WHAT'S GOING ON OVER THERE...?
...IT'S NOT PICCOLO, I KNOW THAT...
HIS CHI... IS GONE...

READ THIS WAY

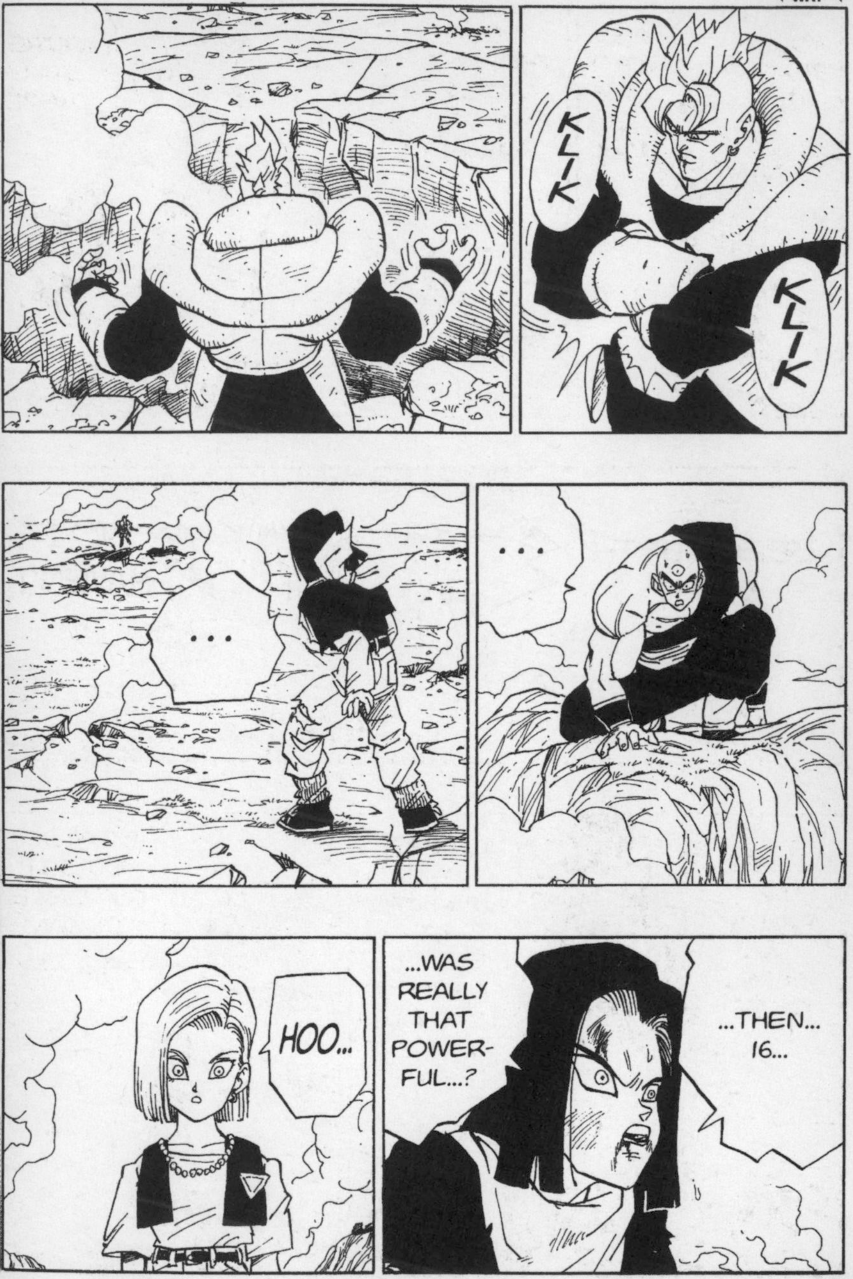
KLIK
KLIK
...
...
...THEN... 16...
...WAS REALLY THAT POWER-FUL...?
HOO...

READ THIS WAY

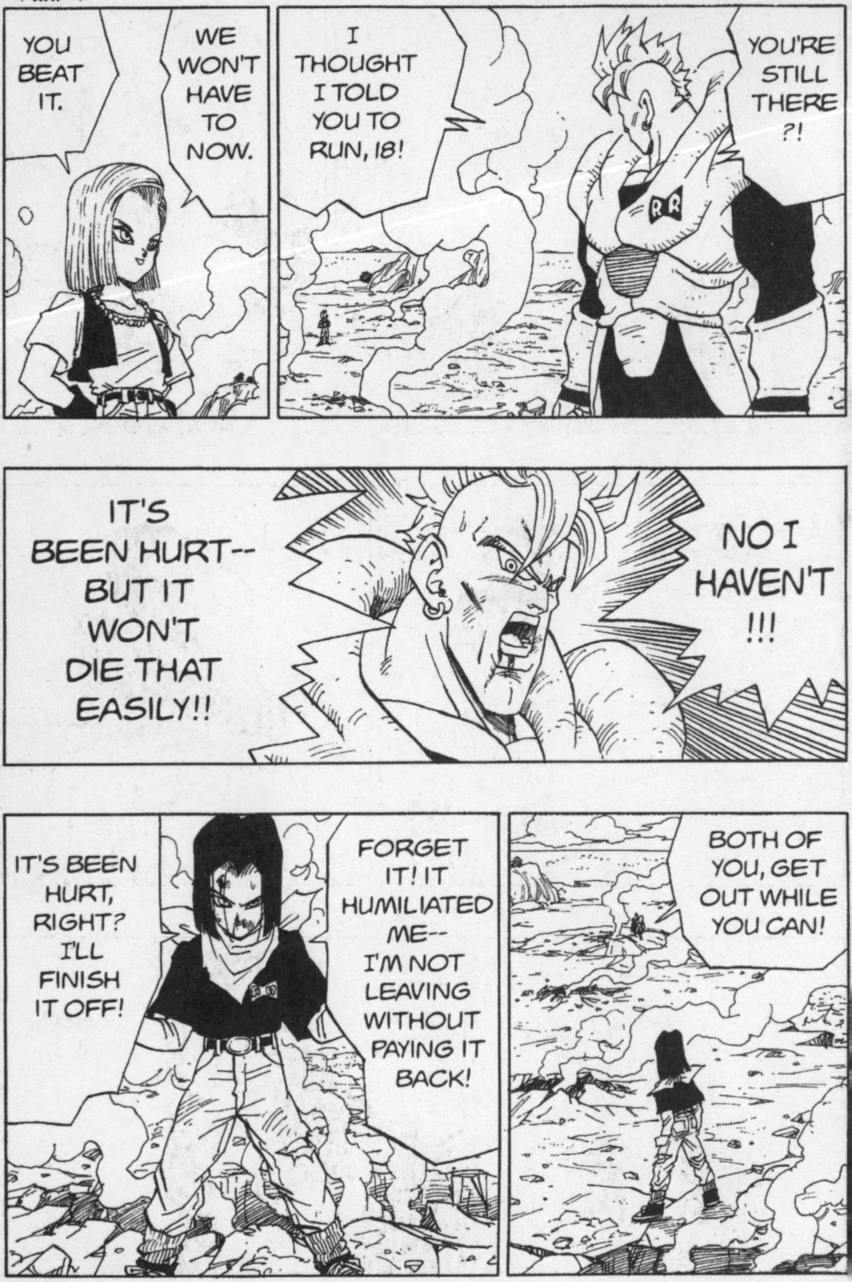
YOU'RE STILL THERE?!
I THOUGHT I TOLD YOU TO RUN, 18!
WE WON'T HAVE TO NOW.
YOU BEAT IT.
NO I HAVEN'T!!!
IT'S BEEN HURT-- BUT IT WON'T DIE THAT EASILY!!
BOTH OF YOU, GET OUT WHILE YOU CAN!
FORGET IT! IT HUMILIATED ME-- I'M NOT LEAVING WITHOUT PAYING IT BACK!
IT'S BEEN HURT, RIGHT? I'LL FINISH IT OFF!

READ THIS WAY

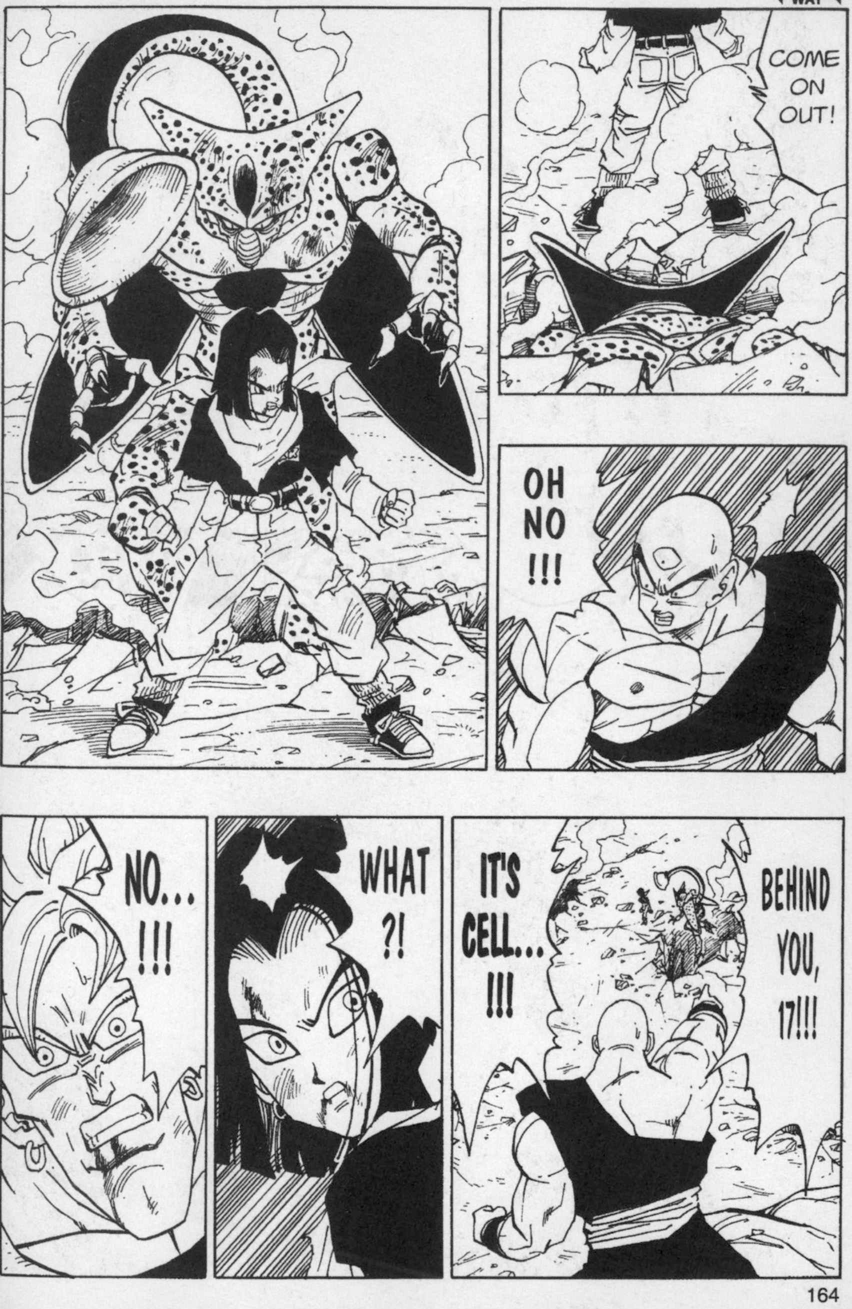
COME ON OUT!
OH NO !!!
BEHIND YOU, 17!!!
IT'S CELL... !!!
WHAT ?!
NO... !!!

READ THIS WAY

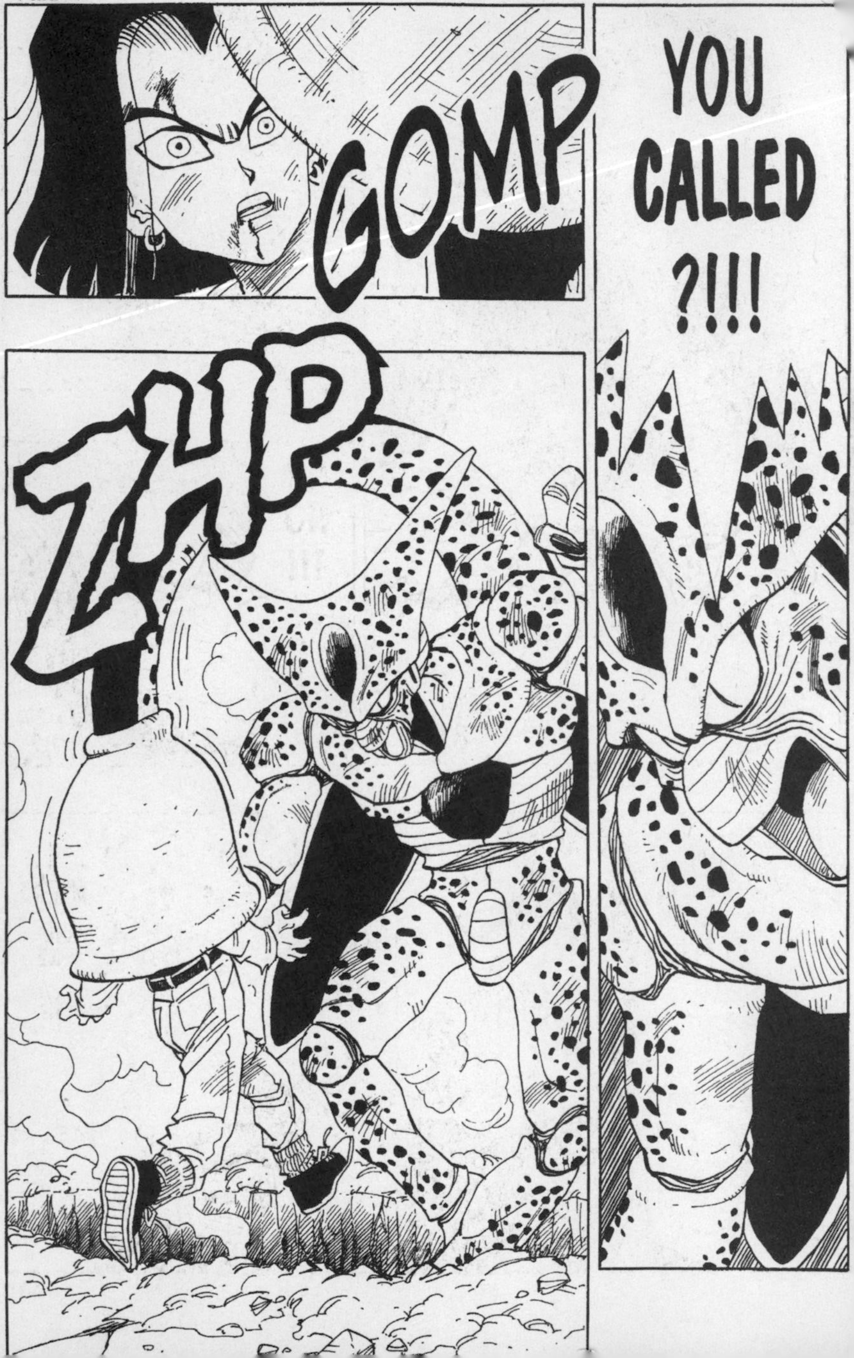
YOU CALLED ?!!!
GOMP
ZIP

READ THIS WAY

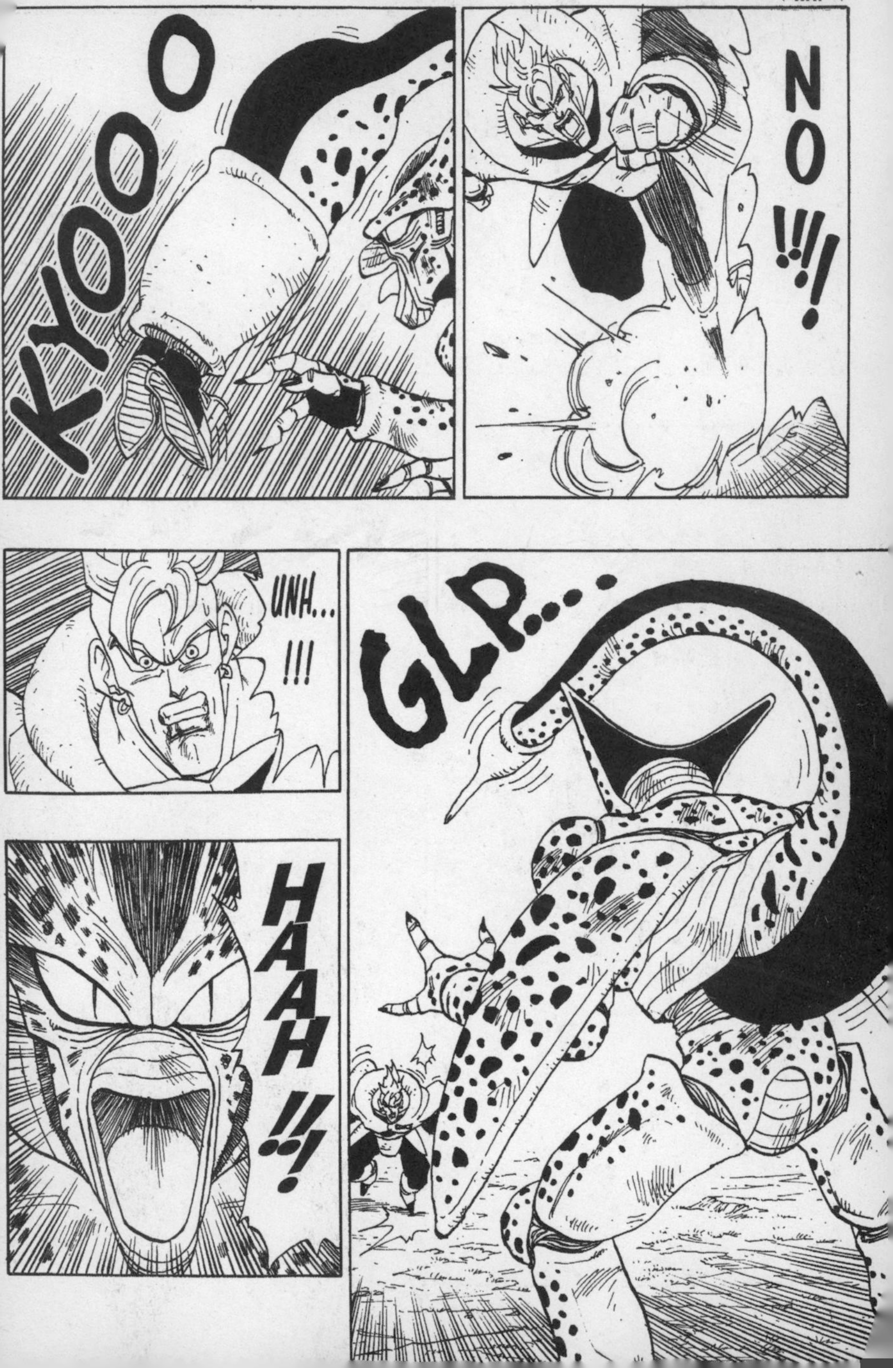

NO!!!!
KYOOO
GLP...
UNH... !!!
HAAH!!!

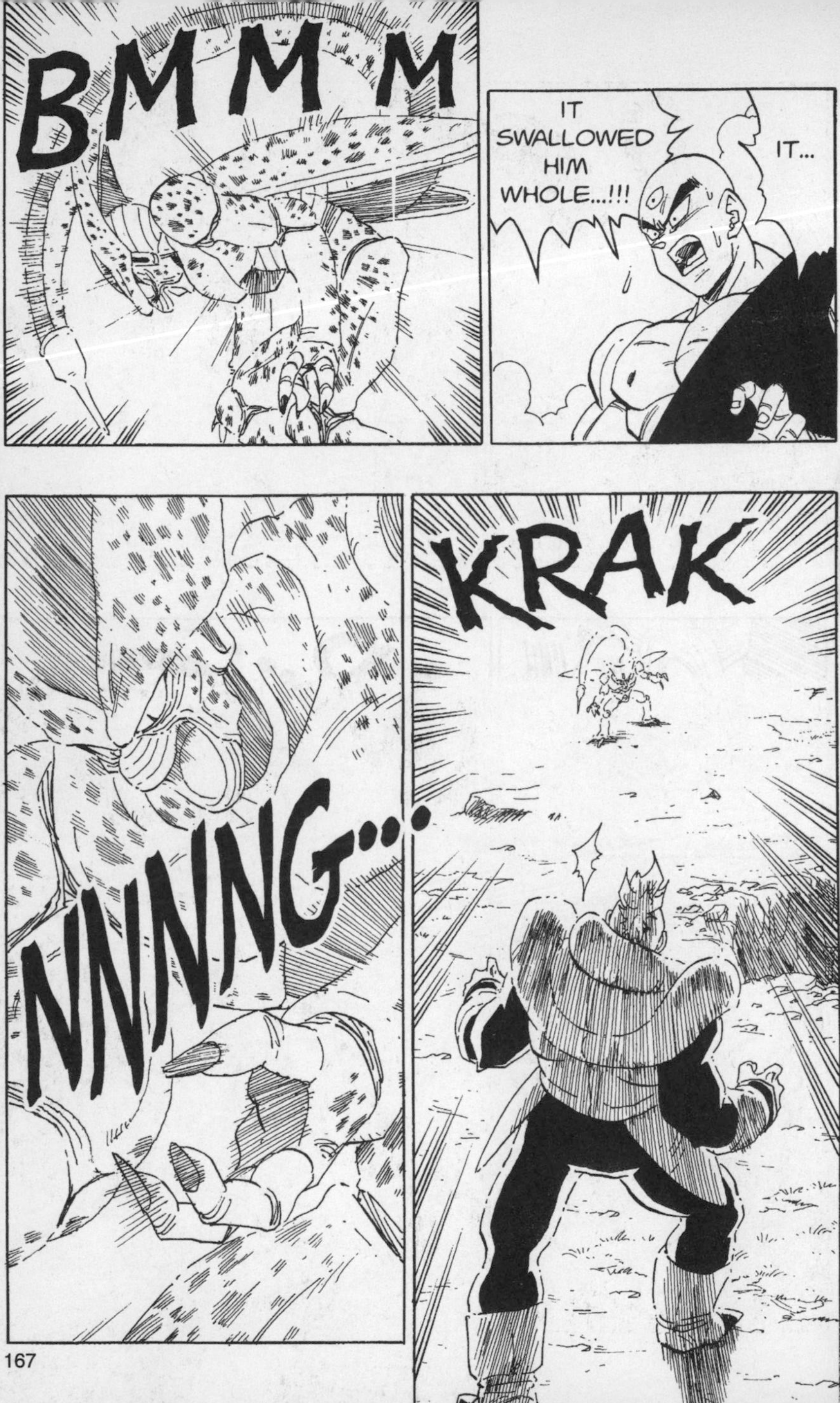
IT...
IT SWALLOWED HIM WHOLE...!!!
BMMM M
KRAK
NNNNG...

READ THIS WAY

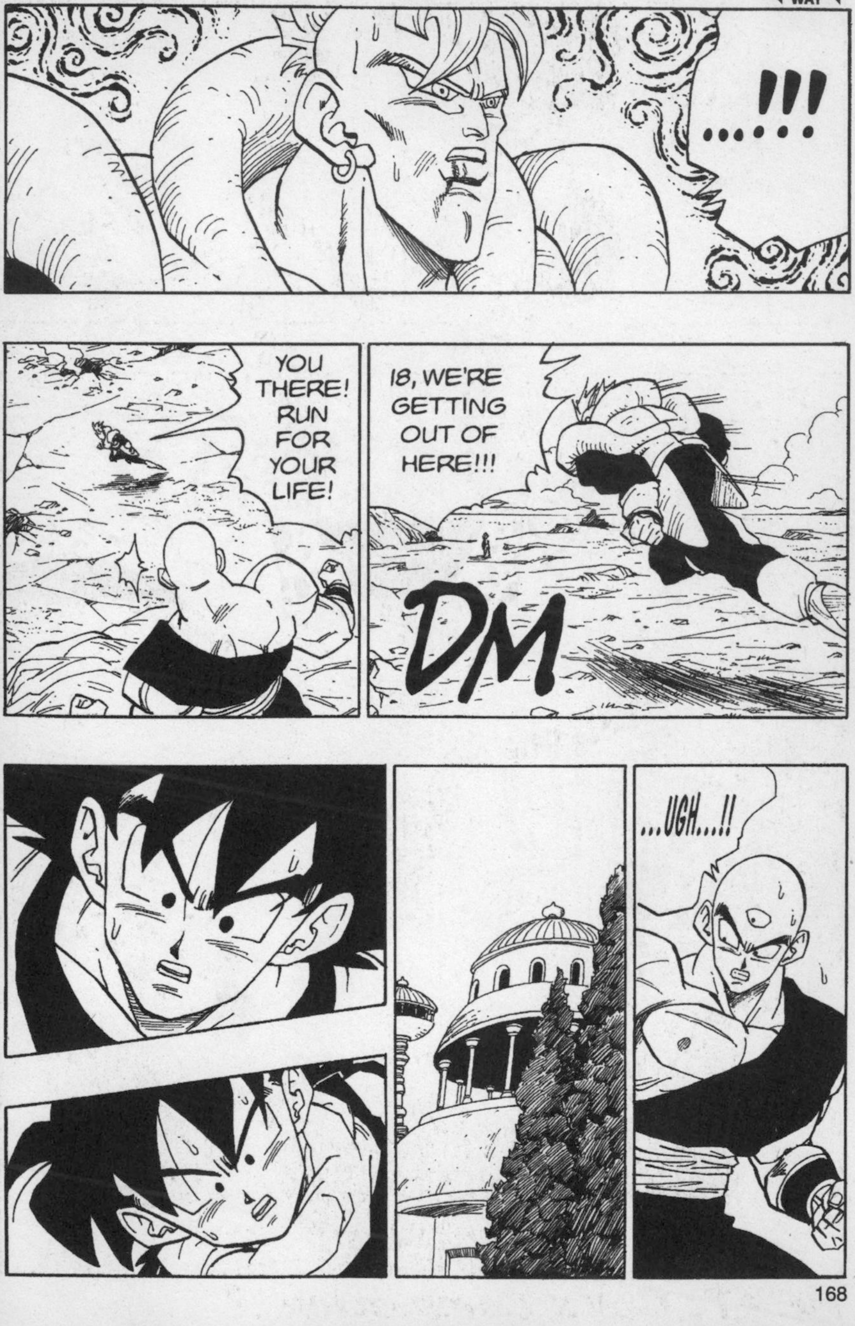
.....!!!
18, WE'RE GETTING OUT OF HERE!!!
DM
YOU THERE! RUN FOR YOUR LIFE!
...UGH...!!

READ THIS WAY

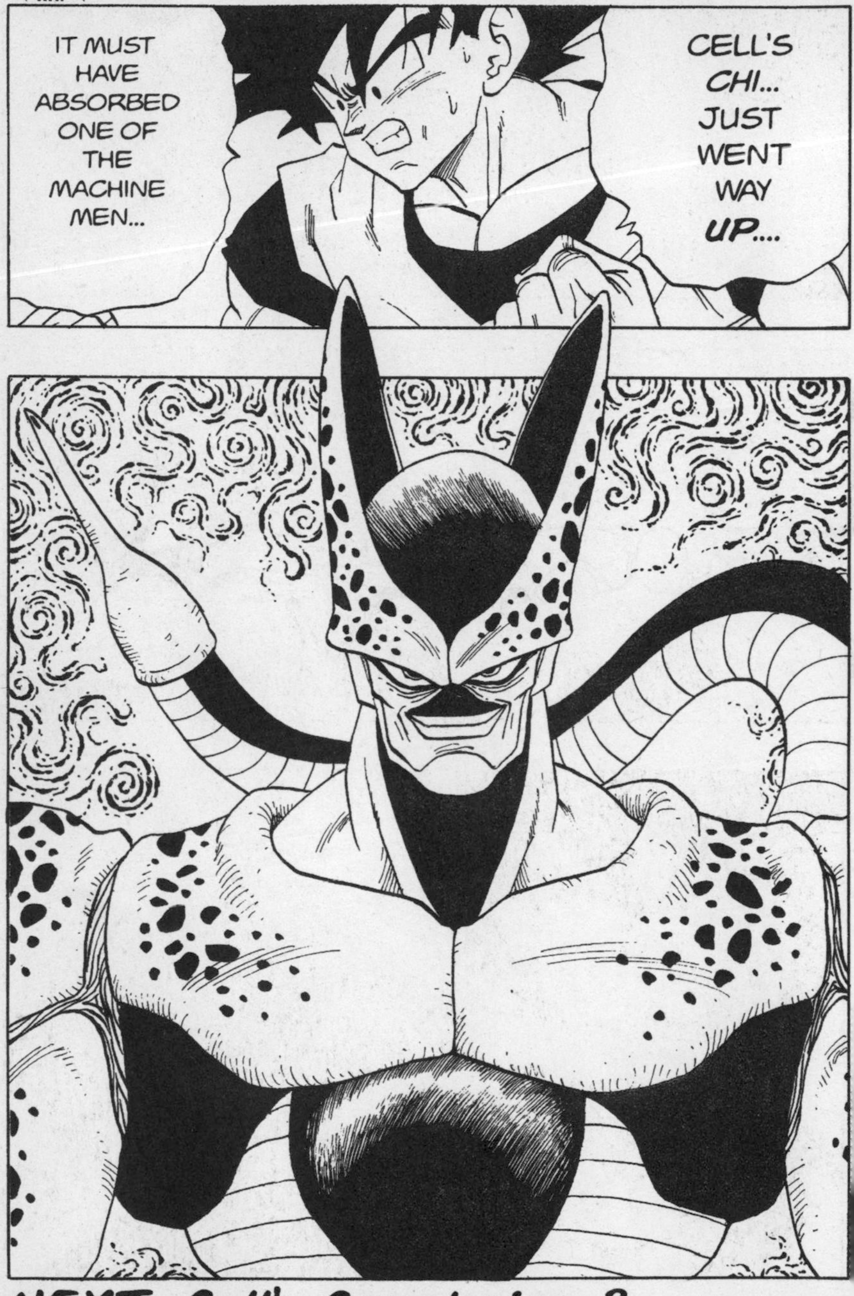
CELL'S CHI... JUST WENT WAY *UP*....
IT MUST HAVE ABSORBED ONE OF THE MACHINE MEN...

NEXT: Cell's Completion...?

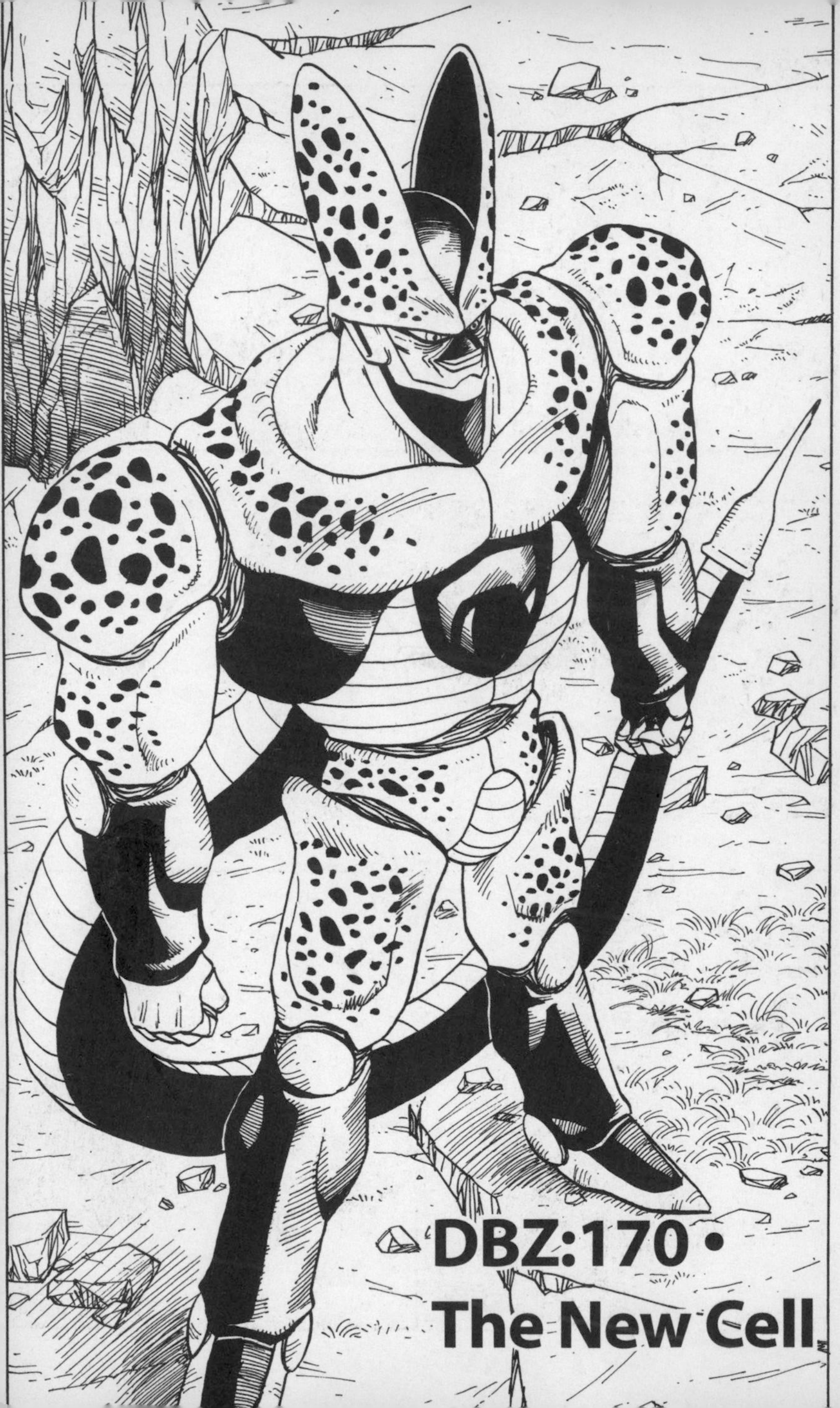

DBZ:170 • The New Cell

READ THIS WAY

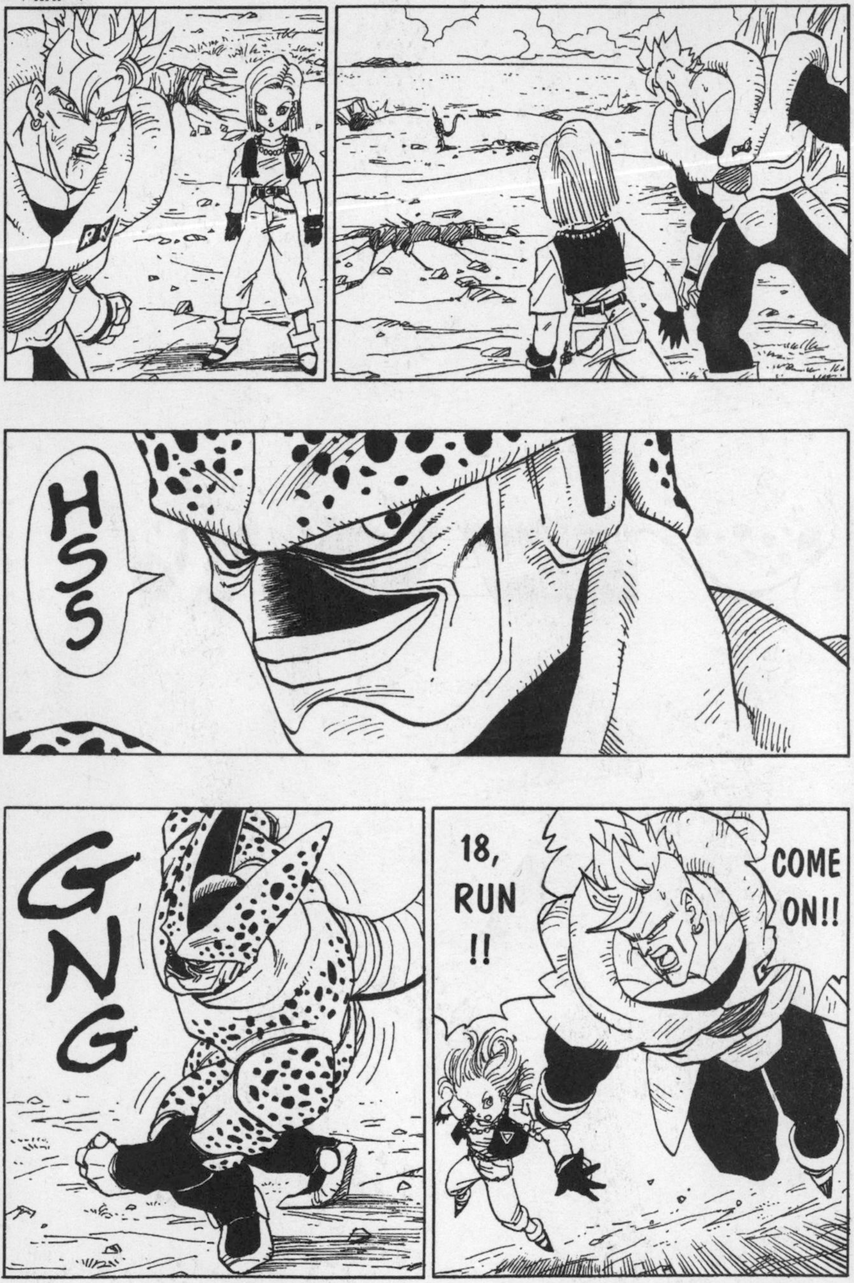
HSS
COME ON!!
18, RUN!!
GNG

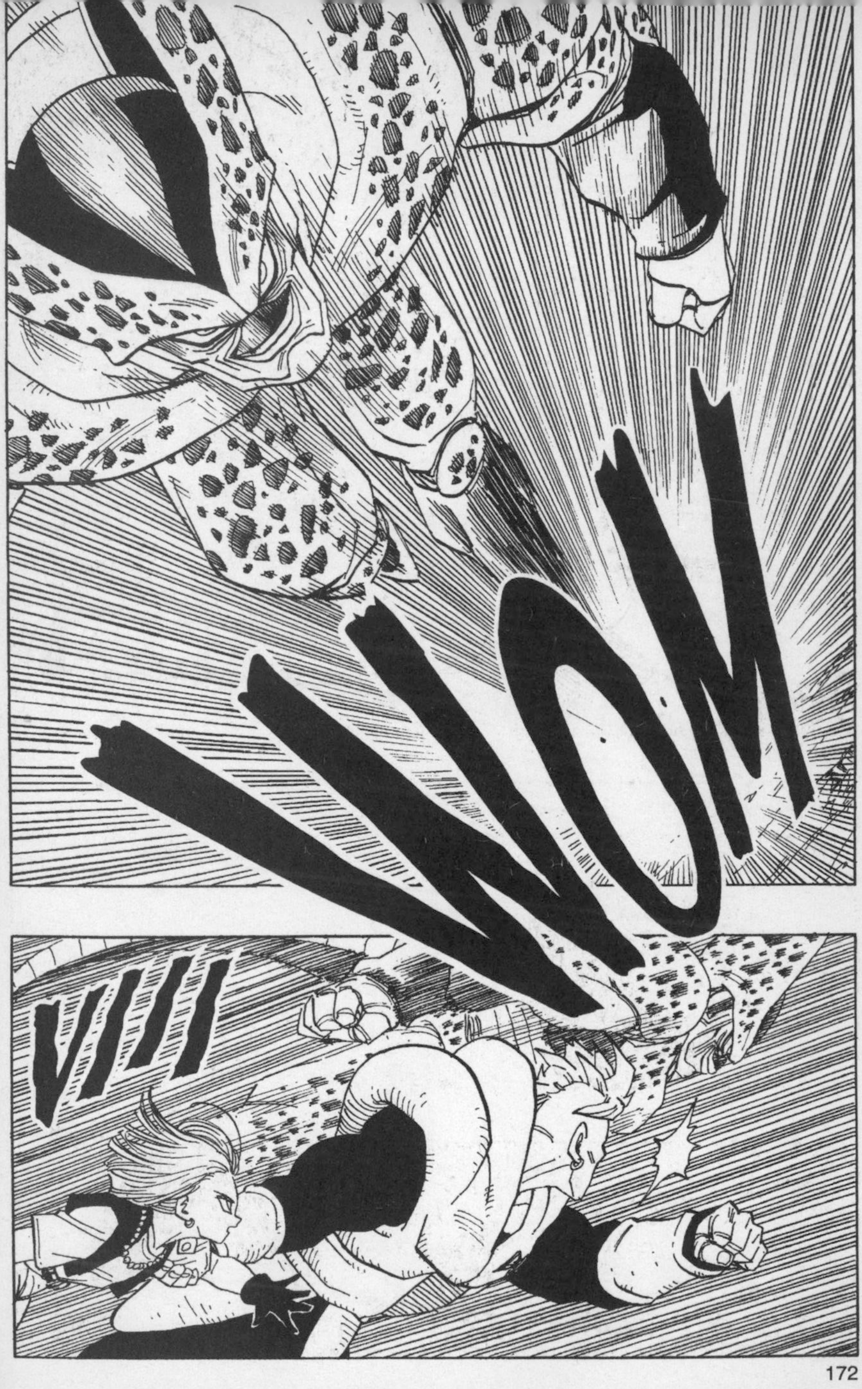
VOOM

READ THIS WAY

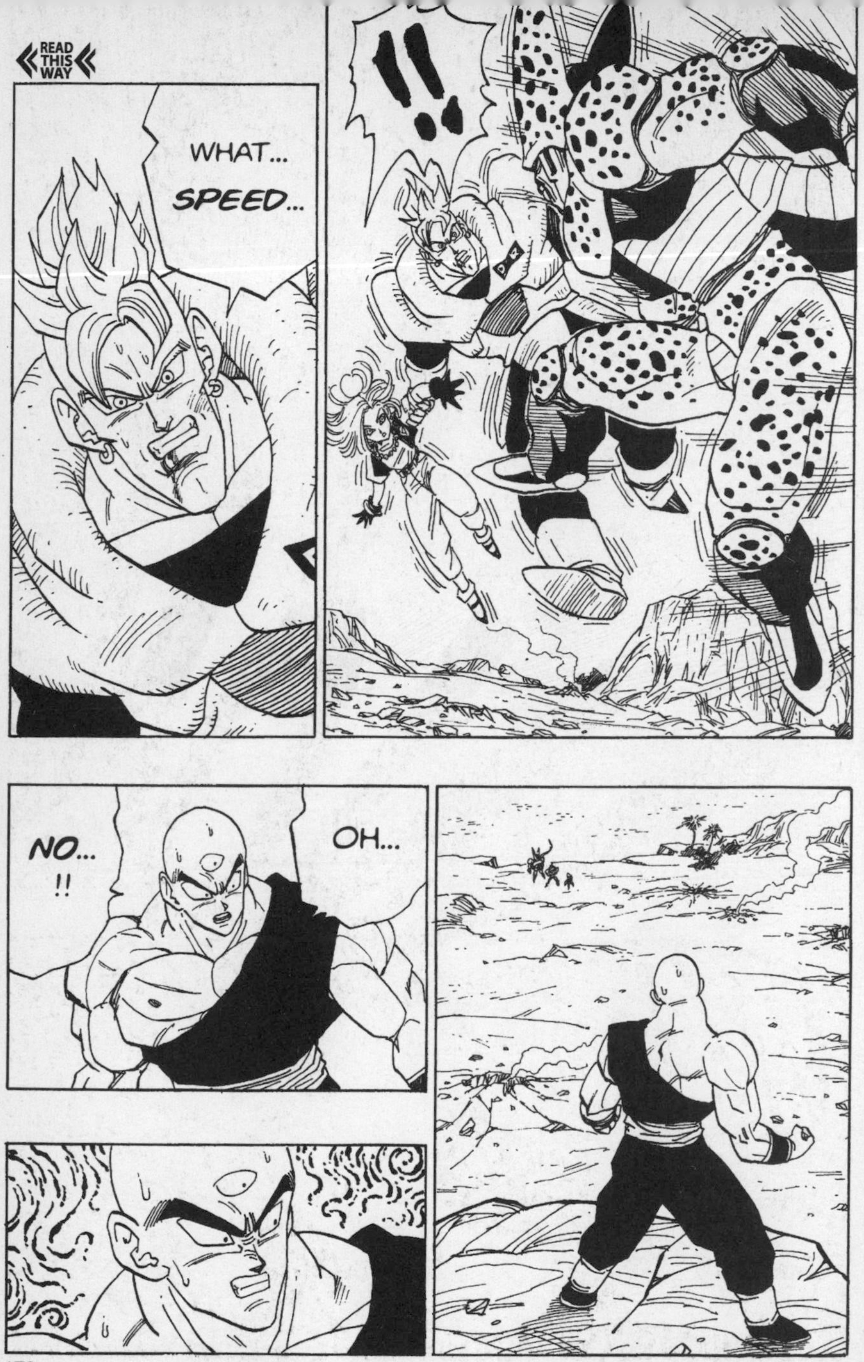
!!
WHAT...
SPEED...
OH...
NO...
!!

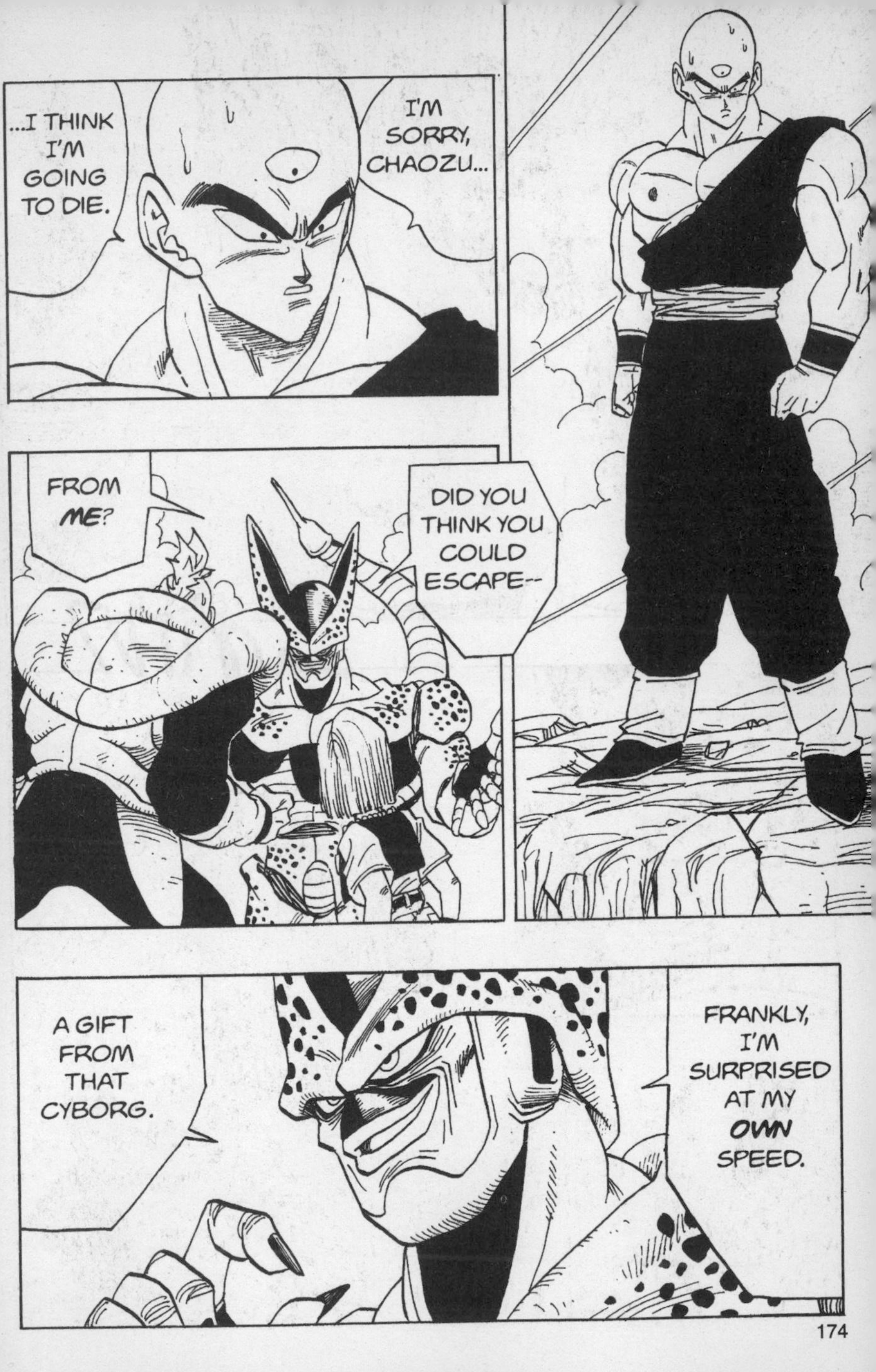
I'M SORRY, CHAOZU...
...I THINK I'M GOING TO DIE.
DID YOU THINK YOU COULD ESCAPE--
FROM *ME*?
FRANKLY, I'M SURPRISED AT MY *OWN* SPEED.
A GIFT FROM THAT CYBORG.

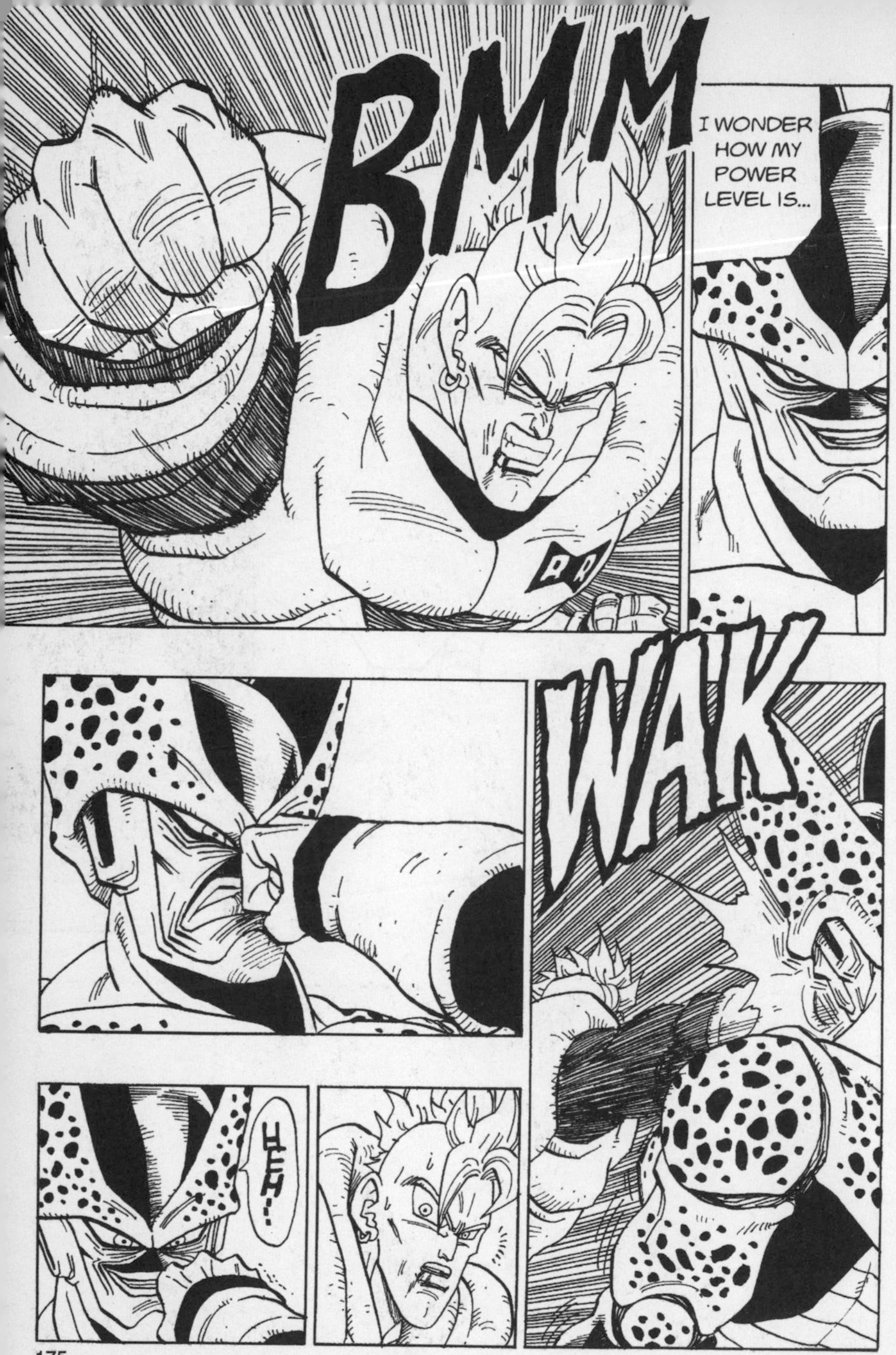
I WONDER HOW MY POWER LEVEL IS...
BMM
WAK
HEH!!

READ THIS WAY

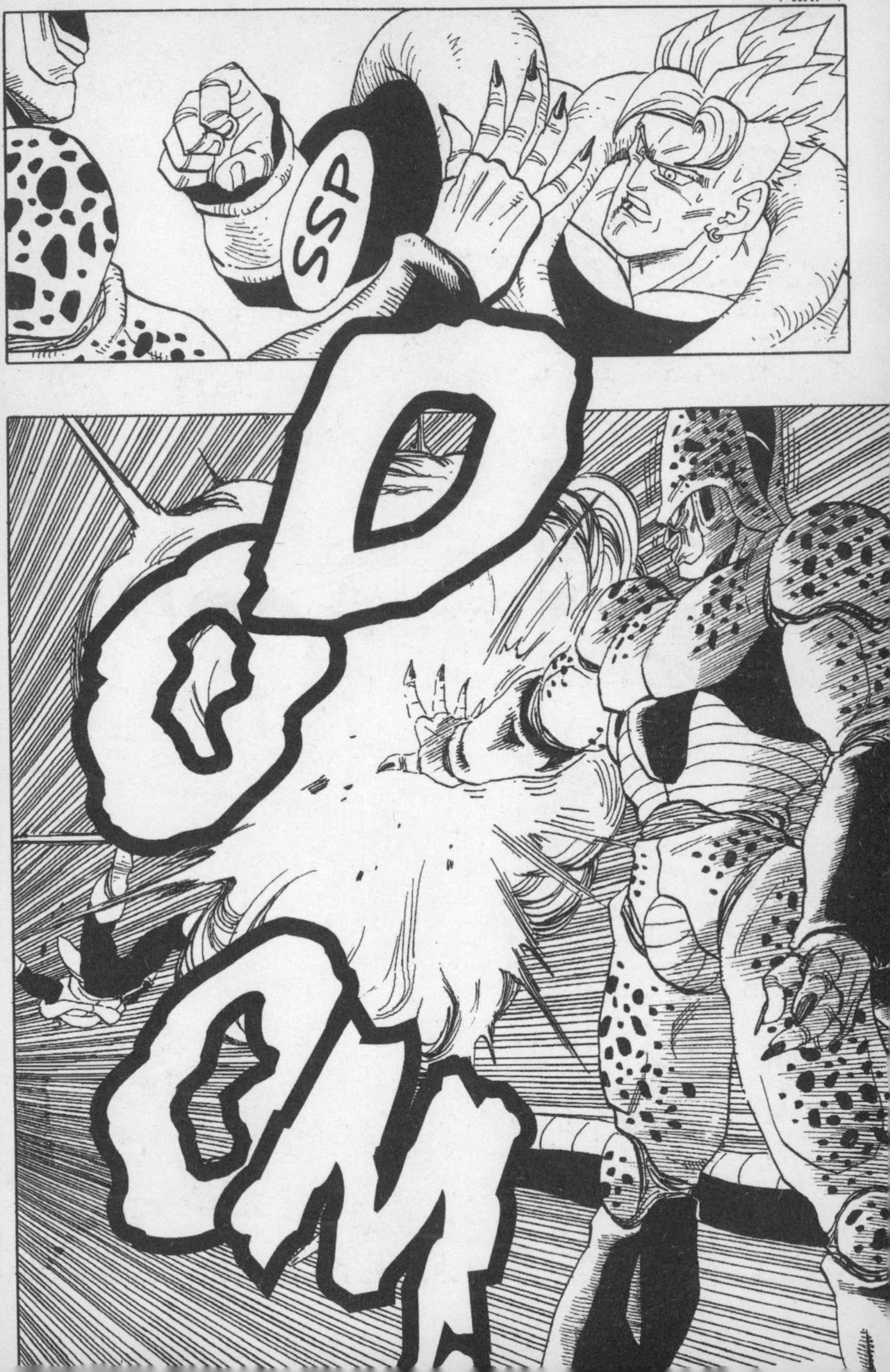
SSP

READ THIS WAY

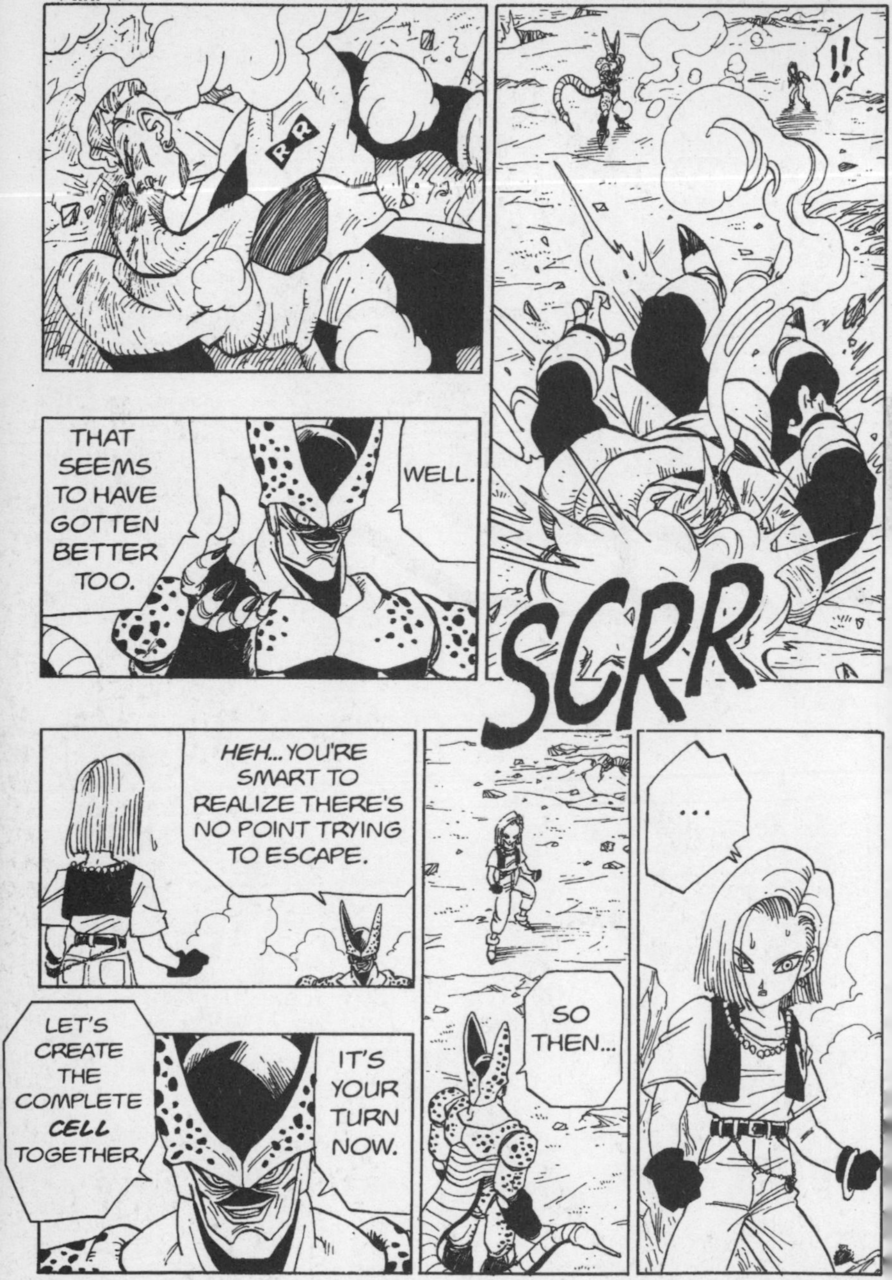
!!
SCRR
WELL.
THAT SEEMS TO HAVE GOTTEN BETTER TOO.
...
SO THEN...
HEH... YOU'RE SMART TO REALIZE THERE'S NO POINT TRYING TO ESCAPE.
IT'S YOUR TURN NOW.
LET'S CREATE THE COMPLETE CELL TOGETHER.

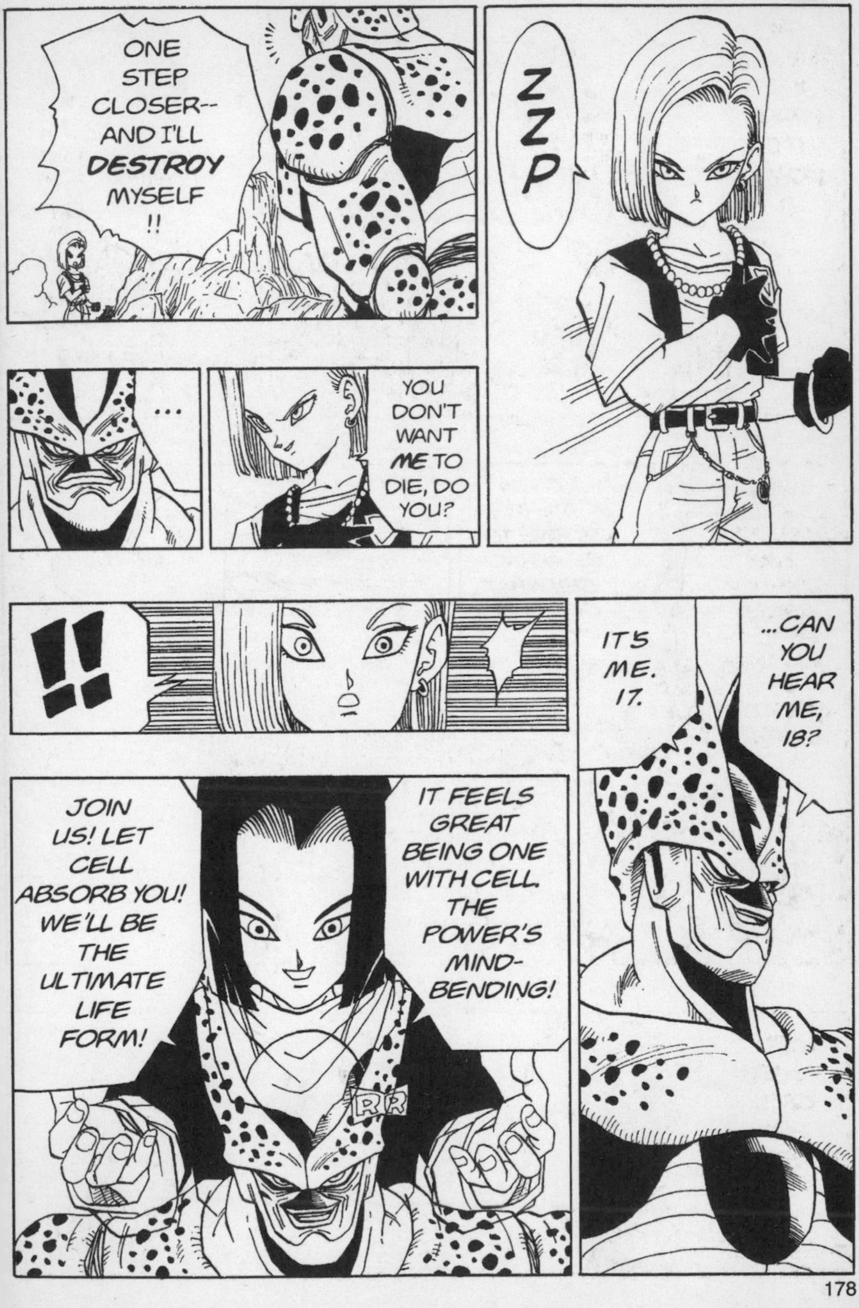
ZZP
ONE STEP CLOSER-- AND I'LL **DESTROY** MYSELF !!
YOU DON'T WANT **ME** TO DIE, DO YOU?
...
...CAN YOU HEAR ME, 18?
IT'S ME. 17.
!!
IT FEELS GREAT BEING ONE WITH CELL. THE POWER'S MIND-BENDING!
JOIN US! LET CELL ABSORB YOU! WE'LL BE THE ULTIMATE LIFE FORM!

READ THIS WAY

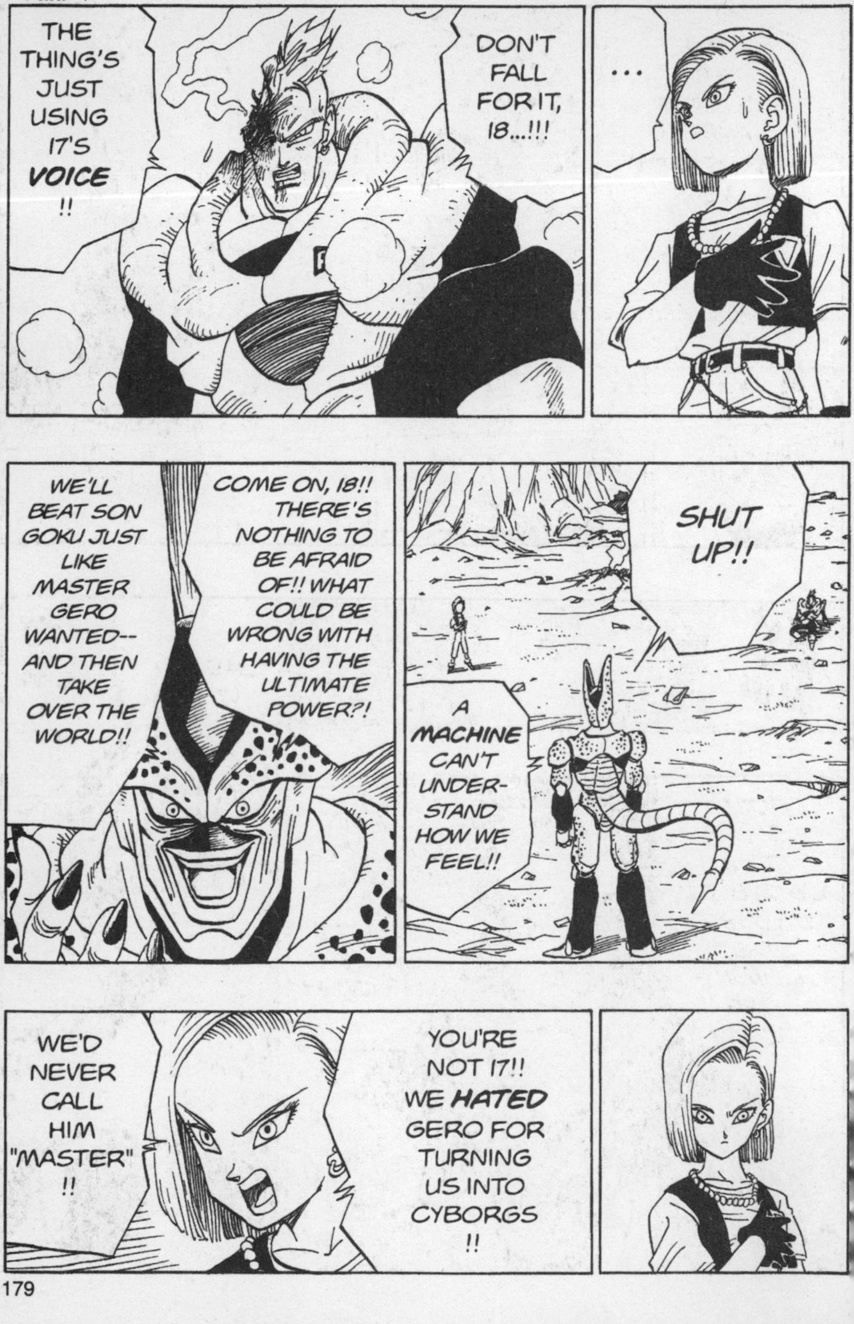
...
DON'T FALL FOR IT, 18...!!!
THE THING'S JUST USING 17'S **VOICE** !!
SHUT UP!!
A **MACHINE** CAN'T UNDERSTAND HOW WE FEEL!!
COME ON, 18!! THERE'S NOTHING TO BE AFRAID OF!! WHAT COULD BE WRONG WITH HAVING THE ULTIMATE POWER?!
WE'LL BEAT SON GOKU JUST LIKE MASTER GERO WANTED-- AND THEN TAKE OVER THE WORLD!!
YOU'RE NOT 17!! WE **HATED** GERO FOR TURNING US INTO CYBORGS !!
WE'D NEVER CALL HIM "MASTER" !!

READ THIS WAY

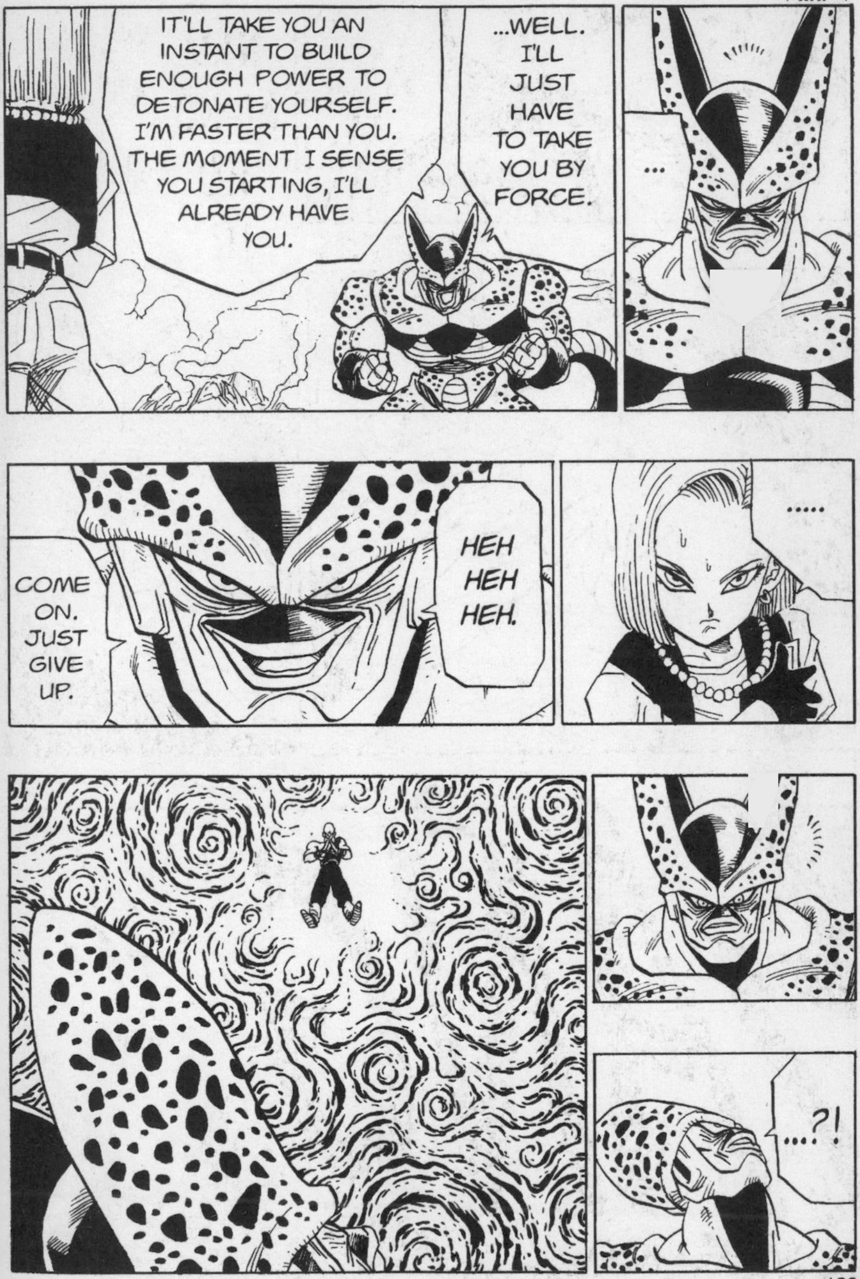

...
...WELL. I'LL JUST HAVE TO TAKE YOU BY FORCE.
IT'LL TAKE YOU AN INSTANT TO BUILD ENOUGH POWER TO DETONATE YOURSELF. I'M FASTER THAN YOU. THE MOMENT I SENSE YOU STARTING, I'LL ALREADY HAVE YOU.
.....
HEH HEH HEH.
COME ON. JUST GIVE UP.
...?!

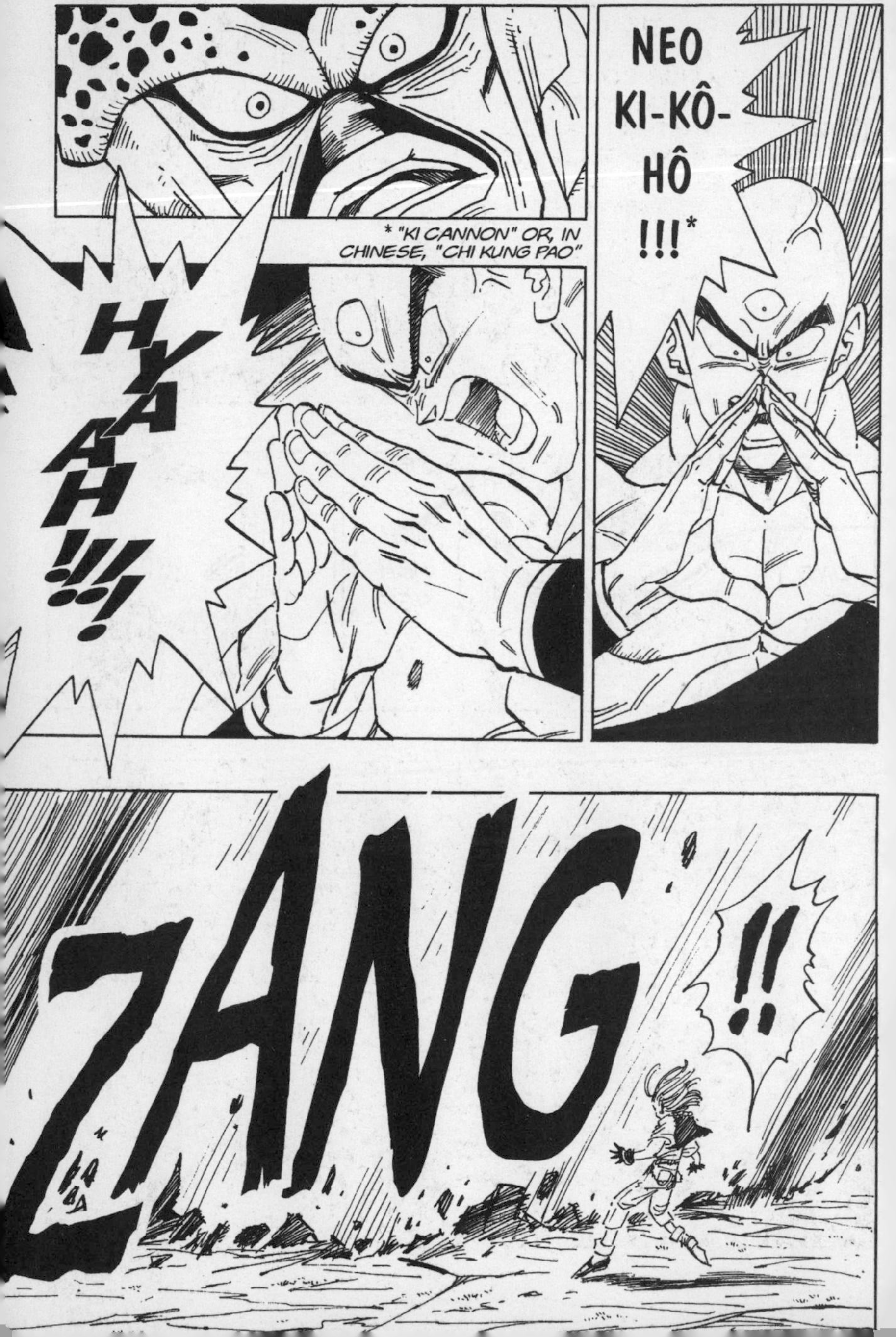
READ THIS WAY
NEO KI-KÔ-HÔ !!!*
* "KI CANNON" OR, IN CHINESE, "CHI KUNG PAO"
HYAAH!!!!
ZANG!!

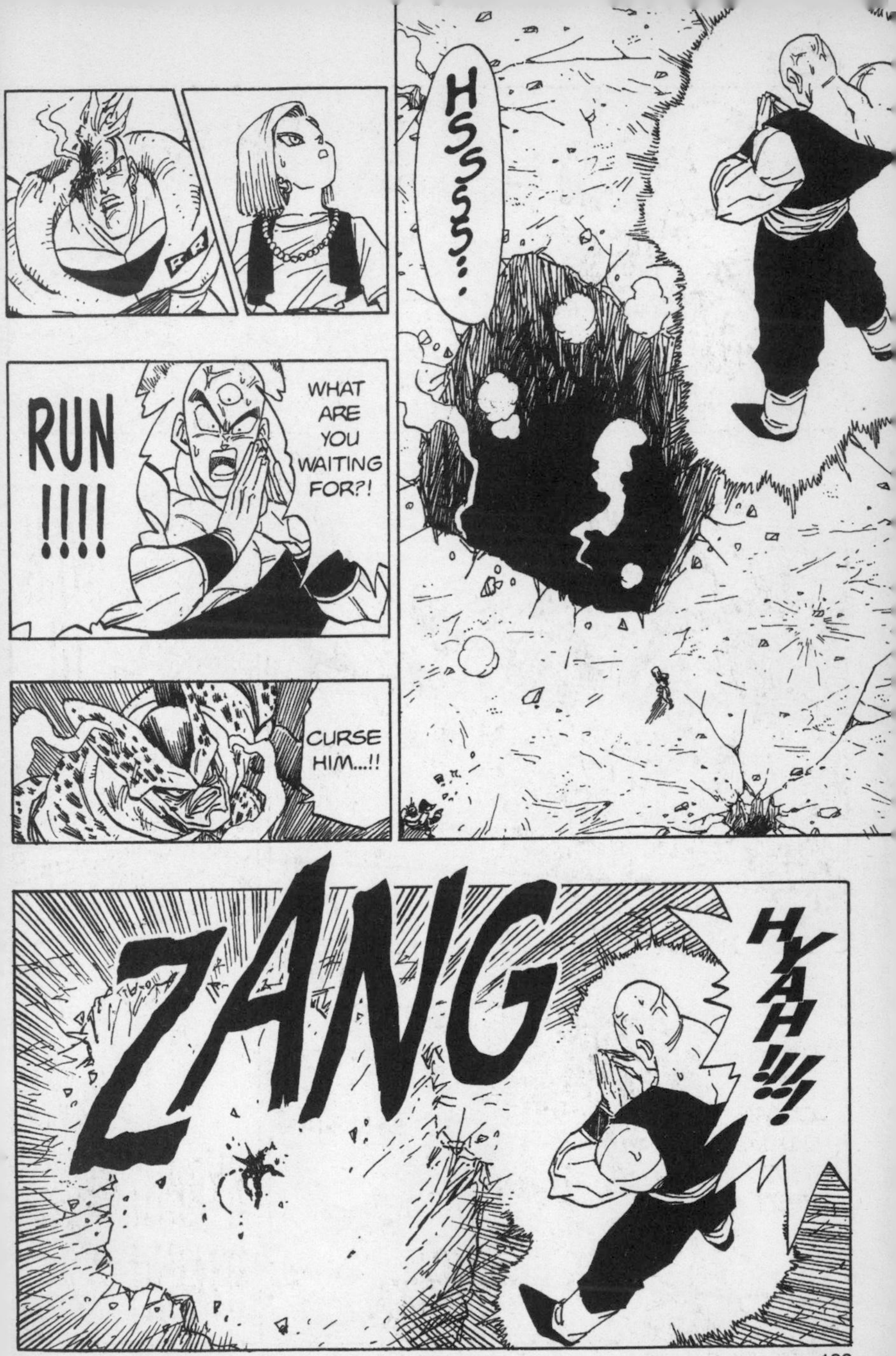
HSSSS...
WHAT ARE YOU WAITING FOR?!
RUN!!!!!
CURSE HIM...!!
HYAH!!!
ZANG

READ THIS WAY

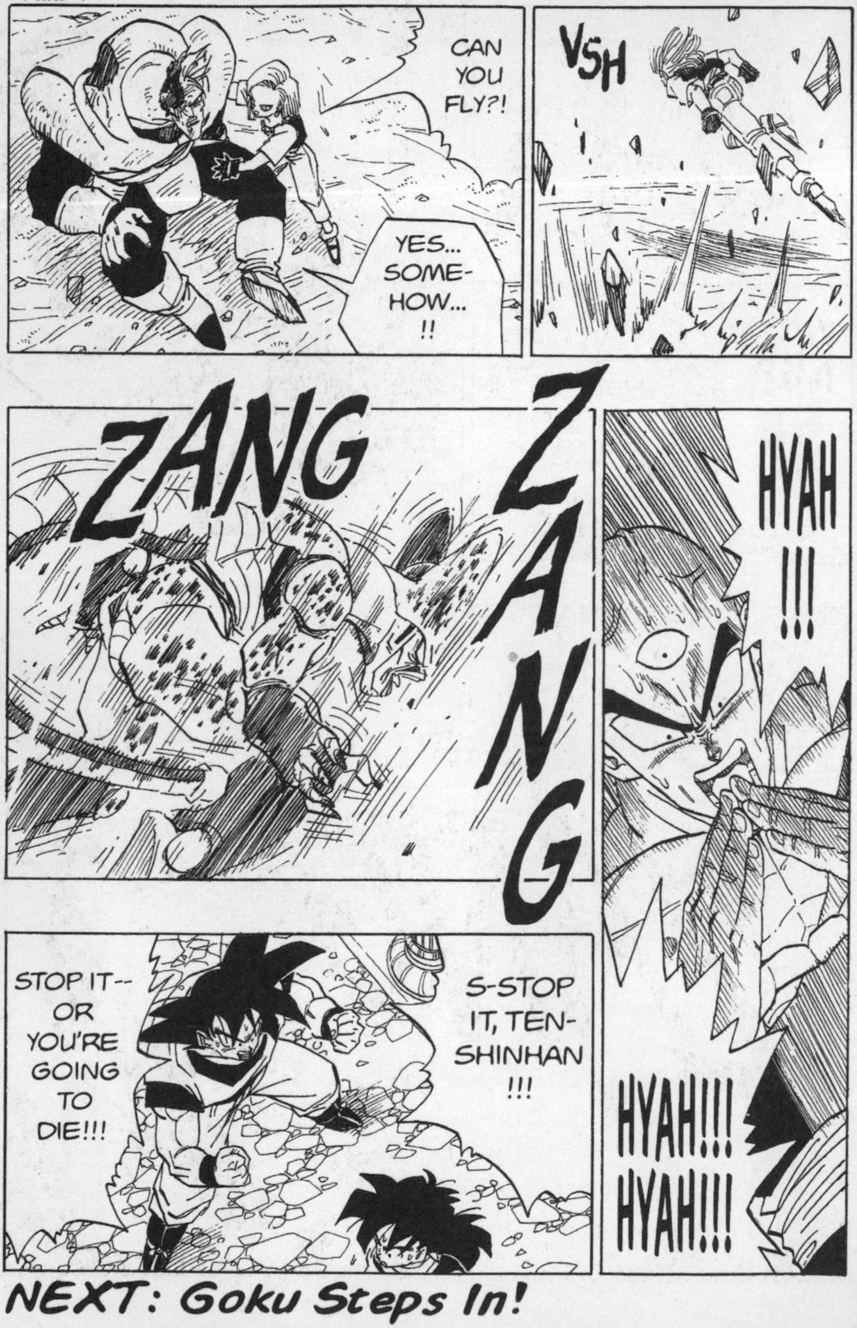
VSH
CAN YOU FLY?!
YES... SOME-HOW... !!
HYAH !!!
HYAH!!! HYAH!!!
ZANG
ZANG
S-STOP IT, TEN-SHINHAN !!!
STOP IT-- OR YOU'RE GOING TO DIE!!!

NEXT: Goku Steps In!

TITLE PAGE GALLERY

DBZ:165
Kami-sama's Vision

WH-WHAT KIND OF MONSTER IS THIS?

These title pages were used when these chapters of **Dragon Ball Z** were originally published in Japan in 1992 in **Weekly Shonen Jump** magazine.

DRAGON BALL

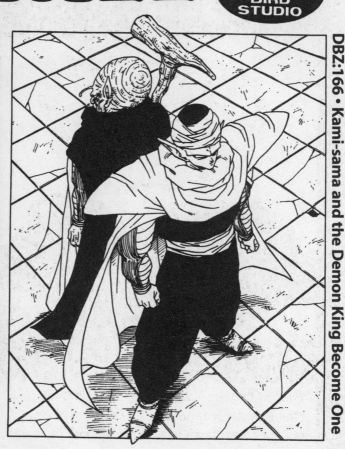

とりやまあきら 鳥山明 BIRD STUDIO

DBZ:166 • Kami-sama and the Demon King Become One

FACING A MONSTER, NOW IS THE TIME TO UNITE!

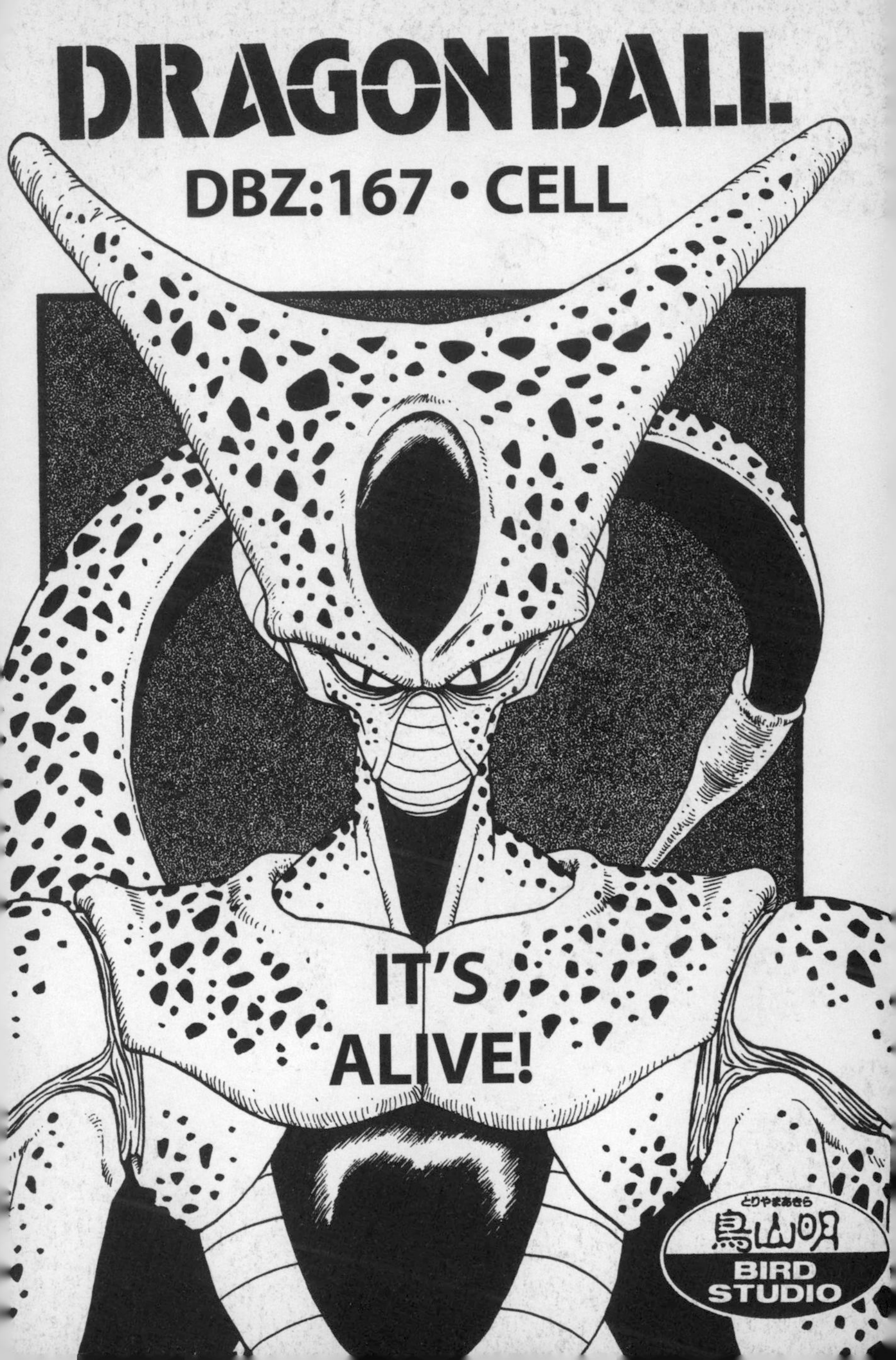
DRAGON BALL
DBZ:167 • CELL
IT'S ALIVE!
とりやまあきら
鳥山明
BIRD STUDIO

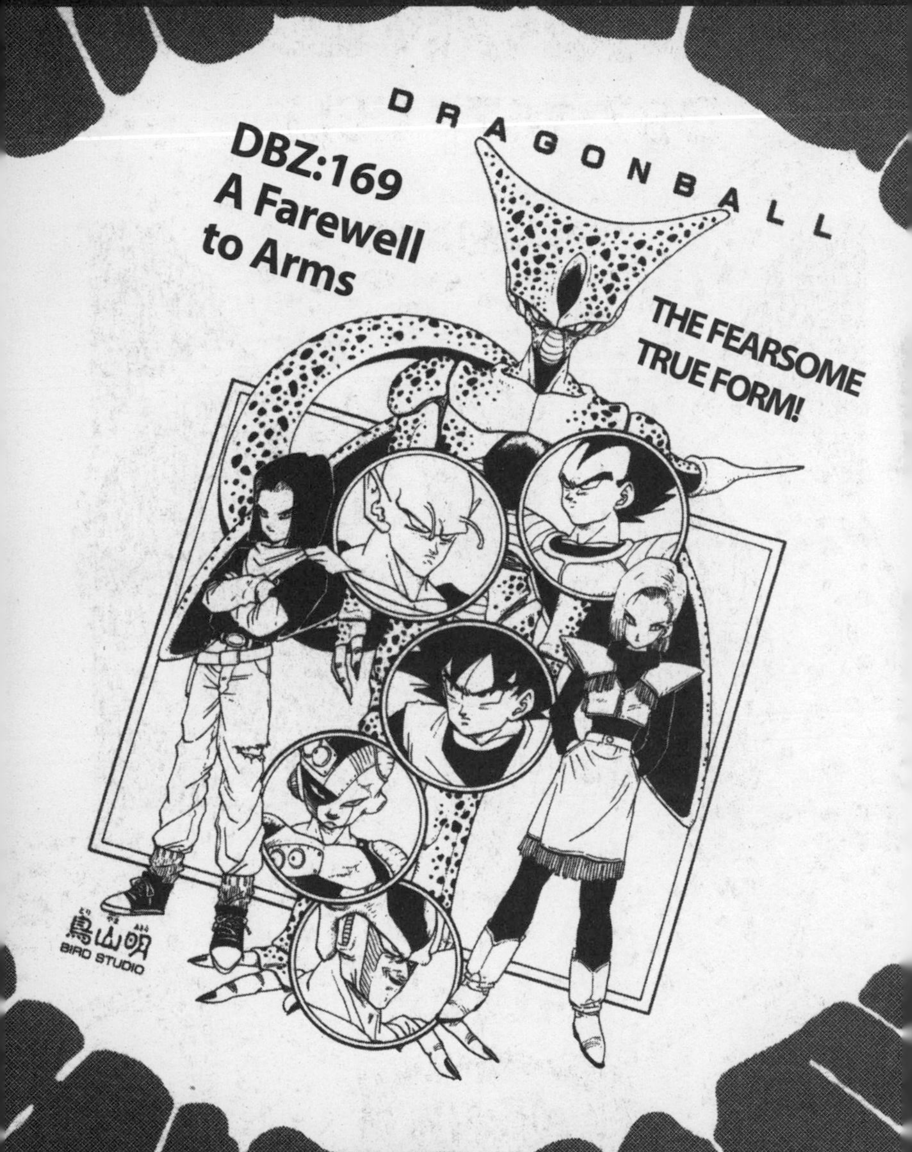
DRAGONBALL
DBZ:169
A Farewell to Arms
THE FEARSOME TRUE FORM!
鳥山明
BIRD STUDIO

DRAGON BALL

DBZ:170
CELL LAUGHS LAST

とりやまあきら
鳥山明
BIRD STUDIO

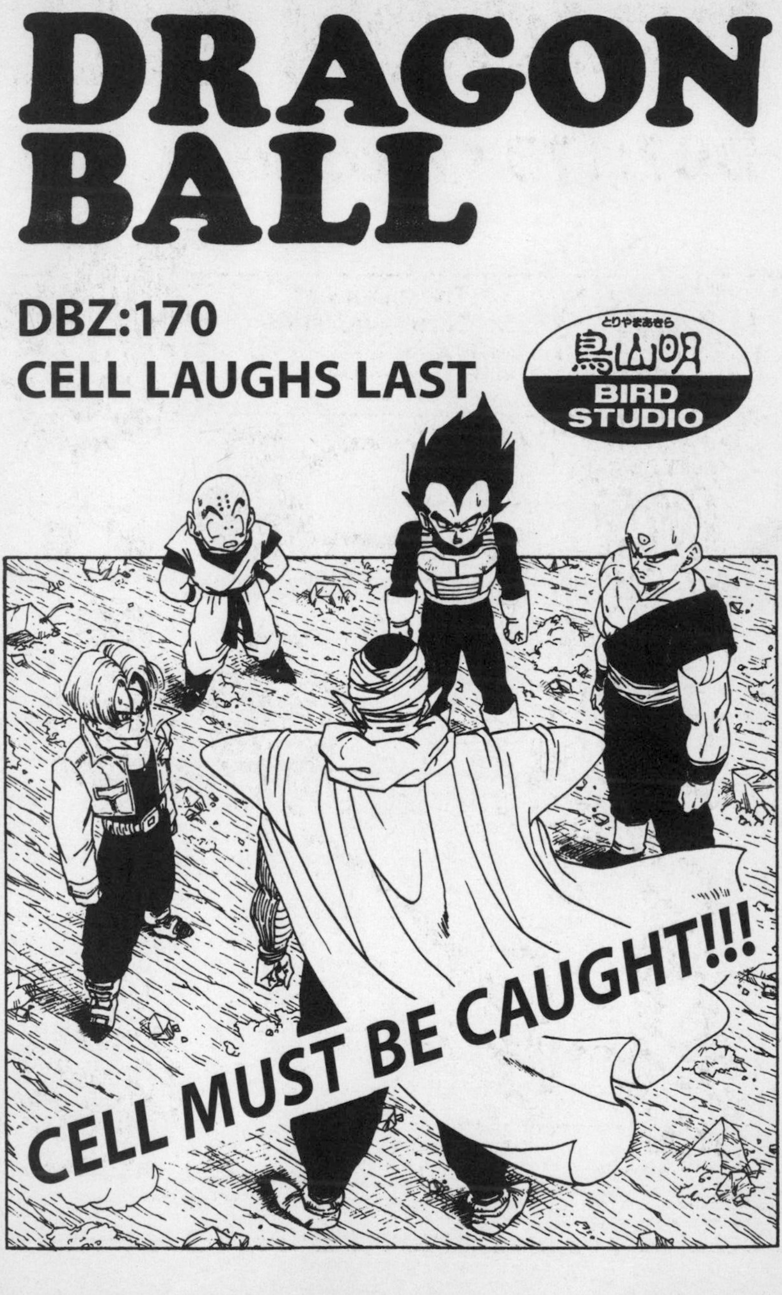
CELL MUST BE CAUGHT!!!

DRAGON BALL

DBZ:173 • Piccolo vs. #17

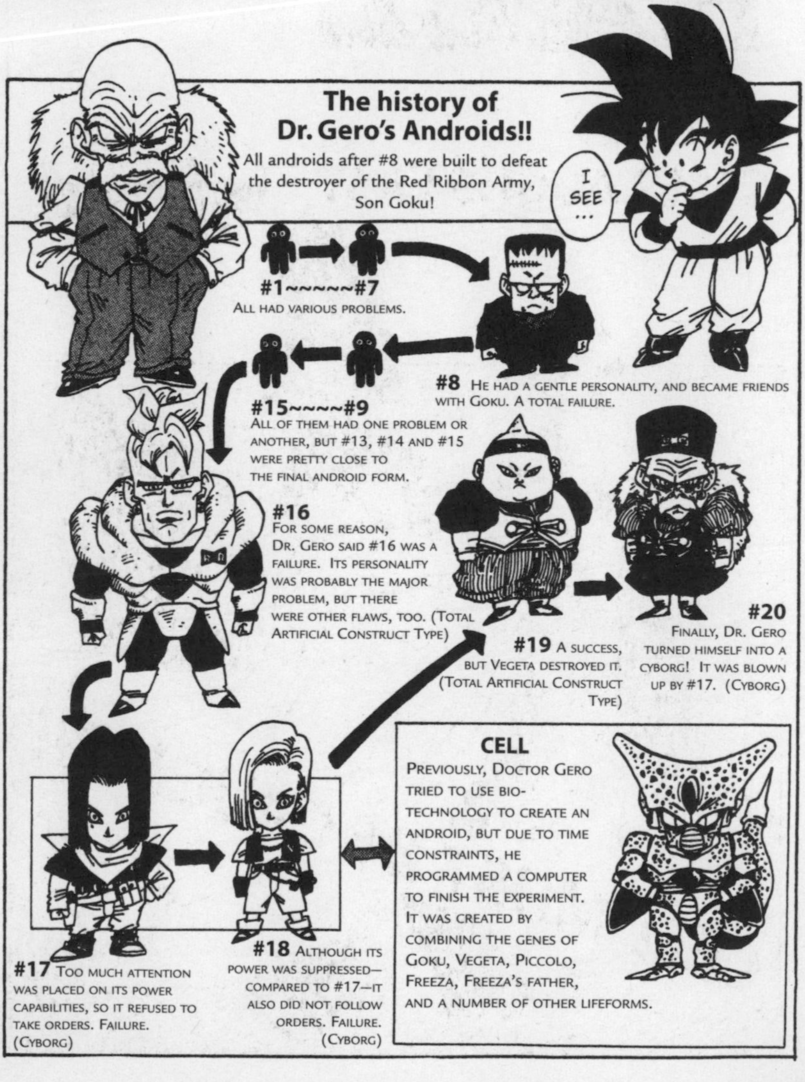

The history of
Dr. Gero's Androids!!
All androids after #8 were built to defeat the destroyer of the Red Ribbon Army, Son Goku!
I SEE ...
#1~~~~~#7
ALL HAD VARIOUS PROBLEMS.
#8 HE HAD A GENTLE PERSONALITY, AND BECAME FRIENDS WITH GOKU. A TOTAL FAILURE.
#15~~~~#9
ALL OF THEM HAD ONE PROBLEM OR ANOTHER, BUT #13, #14 AND #15 WERE PRETTY CLOSE TO THE FINAL ANDROID FORM.
#16
FOR SOME REASON, DR. GERO SAID #16 WAS A FAILURE. ITS PERSONALITY WAS PROBABLY THE MAJOR PROBLEM, BUT THERE WERE OTHER FLAWS, TOO. (TOTAL ARTIFICIAL CONSTRUCT TYPE)
#19 A SUCCESS, BUT VEGETA DESTROYED IT. (TOTAL ARTIFICIAL CONSTRUCT TYPE)
#20
FINALLY, DR. GERO TURNED HIMSELF INTO A CYBORG! IT WAS BLOWN UP BY #17. (CYBORG)
#17 TOO MUCH ATTENTION WAS PLACED ON ITS POWER CAPABILITIES, SO IT REFUSED TO TAKE ORDERS. FAILURE. (CYBORG)
#18 ALTHOUGH ITS POWER WAS SUPPRESSED—COMPARED TO #17—IT ALSO DID NOT FOLLOW ORDERS. FAILURE. (CYBORG)
CELL
PREVIOUSLY, DOCTOR GERO TRIED TO USE BIO-TECHNOLOGY TO CREATE AN ANDROID, BUT DUE TO TIME CONSTRAINTS, HE PROGRAMMED A COMPUTER TO FINISH THE EXPERIMENT. IT WAS CREATED BY COMBINING THE GENES OF GOKU, VEGETA, PICCOLO, FREEZA, FREEZA'S FATHER, AND A NUMBER OF OTHER LIFEFORMS.

DRAGON BALL

とりやまあきら
鳥山明
BIRD STUDIO

DBZ:173 • PICCOLO VS. #17

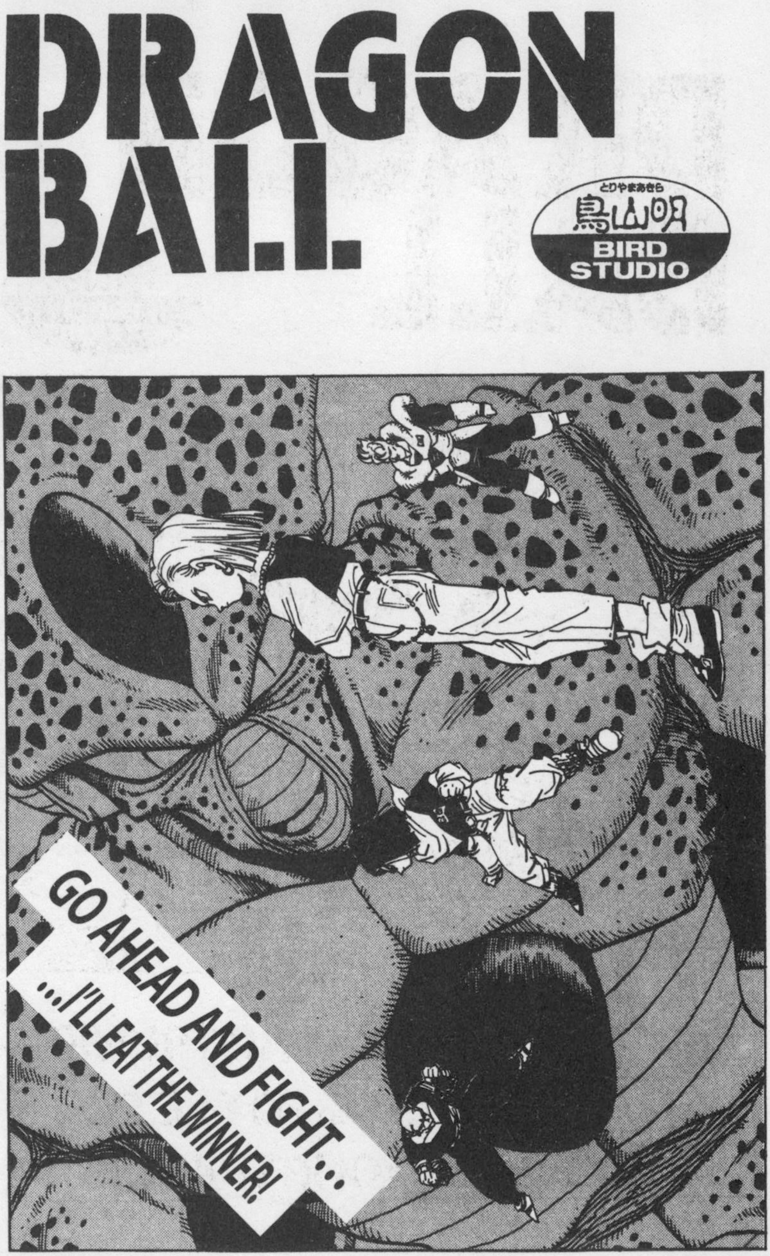
GO AHEAD AND FIGHT...
...I'LL EAT THE WINNER!

DRAGON BALL

とりやまあきら
鳥山明
BIRD STUDIO

DBZ:175 • Cell vs. the Androids

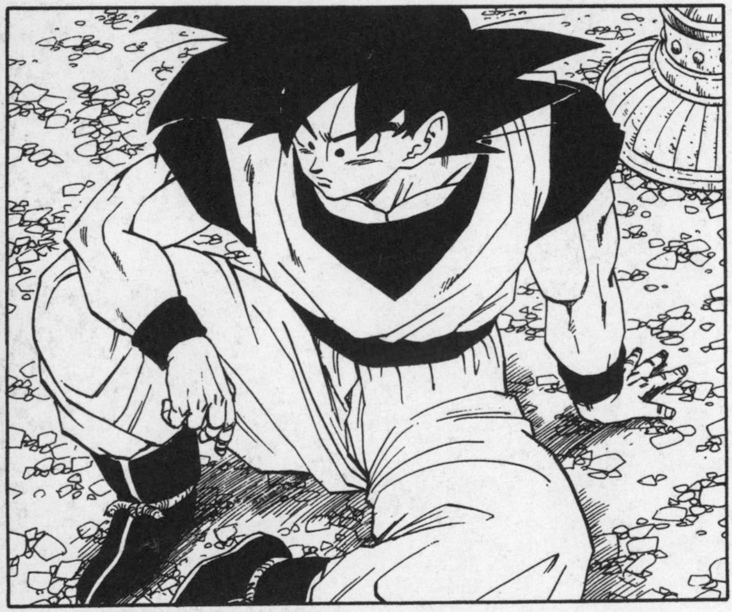

COME ON, VEGETA AND TRUNKS—
WE'RE WAITING TO SEE THE
RESULTS OF YOUR TRAINING!

DRAGON BALL

DBZ:178 • #16
Summons His Power

I WILL PROTECT #17!

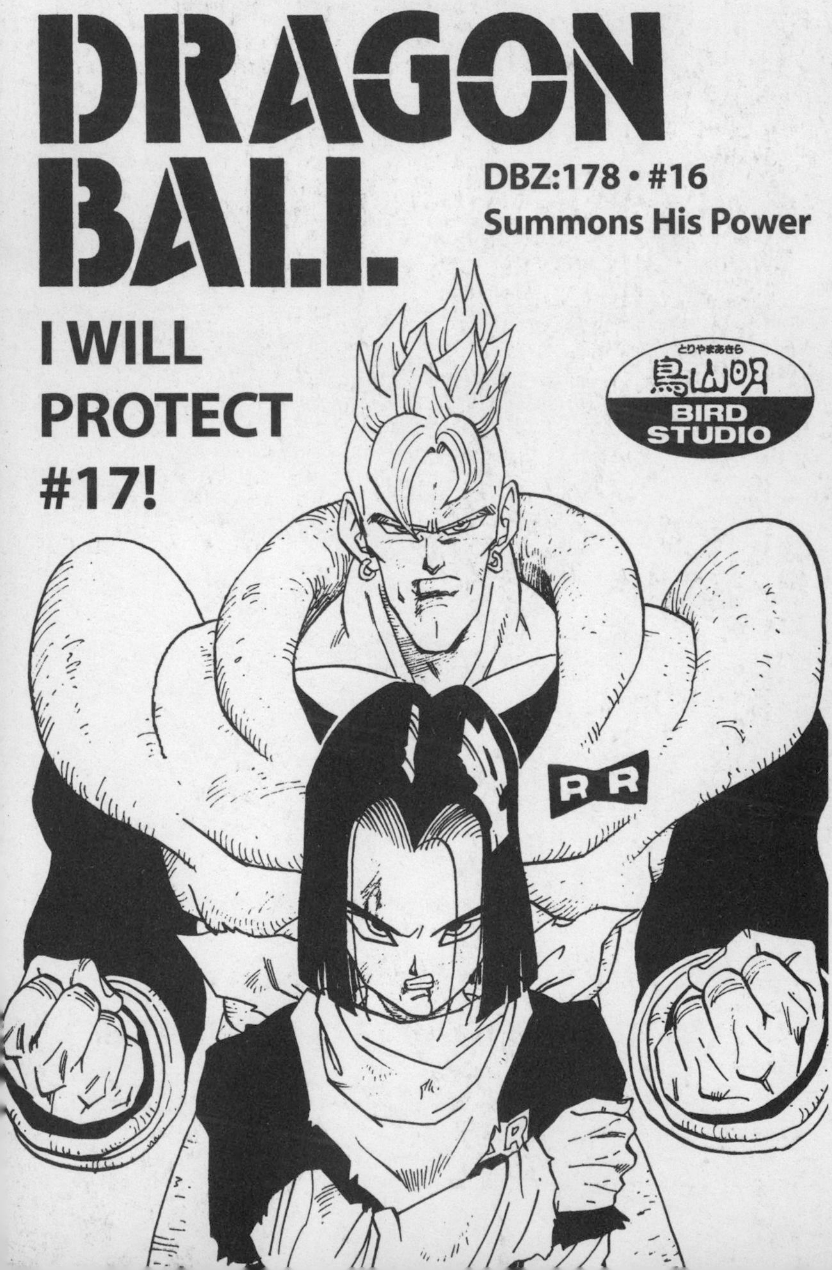

RR

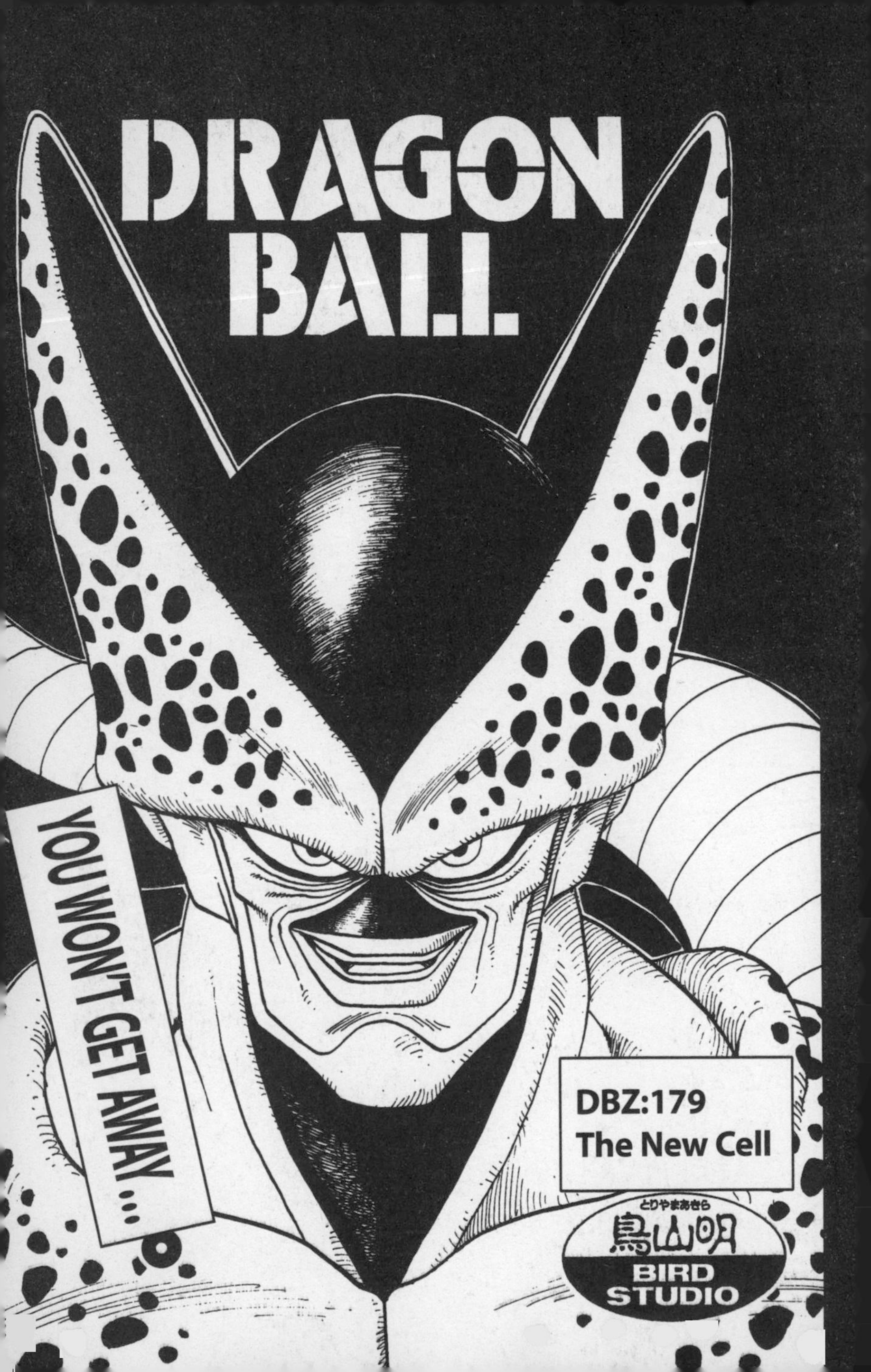
DRAGON BALL
DBZ:179
The New Cell
YOU WON'T GET AWAY...
とりやまあきら
鳥山明
BIRD STUDIO

IN THE NEXT VOLUME...

Cell has fused with android #17, becoming the strongest being in the universe—but how long can its reign of terror last? Training in the Room of Spirit and Time, where a year passes for every day outside, Vegeta and Trunks have gone *beyond* the Super Saiyan, reaching a level of power possibly even greater than second-stage Cell! Can Cell defeat a *Super*-Super Saiyan? Or will android #18 give Cell the key to become even more unimaginably powerful? The battle continues in **the next volume of Dragon Ball Z!**

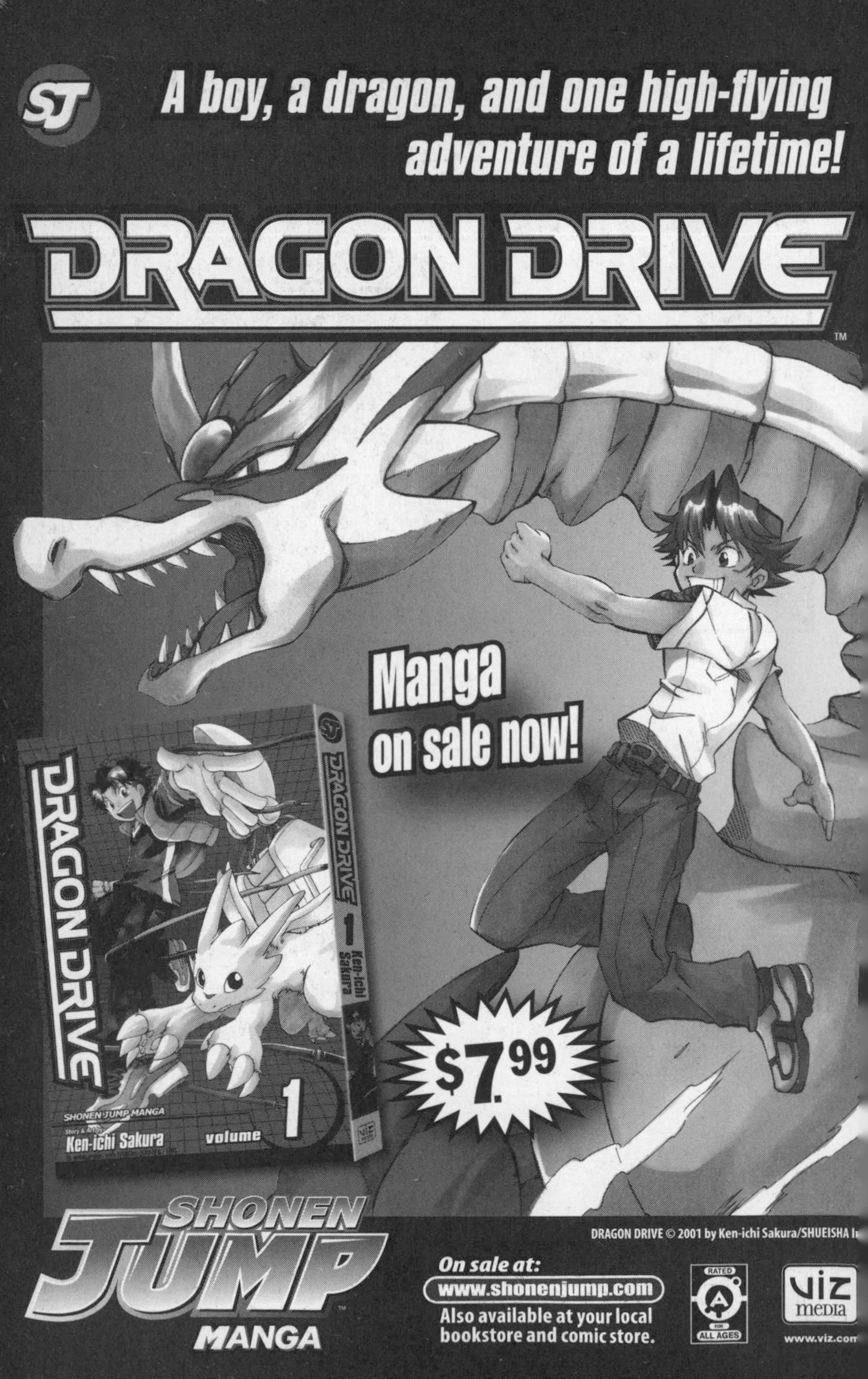
SJ
A boy, a dragon, and one high-flying adventure of a lifetime!
DRAGON DRIVE™
Manga on sale now!
DRAGON DRIVE
SHONEN JUMP MANGA
Story & Art by Ken-ichi Sakura
volume 1
SJ DRAGON DRIVE 1 Ken-ichi Sakura
$7.99
SHONEN JUMP™ MANGA
DRAGON DRIVE © 2001 by Ken-ichi Sakura/SHUEISHA I
On sale at:
www.shonenjump.com
Also available at your local bookstore and comic store.
RATED A FOR ALL AGES
viz media
www.viz.com

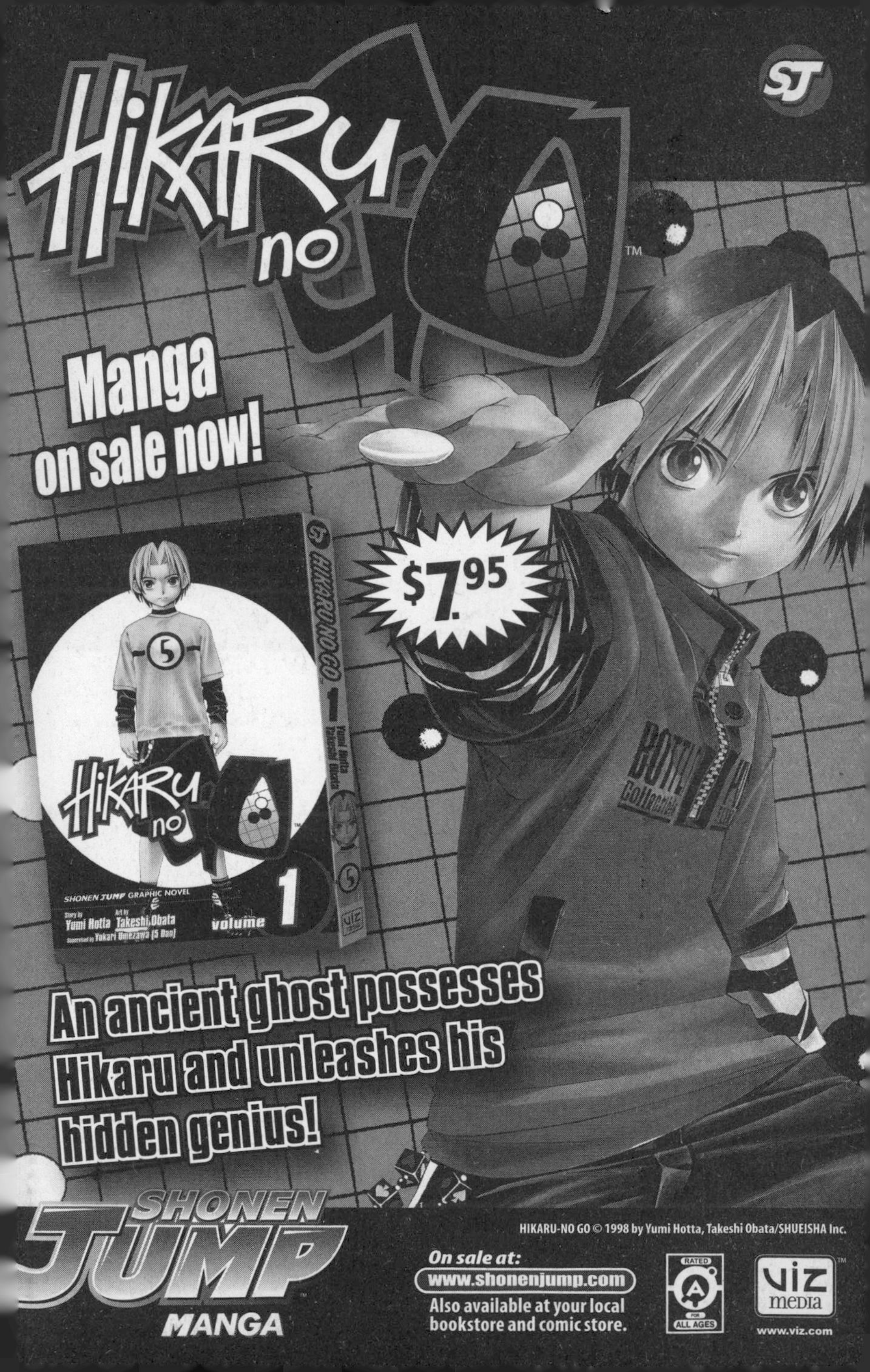
SJ
HIKARU no GO™
Manga on sale now!
$7.95
SJ HIKARU NO GO 1 Yumi Hotta Takeshi Obata
HIKARU no GO™
SHONEN JUMP GRAPHIC NOVEL
Story by Yumi Hotta Art by Takeshi Obata
Supervised by Yukari Umezawa (5 Dan)
volume 1
An ancient ghost possesses Hikaru and unleashes his hidden genius!
SHONEN JUMP MANGA
HIKARU-NO GO © 1998 by Yumi Hotta, Takeshi Obata/SHUEISHA Inc.
On sale at:
www.shonenjump.com
Also available at your local bookstore and comic store.
RATED A FOR ALL AGES
VIZ media
www.viz.com